THE UNPUBLISHED ROLL OF HONOR

THE UNPUBLISHED ROLL OF HONOR

Compiled by
Mark Hughes

Copyright © 1996
Mark Hughes
All Rights Reserved
Published by Genealogical Publishing Co., Inc.
1001 N. Calvert St., Baltimore, MD 21202
Library of Congress Catalogue Card Number 95-79142
International Standard Book Number 0-8063-1487-7

DEDICATION

This book is dedicated to my daughter, Anna Grace Hughes, who spent a lot of quality time with Daddy looking up dead people.

Introduction

The Civil War ended in April 1865. However, the Quartermaster's Department's grim task of reburying the Union soldiers who died during the war had just begun. By 1871 the Department had reinterred over 300,000 bodies, mainly in 74 national cemeteries, but burials were also made in over 250 local and post cemeteries.

In 1865 the Quartermaster's Department published the first volume of the *Roll of Honor* series. These 27 volumes were written to allow "comrades and friends" to find the burial site of Union soldiers. This valuable reference series was all but forgotten until Genealogical Publishing Company began reprinting the series in 1994. In 1995 Genealogical Publishing Company published the first name index to the series, greatly increasing its usefulness.

Nevertheless, the *Roll of Honor* is incomplete. The War Department failed to include two national cemeteries: Ball's Bluff National Cemetery and Grafton National Cemetery. This book, *The Unpublished Roll of* Honor, rectifies this omission by including the first published list of names of soldiers buried at Ball's Bluff and Grafton.

Thousands of Union soldiers died "at home" during the war. Often sick soldiers were sent home to recover only to succumb to disease. These names were also never recorded in the *Roll of Honor*. Many of the names of these soldiers have been lost, but some have been preserved on "headstone" requests. Congress allocated one million dollars for headstones in national cemeteries in 1873. In 1879 Congress authorized the Secretary of War to spend the unused portion of this allocation for headstones for "soldiers who served in the Regular or Volunteer Army of the United States during the War for the Union, and who have been buried in private village or city cemeteries..."

Generally the local GAR post or some local authority (often the postmaster) would write the War Department requesting headstones under the provisions of this act. These letters are the only record of burial of these soldiers. Often it is impossible to determine if these soldiers died during or after the war. However, the Quartermaster's Department carefully checked these headstone requests. No headstone was supplied unless the soldier's regiment was known. Headstones for unknown soldiers who were not buried in a "soldiers lot" were not supplied until 1889.

In 1885, Quartermaster General Samuel B. Holabird sent a headstone request form to all military posts. The quartermaster at each post was to request headstones for all Union veterans buried in the post cemetery. Most quartermasters simply requested markers for all soldiers buried in their post cemetery. Often they requested headstones for civilians also but there was no uniform policy on civilian burials in post cemeteries.

Civilians had been buried in national cemeteries during the Civil War. Often they were employees of the Quartermaster's Department, but sometimes officers' wives or sutlers were buried in the cemetery. These burials were recorded in the *Roll of Honor*; however, the civilian graves were not always marked with permanent headstones.

Later volumes of the *Roll of Honor* also included burials in post cemeteries on the frontier. Volume 19 listed the soldiers killed in the Fetterman Massacre in December 1866. Volume 27 of the series listed burials made as late as 1870. A few burials made before the Civil War are recorded in the *Roll of Honor*.

After the war many soldiers' wives lived on the post with their husbands. If a soldier's wife or children died, they were buried in the post cemetery, and not infrequently these burial records are the only surviving record of the marriage.

Often the post cemetery was the only cemetery in the area. Civilians, such as stage drivers, were sometimes buried there, yet Congress did not allocate money to mark the graves of civilians buried in post cemeteries until $5,000 was allotted in 1904. When a fort closed, the bodies of soldiers from the post cemetery were sometimes moved to either a national cemetery or another post cemetery. There was no set policy on moving the graves of civilians (including soldiers' wives and children). Sometimes they were moved, but normally they were left.

The 1879 bill also required the Secretary of War to "cause to be preserved ... the names and places of burial of all soldiers for whom such headstones have been erected..." Unfortunately these records were not systematically preserved, and only miscellaneous headstone requests are found in the National Archives along with the records of post and national cemeteries. As one archivist put it: "As you know, the material on national cemeteries before 1920 is incomprehensible." He is correct. The surviving records are in poor order. Many records have been lost. For example, there were some 200-odd Union soldiers buried at Saint Elizabeths Hospital in Washington, DC, but apparently the list of names of soldiers buried there has been lost. Neither the National Archives nor Saint Elizabeths Hospital has a copy. Nor were these burials recorded in the *Roll of Honor*.

This book was written to memorialize those soldiers who died in defense of the Union and the expanding frontier but whose names were not recorded in the published *Roll of Honor* or anywhere else. As indicated it is based largely on the records at the National Archives of the two national cemeteries mentioned earlier, on existing records of headstones requests, and on records of post cemeteries.

By continuing the listing of burials of soldiers in post cemeteries and burials of civilians in national and post cemeteries that was begun by the Quartermaster's Department in the *Roll of Honor*, *The Unpublished Roll of Honor* gives the researcher access to previously unpublished records of both soldiers and early settlers on the frontier.

Acknowledgments:

Without the assistance of the following people, this book could not have been written: Dr. Jeffery Olson, Pat Black, and Harold Green of Orangeburg-Calhoun Technical College allowed me time for research. Dr. Mike Myers and D.M. Blanton of the National Archives helped me track down records. Terry Ellison, Director of the Grafton National Cemetery provided valuable information as did Dane B. Freeman, Director of Woodlawn National Cemetery, and Billie Crenshaw, Program Assistant for the Richmond Area National Cemeteries.

Douglas McChristian, Chief Historian of Little Bighorn Battlefield National Monument, provided information on the Fort Keolgh Monument. Ronald G. Wilson, Historian at Appomattox Court House National Historic Site, Crystal Coffey-Avey, ranger at Big Hole National Battlefield, and Terry Kirkland, Jr., ranger at Fort Pulaski National Monument, all shared valuable material with me.

Mr. Larry Freeman, Reference Librarian at Orangeburg-Calhoun Technical College, spent many hours tracking down books. The entire English faculty, especially Hammond Wyle, answered my numerous questions.

My wife, Patty Hughes, typed most of the text. My daughter, Anna Grace Hughes, spent hours in cemeteries without complaining. Without my family's support this book could not have been written. Thanks.

TABLE OF CONTENTS

Livingston	Ala	1
Fort Kodiak	Alaska	1
Camp Date Creek	Ariz	2
Fort Apache	Ariz	3
Fort Bowie	Ariz	4
Fort Grant	Ariz	5
Fort Huachuca	Ariz	6
Fort Lowell	Ariz	6
San Carlos Agency	Ariz	7
Whipple Barracks	Ariz	7
Madison	Ark	9
San Diego Barracks	Calf	10
San Francisco National Cemetery	Calf	11
Cantonment on theUncompahare	Col	14
Fort Lewis	Col	15
Danbury	Con	16
Hartford	Con	18
Hawleyville	Con	19
Brandywine Hundred	Del	20
Battleground Nat Cemetery	D C	21
Fort Clinch	Fla	23
Fort Jefferson	Fla	23
Miami	Fla	25
St. Francis Barracks	Fla	25
Fort Pulaski	Ga	26
Macon	Ga	27
Honolulu	Hawaii	27
Bunker Hill	Ill	28
Carbondale	Ill	29
Chestnut	Ill	29

Colchester	Ill	30
Fort Reno	Indian Territory	30
Fort Sill	Indian Territory	35
Fort Supply	Indian Territory	36
Washita Battlefield	Indian Territory	37
Haney's Corner	Ind	38
Morgan County	Ind	38
Clear Lake	Iowa	39
Clinton	Iowa	40
Paris	Iowa	40
Fort Hays	Kan	41
Fort Riley	Kan	43
Fort Wallace	Kan	45
Towner's Station	Kan	48
Cattlesbury	Ky	48
Mount Vernon	Ky	49
Calais	Maine	50
Nautucket	Maine	50
Annapolis	Md	51
Fort McHenry	Md	53
Port Tobacco	Md	57
Abrigton	Mass	58
Haverhill	Mass	59
Fort Mackinac	Mich	60
Fort Wayne	Mich	61
Big Hole Battlefield	Mont	63
Custer Battlefield	Mont	64
Fort Keogh	Mont	70
Fort Keogh Monument	Mont	71
Fort Maginnis	Mont	74
Fort Misullo	Mont	74
Reno-Benteen Battlefield	Mont	75
Fort McPherson National Cemetery	Neb	77
Fort Robinson	Neb	87
Fort Hallack	Nev	88

Burlington County	NJ	88
Finn's Point National Cemetery	NJ	90
Fort Wingate	NM	94
Cypress Hills National Cemetery	NY	95
Fort Columbus	NY	144
Fort Niagara	NY	152
Fort Wadsworth	NY	153
Jamestown	NY	153
Newburgh	NY	154
Oneida County	NY	155
West Point	NY	156
Cove Creek	NC	156
Fort Macon	NC	157
Fort Yates	ND	158
Gleason	Ohio	159
Hannibal	Ohio	159
Harmon	Ohio	160
Lebanon	Ohio	160
Fort Klamath	Org	161
Camp Cadwalader	Pen	162
Camp Curtin	Pen	166
Shohola	Pen	167
Fort Adams	RI	170
Aiken	SC	171
Chester	SC	172
Orangeburg	SC	172
York	SC	173
Camp Eagle Pass	Tex	174
Camp Pena Colorado	Tex	175
Fort Bliss	Tex	176
Fort Clark	Tex	177
Fort Davis	Tex	179
Fort Hancock	Tex	181
Fort Ringgold	Tex	182
San Antonio National Cemetery	Tex	182

Fort Cameron	Utah	184
Fort Douglas	Utah	186
Alexandria National Cemetery	Va	187
Appomattox Court House	Va	188
Ball's Bluff National Cemetery	Va	189
Cold Harbor National Cemetery	Va	190
Hampton VA National Cemetery	Va	194
U.S. Naval Hospital	Va	195
Fort Spokane	Wash	195
Fort Walla Walla	Wash	196
Vancouver Barracks	Wash	197
Grafton National Cemetery	West Va	198
Fort D. A. Russell	Wyo	215
Fort Laramie	Wyo	217
Fort McKinney	Wyo	219
Fort Washakie	Wyo	220
Fort Yellowstone	Wyo	221
Grattan Massacre	Wyo	222

THE UNPUBLISHED
ROLL OF HONOR

LIVINGSTON
Alabama

In 1876, the Quartermaster General ruled that the bodies of these soldiers, who were buried at Livingston, were not be be moved to a national cemetery.

Name	Rank	Co	Unit
Grayson, James	Pvt	D	7th Cav
Martin, James	Pvt	A	2nd Inf

FORT KODIAK
Alaska

According to an 1870 report, these soldiers were buried at Fort Kodiak between 1868 and 1870. No record of removal of these bodies has been found.

Name	Rank	Co	Unit
Covington, Hugh	Pvt	I	2nd US Art
Donovan, Michael			2nd US Art
Grant, Theo	Sgt	F	2nd US Art
Lauhoef, August	Pvt	F	2nd US Art
Sulloy, John	Pvt	F	2nd US Art

CAMP DATE CREEK
Arizona

This list of the burials in Camp Date Creek's Post Cemetery was made in 1870. The post closed in 1873. Later the bodies were moved to the San Francisco National Cemetery.

Name	Rank	Co	Unit
Allem. John	Pvt	H	14th Inf
Armstrong, Goble	Corp	H	14th Inf
Bellville, Louis F.	Sgt	I	14th Inf
Booth, Ler___	Pvt	H	14th Inf
Brady, Francis	Pvt	H	14th Inf
Croker, John	Pvt	H	14th Inf
Demes, John	Pvt	H	14th Inf
Goffer, Corneilus	Pvt	I	14th Inf
Howell, James	Pvt	C	8th Cav
Keeffee, Maurice	Pvt	H	14th Inf
Keyser, Gustovo	Pvt	I	14th Inf
Kuley, Joh D.	Pvt	H	14th Inf
Kyndiay, Isael	Pvt	H	14th Inf
Linch, Joseph	Pvt	I	14th Inf
McKeron, Patrick	Pvt	I	14th Inf
Miles, Edwin	Pvt	I	14th Inf
Mudgett, Frank	Pvt	C	14th Inf
Parker, Henry	Corp	K	8th Cav
Pemy, Thomas	Pvt	H	14th Inf
Schneidn, Adolphus J.	Pvt	M	3rd Cav

FORT APACHE
Arizona

This list of burials at Fort Apache was dated November 23, 1886.

Name	Rank	Co	Unit
Ansboro, Martin	Pvt	D	6th Cav
Bell, Frank	Pvt	D	6th Cav
Betkic, John	Pvt	A	4th Cav
Blake, Mathew	Pvt	B	6th Cav
Blum, Frank	Pvt	L	1st Cav
Boloton, George H.	Pvt	K	6th Inf
Bowers, William	Post QM Sgt		
Brown, Daniel	Corp	B	1st Inf
Clark, George	Pvt	H	8th Inf
Dell, Peter	Pvt	B	6th Cav
Dougherty, William	Pvt	G	8th Inf
Egh-e-jar	Pvt	E	Indian Scouts
Funk, Phlip	Pvt	E	6th Cav
Girle, William	Sgt	E	8th Inf
Gorman, John	Pvt	D	6th Cav
Griffin, Daniel	Sgt	B	6th Cav
Hafty, Paul	Pvt	F	6th Cav
Hasken, Richard	Hospital Steward		
Hill, Anthony	Pvt	E	8th Inf
Hollis, Frank	Pvt	H	1st Cav
Holmes, Charles	Pvt	B	6th Cav
Hosey, John	1st Sgt	E	8th Inf
Jorgensen, Julius	Pvt	B	6th Cav
Klippl, Adam	Pvt	C	6th Cav
Lacombe, Ernest	Pvt	L	1st Cav
Lesslon, William	Sgt	G	9th Inf
Lyce, Daniel F.	Pvt	B	1st Inf
Lynch, Michael	Sgt	M	1st Cav
Massey, Dawson	Pvt	I	23rd Inf
McEachern, Alexander	Pvt	K	4th Cav
McGuire, John	Pvt	L	1st Cav
Millon, James	Pvt	K	21st Inf

Name	Rank	Co	Unit
Nolan, Thomas	Trumpeter	E	6th Cav
O'Day, Michael	Pvt	E	12th Inf
Olson, Andrew	Corp	I	Scouts
Quinn, Albert	Pvt	L	5th Cav
Platt, Peter	Pvt	D	12th Inf
Pulkugton, Patrick	Pvt	I	6th Cav
Quera, Euele	Corp	A	Indian 1st Cav
Reibel, August	Pvt	M	1st Cav
Shultz, Johann	Pvt	M	1st Cav
Smith, John	Pvt	C	5th Cav
Sweeney, Frank H.	Pvt	D	5th Cav
Walton, Frank	Pvt	L	1st Cav
Winchlon, Paul	Pvt	D	12th Inf

FORT BOWIE
Arizona

Fort Bowie was an active post from 1862 until 1894. These burials were made between 1862 and 1886. There were at least eleven unknown burials in 1886. Later these bodies were moved to the San Francisco National Cemetery.

Name	Rank	Co	Unit
Andrews, A.	Pvt	K	3rd US Cav
Aqueira, Julain	Mail Rider		Civilian
Bice, A.F.			Civilian
Browney, John	Mail driver		Civilian
Carmichael, Wm.	Pvt	L	1st Cal Cav
Carroll, John C	Lt		32nd US Inf
Cass, John M.	Capt.		4th Calf Inf
Durean, J. G.			Civilian
Fisher, Chas. A.B.			1st Cal Cav
Keith, James F.		B	1st Calf Cav
Kelley, John	Pvt	G	1st US Cav
Knowles, George	Pvt	D	32nd US Inf

Name	Rank	Co	Unit
Stone, Cob			Civilian
Luerro, Vivian		A	1st NM Inf
Macom, George	Lt.		32nd US Inf
Macomber, _____			Civilian
infant son of Capt. Macomber - 32nd Inf			
Maloney, Peter A.		B	1st Calf Cav
McIntyre, James	Pvt	G	32nd US Inf
Mooly, Thomas			Civilian
child - burned to death			
Rayson, Samuel		L	1st Cal Cav
Schmidt, Albert		B	1st Calf Cav
Seater, John	Lt		5th Cal Inf
Tapia, Juan C.	Lt		1st NM Inf
Walker, Jas. F.			Civilian
child of emigrants passing through			
Walker, John	Pvt	G	1st US Inf
Wells, Richard W.		E	1st Calf Cav

FORT GRANT
Arizona

Fort Grant was established in 1860. These names are from an undated headstone request. Bodies from the Fort Grant Post Cemetery were moved to the Santa Fe National Cemetery.

Name	Rank	Co	Unit
Brooksea, Frederick		M	5th Cav
Hale, August		I	5th Cav
Hatch, Charles		E	5th Cav
King, Samuel L.	Pvt	L	5th Cav
Spenkius, Walter		A	5th Cav
Zach, Ermsh		I	5th Cav

FORT HUACHUCA
Arizona

Fort Huachuca was first garrisoned in 1877. This is a headstone request made in 1886.

Name	Rank	Co	Unit
Alexander, Isasc	Pvt	B	6th Cav
Haslmck, Augustus	Pvt	B	6th Cav
Kelly, Thomas P.	Pvt	B	6th Cav
King, Peter	Pvt	M	6th Cav
Lebel, Joel	Pvt	B	6th Cav
McCreany, Frank	Wagoner	B	6th Cav
McMorrow, James	Pvt	D	6th Cav
Montgomery, Frank	1st Sgt		4th Cav
Nixon, James	Pvt		1st Inf
Nolen, James	Pvt	A	2nd Cav
O'Brien, James	1st Sgt		8th Inf
Powers, Larry	Pvt	B	6th Cav
Shill, Frank	Pvt		4th Cav
Waskon, Joseph	Pvt	H	6th Cav
Wyatt, Charles		E	4th Cav

FORT LOWELL
Arizona

Fort Lowell (1862 - 1891) was located near Tucson. These names are from an undated headstone request.

Name	Rank	Co	Unit
Deviney, James	Pvt	H	4th Cav
Richardson, Frank D.	Pvt	F	1st Inf

SAN CARLOS AGENCY
Arizona

This list of burials was made in 1891.

Name	Rank	Co	Unit
Blair, William	Pvt	G	10th Inf
Bradley, William	Pvt	I	10th Inf
Carr, Michael	Pvt	F	9th Inf
Crisholm, Samuel	Pvt	G	24th Inf
Daily, John H.	Trumpeter	E	24th Inf
Fleming, Will	Pvt	E	10th Inf
John	Corp	A	Indian Scouts
Johnson, Richard	Pvt	C	10th Inf
Parker, Gustarus	Pvt	A	10th Inf
Royster, William A.	Corp	C	10th Inf
Snowball	Pvt	A	Indian Scouts
Williams, Morgan	Pvt	G	9th Inf

WHIPPLE BARRACKS
Arizona

Whipple Barracks, also known as Camp Clark, was founded in 1863 and deactivated in 1898. These names came from headstone requests for 1886, 1892, 1893, and 1894 and a 1873 report. In 1873 there were 14 unknowns in the post cemetery. These bodies were moved to the San Francisco National Cemetery before 1906.

Name	Rank	Co	Unit
Bungnity, Julius	Pvt	F	12th US Inf
Carleton, David J.	Sgt	B	23rd US Inf
Cressey, E. P.	Pvt	M	3rd US Cav
Curley, Patrick	Pvt	H	9th US Inf
Donaho, Thomas I.	Pvt	F	12th US Inf
Drummond, William	Pvt		8th US Inf

Name	Rank	Co	Unit
Dwyer, Philip	Captain		5th US Cav
Farrell, Wm	Pvt	F	12th US Inf
Fisher, Richard	Pvt	L	8th US Inf
Francis, George	Pvt	L	14th US Inf
Garcia, Marerlino	Pvt	H	1st US Cav
Glasspot, Otto	Pvt	H	14th US Inf
Grist, James K	Pvt	C	9th US Inf
Hibband, John	Pvt	H	14th US Inf
Holway, Theodore	Hospital Steward		
Howell, James	Pvt	C	8th US Cav
Kelley, John D.	Pvt	H	14th US Inf
Kelly, John	Pvt		8th US Cav
Kiefe, Maurice	Pvt	H	14th US Inf
Lee, John	Pvt.		8th US Inf
LeMarquis, Charles A.	Pvt	F	9th US Inf
Linder, John	Chief Musician	Band	23rd US Inf
McGrath, John	Pvt		8th US Inf
Mudgett, Frank	Pvt	I	14th US Inf
Murman, G.		G	11th US Inf
O'shea, Thomas	Pvt	B	11th US Inf
Poojer, Harrison	Pvt	L	14th US Inf
Samdt, John	Pvt	F	5th US Cav
Sands, John	Pvt	F	3rd US Inf
St. Clark, I.W.	Pvt	M	3rd US Cav
Stonnfer, Cornelius	Pvt	I	14th US Inf
Taylor, Joseph	Pvt	L	14th US Inf
Timmerman, T.	Pvt	A	1st Calf Cav
West, Peter G.		I	23rd US Inf
White, John	Pvt	I	9th US Cav
Wilson, Alfred	Hospital Steward		
Wright, Joseph A.	Sgt	H	1st US Cav
Wright, Thomas	Pvt	C	14th US Inf
Zimmerman, F.	Pvt	A	1st US Cav

MADISON COUNTY ARKANSAS

These graves were marked with headstones at the request of the local GAR post. The soldiers marked with an "*" were buried in Saint Paul's Cemetery.

Name	Rank	Co	Unit
Almon, Jacob H.			10th ___
Bennett, H.E.			
Collins, Charles F.			
Gallanher, F.			
Hikle, Jared B. *	Sgt	K	1st Ark Cav
Holmsley, Randolph L. *	Pvt	A	1st Ark Cav
Horton, James *		B	
Hubbard, T.W. *	Pvt	K	1st Ark Cav
Johnson, H.			
Kartins, Teter			
Lahnosenle, U.			
Phillips, Luther P. *	Pvt	K	1st Ark Cav
Prater, Wiley *	Pvt	I	1st Ark Cav
Rose, Jesse M. *	Sgt	K	1st Ark Cav
Taylor, James R. *	Pvt	K	1st Ark Cav
Tendergust, H.			
Tucker, Rob't *		E	6th Mo Cav
Watkins, Issac *	Pvt	K	1st Ark Cav

SAN DIEGO BARRACKS
California

In 1852 the first US military post at San Diego was established. In 1899 the post was renamed in honor of Major General William S. Rosecrans. On October 5, 1934, the post cemetery was designated Fort Rosecrans National Cemetery.

Name	Rank	Co	Unit
Almoudinger, Anthony	Pvt	B	1st Art
Bounke, Thomas	Pvt	G	4th Cal Vol Inf
Burns, John	Pvt	D	8th Inf
Combs, Robert W.	Pvt	E	8th Inf
Craig, L.S.	Lt Col		3rd Inf
Deddridge, Benj.F.	Pvt	G	4th Cal Vol Inf
Dryer, John	Pvt	G	4th Cal Vol Inf
Hammond, Thomas B.	Lt		1st US Dragoons
Holifield, Gotthold	Sgt	M	8th Cav
Holmes, Thomas		G	4th Cal Vol Inf
Letun, Alexander		G	4th Cal Vol Inf
McDonald, Alexander	Sgt	B	12 Inf
McIntyre, Charles L.	Corp	A	8th Inf
McNanny, Owen		G	4th Cal Vol Inf
Moon, Benj.D.			1st US Dragoons
Neill, John O.		B	3rd Art
Phillips, George	Corp	M	1st Cav
Powell, James W.	Cpt		8th Inf
Powell,___			Civilian
infant son of Lt. Jas. W. Powell			
Starkey, Charles	Pvt	D	8th Inf
Welch, John S.	Pvt	J	8th Inf

SAN FRANCISCO NATIONAL CEMETERY
California

Although there was apparently a small post cemetery at the Presidio of San Francisco during the Civil War, the first record of the cemetery in the Quartermaster's files is a report by Brig. General D.B. Saekeh. In 1882 General Saekeh had been sent to inspect the graves of California Volunteers who were buried at Fort Yuma. Because of the poor condition of the cemetery, General Saekeh recommended the establishment of a national cemetery at the Presidio of San Francisco.

Quartermaster General Samuel Holibird recommended the creation of the San Francisco National Cemetery on March 15, 1884. This list shows interments in the cemetery as of December 28, 1886. Bodies from Fort Yuma were not moved to the cemetery until September 1890.

Name	Rank	Co	Unit
____gyrald, John	Pvt	G	9th US Inf
Albers, John	Pvt	F	4th US Art
Atchison, James Jr.	Pvt	A	8th US Cav
Bailey, C.	Lt		
Baker, Wm.	Pvt	H	8th US Cav
Baker, Wm. M.	1st Sgt		2nd Art
Banks, M____	Pvt	A	4th US Art
Barney, Benj. G.	Col		
Barr, Samuel	Corp	F	7th Calf Inf
Beatty, M.	Pvt	D	2nd US Art
Berry, John	Pvt	K	9th US Inf
Boyle, James	Pvt	B	1st US Cav
Britt, James	Pvt.	B	9th US Inf
Brown, B	Pvt		
Brown, Bernard E.			Civilian (Child)
Brown, William	Pvt	C	4th US Art
Carr, Dennis	Pvt.	M	4th US Art
Cassidy, Richard	Pvt	H	2nd US Art
Chamberlin, A.J.	Hospital Steward		
Clarke, J.C.	Pvt	M	2nd US Art
Clawson, John	Pvt	B	21st US Inf

Name	Rank	Co	Unit
Cramston, Authur	Lt		
Crutchfield, Isabella			Civilian
	child of Pvt Crutchfield - 4th US Art		
Crutchfield, James			Civilian
	child of Pvt Crutchfield - 4th US Art		
Crutchfield, Joseph			Civilian
	child of Pvt Crutchfield - 4th US Art		
Cushing, Louis			Civilian
	son of Capt Cushing - 4th US Art		
Daniels, O.E.	Pvt	D	2nd US Art
Davidson, W.D.	Pvt	F	7th US Inf
Decker, Isaac	Pvt		4th US Art
Delaney, John	Pvt	A	2nd US Art
Dempsey, James	Pvt	A	2nd Calf Inf
Dennis, Henry			Civilian
	son of Sgt Dennis - 1st US Art		
Dingee, J.	Pvt	D	14th US Inf
Fishborne, Wm.	Pvt	L	2nd US Cav
Fitzgerald, Jas.	Pvt	D	3rd US Art
Fitzgerald, Richard	Pvt	H	9th US Inf
Ganzert, G.	Pvt		
Haidt, M.L.			
Hallohun, John	Pvt	D	2nd US Art
Hayes, A.A.	Pvt	B	7th Calf Inf
Heintz, B.E.			Band
Henderson, W.H.	Musician		4th US Art
Hope, John	Pvt	F	4th Calf Inf
Hoyard, Michael	Burgler	E	9th Inf
Jones, Mary			
Keeler, C.B.	Pvt		2nd US Art
Kelly, Willie			Civilian
	son of 1st Sgt. Kelly - 1st US Art		
Kelton, John V.			Civilian
	son of Col J.C. Kelton - A.A.G. USA		
Killen, Malachi	Q.M.Sgt		2nd US Art
Klimbeck, James			
L____, W.	Pvt	F	4th US Art
Landrum, John H.	Capt		
Larrimer, John R.	Pvt	B	4th US Art
Leary, D.	Pvt	L	4th US Art
Leonare, Hiram	General		

Name	Rank	Co	Unit
Lubeck, H.E.	Pvt	G	2nd Calf Inf
Mallory, John	Pvt	D	1st Cav
Mansfield, Charles	Pvt	C	4th US Art
Mansfield, T.	Pvt	C	4th US Art
McBride, Michael	Pvt	B	4th US Art
McCarthy, Daniel	Pvt	G	2nd US Art
McCurry, Edward	Lt Col		
McCurthy, daniel	Pvt	G	2nd US Art
McDonald, charles	Pvt	C	14th US Inf
McPherson, Alex.	Pvt	F	9th US Inf
Merrill, Thomas J.	Pvt	D	4th US Art
Miller, Jacob	Pvt	B	4th US Art
Monahan, Millie			Civilian
Montague, James	Pvt.	M	2nd US Art
Mulholland, J.	Hospital Steward		
Philbrick, Wm.			
Preston, Albert W.	Col		
Pryor, Richard L.			Engineer Corps
Pwens, H.G.	Pvt	B	2nd Calf Inf
Reardon, John	Pvt	A	34d Calf Inf
Richenbacker, Martin	Sgt	A	2nd US Art
Seeling, Emima			Civilian
Small, J.F.	Lt		
Stang, Edward	Band		4th US Art
Stewart, Esther			Civilian
	daughter of Lt Col James Stewart		
Sullivan, P.			14th US Art
Sullivan, Phillip	Pvt	A	8th US Cav
Swain, _____			Civilian
Swain, Jas. F.			Civilian
	son of Pvt Swain - 4th US Art		
Swain, Laura			Civilian
	daughter of Pvt. Swain - 4th US Art		
Swain, Lucinda J.			Civilian
	wife of Pvt Swain - 4th US Art		
Taylor, Evan T			Civilian
	son of Lt Taylor - 4th US Art		
Thorington, J.H.	Sgt		2nd Art
Updegraff, Joseph	Major		9th US Inf
Van Hofen, K. Carl			Civilian
	son of Pvt Van Hofen - 1st Art. Band		

Name	Rank	Co	Unit
Watkins, W.	Pvt	K	8th Calf Inf
Werner, Julius	Pv	A	4th US Art
Wiloghy, Marguret			Civilian
Witehall, Edwin B.		G	9th US Inf
Woclfter, Arnold	Pvt	F	4th US Art
Woodall, Wm.	Pvt	F	2nd US Art

CANTONMENT on the UNCOMPAHARE
Colorado

This post was authorized in 1880. In 1886, the post's name was changed to Fort Crawford. These bodies, listed on an 1886 headstone request, were moved to the Fort McPherson National Cemetery sometime before 1909.

Name	Rank	Co	Unit
Barry, Robert M.	1st Sgt	E	23rd Inf
Caldwell, Alvin A.	Sgt	D	23rd Inf
Doyle, Willliam	Pvt	G	14th Inf
Glass, Ferdinand	Corp	G	10th Inf
Hanlon, Peter	Pvt	C	23rd Inf
Hosffle, Theodore	Pvt	F	14th Inf
Maguin, John D.	Pvt	G	14th Inf
O'Riley, Patrick	Pvt	C	23rd Inf
Swift, Benard	Sgt	F	14th Inf
White, James H.	Pvt	Band	9th Cav

FORT LEWIS
Colorado

Fort Lewis was first garrisoned in 1878. The post closed in 1891. These names are from an 1889 headstone request.

Name	Rank	Co	Unit
Armstrong, Alexander	Pvt	G	22nd Inf
Beehler, F.	Pvt	C	13th Inf
Colburn, J.C.	Pvt	F	6th Cav
Donahue, John	Pvt	G	22nd Inf
Doyle, John	Pvt	E	6th Cav
Gaboiel, Jules	Pvt	F	6th Cav
Griesner, Julius	Musician	Band	15th Inf
Hines, William	Pvt	H	15th Inf
Houghtaling, Chas. H.	Pvt	D	13th Inf
Leukel, Wm.	Pvt	A	22nd Inf
Maybrook, George	Sgt	G	22nd Inf
Meneely, Wm. A	Pvt	F	6th Cav
Pringle, John C.	Pvt	H	22nd Inf
Ryan, A.	Sgt	K	22nd Inf
Schwan, F.			
Spencer, F.	Pvt	B	6th Cav
Williams, Wm. A.	Pvt	K	22nd Inf
Wood, Enoch	Pvt	A	22nd Inf
Yost, Wm. V.	Pvt	H	22nd Inf

DANBURY
Connecticut

Acording to a letter received by Col. James Moore, most of the soldiers listed died "at home" during the Civil War.

Key to burial sites:
* Wooster Cemetery   ** Wooster Street Burying Grounds
# Catholic Cemetery   + Mira Broot Burying Grounds
@ Stan's Plain Burying Grounds   & Pembroke Burying Grounds
$ North Burying Grounds

Name	Rank	Co	Unit
Barnum, Homer B. *	Pvt	A	11th Con Vols
Bassett, Patrick #			
Bishop, Joseph *	Musician	B	23rd Col Vols
Bnonson, Aug. E. +	Sgt	C	17th Con Vols
Byerly, John B *			
Chase, E.B.	Pvt		2nd Con Light Batt
Cnofuk, Chas. *	Pvt		23rd Col Vols
Comstock, Wm. L E. *	Pvt	B	23rd Con Vols
Crofut, Henry B. **			17th NY Vols
Daniels, Patrick *			
Demming, Macy #	Capt		
Dikman, William *	Pvt	A	11th Con Vols
Eastwood, Cysus @			(Colored)
Frank Dennis @			(Colored)
Godfrey, G.M. *	Capt	E	23rd Con Vols
Hall, Wm. *	Capt		8th Con Vols
Halstead, Albert Prince *			
Hillson, David F. **	Pvt	C	17th Con Vols
Howerth, James *	Pvt	E	1st Con Vols
Hoyh, E. *			
Hull, Grahame *	Pvt	B	23rd Con Vols
Hyatt, Wm. *	Pvt	B	1st Con Hvy Art
Judson, E.W. *	Pvt	D	7th Con Vols
Judson, Wm *			
Knapp, Michael *	Pvt	B	23rd Con Vols
Lilly, Patrick #			1st Con Art
Mansfield, David B. &	Lt		11th Con vols
Mantz, Wm. *	Pvt.	A	11th Con Vols
McCauley, Frank +			

Name	Rank	Co	Unit
McCauley, Jho. +			
McGuire, John H. +			
Moeging, Wm. C. *	Lt. Col		11th Con Vols
Moore, James E *	Capt.	C	17th Con vols
Morris, Amos *			
Morris, Theodore *	Corp		6th Con Vols
Moses, Wheeton *	Pvt	K	23rd Col Vols
Osim, Christopher *			
Patch, Wm. *	Pvt	A	5th Con Vols
Pelly, Thos. +			
Pinley, John $			1st Con Cav
Pusdy, Amos *			
Raymond, Joseph W. *	Pvt	C	13th Con Vols
Robertson, Aaron L. *	Pvt	A	11th Con Vols
Robinson, T.G. *	Pvt	K	23rd Con Vols
Ryan, James +			
Sears, Geo. *	Pvt.	C	17th Con Vols
Serine, Orrin *	Pvt	K	23rd Con Vols
Skinner, Benj. F. *	Capt.	D	7th Con Vols
Small, Chas. S. *	Pvt	C	17th Con vols
Starr, Fred W. *	Lt	B	23rd Con Vols
Starr, Saml. H. *	Capt		
Stevens, Steven S. *	Lt	I	6th Con Vols
Stratton, Robert *	Pvt	B	23rd Con Vols
Taylor, Henry H. *	Capt	I	8th Con Vols
Trowbridy, Augustus *			
Urmston, _____ **	Lt		12th US Inf
We____, T.S. *			8th Con Vols
Wheeler, Able M *.	Pvt	B	23rd Con Vols
White, Sellick R. *	Capt		
Williams, J. *			

HARTFORD
Connecticut

This is an undated list of burials at Hartford. Many of these bodies were removed from the South after the war.

Name	Rank	Co	Unit
Allen, Amony L.	Sgt	J	14th Con
Allen, Joshua	Sgt	B	17th Ill
Boos, William	Pvt	H	22nd Con
Britton, Henry	Pvt	H	12th Con
Buck, Daniel W.	Corp	A	22th Con
Ciane, Gilbert R	Pvt	D	11th Con
Crabtre, John W.	Pvt	A	7th Con
Cunip, Henry W.	Major		10th Con
DeWams, Geraldo	Pvt	E	14th RI
Dewey, Daniel	Lt	A	25th Con
Dimock, Joseph J.	Major		2nd NY
Drake, John L	Capt	I	16th Con
Eaton, Horato D	Capt	B	6th Con
Ellenberger, Charles	Sgt	H	22nd Con
Ellsworth, James B.	Pvt	B	21st Con
Eusworth, John	Pvt	C	16th Con
Freeman, Horace H.	Corp	H	12th Con
Goodwin, Jinus	Sgt	K	14th Con
Griswold, Eugene W.	Pvt	A	7th Con
Hackney, George	Pvt	F	12th Con
Hayden, Henry	Pvt	H	12th Con
Haywood, John P.	Pvt	F	16th Con
Hills, Albert M.	Pvt	A	16th Con
Honse, William	Pvt	A	25th Con
Jagger, Franklin	Pvt		58th Mafo (?)
Jamison, John L.	Pvt	M	1st Con Cav
Laurie, John D.	Pvt	E	10th Con
Linons, John H.	Corp	E	8th Con
Loomis William T.	Pvt	A	1st Con Hvy Art
Lucas, Clinton J.	Sgt	A	7th Con
Mandvellie	Carp.Mate	K	USN
Marsh, George H.	Sgt	A	8th Con
Nichols, Wm. W.	Pvt	F	16th Con
Niles, Albert H.	Capt	A	1st Con Cav
Noble, Hiram	Corp	A	21st Con

Name	Rank	Co	Unit
Oliver, William A.	Lt	B	25th Con
Owen, Leverelt B.	Sgt		1st Con Hvy Art
P_____, Charles F.	Pvt	K	20th Con
Paul, James P.	Sgt	F	16th Con
Pulkley, Charles E.	Capt	E	1st Con Hvy Art
Quintal, Samuel A.	Pvt	B	7th Con
Rice, Sylvester W.	Lt		1st La. National Guard
Russell, Joseph	Sgt	A	7th Con
Sackett, W.H.	Capt	I	11th Con
Scott, Robert	Pvt	C	16th Con
Shurtleff, James F.	Pvt	E	16th Con
Smith, Henry C.	Capt	C	20th Con
Starkey, Robert	Pvt	E	14th Con
Tenant, Charles H.	Capt	A	16th Con
Terry, Charles E.	Surgeon		
Thomas, E.B.	Corp	K	25th Con
Thomas, John W.	Pvt	J	13th Mass Hvy Art
Tournbull, Thomas L.	Lt. Col		1st Con Hvy Art
Turnbull, James L.	Pay Master		USN
Tuttle, William H.	Pvt	B	25th Con
Very, Edwin	Sgt		116th NY
Wadsworth, Josiah P.	Pvt	D	19th Con
Ward, James H.	Comdr.		USN
Weld, Charles T.	Lt		17th US Inf
Weld, Lewis L.	Lt. Col		4th US CT
Wells, Henry A.	Capt	E	10th Con
Weston, Leverett P.	Sgt.	E	10th Con

HAWLEYVILLE
Connecticut

Name	Rank	Unit
Seeley, Eli	Sgt.	7th Con. Vols
Wilkman, Lenard	Pvt	

BRANDYWINE HUNDRED
Delaware

These names are from an undated list in the Quartermaster's files. Most of these graves were marked with wooden headboards. The majority of these soldiers died during or shortly after the war.

```
*   St. James Episcopal Church     **  Saint Peters (colored) M.E. Church
#   Newark Union M.E. Church       ##  Mount Pleasant M.E. Church
$   Red Clay Creek                 $$  New Port M.E. Church
%   Scranton "Friends" Burying Ground
@   Mount Lebanon M.E. Church
```

Name	Rank	Unit
_____, Thompson #		97th, Pen. Vol.
Bayard, Oliver **	Pvt	24th USCT
Bayard, Wm. Thomas **	Pvt	5th Mass Cav.
Cash, William $	Pvt	4th Del Inf
Dale, Thomas $$	Pvrt	8th Del Inf
Dickerson, Charles %	Pvt	2nd Del Inf
Foulk, Stephen *	Pvt	1st Legion MD Cav
Glatts, Henry	Pvt	4th Del Inf
Goocll, Lewis	Color Sgt	1st Del Vols.
Gregg, Thomas D. *	Pvt	1st Del Battery
Hinsworth, Henry *	Pvt	2nd Del Inf
Hinsworth, Thomas *		2nd Del Inf
Johnson, John K.	Pvt	1st Del Battery
Law, Woodward P.	Pvt	
McNeill, Alexander @	Pvt	4th Del. Inf
Miller, Henry *	Pvt	8th Del Inf
Stepfoe, John C. @	Pvt	4th Del. Inf
Talley, Edwin C. ##	Pvt	4th Del Inf
Wellington, C. Lloyd ##	1st Sgt	1st Del Inf
Williams, William ##	Pvt	1st Del Inf
Wilson, Isaac **		
Yarnall, Symngir *	Pvt	4th Del Inf

BATTLEGROUND NATIONAL CEMETERY
Washington, D. C.

In July 1864, Confederates under General Jubal Early probed the outer defenses of Washington. Even the soldiers assigned to the Quartermaster General's Office, under the command of Quartermaster General Meigs, were sent to help defend the city. In the Battle of Fort Stevens, July 11 and 12, Early was repulsed.

The Union casualties of the battle were later buried in Battleground National Cemetery. No bodies were moved here after the war, nor were burials of Civil War veterans made after the war until Major Edward R. Campbell, age 92, was buried in the cemetery on March 12, 1936. According to the National Park Service, which maintains the cemetery, Major Campbell was the last Union veteran eligible for interment in the cemetery. This list of burials is a corrected version of the list in volume 1 of the Roll of Honor.

Name	Rank	Unit
Ashborough, Andrew	Pvt	61st Pen Inf
Barett, W.S.	Pvt	40th NY Inf
Barrett, E.C.	Pvt	40th NY Inf
Bently, John	Pvt	122nd NY Inf
Bowen, Philip	Pvt	61st Pen Inf
Campbell, Edward R.	Major	
Chandler, Harvey P.B.	Pvt	122nd NY Inf
Christ, C.S.	Pvt	2nd US Art
Davidson, John	Pvt	43rd NY Inf
DeGraft, Matthew J.	Pvt	43rd NY Inf
Dolan, John	Pvt	2nd Mass Cav
Dowen, Andrew J.	Pvt.	77th NY Inf
Ellis, John	Pvt	93rd Pen Inf
Farrar, G.W.	Pvt	43rd NY Inf
Garvin, George	Pvt	93rd Pen Inf
Gillette, William H.	Pvt	49th NY Inf
Gorton, George W.	Corp	1st RI Inf
Hoerle, Bernard	Pvt	89th Pen Inf
Hogebloom, David L.	Pvt	122nd NY Inf
Holtzman, William	Pvt	93rd Pen Inf
Hufletin, Elijah S	Pvt	25th NY Cav

Name	Rank	Unit
Kennedy, John	Pvt	61st Pen Inf
Laughlin, William	Lt	61st Pen Inf
Lovett, Patrick	Pvt	37th Mass Inf
Maloney, Jeremiah	Pvt	40th NY Inf
Manning, Andrew	Pvt	77th NY Inf
Marquet, George	Sgt	89th Pen Inf
Matott, A	Corp	49th NY Inf
McIntire, H.	Pvt	93rd Pen Inf
Mosier, Alason	Pvt	122nd NY Inf
Mowery, Alvarado	Pvt	122nd NY Inf
Pockett, John	Pvt	7th Maine Inf
Richards, John M.	Sgt	139th Pen Inf
Richardson, Thomas B.	Sgt	25th NY Cav
Ruhle, William	Corp	77th NY Inf
Scahouse, Charles	Pvt	139th Pen Inf
Starbird, Alfred C.	Sgt	25th NY Cav
Stevens, Russell L.	Pvt	3rd VT Inf
Stoneham, Mark	Pvt	49th NY Inf
Tray, William	Pvt	40th NY Inf
Walter, Frederick	Pvt	139th Pen Inf

FORT CLINCH
Florida

Construction on Fort Clinch, located on Amelia Island in Nassau County, was begun in 1847. An 1873 report listed eight known burials. At least four unknown soldiers and five unknown members of the US Revenue Service were also buried in the cemetery. At least some of these bodies were moved to the Barrancas National Cemetery.

Name	Rank	Co	Unit
14Notes			
Geary, R.	Pvt	I	97th Pen
Millen, Mot.	Pvt	A	7th US Inf
Morgan, D		E	97th Pen
Oliver, Q.W.		K	97th Pen
Thompson, J.	Pvt	K	97th Pen
Wagner, John	Pvt	A	7th US Inf
Wilson, J.	Pvt	B	97th Pen
Worrie, H.C.	Pvt	B	7th US Inf

FORT JEFFERSON
Florida

This list of burials in the Fort Jefferson Post Cemetery is dated April 15, 1873. Nineteen unknown soldiers were also buried in the cemetery. According to the report, one unknown was buried "along with a woman named Charlotte" in the same grave."

Name	Rank	Co	Unit
Ballagher, John	Pvt	L	5th US Art
Beldin, J.			Citizen
Belding, Jasper L.			Citizen
Benton, Daniel	Pvt	I	5th US Art

Name	Rank	Co	Unit
Biordan, John	Pvt	M	5th US Art
Edwards, Marion	Pvt	L	5th US Art
Evitts, Joseph	Pvt	K	5th US Art
Forsyth, James	Pvt	K	5th US Art
Frankenfield, Leonard	Pvt	J	47th Pen Inf
Fraser, Moser B.	Pvt	L	5th US Art
Holmes, Desato	Pvt	M	5th US Art
Jordan, Mary Louisa			
Mackay, James H.	Pvt	J	7th US Art
May, D.W.	Pvt	I	5th US Art
McCraby, John	Pvt	M	5th US Art
McCue, Patrick	Pvt	I	5th US Art
Menan, Daniel	Pvt	A	5th US Art
Mills, William	Pvt	K	5th US Art
Monahan, Michael	Pvt	L	5th US Art
O'Brien, Martin	Pvt	L	5th US Art
O'Laughlin, Michael	Pvt	M	5th US Art
Plark, William H.	Pvt	M	5th US Art
Pleary, John	Pvt	I	5th US Art
Premens, Patrick	Sgt	L	5th US Art
Roberts, Joseph	Corp	M	5th US Art
Seheutte, H.	Sgt	M	5th US Art
Sharner, Alfred	Hospital Steward	USA	
Sheiner, Ervin	Pvt	J	49th Pen Inf
Wagner, Chris.	Pvt	I	5th US Art
Winters, John	Pvt	J	17th US Inf

MIAMI
Florida

These names are from an undated list found in the Quartermaster Department's files.

Name	Rank	Co	Unit
_____, Wm. M	Pvt		La
Brede, H.			Ala
Davis, Joshua			
Herring, Charles			
Horton, J.F.	Pvt	E	1st Ala Vol
Kirby, D.			Tex
Larsern, Earnst			
Magnam, A.L.			La
Muldoon, Barney			La
Nelson, Jono.D.	1st Lt.	K	2nd La
Schlitz, Chas			2nd Ala
Scott, J.			La
Simmons, S__ H.			Ala
Stewart, James M.	Pvt		1st Ala Vol
Vilanalo, A.			La
Wainwright, James M.	Pvt		La

SAINT FRANCIS BARRACKS
Florida

Burials made at Saint Francis Barracks according to an 1886 headstone request.

Name	Rank	Co	Unit
Chapman, Herbert J.	Pvt	G	2nd Art
Hewliu, Wm.	Pvt	B	33rd USCT
Jackson, Nathaniel N.	Pvt	G	2nd Art
Krueger, Paul	Pvt	D	15th Inf
Proffitt, David	Pvt	G	2nd Art
Rose, Adolf	1st Sgt	L	2nd Art
Smith, Charlie	Pvt	G	3rd Art
Stauley, Wm.			Civilian

infant son of Sgt. H. V. Stauley

FORT PULASKI
Georgia

Construction on Fort Pulaski was begun in 1829. Thirty-one years, twenty-five million bricks and one million dollars later, the fort was still not garrisoned when Confederate forces seized it. Federal forces landed near the fort in December 1861. On April 10, 1862, Federal artillery began bombarding the fort. The Federal's rifled cannon shattered the fort's walls. The fort surrender thirty hours after the bombardment began.

Federal forces occupied Fort Pulaski during the remainder of the war. Some of "The Immortal Six-Hundred," Confederate POWs, were kept as prisoners here to discourage Confederate attacks. Apparently the Confederates buried here were POWs.

By 1880 the post was abandoned. The National Park Service believes the bodies of the Federal troops were moved to the Beaufort National Cemetery shortly after the war ended. However, nothing has been found to confirm this. It appears that only two graves were ever permanently marked, those of Robert Roman and Charles Sellmer.

Name	Rank	Co	Unit
Bradford, M.J.	Capt.		20th NC - CSA
Browly, O.K.	Capt.	B	20th NC - CSA
Bunting, John	Pvt	H	3rd US Inf
Buring, J.L.	Lt.		49th Ga - CSA
Curtis, Edward S.	Pvt	H	16th US inf
Easton, C.B.	Lt.	G	10th Va - CSA
Fisher, S. J.	Musician		16th US Inf
Foster, Thomas	Pvt	E	3rd US Art
Goodloc, F.J.	Lt.		44th Ten - CSA
Gruaway, J.T.	Lt.		50th Va - CSA
Halloran, Michael	Pvt	C	33rd US inf
Hian, Elijah (Colored)	Laborer		Civilian
Hurley, John	Pvt	H	3rd US Inf
Jordan, Harmon	Pvt	E	3rd US Art
Lane, C.C.	Lt.	A	3rd NC - CSA
Lanigan, Mary	Laundress	E	3rd Art
Lingan, John	Pvt	E	18th US Inf
Little, Walter W.	Pvt.	G	18 US Inf

Name	Rank	Co	Unit
Roman, Robert	Lt.		Art & Eng
headstone reads Robert Rowan - died March 3, 1800			
Rosmbalm, E.A.	Lt.		37th Va - CSA
Schaleh, Frdnic (?)	Pvt.	I	7th US Cav
Schweet, Harry	Pvt.	E	15th US Inf
Sillmer, Charles H.			Civilian
infant son of Lt. C. Sillmer - died June 15, 1872			
Smith, W.F.	Pvt.	B	48th NY vols
Wagren, Frederick	Pvt	E	3rd Art
Waters, Q.H.	Pvt		48th NY vols

MACON
Georgia

These Federal occupation troops died in Macon after the Civil War. In 1873, these bodies were moved to Andersonville National Cemetery.

Laur., Ephraim   Co F
Ostrem, A.K.
Warren, Elijah

HONOLULU
Hawaii

These veterans of the Civil War were buried in the "GAR plot" in Honolula.

Name	Rank	Unit
Shipley, George F.	Asst. Surgeron	USN
Wilson, Charles		4th NY Cav

BUNKER HILL
Illinois

These soldiers were buried "in the cemetery at Bunker Hill."

Name	Rank	Co	Unit
Adams, George		B	1st Mo Cav
Atchison, A.C.	1st Lt	A	97th Ill Inf
Bickner, George		F	7th Ill Inf
Bird, James	Corp	A	97th Ill Inf
Bird, Srunder	Sgt	A	97th Ill Inf
Breath, James		A	97th Ill Inf
Davis, Fred		F	7th Ill Inf
Hamilton, George			
Lveick, T. A.		B	1st Mo Cav
Mead, John B	Sgt		28th Ill Inf
Pildermeislie	1st Lt		Marine Bgt
Snedeker, Theadore			80th Ill Inf
Squire, James			97th Ill Inf
Stark, D. H.			142nd Ill Inf
Tipper, Joseph			114th Ill Inf

CARBONDALE
Illinois

These soldiers, who were buried "at the penitentiary" at Carbondale, were listed on an 1870 report.

Name	Rank	Co	Unit
Adams, Albert	Lt		18th Ill Inf
Bowyer, W.L.	Capt		31st Ill Inf
Calvin, Moses		K	18th Ill
Chambers, Lewis		A	93rd US Inf
Collins, E. A.		B	52nd IL Inf
Eldridge, C.L.			15th Ill
Hindman, John		K	18th Ill
Jarboe, L.C.		K	18th Ill
Leftwich, Wm. L.			31st Ill
Marginson, John			15th Ill
Martin, Logan		K	18th Ill
McGee, Joseph			81st Ill Inf
Mulkey, Barton			1st Col Cav
Mulkey, Bejamin	Sgt	G	9th Ill
Powell, Warren			81st Ill Inf
Prickett, John	Corp		31st Ill
Prickett, John	Corp		31st Ill
Richart, F.B.			25th Ohio
Riley, Seaskus	Lt		19 Ill Inf
Roberts, Granville	Capt		Marine Brigade
Robinson, Daniel			13th Ill
Smith, Stewart			2nd Ill
Taylor, Richard			31st Ill
Tiffany, David			Secret Service-USA
White, John H.	Lt Col		31st Ill Inf

CHESTNUT
Illinois

In 1883, a headstone was requested for A. R. Davenport, Company K, 154th Indiana Volunteers, who died in April 1865.

COLCHESTER
Illinios

Name	Rank	Co	Unit
Hindman, David		A	197 Ohio Inf
Prowd, Mathew		C	16 Ill Vet Inf

FORT RENO
Indian Territory

Fort Reno was established in 1874 to protect the Darlington Indian Agency. In the 1880s soldiers from the post guarded the borders of the Oklahoma Territory to keep the "Boomers" from settling in Indian lands. In 1908 the fort was abandoned, but it soon became a remount depot for Army horses and mules. In 1948 the US Department of Agriculture established a research station at the site.

The earliest known burial in the Fort Reno Post Cemetery was made on December 2, 1874. The last burial was that of an infant on May 24, 1948. After World War II, sixty-two German and eight Italian POWs were buried in a separate section of the cemetery.

Name	Rank	Co	Unit
___, Mamie			Civilian (child)
Ackerman, Fred'k		K	5th US Cav
Adair, Italia			Civilian (child)
Aldbigh, Frank		F	25th US Inf
Andrews, J.T.		G	30th US Inf
Argambright, ___			Civilian (child}
Atoli, Jno.			Civilian (infant)
Baker, Robert	Sgt	E	16th US Inf
Barboun, William	Surgeron		
Barnes, I.M.		B	5th US Cav
Beecham, Wm.		E	2nd US Art
Birberick, Geo.			Child
Brinton, Della			Civilian
wife of Joseph Brinton			
Brown, J.H.		E	25th US Inf

Name	Rank	Co	Unit
Brown, John L.			
Brownfield, Stephen N.			
Bucey, Lillie			Civilian
daughter of J.W. and A.L. Bucey			
Bugsell, Ida			Civilian (child}
Burget, Henry			
Burget, Henry			
Burke, ___			Civilian
infant son of Sgt. A.L. Burke			
Butler, Jno.	Sgt	K	5th US Cav
Caldwell, Earl H.			
Calleng, ___			Civilian (infant)
Chalk			Indian Scouts
Clark, Amy			Civilian (infant)
Clark, Ben H.			
Clark, Herman			Civilian (infant)
Clark, Jno.			Civilian (child)
Clark, Julia			Civilian (infant)
Clark, Mary			Civilian (infant)
Clark, Phillip			Civilian (infant)
Clary, Kelly			Civilian (infant)
Cloe, John			
Coleman, James	Pvt	F	9th US Cav
Collins, Mich'l			Employee QMD
Cox, Harley W.			Civilian
son of Pvt H.E. Cox			
Dewn'e, Thomas			Infant
Dolan, John		G	30th US Inf
Dollen, F.M.	Pvt	G	4th US Cav
Elliott, Mary			
Erhardt, Wm. F.			QM Corps
Eubank, Wm.			Child
Fallure, Jas.			Civilian
Farllng, E.J.		H	1st US Cav
Field, Janet Geraldine			Civilian
infant daughter of Pvt Clewold Field			
Finnig, Rich'd		K	5th US Cav
Frass, Lewis A.			Civilian (child)
Freeman, ___			Infant
Furber, Ralph	Pvt		QM Corps
Gilmore, F. W.			Civilian

Name	Rank	Co	Unit	
Glaser, Lizzie			Civilian	(child)
Goldsmith Alex.			Civilian	(child)
Graham, Rob't			Civilian	
Grayard, Jno.			Civilian	(infant)
Gullum, Nancy Patricia				
Halbwachs, Lillian Gertude			Civilian	(infant)
Hall, G.C.	Sgt			
Hamilton, William	Pvt		5th US Cav	
Hamley, Louis F.	Pvt	B	5th Cav	
Hamm, Frank	Pvt	G	4th US Cav	
Hanley, L.F.		B	5th US Cav	
Hanley, Pal'k		C	20th US Inf	
Hannagan, Mich'l			Child	
Harrigom, Q.A.			Civilian	(infant)
Harris, Wm.		F	9th US Cav	
Harrley, Patrick	Pvt	C	20th Inf	
on burial roster, but no headstone				
Hauser, Emil Henry			Child	
Hauser, Herman	Sgt		1st NY Cav	
Hawkins, Marcy				
Herforth, Wm.			Civilian	
Holley, Ester Mae			Civilian	
wife of Pvt. J.A. Holley				
Holmes, Katherine				
Holt, Armstead	Sgt		QM Corps	
Holycross, ____			Civilian	(infant)
Howard, ____zo			Civilian	(child)
Howard, Chas.			QM Employee	
Howard, Joseph Edward			Civilian	
son of Pvt. Joseph Howard - QMC				
Hughes, James Allen			Civilian	
son of Sgt J. L. Hughes				
Hutten, Wm. H.			Civilian	
Hutton, W.H.			13th US Inf	
Indian Child			Civilian	
Jenings, Alb't			Child	
Jennings, Harry			Civilian	
only son of C.M. and E.J. Jennings				
Johnson, Israel		E	34th Ill Inf	
Johnson, ___			Civilian	(child)

Name	Rank	Co	Unit
Johnson, Israel M.			
member GAR Reno Post 10			
Jones, G.D.		F	25th US Inf
Jones, Thomas A.			Civilian (infant)
Kearns, Jos.	Sgt	F	5th US Cav
Kemp, Sam'l		F	9th US Cav
King, Alex		H	25th US Inf
Lanahan, John			
Laueaeyghe, ___			Civilian (infant)
Lee, Edward		H	25th US Inf
Lee, James		F	9th US Cav
Lynch, Patrick	Corp	G	4th Cav
Mason, Annie			
McAdoo, Major			
McCauley, Mary			Civilian
McDonald, Bosswell		B	5th US Cav
McNeil, Fred			Civilian (child)
Michan, And'w		C	13th US Inf
Mistucitt, ___			
Modinger, Wm.		G	4th US Cav
Moore, Henry	Pvt	H	2nd Art
on burial roster, but no headstone			
Morgan, Maralou			
Mosu, Henry		H	2nd US Art
Mucker, Viola			
Mulcahy, T.F.	Corp	I	23rd US Inf
Murphy, W.F.			Civilian
Newham, Rudolph			Civilian (infant)
Niebuhr, Gustaw		B	5th US Inf
O'Connel, Tim			Employee OM Corps
Orayard, Bertha			Civilian (infant)
Otterby, Thos.			Civilian (child)
Pitts, Wm. P.	Musician	F	25th US Inf
Redamore, Columbus	Sgt	L	4th US Cav
Ridgeway, Edward	Corp	G	4th Cav
Robinson, William C.		F	15th US Inf
prior service - NY Vols. Troop G			
Ross, Frank			Civilian
Ross, Frank			2nd Iowa Cav
Ruffing, Sharon Kay			Civilian
daughter of Sgt. Harold Ruffing			

Name	Rank	Co	Unit	
Russell, Auther			Civilian	(child)
Schiffer, ___	Sgt	B	5th US Cav	
Shaffer, J.E.		B	5th US Cav	
Shipley, Saul		F	9th US Cav	
Shoenberg,, F.G.				
Shoenberg,, Paul G.			Civilian	
	son of Henry and Emma Shoenburg			
Shumate, Joseph	Master Sgt		Mo	
Snow, W.S.		I	18th Ind Inf	
Stevens, H.F.			Civilian	
Stogkwell, Wm.			Civilian	
Strang, Wm.		E	5th US Cav	
Stratton, J.H.			Employee	
Struad, Frank		H	4th US Cav	
Swift, Paul				
Sykes, Horace F. (Jr.)			Civilian	(infant)
Tempany, Fred			Infant	
Torrey, E.P.			Civilian	(infant)
Trass, ___			Civilian	(child)
Tucker, Bessie			Civilian	
	infant daughter of R.J. Tucker			
Tucker, John				
V___son, S			25th US Inf	
Vanatta, L.R.		D	22th US Inf	
Waggott, Henry		K	5th US Cav	
Walsh, Sonny			Civilian	(infant)
Walters, William F.				
Ward, Frank J.	Pvt			
Watkins, Alex				
Webster, Porter		A	24th US Inf	
Weeks, Henry	Major			
Wetzel, Philip			Employee QMD	
Wheeler, John (Jr.)			Civilian	(infant)
Wheeler, Maria			Civilian	(child)
White Elk	Pvt	A	Indian Scouts	
Willett, Elmer G.			Employee QMC	
Williams, Jno		G	9th US Cav	
Williams, John	Pvt		9th Cav	
Wilson, Clarence	Pvt			
Wilson, Martha F.				
Wilson, Sarsh Alice				

Name	Rank	Co	Unit
Wilson, Wm. A.			Civilian
Woodman, Patties A.			
Wunterlick, Freda___l			
Young Old Crow			Infant
Young, Clark		M	10th US Cav
Zellmeger, Jacob			

FORT SILL
Indian Territory

This is a list of some of the civilians buried in Fort Sill's Post Cemetery.

Name	Unit
Allen, Emma	Civilian
Anderson, Homer	Civilian
Anderson, Mrs. S.J.	Civilian
Burton, Erwin	Civilian
Carroll, Hazel Beatrice	Civilian
Cartell, M.J.	Civilian
Cook, M.B.	Civilian
Florian, W.M.	Civilian
Griffih, C.C.	Civilian
Hazer, M.	Civilian
Kenwood, A.C.	Civilian
Key, L.E.	Civilian
Litel. Bessie M.	Civilian
Malone, Jno	Civilian
McCune, Henry P.	Civilian
Mocline, E.F.	Civilian
Orudington, A.E.	Civilian
Pager, H.H.	Civilian
Smith, L.B.	Civilian
Srewaet, Mrs A.C.	Civilian
Steeley, W.F.	Civilian
Stout, C.A.	Civilian
Stout, M.M.	Civilian
Thompson, H.W.	Civilian

FORT SUPPLY
Indian Territory

Fort Supply was established in November 1868. On November 22, 1868, Colonel George Armstrong Custer left the post to find hostile Indians. Six days later he attacked Black Kettle's camp on the Washita River. The post closed in 1894. The bodies from the post cemetery were moved to Fort Leavenworth National Cemetery. These names came from an 1886 headstone request.

Name	Rank	Co	Unit
Badface	Pvt	B	Indian Scouts
Christopher, Rex	Pvt	G	6th Cav
Clay, Henry	Sgt	A	24th Inf
Funcy, Michael	Pvt	I	4th Cav.
Funcy, Michael	Pvt	H	23rd Inf
Goodwin, Edwin	Corp	F	5th Cav
Halt, Thomas	Pvt	Band	24th Inf
Higgins, William	Pvt.	F	3rd Inf
Kelley, James	Pvt	F	19th Inf
King, Joseph H.	Pvt	Band	24th Inf
Kinsch, Charles	Pvt	F.	23rd Inf
Lareny, Anderson	Sgt	I	3rd Inf
Mason, _____	child		Civilian
Mayer, Gustavo	Pvt	F	5th Cav
McDonald, John A.	Sgt	H	6th Inf
McDonell, James	Pvt	I	6th Cav
McKelvey, Edm'd B.	Pvt	E	23rd Inf
McSwain, Henry	Pvt	G	6th Cav
Morris, John	Pvt	H	19th Inf
Nash, John A.	Pvt	A	6th Cav
Nehl, Joseph A	Pvt	G	6th Cav
Pegram, Julia			Civilian
Reed, Frank	child		Civilian
Reussin, Je___	Pvt	K	6th Cav
Ringally, Edward	Pvt	C	8th Cav
Saris, Robert	Sgt Major		24th Inf
Scott, B_____	Pvt.	D	10th Cav
Shaw, H. C.			Civilian
Stone, Robert T.	Sgt	I	3rd Inf
Wardnell, William	Pvt	C	6th Cav

WASHITA BATTLEFIELD
Indian Territory

On the morning of November 27, 1868, Col. George Armstrong Custer carried out Lt. Gen. Philip Sheridan's plan of attacking "hostile" Indians in their winter camps by attacking Cheyenne Chief Black Kettle's camp near the Washita River. Custer killed over one hundred Cheyenne and captured fifty-three women and children. Custer took his known wounded and dead back to Camp Supply, but Major Joel Elliott and fourteen troopers were cut off and killed.

In December Custer revisited the battlefield and discovered the bodies of Elliott's command. Elliott's body was moved to Fort Arbuckle. The others were buried in a trench near the battle site. None of these graves have been marked, including the graves of the soldiers who died at Camp Supply.

Name	Rank	Co	Unit
Carrick, William	Corp	H	7th Cav
Christie, Thomas	Pvt	E	7th Cav
Clover, Eugene	Pvt	H	7th Cav
Cuddy, Charles	Pvt	B	7th Cav
KIA - body moved to Camp Supply			
Delaney, Augustus	Pvt		7th Cav
died of wounds at Camp Supply			
Downey, Thomas	Pvt	I	7th Cav
Elliott, Joel H.	Major		7th Cav
Fitzpatrick, Thomas	Farrier	M	7th Cav
George, John	Pvt	H	7th Cav
Hamilton, Louis M.	Captain		7th Cav
body moved to Fort Supply			
Kenedy, Walter	Sgt Major		7th Cav
Lineback, Fredinand	Pvt	M	7th Cav
McCasey, Benjamin	Pvt		7th Cav
died of wounds at Camp Supply			
McClernan, John	Pvt	E	7th Cav
Mercer, Harry	Corp	E	7th Cav
Milligan, William	Pvt	H	7th Cav
Myers, Carson	Pvt	M	7th Cav
Myers, John	Pvt	M	7th Cav
Sharpe, Cal	Pvt	M	7th Cav

Name	Rank	Co	Unit
Stobacus, Frederick	Pvt	M	7th Cav
Vanousky, Irwin	Sgt	M	7th Cav
Williams, James F.	Corp	I	7th Cav

HANEY'S CORNER
Indiana

The Gordon Post of the GAR requested headstones for the following "soldiers interred in our midst that have no tablet to mark their graves."

Name	Rank	Co	Unit
Bates, Alfred	Pvt.	D	6th Ind Inf
buried in the Concord Cemetery			
Buckhamman, John W.	Pvt.	A	37th Ind Inf
buried in the McGlophlin Cemetery			
Kelly, Charles F.	Pvt	A	37th Ind Inf
Young, George W.			17th Inf

MORGAN COUNTY
Indiana

Name	Rank	Co	Unit
Cummins, John	Pvt	K	132nd Ind
Johnson, Joseph H.	Pvt	K	132nd Ind.
Lyman, Daniel	Pvt	F	21st Ill
Lynch, Benjamin D.	Pvt	A	33rd Ind
Lynch, Benoni P.	Pvt	C	71st Ill
Pike, Meanton	Pvt	H	43rd Ind

CLEAR LAKE
Iowa

These names were listed on an 1884 headstone request.

Name	Rank	Co	Unit
Allen, James		H	15th Mass Inf
Baker, Edward D.	Col		71st Pen Inf
Booth, Cyrus			
Booth, Wm.		B	25th Wisc Inf
Carlyon, Thos.		H	1st Wisc Art
Fay, Charles		H	96th Ill Inf
Gilmor, George		G	37th Iowa Inf
Hatcher, Clinton		F	8th Va - CSA
Howard, Tom	1st Sgt	B	32nd Iowa Inf
Martin, Augustus	1st Sgt	H	98th NY Inf
Sirrine, David		C	12th US Inf

CLINTON
Iowa

In 1885, Jno. F. McGuire requested headstones for the following soldiers buried at Clinton.

Name	Rank	Co	Unit
Adams, B.P.	Pvt	A	1st Ind Cav
Godskesen, Seneus	Corp	M	1st Ohio Battery
Morey, Ira F.	Pvt	B	26th Iowa Inf
Rexford, D.A.	2nd Lt	F	6th Inf
Walker, W.A.	Pvt	B	16th Mich Sharpshooters

PARIS
Iowa

Name	Rank	Co	Unit
Bice, George		F	20th Iowa
Breneman, Finally		C	24th Iowa
Hesaton, Semer C.		D	47th Iowa
Jordan, Hanson		E	20th Iowa
Joshlyn, Joseph J.		G	96th Ill
Wheeler, Wm. N.		E	46th Iowa
Yazel, William		C	19th Ohio

FORT HAYES
Kansas

Fort Hayes (originally known as Camp Fletcher) was founded in 1865. This undated list includes burials in the post cemetery from 1867 - 1884. There were also 120 unknown burials in the post cemetery. The post closed in 1880. Sometime before 1909 a total of 180 bodies were moved to Fort Leavenworth National Cemetery.

Name	Rank	Co	Unit
Anderson, Bascom C.	Pvt	A	19th Inf
Anderson, Thomas S.	Pvt	E	38th Inf
Armstrong, William	Pvt	F	10th Cav
Ash, Robert	Pvt	E	38th Inf
Beman, James	Pvt	F	7th Cav
Blackman, Louis A.	Pvt	M	6th Cav
Brich, James	Pvt	G	38th Inf
Buser, Charles	Pvt	F	10th Cav
Cheale, William	Corp	B	20th Inf
Christian, R.A.	A.A. Surgeon		USA
Clark, George L.	Pvt	F	6th Cav
Coleman, Jordon	Pvt	C	38th Inf
Cullen, Patrick	Pvt	F	6th Cav
Dandridge, Richard	Pvt	F	10th Cav
Donnelly, Michael	Pvt	Band	6th Cav
Duncan, Austiso	Pvt	J	10th Cav
Eikius, Peter	Pvt	F	10th Cav
Filbery, Albert	Pvt	E	38th Inf
Filmore, Willston	Pvt	F	10th Cav
Fugan, Jacob		G	5th Inf
Gaines, Harry	Pvt	G	38th Inf
Gaines, Leven	Corp	E	38th Inf
Glisman, Frank	Pvt	C	3rd Inf
Green, George	Pvt	F	10th Cav
Ingrass, Hardin	Pvt	C	38th Inf
Jackson, Thomton	Pvt	E	9th Cav
Johnston, Edward	Pvt	F	10th Cav
Keah, Wilber D.	Pvt	B	18th Inf
Kelly, John	Pvt	H	7th Cav
Kelly, Robert	Pvt	K	7th Cav
Kihok, Richard	Pvt	G	10th Cav

Name	Rank	Co	Unit
Kober, William	Pvt	G	6th Cav
Kraesuer, Charles	Pvt	F	6th Cav
Labor, Dones	Pvt	G	20th Inf
Lankeu, John	Pvt	D	18th Inf
Lealey, E.M.	Pvt	A	3rd Inf
Leggih, Robert	Pvt	C	38th Inf.
Limpson, William	Corp	G	38th Inf
Logan, John	Pvt	F	10th Cav
Lutz, George	Pvt	G	5th Inf
Marsh, James	Pvt	E	3rd Inf
McMahon, Andrew	Pvt	C	38th Inf
Miller, Henry	Pvt	G	5th Inf
Miller, William	Pvt	L	19th Kan Cav
Neil, Jeff J.	Pvt	E	20th Inf
Olson, Edward	Pvt	G	5th Inf
P___eth, Hugh	Pvt	G	38th Inf
Parker, Henry	Pvt	C	38th Inf
Rogers, Nathan	Pvt	E	6th Cav
Romey, Michael	Sgt	E	5th Inf
Scott, Starling	Pvt	E	38th Inf
Scusn, Peter	Pvt	G	20th Inf
Sirethy, James	Pvt	E	3rd Inf
Smith, John	Pvt	G	6th Cav
Smith, Joseph	Pvt	G	38th Inf
Sumnor, George H.	Pvt	L	6th Cav
Thayer, James B.	Pvt	G	20th Inf
Thompson, Frank	Pvt	G	38th Inf
Torrell, James H.	Pvt	C	18th Inf
Tugan, James	Pvt	G	5th Inf
Turpin, Edward	Pvt	C	38th Inf
Vircn, Clemens	Pvt	F	20th Inf
Vooman, Adolph	Sadler	C	6th Cav
Waldm, George B.	Pvt	C	6th Cav
Walters, Joseph	Pvt	E	9th Cav
Warren, Samuel	Pvt	E	38th Inf
Welch, Peter	Pvt	L	6th Cav
Wesley, August	Pvt	F	10th Cav
Williams, George	Pvt	C	38th Inf
Wright, John A.	Pvt	J	7th Cav

FORT RILEY
Kansas

Fort Riley was founded in May 1853. During the summer of 1867 a cholera epidemic claimed 67 lives. By 1880 there were over 200 burials in the cemetery. These names are from an 1886 headstone request. At least two bodies from the post cemetery were removed to Fort Leavenworth National Cemetery, but today the cemetery is an active army post cemetery.

Name	Rank	Co	Unit
Batteree, Thos. J.	Pvt	F	2nd Vols
Brown, W.J.	Pvt.	C	13th Wis Vols
Deanholdt, H.	Pvt	B	12th Wis
Gregory, William	Pvt	G	2nd Wis Vols
Ilsoone, T.B.	Pvt	F	2nd Col Cav
James, Thomas	Pvt	G	2nd Vols
Jones, B.R.	Sgt	G	7th Cav
Jones, Joseph	Pvt	H	5th Wis Vols
Kennedy, Robert	Pvt	A	38th Inf
Kenney, Thos. S.	Sgt	G	5th Vols
L'Duncan, Wm.	Pvt	G	2nd Vols
Long, Wm. R.	Pvt	K	5th Wis Vols
Lung, John	Pvt		3rd Wis Cav
Maloy, John	Pvt	G	7th US Cav
Manning, Thomas	Pvt	I	7th US Cav
Moiole, Richard W.	Pvt	E	14th MO Cav
Monle, Richard W.	Pvt.	E	4th Wis Cav
Moore, Rebulon	Pvt	L	2nd Col Vols
O'Donnell, Joesph	Sgt	B	6th US Inf
O'Donnell, Nicholas	Pvt	K	7th US Cav
Parker, James	Pvt		3rd Wis Art
Prickett, Jacob	Pvt	E	7th US Cav
Ratteree, Thomas J.	Pvt	F	2nd US Vols
Rogers, Albert	Pvt	A	7th US Cav
Rolfe, R.L.	Pvt	F	13th Wis Vols
Rolfe, R.L.	Pvt	I	7th US Cav
Schnitz, K.	Pvt		
Shine, Geo.	Corp	G	37th Inf
Smith, James	Pvt	E	2nd Kan Cav
Stangler, Thomas	Corp	A	13th US Inf

Name	Rank	Co	Unit
Swane, J.	Pvt	K	1st US Cav
T_____, E.H.			
Thompson, W.W.	Pvt	F	7th Kan Cav
Valier, Vincent	Pvt	I	9th Kan Cav
W_____, J.W.			
Watts, William H.	Com. Sgt.		7th US Cav
Winters, Owen	Pvt	H	2nd Col Vols
Withens, George	Pvt	D	7th US Cav

FORT WALLACE
Kansas

This list of burials at Fort Wallace is dated 1886. Soldiers marked with an "*" were killed by Indians on July 1, 1867. The bodies of soldiers who were removed from Fort Craig, New Mexico, are marked with an "#". However most of the bodies (147) in the Fort Craig Post Cemetery were moved to the Santa Fe National Cemetery in March of 1876.

This list apparently was made before these bodies were moved to the Fort Leavenworth National Cemetery.

Name	Rank	Co	Unit
Abbing, Charles	Pvt	A	7th Cav
Adams, Alex.	Corp	H	10th Cav
Bacen, Fred. A,	Pvt	I	7th Cav
Bacon, Julius	1st Sgt	F	5th Cav
Bersee, Seth	Pvt	K	7th Cav
Blackman, James	Pvt	E	5th Cav
Blair, William	Pvt	B	5th Inf
Bonthron, James	Corp	G	5th Cav
Brown, Charles	Pvt	F	5th Cav
Brown, James	Pvt	G	7th Cav
Burch, Charles	Pvt	E	7th Cav
Burk, Thomas	Pvt	I	5th Inf
Burns, James	Pvt	I	5th Cav
Carry, Rodgers *	Pvt	M	2nd Cav
Cavender, James S.	Sgt	G	16th Inf
Clark, James	Pvt	D	5th Cav
Clise, Oscar *	Sgt	M	2nd Cav
Cmigan, Patrick	Pvt	I	5th Cav
Cnuneu, Michael	Pvt	C	5th Cav
Conway, J.M. #	Pvt	E	23rd Inf
Cormell, Michael *	Pvt	M	2nd Cav
Culvay, C.W.			Scouts
Davenport, Samuel	Sgt	K	7th Cav
Davis, Henry	Pvt	I	38th Inf
Davis, James	1st Sgt	I	10th Cav
Douglass, James	Corp	G	7th Cav
Duggan, Daniel	Corp	G	5th Cav
Dummell, Wm. H.	Sgt	G	7th Cav

Name	Rank	Co	Unit
Elam, Charles	Burgler	G	7th Cav
Ericksin, Louis M.	Pvt	H	3rd Inf
Farley, Lewis			Scouts
Fisher, Jacob	Pvt	I	5th Cav
Fleming, John	Drum Major		5th Cav
Floyd, William *	Pvt	M	2nd Cav
Foster, Joseph	Pvt	M	2nd Cav
Gloltery, John	Pvt	H	3rd Inf
Gnman, Michael *	Pvt	M	2nd Cav
Gordon, Charles	Corp	D	3rd Inf
Green, John	Pvt	I	10th Cav
Habl, Richard	Pvt	K	19th Inf
Haines, Chas. S. *	Corp	M	2nd Cav
Haley, Michael *	Pvt	M	2nd Cav
Hatchett, J. #	Pvt	D	9th Cav
Heiser, Thos. R.	Pvt	A	3rd Inf
Henderson, John	Ord Sgt		
Hill, William	Pvt	H	5th Cav
Humphries, N. J. *	Pvt	M	2nd Cav
John, Thomas	Pvt	B	5th Cav
Johnson, Charles	Pvt	K	7th Cav
Junker, Joesph	Hospital Steward		
Kelsey, Edward #	Pvt	D	9th Cav
Kerr, William	Wagoner	D	5th Inf
Kirrney, Isaac	Pvt	I	10th Cav
Klink, Fred	Pvt	E	7th Cav
Knadesville, Forest	Pvt	C	5th Cav
Kriser, Christian	Pvt	I	5th Cav
Lawler, Michael *	Pvt	M	2nd Cav
Legnon, Frank	Pvt	C	5th Inf
LeRoy, Eugene	Sgt	G	16th Inf
Maquire, Peter	Pvt	G	5th Cav
McNally, Ed	Pvt	E	3rd Inf
Miller, Jacob S.	Pvt	E	3rd Inf
Morris, John	Pvt	D	3rd Inf
Morton, Frank A. #	Pvt	D	15th Inf
Mremu, Joseph	Pvt	D	3rd Inf
Murphy, Michael	1st Sgt	L	7th Cav
Nesmith, C.E.	Capt	A	6th Inf
Nolan, Palmer #	1st Sgt	K	15th Inf
Papar, Theodore	Sgt	H	6th Inf

Name	Rank	Co	Unit
Reahme, Frank	Pvt	G	7th Cav
Reur, Gethard	Pvt	D	7th Cav
Reynolds, Joseph J.	Pvt	K	7th Cav
Richardson, Wm. #	Pvt	D	9th Cav
Riley, John	Pvt	K	7th Cav
Rogers, Amscah	Pvt	F	5th Cav
Ross, Robert	Pvt	E	7th Cav
Sa_____idt, Michael	Pvt	C	5th Inf
Saunders, Charles		L	7th Cav
Sines, Gotthardt	Pvt	B	5th Inf
Smith, Euring	Sgt	C	10th Cav
Talbot, Thomas #	Pvt	E	4th Cav
Thomas, Charles	Pvt	F	10th Cav
Thomas, Henry	Pvt	F	10th Cav
Thomas, Robert	Pvt	H	6th Inf
Thompson, Wellington	Pvt	H	5th Cav
Tolton, Charles *	Pvt	M	2nd Cav
Trail, Nathan	Pvt	G	7th Cav
Trestee, Emile	Pvt	M	7th Cav
Turner, John	Sgt	A	7th Cav
Unknown *			
Waldnuff, Jas.	Pvt	E	3rd Inf
Walker, H.W.	Corp	C	7th Cav
Washington, John	Pvt	I	10th Cav
Weaver, John A. #	Pvt	F	23rd Inf
Wells, Frank	Sgt		5th Cav
Williams, Benjamin	Pvt	I	10th Cav
Williams, Edward	Corp	I	38th Inf
Williams, John	Pvt	C	5th Cav
Wilson, Samuel	Pvt	C	10th Cav
Wyllyaws, Fred.	Sgt	G	7th Cav
Young, John	Corp	C	5th Inf
Zuinke, James	Pvt	D	7th Cav

TOWNER'S STATION
Kansas

The following soldiers were buried at Towner's Station according to an 1867 report.

Burket, Casper
Hanrey, _____
Rudolph, Teadore

CATTLESBURY
Kentucky

According to an 1866 report these bodies were "buried indiscriminately. Only a few headboards have been erected ... marked in pencil." These bodies were later moved to the New Albany National Cemetery.

Name	Rank	Co	Unit
Armstrong, Ralph	Maj		5th Iowa Inf
B_____, A.			43rd Ind Inf
B_____, T.	Pvt	D	44th Ind Inf
Baldwin,			
Brown, J.T.	Pvt	C	___ Ind. Inf.
Burk, W. B.	Maj		14th Ky Inf
Burkhant, Emanuel	Pvt	A	43rd Ind Inf
Caffin, G.			___ Ind Inf
Childers, J.	Pvt	C	14th Ky Inf
D_____, H.	Pvt	E	44th Ind Inf
Dunn, A.	Pvt	I	17th KY Inf
Fish, Leo M.	Pvt		44th Ind Inf
Gerrh, J.A.			
H____, B.E.			
H_____, C.T.	Pvt	G	44th Ind Inf
Hampton, J.	Adjutant		89th Ky Inf
Hleole, _____			11th KY
Hollis, H.P.	Pvt	C	1st Ky
Jackson, H.G.	Pvt	H	___Ind Inf

Name	Rank	Co	Unit
Keichaels, K.		C	1st Ky Inf
Kglin, R.A.			
L . T. A.			
Levington, J.			
Little, William			17th Ky Inf
McBryer, Solomon	Pvt		89th Ky Inf
S_____, T.			
Stack, H.	Pvt		44th Ind Inf
Stinger, W.D.			
Williamson, J. E.	Pvt	C	14th Ky Inf
Young, J.		C	1st Ky Inf

MOUNT VERNON
Kentucky

These soldiers were buried at Mount Vernon according to an undated report. It appears these bodies were moved to the London National Cemetery. Later that cemetery was moved to the Camp Nelson National Cemetery.

Name	Rank	Unit
Augle, John	Pvt	100th Ohio
Auglunyer, J. H.	Pvt	104th Ohio
Baldwin, M.L.	Pvt	104th Ohio
Gesselmen, John	Pvt	100th Ohio
Kruses, D	Pvt	100th Ohio
S____, W.	Pvt	86th Ind
Strewple, C		
Woody, E.	Pvt	14th Ohio

CALAIS
Maine

This list of Union soldiers who died during the war is dated 1866.

Name	Rank	Unit
Barnard, Frank	Sgt	6th Maine Inf
Beruly, Simeon		12th Maine Inf
Choal, Charles		12th Maine Inf
Coy, John Hamer	Sgt	6th Maine Inf
Coy, William		6th Maine Inf
Dunn, Russel	Sgt	6th Maine Inf
Foster, Charles A.		22nd Maine Inf
Furlong, Ruel	Capt	6th Maine Inf
Gass, Henry		12th Maine Inf
Geer, John		1st Maine Cav
Lahan, Edward		22nd Maine Inf
Learik, Zacharias		20th Maine Inf
Munson, Warren		20th Maine Inf
Sears, Adolphus		1st Maine Cav
Shay, Michael		6th Maine Inf
Townsend, Edgar		22nd Maine Inf
Wail, Henry	Lt	6th Maine Inf

NAUTUCKET
Maine

This 1866 list is of soldiers and sailors who died in Nautucket during the war.

Name	Notes
Alley, George	
Alley, L.T.	
Chace, Seth	
Chrain, John	Newtown Cemetery
Coffin, Charles	Newtown Cemetery
Ellis, Wm	
Fisher, Charles	

Name	Notes
Folger, James	
Fredinian, Alley	
Fuiens, William H.	North Congregational Church
Fyher, Hirman	
Gruber, Charles	Navy - Newtown Cemetery
Gruber, Wm	Unitarian Cemetery
Hany, Robert	
Inho, George W.	
Lavarn, Wm. H.	
Lefrey, F.W.	
Loffin, Rufus	
Luarin, George H.	
Macy, Charles	
Mender, Lamhel B.	
Mitcheal, Beng.	
Moore, Alex	
Morgan, Peley	Navy - U.S. Dawn
Nuchews, Fred. W.	
Perry, William	Newtown Cemetery
Rogers, David N.	
Russell, Henry	
Tracy, George	
Wimlow, S.M.	Newtown Cemetery

US NAVAL ACADEMY
Annapolis
Maryland

These names are on an 1887 request for headstones for unmarked graves in the Naval Academy Cemetery.

Name	Rate	Unit	Notes
Bailey, Thomas	1st g Stwd.	USN	
Briscod, James	2 CL Boy	USN	
Brown, John	Gun mate	USN	U.S.S. Dale

Name	Rate	Unit	Notes
Carroll, Eugene		USN	
Carson, Robert	Seaman	USN	U.S.S. Hassle
Clarke, William	1 C.F.	USN	
Cloyd, Charles L.	Q.M.	USN	U.S.S. Dale
Colson, Peter	Seaman	USN	
Crown, Joseph	Cox	USN	U.S.S. Santee
Gardner, William	Pvt	USMC	
Harrison, William		USN	USS Macedonian
Hartland, David	Seaman	USN	USS Constellation
Iynde, Henry	Chief Gunmate	USN	U.S.S. Santee
James, Henry	g. Gr. (sic)	USN	U.S.S. Santee
Jarrard, Thomas			
Knost, John	Mus.	USMC	
McIntyre, Thomas	Seaman	USN	
Miller, Conrad	Pvt	USMC	
Morse, Albert	Seaman	USN	
Morton, Gilbert	Pvt	USMC	
Nulte, Conrad	Pvt	USMC	
Parks, Alexander	Carpt. Mate	USN	U.S.S. Dale
Parks, George	Master's Mate	USN	USS Brandywine
Pinkham, Edward S.	Q.M.	USN	U.S.S. Santee
Schreyer, John	Musician	USN	
Tripp, John Ellis		USN	
Walker, Samuel	Seaman	USN	U.S.S. Dale

FORT McHENRY
Maryland

This is an 1866 list of burials in the Fort McHenry Post Cemetery. These graves were marked with headstones in 1874. This post was still active as late as 1893.

Name	Rank	Co	Unit
Armsby, John	Pvt	F	91st NY Inf
Arnold, William	Pvt	J	6th NY Art
Bailey, Edmond	Pvt	D	7th USCT
Barcheis, F.	Pvt	K	Purnell Legion
Barry, Thomas	Pvt		2nd US Art
Bison, Jacob S.	Pvt		
Bloo____, Philamer	Pvt	E	6th NY Art
Bradigan, Martin	Pvt	E	5th Mo Inf
Bragg, W.	Pvt	F	6th NY Art
Bransom, B.F.	Pvt	J	11th Ind Inf
Brown, P.C.	Pvt	A	Purnell's Legion (Md)
Buegler, William	Pvt	F	7th NU Art
Burry, W.	Pvt	C	11th Ind Inf
Bush, Henry	Pvt	A	122nd USCT
Campbell, thomas	Pvt	J	2nd US Art
Chueer, Samuel A.	Pvt	B	91st NY Inf
Collins, Lewis (Colored)	unassigned		
Culoer, Theodore	Pvt	C	27th NJ Inf
Darrell, Geo.	Pvt	A	White's Battallion
Davis, Edwin	Pvt	B	8th NY Art
Dean, James	Pvt	J	2nd US Art
Dennison, W.A.	Pvt	K	85th Pen Inf
Denny, Joseph	Pvt	B	91st NY Inf
Dodge, W.	Pvt	C	5th NJ Inf
Dorabush, Charles	Pvt	H	2nd US Art
Duxburry, J.	Pvt	G	29th Mass Inf
Ellsworth, Henry S.	Hospital Steward		
Emory, W.H.	Pvt	J	2nd US Inf
Eugene, Max	Pvt	K	2nd US Art
Fisher, J.W.	Pvt	D	160th Ohio Inf
Francis, J.H.	Pvt	B	5th NY Art
Frank, Geo.	Pvt	K	8th NY Art
French, G.Q.	Pvt	E	3rd US Inf
Gibson, William	Pvt	E	6th US Inf
Glasgow, Adam (Colored)	unassigned		

Name	Rank	Co	Unit
Glears, Henry	Pvt	E	39th USCT
Gowan, San	Pvt	F	5th Wis Inf
Haight, Geo.	Musician	H	8th NY Art
Hall, C.H.	Pvt	E	5th NY Inf
Harrington, A.J.	Pvt	J	137th NY Inf
Hill, James	Pvt	B	5th NY Art
Hizelberger, Joseph	Pvt	A	3rd Md Inf
Hoffman, Charles	Pvt	A	91st NY Inf
Holmes, Jonoas	Pvt	H	
Holse, Charles	unassigned		
Houston, Samuel (Colored)	unassigned		
Huggins, J.C.L.	Pvt	J	3rd US Inf
Hull, Marion	Pvt	K	44th NY Inf
Jones, Wilber	Pvt	A	49th NY Inf
Karsy, Patrick	Pvt	C	91st NY Inf
Keaton, W.	Pvt	A	49th Pen Inf
Kerris, Th. E.	Pvt	G	12th US Inf
Kuhn, Daniel	Pvt	F	3rd Md Inf
LaBounsy, Ira	Pvt	C	91st NY Inf
Lachenal, Andrew	Pvt	H	2nd US Art
Lajorge, John	Pvt	F	6th NY Art
Lampburg, W.	Pvt	M	14th Pen Cav
Lamure, Alphonso	Pvt	K	2nd US Art
Laughlin, Th.	Pvt	G	3rd US Art
Leoy, James	Pvt	E	87th NY Inf
Link, M.A.	Pvt	D	103rd NY Inf
Lissleson, Leoan	Pvt		Independent Cav
Loolam, Henry	Pvt	A	4th US Inf
Lowton, Charles	Pvt	C	5th NY Art
Lsockson, L.T.	Pvt	H	99th Pen Inf
Masherson, John	Pvt	K	2nd US Art
Maury, James	Pvt	K	2nd US Art
McDaniels, F. L.	Pvt	E	1st US Cav
McGill, Henry	Pvt	H	2nd US Art
McGin, James	Pvt		2nd US Art
McGuire, W.	Pvt	J	
Micku, Peter	Musician	Band	2nd US Art
Miller, P.W.	Pvt	A	184th Ohio
Monehousr, E.	Pvt	C	8th NY Art
Montanye, Washington	Pvt	F	53rd Pen Inf
Moore, W.	Pvt		Anderson's MA Sharps

Name	Rank	Co	Unit
Mullen, Hugh	Pvt	C	3rd Md Inf
Nelson, Th.	Pvt	D	33rd NJ Inf
O'Connell, John	Pvt	A	91st NY Inf
Owens, George	Pvt	J	91st NY Inf
Peck, Cornelius	Pvt	J	77th NY Inf
Pendergraph, Joshua	Pvt	K	11th Ind Inf
Percival, Simon B.	Pvt	E	5th NY
Peterson, John	Pvt	H	15th NY Cav
Playford, Edward	Pvt	A	91st NY Inf
Pollard, Barsless	Pvt	D	19th NYSM Inf
Prass, Sh.	Pvt	C	111th Pen Inf
Precoss, S.	Pvt	A	5th NH Inf
Quinn, Elias (Colored)	unassigned		
Quinn, Th. (Colored)	unassigned		
Quinn, Thomas	Pvt	D	5th NY Art
Rarick, M.	Pvt		NY Inf
Reily, John	Pvt	K	33rd NY Inf
Rickets, Geo.	Pvt	G	8th Md Inf
Riley, Peter	Pvt	A	4th MO Inf
Rum, Phillip	Pvt		1st US CT
Rutherford, Th	Pvt	K	8th Va Inf CSA
name struck out on roll			
Sayers, Thomas	Pvt	E	2nd US Art
Schawb, L.	Pvt	K	74th Pen Inf
Scoss, George	Pvt		5th NY Cav
Serlis, Harry	Pvt	J	6th NY Art
Sewart, John	Musician	Band	2nd US Art
Shage, Aaron	Pvt	J	51st Pen Inf
Sirling, C.	Pvt	D	5th NY Art
Smith, W.H.	Sgt	K	6th Ohio Cav
Springer, Charles S.	General Service		
Sruler, Wm.	Pvt	B	111th Pen Inf
Steward, James	Pvt	C	11th Ind Inf
Stuckman, W.J.	Pvt	F	91st NY Inf
Sullivan, Dennis	Pvt	J	2nd US Art
Suocking, Henry	Pvt	G	91st NY Inf
Thompson, T.	Pvt	K	108th NY Inf
Thorburn, Alexander	Pvt	B	98th Ohio Inf
Tucker, W.T.	Pvt	G	11th Ind Inf
Turpin, James	Pvt	F	37th USCT
VanValkinburg, Peter	Pvt	C	91st NY Inf

Name	Rank	Co	Unit
Vickers, Charles	Pvt	E	10 Md Inf
Vinal, Lrupet	Pvt		5th NY Art
Walter, Thomas	Pvt	E	10th Md Inf
Warner, Edward	Pvt	H	6th NY Art
Was_____, Greenbery G.	Pvt	K	1st Md Inf
Waterman, S.F.	Pvt	G	8th NY Art
Wiard, John	Pvt	B	8th NY Art
Wims, Peter (Colored)	unassigned		
Wolfe, J.	Pvt	K	107th Ohio Inf
Zlarding, J.W.	Pvt	J	2nd US Art

PORT TOBACCO
Maryland

These names are from a list of bodies (including 38 unknowns) moved from the Port Tobacco area to Arlington National Cemetery in July 1867.

Name	Rank	Co	Unit
Aollington, W.S.		E	11th US Vols
Bell, John		I	5th NJ
Bliss, E.W.		B	3rd Reg Exlisor Brig
Borber, A. J.		I	3rd Reg Exlisor Brig
Bryce, Petter			NYV
Cadey, Hurbert			
Chew, Andrew		I	6th NJ
Clark, Sevi			
Dolin, Steverson			
H_____, F..			2nd NJ
Heff, Jacob		A	3rd Reg Exlisor Brig
Hurt, Josh.		H	5th NJ
Hyman, _____			
Jaco, Wm.		E	14th Pen
Jones, Charles W.		G	3rd Reg Exlisor Brig
Jones, Wm.			14th Pen
Long, Wm. C.	Corp	G	Maryland Vols
McNee, T.		I	3rd Reg Exlisor Brig
Nelson, Otto		B	3rd Reg Exlisor Brig
Pette, Davis		B	6th NJ
Porter, Ed		B	3rd Reg Exlisor Brig
Quinn, P.J.			5th Reg Mags
Shaw, John F.		H	7th NJ
Smith, Ephraim B.		E	3rd Reg Exlisor Brig
Smith, W.B		I	3rd Reg Exlisor Brig
Sowe, Max		H	3rd Reg Exlsior Brig
Teal, John H.		G	3rd Reg Exlisor Brig
Warren, D.		G	3rd Reg Exlisor Brig
Whaland, Thomas		G	1st Reg Exlisor Brig
Wheeler, J.B.		G	3rd Reg Exlisor Brig
Wheeler, L. Curtis		B	3rd Reg Exlisor Brig
Wlhitney, Wm. H.		C	13th Reg USV
Wood, Isral			
Zahn, H.		H	3rd Reg Exlisor Brig

ABRIGTON
Massachusetts

This is an undated list sent to the War Department by Abrigton's GAR post.

Name	Rank	Co	Unit
Cook, Fred	Pvt		7th Mass
F__nch, George	Pvt		
Fenno, James A.	Pvt	G	48th Mass
also Co A - 60th Mass			
Gurney, Windfield	Pvt	D	5th NJ
Launders, Edward	Pvt	A	11th Mass
Nash, Edward E.	Pvt	C	38th Mass
Newton, H.O.F.	Pvt	C	38th Mass
Oldham, Walter S.	Pvt		16th Mass Batt
Oveutt, Lowell	Pvt	I	
Perry, Jonothan	Pvt	C	38th Mass
Small, John M.	Corp.		23rd Mass
Snell, Samuel L.			3rd Mass Cav
Sprague, Lucus A	Pvt		20th Mass
Steison, Charles	Pvt	F	4th Mass Cav
Stetson, Charles	Pvt	F	4th Mass Cav
Thompson, Josiah	Pvt	D	42nd Mass
Winston, J. B.	Pvt	H	12th Mass

HAVERHILL
Massachusetts

This list of burials at Haverhill was attached to a letter from the local GAR post.

Name	Co	Unit
Batchilclan, John		
Brachett, Ambrose	E	
Chein, John		1st Mass Hvy Art
Church, Wm.		
Cumier, J. H.		
Davidson, William	K	11th Mass Inf
Ellis, Hiram W.		
Frye, J.L.	C	2nd Mass Hvy Art
Gross, LD.N.	K	11th Mass Inf
Hamwood, Andrew J.	G	50th Mass Inf
Mahoney, John	E	17th Mass Inf
Minnuns, Wm. H.		
Morgan, Geo. E.		
Palmer, Charles		
Permbenton, Robert		
Pier, Charles		
Putnam, Henry		
Stevens, J.M.	E	11th Mass Inf
Whitter, Charles	C	12th Mass Inf
Witharm, Charles O.		

FORT MACKINAC
Michigan

This undated report lists burials in the post cemetery at Fort Mackinac.

Name	Rank	Co	Unit
Clitz, John	Capt		2nd US Inf
DeRussy, R.E.			Civilian (child)
Fires, J.P.	Pvt		4th VRC
Fisher, Chas.	Pvt	B	43rd US Inf
Goldhofer, J.	Pvt	F	1st US Inf
Granger, H.W.			
Hughes, J.	Pvt		4th VRC
L_____mmson, A.C.	Pvt	F	1st US Inf
Lawrence, A.			2nd US Inf
McCabe, W.	Pvt		4th US Art
Mills, J.R.			
O'Brian, A.E.			Civilian
O'Brian, Charles			Civilian
burried in the O'Brian Family Lot			
Perry, Louis	Sgt	F	1st US Inf
Ragen, George			2nd US Inf
Slingerland, R.H.	Pvt		4th VRC
Stoner, Saul	Pvt		4th VRC

FORT WAYNE
Michigan

After the Civil War bodies were moved to the Fort Wayne Post Cemetery from Flint, Kalamazoo, Niles, and Ypsilanti. This list of burials at Fort Wayne is from an 1886 headstone request. Unfortunately the first page, listing 38 names, is missing.

Name	Rank	Co	Unit
Bartell, John	Pvt	G	4th US Art
Beutly, Orin	Pvt	E	1st US Inf
Brook, William		G	4th US Cav
Brown, Peter	Pvt	H	22nd US Inf
Bugman, Adolph	Pvt	Band	1st US Inf
Bullock, Charles	Pvt	A	10th US Inf
Burns, William			A Batt.-19th US Inf
Butler, John		A	2nd Batt-19th US Inf
Castell, George			
Dawsen, William J.	Musician	C	1st US Inf
Dorer, William	Pvt	A	1st US Inf
Dufficks, Leroy			
Duffy, Edward	Pvt	D	1st US Inf
Fagan, Michael			General Service-USA
Flanagan, Jeremiah	Pvt	J	1st US Inf
Flynn, Michael		B	A Batt.-19th US Inf
Green, wlilliam H.	Pvt	I	1st US Inf
Hall, Weruer	Pvt	F	3rd US Cav
Haterman, William F.	Pvt	E	10th US Inf
Haudy, Charles	Rect		19th US Inf
Hildreth, Norris	Pvt	B	2nd Batt-19th US. Inf
Holmes, Dewis	Pvt	C	10th US Inf
Kahn, John	Pvt	G	1st US Inf
Kelly, John D.	Pvt	J	23rd US Inf
Kelly, Thamos	Pvt	A	1st US Inf
Kile, Joseph W.	Sgt	G	5th Mich Inf
Lehman, N.B.		B	1st batt-19th US Inf
Ltein, John	Pvt	K	10th US Inf
Lutton, George	Pvt	E	1st US Inf
Lynch, Patrick	Pvt	E	1st US Inf
McAllister, Wreman	Sgt	J	1st US Inf
McCooly, ___			
McHugh, John	Pvt		1st US Inf
McMahon, Patrick		E	2nd Batt-19th US Inf

Name	Rank	Co	Unit
Meahau, Charles	Pvt	A	1st US Inf
Morrison, Norman		A	2nd Batt-19th US Inf
Pelit, Clinton	Pvt	K	10th US Inf
Perry, George	Pvt	H	10th US Inf
Potts, John	Musician	Band	1st US Inf
Pratt, Henry C.	Major		
Rice, Wm. J.	1st Lt		23rd US Inf
Richards, John	Pvt	H	10th US Inf
Russell, William	Pvt	E	1st US Inf
Silver, Stephen		J	43rd VRT
Walsh, James			A Batt.-19th US Inf

BIG HOLE BATTLEFIELD
Montana

The Battle of Big Hole was fought between the Nez Perce Indians and about 200 soldiers and civilians under Col. John Gibbon. Despite being surprised, the Nez Perce repelled Gibbon's men before retreating. After the battle the majority of the casualties were buried on the field. It appears their remains were later moved to a common grave on the battlefield that was marked by a monument.

Name	Rank	Co	Unit
Bradley, James H.	1st Lt	B	7th Inf
Broetz, Herman	Pvt	I	7th Inf
Butterly, Mathew	Pvt	E	7th Inf
Drake, McKindra L.	Pvt	H	7th Inf
Edgeworth, Robert L.	1st Sgt	G	7th Inf
Eisenhut, Jacob	Corp	D	7th Inf
English, William	1st Lt	I	7th Inf
died at Deer Lodge, Mt.. Body moved to Jacksonville, Ind.			
Gallagher, Michael	Musican	D	7th Inf
Hogan, Michael	Sgt	J	7th Inf
Klies, John	Artificer	K	7th Inf
Logan, William	Capt	A	7th Inf
remains moved to Custer Battlefield in 1892			
Mantz, Gottieb	Pvt	G	7th Inf
Martin, William H.	Sgt	G	7th Inf
McCafferey, Daniel	Corp	I	7th Inf
McGuire, James	Pvt	F	7th Inf
O'Brian, F. John	Pvt	G	7th Inf
O'Conner, Dominick	Corp	G	7th Inf
Page, Edward	Sgt	L	2nd Inf
Payne, William H.	Corp	D	7th Inf
Pomeroy, Noah G.	Corp	K	7th Inf
Sale, Robert E.	Corp	G	7th Inf
Smith, John B.	Pvt	A	7th Inf
Stinebaker. Thomas P.	Musician	K	7th Inf
Stortz, Frederick	!st Sgt	K	7th Inf
Watson, William W.	Sgt	F	7th Inf

CUSTER BATTLEFIELD
Montana

On June 28, 1876, five companies of the 7th Cavalry, some 225 men, were wiped out by the Sioux and Cheyenne Indians in what became known as "Custer's Last Stand." After the battle the dead were buried on the battlefield. The next year the 7th Cavalry revisited the battlefield to remove most of the bodies of the officers. No bodies of the enlisted men were removed. Two years later the remaining graves were remounded. The site was declared a national cemetery in 1879. In 1881 the bodies were moved to a common grave around a granite monument on Custer Hill. No attempt was ever made to recover the bodies of the casualties of Reno's command, even though they were buried less than six miles away. This is a list of men killed with Custer.

Name	Rank	Co	Unit
Adams, George E.	Pvt	L	7th Cav
Allan, Fred C.	Pvt	C	7th Cav
Andrews, William	Pvt	L	7th Cav
Assadley, Anthony	Pvt	L	7th Cav
Atchison, Thomas	Pvt	F	7th Cav
Babcock, Elmer	Pvt	L	7th Cav
Bailey, Henry A.	Blacksmith	I	7th Cav
Baker, William H.	Pvt	E	7th Cav
Barry, John	Pvt	I	7th Cav
Barth, Robert	Pvt	E	7th Cav
Bobo, Edwin	1st Sgt	C	7th Cav
Boyle, Owen	Pvt	E	7th Cav
Brady, William	Pvt	F	7th Cav
Brandon, Benjamin	Farrier	F	7th Cav
Brightfield, John	Pvt	C	7th Cav
Briody, John	Corp	F	7th Cav
Broadhurst, Joesph H.	Pvt	I	7th Cav
Brogan, James	Pvt	E	7th Cav
Brown, Benjamin F.	Pvt	F	7th Cav
Brown, Geoge C.	Corp	E	7th Cav
Brown, William	Pvt	F	7th Cav
Bruce, Patrick	Pvt	F	7th Cav
Bucknell, Thomas J.	Trumpeter	C	7th Cav
Burke, John	Pvt	L	7th Cav

Name	Rank	Co	Unit
Burnham, Lucien	Pvt	F	7th Cav
Bustard, James	Sgt	I	7th Cav
Butler, James	1st Sgt	L	7th Cav
Calhoun, James	1st Lt	L	7th Cav
body removed to Fort Leavenworth National Cemetery			
Callahan, John J.		K	7th Cav
Carney, James	Pvt	F	7th Cav
Cashan, William	Sgt	L	7th Cav
Cather, Armantheus D.	Pvt	F	7th Cav
Cheever, Ami	Pvt	L	7th Cav
Coleman, Charles	Corp	F	7th Cav
Conner, Edward	Pvt	E	7th Cav
Conners, Thomas	Pvt	I	7th Cav
Cooke, William W.	Lt	HQ	7th Cav
body moved to Hamilton, Ontario			
Criddle, Christopher	Pvt	C	7th Cav
Crisfield, William B.	Pvt	L	7th Cav
Crittenden, John J.	2nd Lt	L	7th Cav
body moved from the battlefield to Custer National Cemetery			
Custer, George A.	Lt Col	HQ	7th Cav
body moved to West Point			
Custer, Thomas W.	Capt	C	7th Cav
body moved to Fort Leavenworth			
Darris, John	Pvt	E	7th Cav
Davern, Edward	Pvt	F	7th Cav
Davis, William	Pvt	E	7th Cav
Dohman, Anton	Pvt	F	7th Cav
Donnelly, Timothy	Pvt	F	7th Cav
Doss, Henry C.	Trumpeter	G	7th Cav
Downing, Thomas P.	Pvt	I	7th Cav
Driscoll. Edward	Pvt	I	7th Cav
Duggan, John	Pvt	L	7th Cav
Dye, William	Pvt	L	7th Cav
Eiseman, George	Pvt	C	7th Cav
Engle, Gustave	Pvt	C	7th Cav
Farrand, James	Pvt	C	7th Cav
Farrell, Richard	Pvt	E	7th Cav
Finckle, August	Sgt	C	7th Cav
Finley, Jeremiah	Sgt	C	7th Cav
Foley, John	Corp	C	7th Cav
French, Henry E.	Corp	C	7th Cav

Name	Rank	Co	Unit
Galvan, James J.	Pvt	L	7th Cav
Gardiner, William	Pvt	F	7th Cav
Gilbert, William H.	Corp	L	7th Cav
Gillette, David C.	Pvt	I	7th Cav
Graham, Charles	Pvt	L	7th Cav
Griffen, Patrick	Pvt	C	7th Cav
Gross, George H.	Pvt	I	7th Cav
Hagan, Thomas	Corp	E	7th Cav
Hamilton, Henry	Pvt	L	7th Cav
Hammon, George W.	Pvt	F	7th Cav
Harrington, Henry M.	Lt	C	7th Cav
Harrington, Weston	Pvt	L	7th Cav
Harrison, William H,	Corp	L	7th Cav
Hartersall, James	Pvt	C	7th Cav
Haugge, Louis	Pvt	L	7th Cav
Heath, William H.	Farrier	L	7th Cav
Helm, John	Pvt	E	7th Cav
Henderson, John	Pvt	E	7th Cav
Henderson, Sykes	Pvt	E	7th Cav
Hetsimer, Adam	Pvt	I	7th Cav
Hieber, William	Pvt	E	7th Cav
Hiley, John	Pvt	E	7th Cav
Holcomb, Edward P.	Pvt	I	7th Cav
Horn, Marion E.	Pvt	I	7th Cav
Howell, George	Saddler	C	7th Cav
Hughes, Francis T.	Pvt	L	7th Cav
Hughes, Robert H.	Sgt	K	7th Cav
James, William B.	Sgt	E	7th Cav
Kavanagh, Thomas G.	Pvt	L	7th Cav
Kelly, John	Pvt	F	7th Cav
Kelly, Patrick	Pvt	I	7th Cav
Kenny, Michael	1st Sgt	F	7th Cav
Keogh, Myles W.	Capt	I	7th Cav
body moved to Fort Hill Cemetery, Auburn, NY in 1877			
King, John	Farrier	C	7th Cav
Klein, Gustave	Pvt	F	7th Cav
Knauth, Herman	Pvt	F	7th Cav
Knecht, Andy	Pvt	E	7th Cav
Kramer, William	Trumpeter	C	7th Cav
Leham, Henry	Pvt	I	7th Cav
Lehman, Frederick	Pvt	I	7th Cav

Name	Rank	Co	Unit
Lerock, William H.	Pvt	F	7th Cav
Lewis, John	Pvt	C	7th Cav
Liddiard, Herod	Pvt	E	7th Cav
Lieman, Werner L.	Pvt	F	7th Cav
Lloyd, Edward W.	Pvt	I	7th Cav
Lobering, Louis	Pvt	L	7th Cav
Lossee, William A.	Pvt	F	7th Cav
Madsen, Christian	Pvt	F	7th Cav
Mahoney, Bartholomew	Pvt	L	7th Cav
Manning, James	Blacksmith	F	7th Cav
Mason, Henry S.	Corp	E	7th Cav
Maxwell, Thomas E.	Pvt	L	7th Cav
McCarthy, Charlrs	Pvt	L	7th Cav
McElroy, Thomas	Trumpeter	E	7th Cav
McGucker, _____	Trumpeter	I	7th Cav
McGue, Peter	Pvt	L	7th Cav
McIlhargey, Archibald	Pvt	I	7th Cav
Meier, Frederick	Pvt	C	7th Cav
Meyer, Albert H.	Corp	E	7th Cav
Meyer, August	Pvt	C	7th Cav
Miller, John	Pvt	L	7th Cav
Milton, Francis E.	Pvt	F	7th Cav
Mitchell, John	Pvt	I	7th Cav
Monroe, Joseph	Pvt	F	7th Cav
Moonie, George A.	Trumpeter	E	7th Cav
Morriss, George C.	Corp	I	7th Cav
Noshang, Jacob	Pvt	I	7th Cav
Nursey, Frederick	Sgt	F	7th Cav
O'Bryan, John	Pvt	I	7th Cav
O'Connell, David J.	Pvt	L	7th Cav
O'Conner, Patrick	Pvt	E	7th Cav
Ogden, John S.	Sgt	E	7th Cav
Omling, Sebastian	Pvt	F	7th Cav
Parker, John	Pvt	I	7th Cav
Patton, John W.	Trumpeter	I	7th Cav
Perkins, Charles	Saddler	L	7th Cav
Phillips, Edgar	Pvt	C	7th Cav
Pitter, Felix James	Pvt	I	7th Cav
Pix, Edward	Pvt	C	7th Cav
Porter, James E.	1st Lt	I	7th Cav
Post, George	Pvt	I	7th Cav

Name	Rank	Co	Unit
Quinn, James	Pvt	I	7th Cav
Rauter, John	Pvt	C	7th Cav
Reed, William	Pvt	I	7th Cav
Rees, William H.	Pvt	E	7th Cav
Reibold, Christan	Pvt	L	7th Cav
Reily, William Van W.	2nd Lt	F	7th Cav
body moved to Washington, DC.			
Roberts, Henry	Pvt	L	7th Cav
Rogers, Walter B.	Pvt	L	7th Cav
Rood, Edward	Pvt	E	7th Cav
Rossbury, John W.	Pvt	I	7th Cav
Rudden, Patrick	Pvt	F	7th Cav
Russell, James H.	Pvt	C	7th Cav
Ryan, Daniel	Corp	C	7th Cav
Saunders, Richard	Pvt	F	7th Cav
Schele, Henry	Pvt	E	7th Cav
Schmidt, Charles	Pvt	L	7th Cav
Scott, Charles	Pvt	L	7th Cav
Seiler, John	Corp	L	7th Cav
Shade, Samuel	Pvt	C	7th Cav
Shea, Jeremiah	Pvt	C	7th Cav
Shorrow, William H.	Sgt Major	HQ	7th Cav
Short, Nahan	Pvt	C	7th Cav
Siefous, Francis W.	Pvt	F	7th Cav
Siemon, Charles	Blacksmith	L	7th Cav
Siemonson, Bent	Pvt	L	7th Cav
Smallwood, William	Pvt	E	7th Cav
Smith, Albert A.	Pvt	E	7th Cav
Smith, Algernon	1st Lt	E	7th Cav
body moved to Fort Leavenworth			
Smith, James	Pvt	E	7th Cav.
Snow, Andrew	Pvt	L	7th Cav
St John, Ludwick	Pvt	C	7th Cav
Stafford, Benjamin	Pvt	E	7th Cav
Staples, Samuel	Corp	I	7th Cav
Starck. Frank	Wagoner	C	7th Cav
Stella, Alexander	Pvt	E	7th Cav
Stuart, Alpheus	Pvt	C	7th Cav
Stungwitz, Ignatz	Pvt	C	7th Cav
Sturgis, James G.	2nd Lt	E	7th Cav
Symms, Darwin L.	Pvt	I	7th Cav

Name	Rank	Co	Unit
Tarbox, Bryon	Pvt	L	7th Cav
Teeman, William	Corp	F	7th Cav
Tessier, Edward D.	Pvt	L	7th Cav
Thadus, John	Pvt	C	7th Cav
Torrey, William A.	Pvt	E	7th Cav
Troy, James E.	Pvt	I	7th Cav
Tweed, Thomas S.	Pvt	L	7th Cav
Van Allen, Garret	Pvt	C	7th Cav
Van Sant, Cornelius	Pvt	E	7th Cav
Varden, Frank E.	1st Sgt	I	7th Cav
Vetter, Michael	Pvt	L	7th Cav
Vickory, John	Sgt	F	7th Cav
Von Bramer, charles	Pvt	I	7th Cav
Warren, George A.	Pvt	F	7th Cav
Way, Thomas N.	Pvt	F	7th Cav
Whaley, William B.	Pvt	I	7th Cav
Wild, John	Corp	I	7th Cav
Wilkinson, John R.	Sgt	F	7th Cav
Wright, Willis B.	Pvt	C	7th Cav
Wyman, Henry	Pvt	C	7th Cav
Yates, George	Capt	F	7th Cav

body moved to Fort Leavenworth National Cemetery in 1877

FORT KEOGH
Montona

These names are from an 1886 headstone request. These bodies were moved to Custer National Cemetery.

Name	Rank	Co	Unit
Braitsch, Charles	Pvt	G	22nd Inf
Gray, Thomas	Sgt	D	5th Inf
Nohles, Johu P.	Bandleader		5th Inf
O'Neill, Henry	Pvt	G	18th Con. Vol.

FORT KEOGH MONUMENT
Montana

These names appear on a large, red granite monument located in Custer National Cemetery. The inscription reads: **To the officers and soldiers killed, or who died of wounds received in action, while clearing the District of the Yellowstone of hostile Indians.** The only information in the Quartermaster General's files is a sketch dated October 22, 1881 filed as "monument." It appears this monument was first erected at Fort Keogh. Perhaps the soldiers there raised the funds to erect it.

After Fort Keogh closed, the "remains, monuments, and headstones" from the post cemetery were shipped to Custer Battlefield National Cemetery (the name was changed in 1991). The monument arrived at the railroad station at Crow Agency in the summer of 1908. However, because the monument weighed several tons it could not be moved to the cemetery a few miles away. After much bureaucratic red tape (the officials in Washington could not accept the bid of $273.00 to move the monument) the monument was finally moved to the cemetery in May 1910.

Name	Rank	Co	Unit
Alberts, James S.	Sgt	D	7th US Cav
KIA at Bear Paw Mountains			
Archer, Elire	Pvt	L	7th US Cav
KIA at Caynon Creek			
Baader, Lee	Pvt	E	5th US Inf
KIA at Mispah Creek			
Batty, William H.	Pvt	C	5th US Inf
KIA at Tongue River			
Bennett, Andrew S.	Capt		5th US Inf
KIA at Clark's Fork			
Biddle, J.W.	2nd Lt		7th US Cav
KIA at Bear Paw			
Brown, Matthew F.	Pvt	L	7th US Cav
KIA at Caynon Creek			
Cable, Joseph A.	Sgt	I	5th US Inf
KIA at Bear Paw Mountains			
Cleaveland, John E.	Pvt	A	7th US Cav
KIA at Bear Paw Mountains			

Name	Rank	Co	Unit
Dawsey, David E.	Pvt	D	7th US Cav
KIA at Bear Paw Mountains			
Derchew, Otto	Sgt	A	7th US Cav
KIA at Bear Paw Mountains			
Douglas, George E.	Pvt	E	5th US Inf
KIA at Pumpkin Creek			
Gasselin, Frank J.	Pvt		7th US Cav
KIA at Caynon Creek			
Georghegan, Thomas	Pvt	C	5th US Inf
KIA at Bear Paw Mountains			
Glackousaky, Frank	Pvt	F	5th US Inf
KIA at Rosebud			
Haddo, John	Corp	B	5th US Inf
KIA at Bear Paw Mountains			
Hale, Owen	Capt		7th US Cav
KIA at Bear Paw Mountains			
Hurdick, George	Pvt	K	7th US Cav
KIA at Bear Paw Mountains			
Irving, John	Pvt	G	2nd US Cav
KIA at Bear Paw Mountains			
Johnson, Joseph	Sgt	C	5th US Inf
KIA at O'Fallon Creek			
Kelly, Lewis	Pvt	A	7th US Cav
KIA at Bear Paw Mountains			
Khaupp, Frank	Pvt	K	7th US Cav
KIA at Bear Paw Mountains			
Kohler, Joseph	Pvt	I	5th US Inf
KIA at Bear Paw Mountains			
Lawlin, James	Pvt	G	7th US Cav
KIA at Caynon Creek			
Loreys, Peter	Pvt	H	5th US Inf
KIA at Rosebud			
Martin, Michael	1st Sgt	D	7th US Cav
KIA at Bear Paw Mountains			
Martindale, Charles A.	Pvt	F	5th US Inf
KIA at Rosebud			
McCauu, Bernard	Pvt	F	22nd US Inf
KIA at Wolf Mountains			
McDermott, Geo.	1st Sgt	A	7th US Cav
KIA at Bear Paw Mountains			

Name	Rank	Co	Unit
McIntyre, Samuel	Pvt	A	7th US Cav
KIA at Bear Paw Mountains			
Meilke, Max	Sgt	K	7th US Cav
KIA at Bear Paw Mountains			
Peshall, Richard M.	Pvt	G	5th US Inf
KIA at Bear Paw Mountains			
Randall, Wm. J.	Pvt	D	7th US Cav
KIA at Bear Paw Mountains			
Roth, Francis	Pvt	K	7th US Cav
KIA at Bear Paw Mountains			
Rotheman, Augustus	Corp	A	5th US Inf
KIA at Wolf Mountains			
Shreuger, Charles	Pvt	H	5th US Inf
KIA at Rosebud			
Whitlow, William	Pvt	K	7th US Cav
KIA at Bear Paw Mountains			
Wilde, Otto	1st Sgt	K	7th US Cav
KIA at Bear Paw Mountains			

FORT MAGINNIS
Montana Territory

Fort Maginnis was founded in 1880. This list of burials in the post cemetery is from an 1886 headstone request. These bodies were later moved to the Custer Battlefield National Cemetery.

Name	Rank	Co	Unit
Adams, Henderson	Corp		1st Cav
Baur, Frederick	Ord Sgt		
Burt, Chas. E.	Pvt	G	18th Inf
DeJrak, E.L.	Pvt	I	18th Inf
Herline, Alonzo	Pvt	K	3rd Inf
Neal, Henry	Pvt	F	1st Cav
Parker, Joseph	Sgt	K	2nd Cav
Roberts, Robert	Pvt	I	18th Inf
Waters, Frederick O.	Sgt	I	18th Inf

FORT MISULLO
Montana

Fort Missullo was an active Army post from 1876 through World War I. This list of burials in the post cemetery is taken from an 1886 headstone request.

Name	Rank	Co	Unit
Beck, Charles	Pvt	D	3rd Inf
Burleigh, Charles J.	Pvt	B	3rd Inf
Girick, Wm.	Pvt	H	3rd Inf
Jenkzer, Walter Kendig	Pvt	H	3rd Inf
Mahan, John	Pvt	I	3rd Inf
McMahon, John	Pvt	B	3rd Inf
O'Neil, James J.	Pvt	D	3rd Inf
Smith, John	Pvt	F	3rd Inf
Stewart, Robert	Sgt	D	

RENO - BENTEEN BATTLEFIELD
Montana

On June 25, 1876, five troops of the 7th Cavalry under Col. George Armstrong Custer were wiped out by Sioux and Cheyenne Indians. Maj. Marcus Reno and Capt. Frederick Benteen's commands were trapped by the Indians and almost wiped out also.

The two officers' bodies were recovered and moved back East, but there was never an attempt to move the bodies of the enlisted men to the national cemetery less than five miles away.

Name	Rank	Co	Unit
Armstrong, John E.	Pvt	A	7th Cav
Bloody Knife	Indian Scout		7th Cav
Bobtail Bull	Indian Scout		7th Cav
Botzer, Edward	Sgt	G	7th Cav
Charley, Vincent	Farrier	D	7th Cav
Clear, Elihu F.	Pvy	K	7th Cav
Considine, Martin	Sgt	G	7th Cav
Dalious, James	Corp	A	7th Cav
DeWolf, James M.	Surgeon		USA
Dorman, Isaiah			7th Cav
Dorn, Richard B.	Pvt	A	7th Cav
Golden, Pat M.	Pvt	D	7th Cav
Gordon, Henry	Pvt	M	7th Cav
Hageman, Otto	Corp	G	7th Cav
Hodgson, Benjamin (II)	2nd Lt	B	7th Cav
body moved to Philadelphia			
Holmer, Julius	Pvt	K	7th Cav
Jones, Julien D.	Pvt	H	7th Cav
Koltzbucher, Henry	Pvt	M	7th Cav
Lell, George			
Liddiard, Herod T.			
Little Brave	Indian Scout		7th Cav
Lorentz, George	Pvt	M	7th Cav
Mann, Frank C.			
Martin, James	Corp	G	7th Cav
McGinnis, John J.	Pvt	G	7th Cav
McIntosh, Donald	1st Lt	G	7th Cav
body moved to Fort Leavenworth then to Arlington in 1909			
Meador, Thomas B.	Pvt	H	7th Cav

Name	Rank	Co	Unit
Meyer, William D.	Pvt	M	7th Cav
Moody, William	Pvt	A	7th Cav
Moore, Andrew J.	Pvt	G	7th Cav
O'Hara, Miles F.	Sgt	M	7th Cav
Rapp, John	Pvt	G	7th Cav
Reynolds, Charles A.			
Scollin, Henry M.	Corp	M	7th Cav
Seafferman, Henry			
Smith, George	Pvt	M	7th Cav
Streing, Frederick	Corp	M	7th Cav
Sullivan, John	Pvt	A	7th Cav
Summers, David	Pvt	M	7th Cav
Tanner, James J.	Pvt	M	7th Cav
Turly, James	Pvt	M	7th Cav
Voight, Henry C.	Pvt	M	7th Cav
Wells, Benjamin	Farrier	G	7th Cav
Winney, DeWitte			

FORT McPHERSON NATIONAL CEMETERY
Nebraska

Fort McPherson National Cemetery was established on March 3, 1873, to provide a convenient location for reburial of bodies from the post cemeteries at abandoned forts. By the time Lt. Col. Oscar Mack, the Inspector of National Cemeteries, inspected the cemetery in 1874, a total of 389 burials (only 118 known) had been made in the cemetery.

When the bodies from the Fort Laramie Post Cemetery were moved to the cemetery in 1891, the remains of 28 enlisted men of the 6th Infantry who were killed in the "Gratton Massacre" were moved and reburied in a mass grave. Their names are listed in a separate entry in this book.

The names here are from tombstones in the cemetery.

Name	Rank	Co	Unit
____, James C.			
____, Katherine M.			
____, S. H.			
____, Evelyn			
____, F. H.			
Alegan, Hopkins			
Allen, Lizzie			
daughter of C.W. and K. E. Allen			
Anderson, John			___ Cav
Arlington, N			
Ayers, Austin E.			Neb
Bahr, Conrad	1st Sgt	G	4th US Inf
died Ft. Sanders			
Bakers, Wm.	Corp		
Barhard, Annie May			Civilian
infant daughter of H. & A. Barhard,			
Barry, R. M.	Sgt	E	23rd US Inf
Bartels, Charles F.J.	Pvt		36th Inf
Bartlett, Alice			
Bartlett, Mathew	Civilian		
Bates, Albert			
Beehler, Fred'k		C	13th US Inf
Beerman, August		C	6 Regt Minn Inf
Berlinn, Chas.			

Name	Rank	Co	Unit
Berry, W. J.			
Bid, Andrew			Civilian
son of Andrew & Nettie W. Bid			
Blackwood, Rob't			
Bond, F.W.			
Bott, John A.	Farrier		
Brandon, Wm.			
Brooks, Jno.			
Brown, Alva W.			Nebr
Brown, Hugo		H	14th US Inf
Brown, James W.	Farrier	F	2nd Kans. Cav
Brownwell, Dan'l			
Brund, G.W.			
Bryan, T.D.			
Bulhand, Joseph L.		M	1st Mich Cav
Burke, JNO		G	10th US Inf
Burke, Wm	Sgt		
Burmann, Jno.			
Byerson, Chas.			USCT
Byrne, Geo.			
C.T.J.			
Caffrey, Bernard			
Carter, B.			
Chindler, ____			
Chon, Lewis			
Chorpening, Samuel		G	13th Inf
Christ, Dan'l			Ohio
Clark, Jno.			Pen
Clary, Blanche Irene			
daughter of F.E. and Rose E. Clary			
Clear, G.W.	Sgt		
Clemens, W.H.		A	2nd US Cav
Clifford, Timothy		F	4th US Inf
Coats, R.S. (Mrs.)			
Coffey, Dan'l	Corp		
Coker, J.W.			
Colbur, J.C.		F	6th US Cav
Collins, James			
Colyer, Clarence R.			
Corcoran, Edmond	Corp		
Cortell, Edw'd			USA

Name	Rank	Co	Unit
Costello, Wm.			
Crier, Sam'l			
Croker, S.A.			
Croker, Wm.			
Crosey, John	Recruit		2nd US Cav
Cumming, Lester A			
son of A and M Cumming			
Cunningham, ___			
Dany, Bernard	Ord'n. Sgt.		
Davis, David			
Dawson, Rich'd	Sgt		
Day, N. K.			Ohio
Delarid, J.M.			
Deuel, William A.			
son of G and C Deuel			
Diffley, Edward T.	Pvt	D	4th Inf
killed by lightning at Fort Laramie			
Doi, Edward			3rd US Cav
Dolan, Thomas			
Doyle, Jno.			
Duis, William	Corp		1st US Inf
Dyer, Fred'k			Iowa
Edgar, L..G.	Corp	G	3rd US Cav
Elia, Lizzie			
Ellison, C.			
Eltz, Frederick		I	3rd Calif Inf
Everly, Martha			
wife of Pvt. C. Wilson			
Feay, C.F.			
Feeterle, E.			
Fera, C.F.			
Fink, J.E.			
Finn, ___			
Fish, Mary J.			Civilian
daughter of E.D. & J.A. Fish			
Fisher, Lulu			Civilian
daughter of J.S. & M.A. Fisher			
Fisk, James	Pvt		2nd US Cav
Flynn, Thos.			
Forrest, J. A.			Ohio
Fouts, William	Capt	D	7th Iowa Cav

Name	Rank	Co	Unit
Fox, Cyrus		C	7th Iowa Cav
Frawley, James		G	4th US Inf
Froendall, Theodore			
Gabriel, Jules			
Gaffery, Thos.			
Gale, Henry C.	Comsy Sgt	A	11th Kan Cav
Ganham, Alf'd	Corp	H	4th US Inf
Garr, H.			Kan
Garrons, Louis		G	3rd US Cav
Gaus, Christian		K	4th US Inf
Gillberg, Edw'd			
Glass, Ferd.	Corp	G	10th US Inf
Gleason, Dan'l			
Glover, Peter			
Goble, Jno.			
Godfrey, Mary L.			
wife of W.R. Godfrey			
Gore, Robert		D	48th Ill Inf
Grady, J. O.		F	17th US Inf
Graves, Wm. H.	Pvt		2nd US Cav
Gray, Henry	Q.M. Sgt	H	16th Kan Cav
Grelen, L.G. (Mrs)			
Griesner, Julius	Band		15th US Inf
Griffin, Daniel		M	2nd Calif. Cav.
Groms, Benj.			Iowa
Grossman, Ira		B	11th Ohio Cav
Guire, J.D.		G	14th US Inf
H____, Jno.			
Hagen, Michael			
Hailman, Martin		I	3rd Calif. Inf
Hallauer, Jno			
Halliley, Dennis		G	2nd US Cav
Hammond, A. M.			
Hanaway, Rob't		B	9th US Inf
Hanlon, Peter		C	23rd US Inf
Haughey, James A.			
Hayden, Charles			
Healy, M.			
Heath, George W	2nd Lieut	G	7th Iowa Cav
Heath, W.H.			
Henderson, James		M	16th Kansas Cav

Name	Rank	Co	Unit
Highland, James			
Highterver, J.F.			
Hines, A.G.	Corp		
Hines, Wm.		H	15th US Inf
Hinze, Wm.			
Hugely, Argine			
Hughes, James		F	7th Iowa Cav
Hunt, James			
Hurley, James		I	3rd Calif Inf
Hutchinson, ___			
Hutchinson, V.A.A.			
Hutchison, Blanche			Civilian
daughter of Joab & Sarah Hutchison			
Ibwin, Basgom G.	1st Sgt	U	14th US Inf
Jenkins, L			
Johnson, Almond			
Johnson, Peter	Civilian		
Johnston, J.F.			
Jones, C.L.			
Jones, Henry			
Jones, Wm.			
Jones, Wm.	Sgt		
Jordon, Jos			
Jost, William	Pvt		22nd US Inf
Julin, Lilly Sophia			
daughter of Henry and Mary Julin			
Kearns, A.			
Keating, James			
Keeb, Louis			
Keefer, Barney			
Kelly, Rob't			
Kelsey, James			
Kesner, ___			
Khiner, ___	Sgt		
King, Chas.			
Kitchen, W.M.			
Krohn, J.M.			
Laied, John D.			
Lasen, Henry			
Leighty, Roy C.			
Lellen, C.B.			Iowa

Name	Rank	Co	Unit
Leunel, Wm.			22nd US Inf
Lewis, George		A	206th Pa Inf
Litz, Jacob		F	13th US Inf
Lizieelder, Alvin G.			Civilian
son of Thomas G.			
Lloyd, Julia H.			Civilian
wife of B.L. Lloyd			
Low, A.S.			
Lucas, Isaac J.			Ind
Lucksinger, ___			
Lustig, Carol			
Lutz, Frederic		A	14th Inf
Lynch, ___			
Lyons, B.M.	Corp	G	7th Iowa Cav
Macomber, Lorenzo S.			
16 Indpt. Btry. Mass. Lt. Arty.			
Maddox, Samuel	Blacksmith	B	11th Ohio Cav
Madsen, Anders			
Mahedy, E.F.			
Mahoney, Dennis J.	Pvt		3rd US Cav
Maker, ___			
Mallatt, Chas.			
Manker, C.A.	Sgt.		Ohio
Mardorf, Wilhelm			
Mares, William C.	Pvt		3rd US Cav
Marte, Jas.			
Mason, ___			
Mathlenesen, Ludwig		M	1st Neb Cav
Maybrook, Geo.	Sgt	G	22nd US Inf
McAllister, J.A.			
McCabe, Pat'k			
McCanner, William			
McDonald, George			
McGhee, ___			
McGowan, Wm.			
McKay, Robt		E	4th US Inf
McKenna, Geo.			
McKenzie, John R.	Corp	F	9th US Inf
McMillin, John W.	Bglr	K	12th Mo Cav
Meglie, James			
Mernagh, Michael	Pvt	K	USA

Name	Rank	Co	Unit
Merrick, Rob't			
Merrill, Loring	Corp	B	14th US Inf
Meyers, Edward F.	Farrier	I	__th Cav
Miller, Daniel H.		F	3rd US Cav
Medal of Honor - Indian Wars			
Miller, R.A.			
Mitchell, E.			
Montgomery, J.O.			
Moorehead, Phillip			Ohio
Morey, W.H.			
Morris, David			
Morris, Moore		G	3rd US Cav
Morton, G.			
Morwig, ___			
Morwig, Fred'k			
Morwig, L.			
Muller, William			
Murphy, Wm.			
Murray, ___			
Murray, John	Sgt		
Muteay, John	Pvt		9th US Inf
Myers, Herman			
Nehnardt, August E.			
Newman, James			
Newton, A.S.			
Nolan, Matthew			
Nolitor, Jno.		D	4th US Inf
Norton, G. H.			
O'Brien, J.		G	4th US Inf
O'Connell, Daniel			
O'Hara John			
O'Neal, Anges			
O'Rourke, Patrick,J.	Capt	E	1st Pa. Res. Inf
Orr, R.			
Osterhout, Jesse			15th Ill Cav
Ott, Frank	Corp	G	14th US Inf
born in Baden, Germany			
Parker, ___			
Parsons, James			
Patterson, ___			

Name	Rank	Co	Unit
Pinkston, James			
murdered Sept. 16, 1885			
Pinkston, John W.			
murdered Sept. 16, 1885			
Piterman, Andrew			
Pollock, Edwin			
son of ___ Annie			
Potter, ___			
Power, A.			
Pownley, ___			
Pressher, Havy			
Ray, James M.		B	44th Iowa Inf
Reames, Elmer E.			Civilian (infant)
Reames, Nettie B.			
Reames, Peter			age 17
Reed, ___			
Reed, Clifton			
Reiley, James			
Remington, Asa			
Reynolds, Henry			
Righardson, S.N..			
Roach, Henry			
Roach, Herman			
Roagh, M.J.			
Roberts, R.F.			
Roberts, William		F	5th Mo SM Cav
Robinson, L.L.		L	1st Mich Cav
Roma, Cottlier			
Ryan, Alpheus	Sgt	K	22nd US Inf
Ryan, Jno			
Ryan, Thomas			
Ryan, Thos.			
Saardort, Rey F.			Civilian
Schaeffer, J.F.			Ind
Schmutz, Magdeline			
Schulz, Rob't			
Schwan, F.			
Scott, Louis			
Seneff, Albert			Neb
Shaw, James R.	Col		3rd NJ Cav
Sheridan, K.			

Name	Rank	Co	Unit
Sicking, Bernard	Pvt	G	13th Inf
Silva, Louis	Pvt		14th US Inf
Smead, A. L.			
Smith, _____			
Smith, G.S.			
Smith, Isaac C.			Iowa
Smith, JNO		E	4th US Inf
Smith, Joseph			
Smith, Phillip			Neb
Smith, W. G.			
Smith, Wm.			
Sneld, W.M.			
Snyder, _____			
Snyder, Robert		B	6th Inf
Sonnelly, Jas	Sgt. Maj		USA
Southwick, _____			
Spencer, Frederick	Pvt		6th US Cav
Spotted Horse			
Staley,		F	3rd US Cav
Stewart, Perry			Ohio
Stine, Chas.			Mich
Strong, Alex.		G	22nd US Inf
Sullivan, J.W.			
Sullivan, James	Sgt		
Sullivan, Jno.			
Sullivan, Patrick J.		E	9th Inf
Sweeny, James			
Sweeny, P.J.		B	6th US Inf
Swift, Bernard	Sgt	F	14th US Inf
Tailor, And'w	Sgt		Ord. Dept.
Taylor, Daniel H.	Pvt		3rd US Cav
Taylor, Wm.		G	3rd US Cav
Thomas, J.C.			
Thompson, Jos			Nevada
Tieney, Dan	Pvt		1st US Inf
Tivens, J.C.			
Totten, J.H.			
Twist, Leon			
Tyrrell, William	Corp		2nd US Cav
Van Moll, John H.	1st Sgt	A	3rd US Cav

assasinated Dec. 15, 1877 - age 30

Name	Rank	Co	Unit
Voght, Rich D.	Civilian		
Walss, Edw'd			
Walter, Jos.			
Ward, J.W.			
Ward, James			
Wareham, James	Corp		1st PA Res. Lt. Art
Warnock, Jessie May			
daughter of Mr. and Mrs. S. W. Warnock			
Watson, Julia A.			Civilian
wife of Hugh Watson			
Webb, James			
Webster, J.C.			
Welsch, E.M.			
Wesson, R.			
Wheeler, Chas		E	4th US Inf
White, _____			
White, J. H.	Band		9th US Cav
White, Jnd.			
Wilis, Robert	Sgt		
William, Sherman			NY
Williams, JC			
Williams, W.A.		K	22nd US Inf
Wilson, Cornelius			Mo
Wilson, Jno.			Ill
Wilson, R.			
Wilson, S.S.			Kan
Wilson, Wm.	Sgt		
Wood, Enoch		A	22nd US Inf
Wright, D			
Yelle, Casper E.			
born in Norway			
Yount, Jefferson			Civilian

FORT ROBINSON
Nebraska

Fort Robinson was an active post from 1871 until 1948. These names are from an 1886 headstone request.

Name	Rank	Co	Unit
Allen, Joseph	Pvt	M	4th Cav
Barber, A.J.	Pvt	H	3rd Cav
Barbour, Amos	Pvt	H	3rd Cav
Barth, Frances	Pvt	E	3rd Cav
Brogau, James	Pvt	A	9th Inf.
Brown, George	Farier	A	3rd Cav
Caraley, James	Pvt	M	3rd Cav
Carlton, Eugene	Pvt	D	9th Inf
Caual, Charles	Pvt	E	4th Cav
Chaffin, Henry W.	Pvt	K	9th Inf
Chambers, Henry	Pvt	C	4th Inf
Cogan, John	Pvt	C	14th Inf
Conally, James	Pvt	D	3rd Cav
De Llois	Pvt	H	3rd Cav
Edwards, William	Trumpeter	L	3rd Cav
Everett, Wm. W.	Pvt	H	3rd Cav
Getts, John	Pvt	D	14th Inf
Good, Wm. H.	Pvt	L	3rd Cav
Green, Martin V.	Pvt	M	5th Cav
Hinley, John E	Pvt	F	3rd Inf
Hulse, Peter	Pvt	A	3rd Cav
Johnson, Charles	Pvt	C	9th Cav
Kaley, Joh G.	Pvt	D	9th Inf
Kellog, Bernard	Pvt	E	3rd Cav
McFarland, Pete	Sgt	C	4th Inf
Miller, Wm. M.	1st class Pvt		U.S. Sig Corps
Morton, Thomas	Pvt	C	9th Cav
Nelson, George	Pvt	A	3rd Cav
Ollis, John	Pvt	M	5th Cav
Phel, Jacob	Pvt	K	3rd Cav
Reardon, Con	Pvt	G	9th Inf
Sfmowl, George	Pvt	L	3rd Cav
Smidt, Frank	Pvt	A	3rd Cav
Sullivan, Timothy	Pvt	F	5th Cav
Taggart, James	Sgt	A	3rd Cav

FORT HALLACK
Nevada

In 1886 Fort Hallack's post quartermaster requested a headstone for Fritz Soupe'. The next year Soupe's body was moved to the San Francisco National cemetery.

Name	Rank	Co	Unit
Soupe', Fritz	Pvt	E	8th Inf

BURLINGTON COUNTY
New Jersey

This is a list of Union soldiers buried in the Little Eggharbor and Bass River Townships of Burlington County. Most of the soldiers in this 1870 list had died in the South.

Name	Co	Unit
Adams, Jesse	K	10th NJ
Algar, Bloomfield	K	10th NJ
cemetery at Tuckerton		
Allen, Musgrove	K	10th NJ
Allen, W.L.	K	23rd NJ
cemetery at Tuckerton		
Bennett, Joshua	K	10th NJ
M.E. Church Yard at Tuckerton		
Berry Wm. H.	K	10th NJ
cemetery at Tuckerton		
Berry, Joseph		
cemetery at Tuckerton		
Bird, James (Jr.)	K	23rd NJ
cemetery at Tuckerton		
Crammer, Josiah N.	K	10th NJ
M.E. Church Yard at Tuckerton		
Curl, William	K	10th NJ

Name	Rank	Co
Driscall, Edw. (Jr.)	K	10th NJ
cemetery at Tuckerton		
Gale, John A	K	10th NJ
Gale, Oliver	K	10th NJ
cemetery at Tuckerton		
Gale, William	K	10th NJ
cemetery at Tuckerton		
Gashill, Reuben	K	23th NJ
Gaskill, James R.	K	10th NJ
M.E. Church Yard at Tuckerton		
Hewlings, Nyent	K	10th NJ
Jones, Timothy W. Jones	K	10th NJ
Lippincott, John	K	10th NJ
Lruax, Joesph R.	K	10th NJ
cemetery at Tuckerton		
Miller, Edw.		
Mott, Geo. E.	K	10th NJ
cemetery at Tuckerton		
Parker, Enoch		2nd NJ Cav
Parker, Joshua	K	10th NJ
West Creek		
Ruttan, John	K	10th NJ
Seaman, Chas. D.		5th NJ
Soper, Reuben	K	23rd NJ
Friends Ground at Tuckerton		
Watson, Samual	G	6th NJ

FINN'S POINT NATIONAL CEMETERY
New Jersey

During the Civil War the Union built a large POW camp at Fort Delaware. Fort Delaware was located on Pea Patch Island in the Delaware River about 1 1/2 miles from Finn's Point. As the POW exchange cartel broke down in 1863, the prison population soared. By August 1865, the camp held 8,932 POWs. Over 2,500 Confederates died in the camp. Because of the high water table on the island, most of the bodies were taken to the military post cemetery at Finn's Point.

After the war the cemetery was neglected. In 1875 Governer James Kemper of Virginia wrote the Secretary of War about the neglected Confederate graves on Pea Patch Island. The cemetery was named a national cemetery on October 3, 1875. The Quartermaster General was instructed to move any bodies from Pea Patch Island to the new cemetery at Finn's Point.

The Union soldiers were buried in individual graves, but soon the wooden headboards rotted leaving the graves unidentifiable. In 1879 Congress provided funds for a monument with the names of 105 known Union soldiers buried at Finn's Point. However, the monument only lists 104 names. (There were 30 burials of unknown soldiers.)

In 1906 Congress authorized marking the graves of Confederates who died in Northern prisons. The Confederates had been buried in trenches, so in 1910 an 85 foot monument was erected. Bronze plates listing the names of 2,436 Confederate POWs who died on Pea Patch Island were attached to the monument. Other records state there were 2,509 Confederates buried in the cemetery.

Name	**Rank**	**Co**	**Unit**
Andrews, C.B.	Drummer	A	Md Inf
Bathurst, Benjamin M.	Pvt	A	157 Pen Inf
Bertsch, Jacob	Recruit		USA
Bigger, Robert M.	Pvt	G	2nd Pen Light Art
Bradfield, George E.	Pvt	H	11 Md Inf
Bradley, Robert K.	Pvt		Ahls Ind Co.- Del Hvy Art
Brower, John M.	Pvt	H	27th Ind Inf
Burgner, David W.	Pvt		Ahls Ind Co.-Del Hvy Art

Name	Rank	Co	Unit
Butler, William	Pvt	A	2nd Pen Light Art
Cain, William S.	Recruit		USA
Callahan, Geo.			
Cargill, George M.	Pvt	I	29th Ohio Inf
Chiveral, Alexander	Pvt	C	Purnell Legion-Md In
Conoway, William H.	Pvt	D	5th Md Inf
Cook, C.P.	Pvt		Ahls Ind Co.-Del Hvy Art
Cook, Urban S.	Lt	M	2nd Pen Hvy Art
Cookes, James M.	Pvt	I	66th Ohio Inf
Cowperthwait, Joseph			
Crawford, John M.	Pvt	G	157th Ohio Inf
Cross, Warnell	Pvt	A	5th Md Inf
Deem, William	Pvt	M	3rd Pen Hvy Art
Dietz, John	Pvt	A	2nd Pen Light Art
Dodge, Joseph	Pvt	B	6th Mass Inf
Donely, John	Corp	K	66th Pen Inf
Downing, Fritz R.	Pvt	B	20th Mass Inf
Durant, Geo	Pvt		Ahls Ind Co.-Del Hvy Art
Eigleston, Jno.	Pvt	B	5th Md Inf
Evans, Geo.	Pvt	B	2nd Pen Hvy Art
Flowers, William H.	Pvt	B	9th Del Inf
Fowler, George	Pvt	M	3rd Pen Hvy Art
Freeman, James	Pvt	A	2nd Pen Light Art
Gallon, Charles	Pvt	A	2nd Pen Light Art
Gallon, Charles	Pvt	B	3rd Pen Hvy Art
Gillian, James K.	Pvt		Ahls Ind Co.-Del Hvy Art
Grade, August	Pvt	A	2nd Pen Light Art
Graham, Henry M.	Pvt	G	2nd Pen Light Art
Grooms, Edward	Pvt	B	Punrell Legion-2nd I
Hamilton, Edw. C.	Pvt	B	157th Ohio Inf
Hart, William H.	Pvt	B	3rd Pen Hvy Art
Hassley, John	Pvt		VRC
Henderson, John	Pvt	F	1st Del Cav
Henhoefer, Alexander	Pvt	A	2nd Pen Lt Art
Herrin, John	Pvt	A	2nd Pen Lt Art
Higgins, William	Sgt	C	5th Con Inf
Hill, Amos	Pvt		Ahls Ind Co.-Del Hvy Art
Hughes, _____	Pvt	F	1st Del Cav
Humes, David M.	Pvt	A	65th Ohio Inf
Hutchins, Abel W.	Pvt	D	2nd US Sharp Shooters
Johnson, W.M.			

Name	Rank	Co	Unit
Kelly, Bernard	Pvt	F	14th US Inf
Kinsley, Dennis	Pvt		Ahls Ind Co.-Del Hvy Art
Laforge, James			NY
Long, John	Pvt	D	6th Mass Inf
Martin, Peter	Pvt	M	3rd Pen Hvy Art
Mathews, James	Sgt	D	2nd Pen Hvy Art
Maynard, James L.	Pvt	G	2nd Pen Light Art
McCartney, Jno.			Pen
McCollister, John W.	Pvt	F	5th Md Inf
McPhee, Angus	Pvt	K	6th Mass Inf
Meehan, Joseph	Seaman		USN-Rev.Cutter-Varin
Miller, Dan'l			
Mills, Edward	Pvt	D	5th Md Inf
Moore, Andrew N.	Pvt	G	4th Ohio Inf
Moses, Joshua	Pvt	A	2nd Pen Light Art
Mossey, Jepther	Pvt	B	151th NY Inf
Neely, George	Pvt	G	2nd Pen Light Art
Negis, william	Pvt	F	157th Ohio Inf
Neidner, Frederick	Pvt	K	5th Md Inf
Overtt, Abijah	Pvt	D	4th NY Hvy Art
Pascher, Henry	Pvt	D	3rd Pen Hvy Art
Phillips, George N.	Pvt	G	11th Md Inf
Post, William	Pvt	D	3rd Pen Hvy Art
Rager, James	D		49 Pen Inf
Rais, Jacob F.	Pvt	A	2nd Pen Light Art
Ralston, John	Pvt	G	29 Pen Inf
Reintz, Augustus			
Ritchie, William	Pvt	E	11th Md Inf
Scan, Johnathan	Pvt		Ahls Ind Co.-Del Hvy Art
Shoemaker, C.P.	Pvt		Pen
Shultz, Geo. W.	Pvt	L	18th Pen Cav
Simpson, Thomas H.	Pvt	E	9th Del Inf
Smith, George W.	Corp	E	9th Del Inf
Smith, Marion F.	Pvt		Ahls Ind Co.-Del Hvy Art
Sparks, Joseph W.	Pvt	E	3rd Del Inf
Speckmon, James	Pvt	K	1st Del Cav
Speedy, John	Pvt	K	157th Ohio Inf
Spicer, John K.	Pvt	D	9th Del Inf
Spoenla, Moritz	Pvt	M	3rd Pen Hvy Art
Sprague, Charles A.	Pvt	F	10th NY Hvy Art
Sreffen, George O.	Pvt	A	2nd Pen Light Art

Name	Rank	Co	Unit
St. Vrain, Felix	Pvt	A	2nd Pen Light Art
Sterlin, Daring	Pvt	F	66th Ohio Inf
Stranpler, George O.			NY
Thacher, George W.	Pvt	H	6th Mass Inf
Tharp, James D.	Pvt	G	2nd Pen Light Art
Underwood, Robert C.	Hospital Steward		USA
Vance, James	Pvt	G	2nd Pen Light Art
Walker, Thomas E.	Pvt	E	11th Md Inf
Walters, James	Pvt	D	157th Ohio Inf
Waples, George B.	Pvt	C	9th Del Inf
Williams, Samuel G.	Pvt	B	Ahls Ind Co.-Del Hvy Art
Willis, Charles H.	Pvt	G	11th Md Inf
Wixon, David E.	Pvt	L	2nd Pen Hvy Art
Young, Robert A.	Cpl	B	2nd Pen Light Art

FORT WINGATE
New Mexico

These names of burials in the Fort Wingate Post Cemetery are from an 1886 headstone request. Some of the bodies of soldiers buried at Fort Wingate before 1868 may have been moved to Fort Lyon. At least one body from this cemetery was moved to Fort Leavenworth National Cemetery sometime before 1909.

Name	Rank	Co	Unit
Airey, Thomas	Pvt	Band	15th US Inf
Anderson, Augustus	Pvt	A	15th Inf
Arthur, Thomas	Pvt	K	8th US Cav
Barton, Alfred	Pvt	L	3rd Inf
Blair, Andrew M.	Pvt	B	5th Inf
Blake, Samuel A.	Pvt	I	18th Inf
Brown, John	Pvt	K	9th Cav
Burns, Daniel	Pvt	K	15th US Inf
Burns, James	Capt.		5th Cav
Chandler, Richard	Pvt	I	9th US Cav
Fieldman, Wm.	Pvt	H	8th Cav
Fitzsimmons, John	Pvt	A	15th Inf
Flaherty, Daniel	Pvt	A	15th US Inf
Gier, Laurnice	Pvt	K	4th Cav
Gunther, Jacob	Corp	E	8th US Cav
Haley, Owem	Sgt	K	5th Inf
Hurley, Timothy	Pvt	K	6th Cav
Jones, _n.	Pvt	B	5th Inf
McCormick, Conelius	Pvt	K	8th US Cav
Meitzel, Conrad	Pvt	K	15th Inf
Miller, Frank	Pvt	B	21st US Inf
Miughes, John	Sgt		13th Inf
Nolan, Nicholas	Major		3rd Cav
Perkins, Erskine	Pvt	G	13th US Inf
Price, Daniel	Pvt	K	15th US Inf
Robinson, James	Pvt	D	5th Inf
Shepard, Benjamin	Pvt	E	8th Cav
Shuetters, Austaonio	Pvt	L	3rd Inf

CYPRESS HILLS NATIONAL CEMETERY
New York

Cypress Hills National Cemetery was one of the twelve original national cemeteries established by President Lincoln under the provisions of an 1862 act that authorized the establishment of national cemeteries. The first interments were the bodies of Confederate POWs and their guards who were killed in a train wreck.

By the time volume 16 of the *Roll of Honor* was published (1868) a total of 3,277 soldiers (3,002 known) had been buried in the cemetery. In January 1872, the cemetery published a revised list of 3,874 soldiers buried at Cypress Hills.

These burials are listed by states.

Alabama
Ames, David
Banes, James
Brossis, William S.
Carroll, Albert
Cash, P.C.
Davidson, W. F.
Davis, Sampson
Fleming, J. E.
Furnham, Thomas F.
Gice, E. M.
Horton, H. C.
Johnson, John B.
King, Thomas J.
Lawsden, John
McDermott, A. H.
McHarley, Daniel
Phelps, David
Sapp, Francis M.
Shelworth, Samuel
Smith, W. R.
Sullivan, James
Vi, J. William
Watson, Jefferson

Confederate POWs
Adams, A. B.
Bradley, _____
Bradshaw, J.P.
Bryan, J. P.
Bushing, _____
Campbell, R. J.
Carnhill, Charles
Chambers. Harvey
Clarke, _____
Collins, James
Crimp, James
De Brady, De Young
Dickman, A. D.
Doner, Frank
Felons, John C.
Gatt, Jacob
Gay, N.
Gibbs, George T.
Gilder, G. A.
Hale, P. P.
Hicks, Jacob A.
Hoffman, _____
Hughes, Anthony
Humphrey, J. J.

Confederate POWs
(continued)
Indian, Billy
Jowers, F. M.
Keyser, William
Little, James H.
Martin, B. E.
Mathews, James
McRielty, Samuel
Medlin, Francis
Miller, Carl
Owens, A. P.
Patterson, Benjamin
Pegram, J. E.
Pletmons, W. C.
Pugh, Eli
Pyle, A. J.
Schraeder, Samuel E.
Scott, Henry
Shuber, _____
Slaughter, Selim
Stephens, C. S. T.
Tindall, Peter
Tinole, Peter L.
Tranler, J. J.
Tryon, William L.
Tutt, John G.
Williams, S.
Williams,_____
Young, John
Yuderiffe, J.

Connecticut
Andrew, Leroy
Appleby, Simon
Baldwin, Luserne
Beer, Joseph
Bodine, Napoleon
Brick, John
Burt, Chas. H.
Burton, Horace

Connecticut
(continued)
Cauldell, Sam'l
Colby, Henry
Doe, Patrick
Edwards, Geo. S.
Fox, E. J.
Fuller, T.P.
Gaylord, Albert
Geary, Wm. F.
Graff, Leo
Graham, Charles
Gursmann, Wm.
Hart, Francis T.
Jackson, Abraham
Jennan, George
Lynch, Thos.
Mickel, W. A.
Mills, Floyd
Moftitt, Aaron
O'Hara, Michael
Pashe, Antone
Peckham, Henry
Peter, Elijah
Phagan, Sanford
Ramsdell, James B.
Reder, Charles
Royol, Andrew C.
Seinfor, James
Sheehan, Joseph
Shipley, Miller O.
Simmons, Horace
Spencer, Cyrus
Starr, Benjamin
Stone, Walter
Thomas, Geo. S.
Thorne, M. H.
Webb, Wm. F.
Wellman, John C.
Woodins, Walter
Young, Milo

Delaware
Briggs, R. J.
Corpium, James
Dodd, John
Draper, Isaac F.
Hendricks, M.
Jackson, Joel P.
Mack, Tsbias
Norris, Charles
Perry, William
Rose, James
Simmons, R.
Williams, Willington

Florida
Browne, James
Cannon, John
Carleton, James
Dixon, John J.
Hartfield, John
Kelly, John J.
Weeks, Levi

Georgia
Baker, Gilford D.
Bazeman, M.
Blunt, E. H.
Bradbury, Wiley
Cook, S. T.
Dollis, J. J.
Farmer, William F.
Fraiton, William
Griffith, F. O.
Hollingsworth, W__, J.
Jordan, John J.
Kennedy, Patrick
King, M.
Lawrence, J. L.
Maxon, Richard

Georgia
(continued)
McConnell, R. T.
McKenzie, Hardy T.
Mitchell, William L.
Mull, J. H.
Murdoch, James
Perry, H. B.
Powell, Thomas
Rainey, James
Ramsay, J. H.
Richardson, Robert M.
Roberts, George M.
Roberts, John A. W.
Ryan, Patrick
Savage, Baxton
Smith, Henry
Smith, J. A.
Vaughan, A. G.
Webb, John W.
York, P.C.

Illinois
Agoost, William
Allison, F. S.
Bigelow, Barnard
Bishop, William H.
Bliss, Seth
Brown, Theodore
Buckhart, G.
Burton, James
Caldwell, W. R.
Campbell, John W.
Charm, Thomas
Clark, Jerome G.
Claudell, Nicholas
Conn, George W.
Cookman, William
Cowden, George H.
Davison, James
Deck, M.

Illinois
(continued)
Dennis, E. A.
Dickinson, Barrow
Door, Joseph
Dyarnett, _____
Ellerty, J.
Esaac, Frederick
Fair, H. H.
Fanning, Thomas M.
Floyd, Robert
Franklin, Jonathan
Franklin, Robert
Gear, John
Gilbert, James
Glenn, Samuel R.
Hagner, Andrew
Hallenbeck, William
Hammond, Oliver
Harney, James V.
Havell, William
Hemer, Samuel
Hendrick, Moses B.
Huggins, W. M.
Johnson, David
Johnson, Davin
Johnson, Thomas N.
Jones, Willis
Kennedy, George
Lamb, Matthew W.
Lewis, Giles B.
Little, Henry M.
Logan, R. J.
Lovelady, Samuel D.
Mack, James
McClave, John
Mettler, J.H.
Miles, James W.
Moore, Carlos T.
Moore, George F.
Musgeire, Jonathan J.
Myers, George W.

Illinois
(continued)
Nick, John
O'Connell, Patrick
Oliver, Robert
Parker, Nathan
Pool, Winfield S.
Price, Henry V.
Roach, Henry
Scott, Henry
Sheaver, David
Sherman, E.
Sholle, Henry
Six, James
Stamford, James P.
Stone, Adonison J.
Sylvester, Silas
Thomson, Henry
Uhl, Christian C.
Wayne, Isaac W.
Whitaker, Joshua
Wood, John
Zumwalk, Simon

Indiana
Andrews, Jacob B.
Asdell, A. N.
Berry, Lewis
Bledsoe, David R.
Bogart, John
Bokinger, George
Boothwick, William
Boyd, Thomas
Burns, James T.
Burns, John
Burrell, Green
Callahan, Andrew
Cassel, George A.
Clark, George

Indiana
{continued)
Clark, William F.
Clendersing, Andrew
Coleman, Daniel T.
Comforth, John
Conniss, Michael O.
Cook, Isaac
Curtis, Joseph
Dagram, Nicholas
Davidson, E. H.
Davis, William
Day, Ira W.
Detrick, Eli
Dispenett, Newton
Dorrance, W. B.
Downer, Job
Eckler, Peter
Edwards, E. H.
Edwards, Isaac J.
Ellige, William
Eskew, Henry
Felton, Frederick
Fileson, George
Flemer, John
Fraser, Edwin
Fuller, George
Garrett, Samuel
Gowan, Martin G.
Griesall, John
Griffin, J.
Gromer, George
Hamilton, James
Harmon, James
Harris, Benjamin
Hartman, David
Hendricks, Jas J.
Hollerfield, Joseph
House, Israel W.
Humphrey, A. M.
Husker, Leander
Imboden, Eli

Indiana
{continued)
Jackson, Geo. W.
Johnson, Thomas
Jones, Adams
Kelley, John
Kemple, Jacob
King, Anthony H.
Kirkpatrick, Wm.
Lens, Peter
Libbett, Oliver P.
Llewellen, Jacob
McCart, James M.
McHenry, Charles
McNutt, John H.
McPherson, Wright
Meine, Amos
Miller, Levi
Mitchell, Isaac N.
Moorman, Stephen
Morgan, Alfred
Mott, J.
Ockners, Frederick
Plotney, Samuel
Potter, James
Purnell, Andrew
Raider, Richard M.
Reeves, Henry B.
Reiker, J. H.
Risk, Chester C.
Robbins, R. R.
Roberts, Harden
Seisman, Peter
Silver, John
Slater, J. A.
Smith, Anderson C.
Smith, B.
Smith, William
Smith, William H.
Sparrow, Jacob
Spear, Samuel
Stroman, Absden

Indiana
(continued)
Sutton, James

Iowa
Allen, James
Burgess, William
Burns, A.P.
Carson, Ezra
Chamberlain, Francis J.
Chum, Barney
Commiky, Phillip
Coulthart, W. A.
Easton, John
Filder, Chester G.
Fisher, William M.
Hockersmith, George
Keasy, M. H.
Lenhart, Paul
Levee, James
Lopert, Thomas C.
McCafferty, James H.
Milton, Robert
Severson, Leslie C.
Slatterly, John
Smith, George H.
Spain, P. D.
Trusdell, Seth
Wade, John
Westfall, George
Williams, J.
Wilson, James
Woocox, J. Ira R.
Wyllie, James

Kentucky
Angle, David
Dewitt, C.
Foster, Rufus
Grinstaff, Green
Merrifield, Samuel
Randall, John
Sheridan, John
Smith, Burr N.

Louisiana
Fisher, U. W.
Murray, John
Olevica, P.D.
Sing, S.
Siveley, George
Young, Beverly D.

Maine
Ackley, William
Alwood, Charles H.
Anderson, S.
Armstrong, Wm.
Austin, Thomas
Averill, Edward
Baldwin, Jerome
Barlow, F. R.
Barney, Redmond
Barr, Robert
Beating, A. H.
Benton, George W.
Betts, B. W.
Bogger, Alex.
Bray, T.E.
Brayden, John J.
Briggs, John H.
Brookings, A. L.
Brown, Brodish
Brown, F. M.
Brown, Wm. S.

Maine
(continued)
Candage, Geo. B.
Clarry, Edward B.
Cobb, Franklin B.
Coburn, Isaiah
Collamore, F. H.
Colson, John O.
Connolly, Patrick
Coombs, George E.
Cunningham, Sorvell
Dandall, Isaiah
Davis, James
Dawilson, Charles E.
Denias, Clement
Denny, Edward M.
Dickey, Charles H.
Dixon, William
Doughty, Robert H.
Downey, John
Dunham, Daniel J.
Eastman, Chas. A.
Eaton, F.
Eldridge, Lewis
Emmeroth, Peter
Erskine, John
Fogg, Geo. K.
Folger, Henry
Foster, G. W.
Foyle, T. W.
Furner, Benjamin
Gartner, Albert T.
Gary, Charles
Gay, Abner
Gerald, Geo. W.
Glidden, Benj. F.
Goodwin, Samuel
Gould, Luther H.
Gove, Geo.
Gray, Albert J.
Gray, John
Grey, Francis

Maine
(continued)
Grey, Washburn
Griffin, Thos.
Grover, Dennis
Hanford, Joseph
Hanscome, T. P.
Hanscome, T. P.
Harford, John W.
Hitchhen, Daniel
Holmes, H. P.
Howe, Henry H.
Hubbard, George M. C.
Hubbard, Thomas
Hughes, Martin
Hutchings, George
Jenkins, Hiram
Jolman, Moses B.
Judkins, Moses H.
Kimball, Moses F.
Knox, Wm.
Lamont, Thomas
Lillison, Daniel
Lindsay, Gaff. O.
Lowell, Wm. H.
Luskins, James
Mains, Herd. S.
McCole, Daniel
McDermott, John
McDonald, D.
McDonald, Samuel
McDongal, Stephen
McFarland, John D.
Merrill, Miner
Mich____, Zina
Mitchell, ____
Modeny, John
Moody, H. C.
Moore, Ephraim
Morrison, Daniel H.
Murphey, Wesley
Nicholas, Chas. L.

Maine
(continued)
Norcop, Joseph D.
Norton, Edmond
Parks, Hoyt R.
Perkins, Thomas B.
Pierson, F.
Pouler, Tos.
Powers, Charles R.
Powers, F. L.
Rachard, G. R.
Ramsdell, J. F.
Rayner, Calvin
Roberts, A. U.
Rook, Gilmore B.
Rowe, E.
Russell, William
Sanfs____, Prim
Savage, George
Sephan, Amos
Slothezse, Henry
Small, Daniel
Smith, Benjamin
Smith, Edward H.
Smith, James H.
Stacl[p;e. Eugene
Staples, Geo. D.
Stephens, F. N.
Stone, George
Sweet, T.
Tarbox, Wm. S.
Tates, Cyrus
Taylor, T. W.
Teron, Benjamin
Tompkins, N. M.
Toy, Granville W.
Tuttle, Luther
Walton, Charles M.
Ward, Ebenezer
Webb, Woodbridge
Webber, H. S.
Weymouth, Fred

Maine
(continued)
Whitney, Thos. B.
Whitten, C. F.
Williams, Dennis
Williams, William
Wooster, Aaron
Woter, Warren
York, John K.

Maryland
Anderson, Leroy
Beers, James
Bennett, Theopholis
Clark, William F.
Farrington, John
Folsom, Ephraim P.
Gibson, Charles
Gosnell, Joshua
Harrington, G.
Koch, D.
Longer, Samuel
McCall, A.
Ness, William
Shack, Charles W.
Stacy, F.
Weaver, Henry

Massachusetts
Alarick, John H.
Andrews, Luerren
Ash, David B.
Ashton, Thomas
Barker, R.C.
Barnes, Jas. T.
Basseter, Wm. C.
Belden, Henry
Bennet, Geo. N.
Bonaparte, Wilson
Borrers, James

Massachusetts
(continued)
Brown, Henry
Burdett, Aaron
Bushy, Henry
Cartright, John
Charles, James H.
Clemens, A.
Comedy, Philo
Croht, Henry
Cutling, Horatio A.
Daley, Daniel
Daley, Jeremiah
Dally, Michael
Davis, George L.
Dean, C.
Dickey, Madison
Diescher, Lewis
Driscott, James
Fairbanks, Chas. H.
Farrington, Henry
Fetra, Jeremiah
Foser, William
Francis, Joseph
Fuller, Amos L.
Gardner, W.H.
Gladding, Edward
Glover, Harrison
Gould, Joshua
Grobut, Augustus
Guard, Samuel
Harkell, Abraham
Haskins, James D.
Hawley, Daniel
Heenan, Hugh
Henneck, Jas. W.
Holbrook, W.A.
Howard, Henry
Jones, Fred. O.
Lancaster, Ezra G.
Lawrence, J.
Leonard, G.E.

Massachusetts
(continued)
Leonard, James
Lord, J.M.
Loveland, Edward L.
Malcahy, William
Manning, Martin
Mason, Geo. H.
McGrade, Jerry
McGuire, Patrick
Neil, John F.
Newport, F.H.
Nichols, L.A.
Noland, H.J.
O'Brien, William
O'Neil, James
Phillips, Lyman D.
Ramsey, John
Reynolds, Patrick
Richards, B.B.
Sanderick, Frederick
Sandree, Joseph
Smith, Francis E.
Smith, Fred. C.
Snow, Philo
Spinney, Alex
Splain, James B.
Spring, Henry G.
Statuf, Stephen G.
Stoerza, Henry
Stracks, Harman
Sulllivan, James
Tillinghast, Wm. H.
Weysser, Chas. W.
Willcott, E.
Wood, J.D.C.
Woodbury, Charles M.
Wright, J.

Michigan
Abbott, James
Alimany, Jacob
Baker, Joseph
Banderberg, J.
Barstow, Elijah H.
Bates, Charles S.
Bathlain, J. A.
Beard, Alexander
Bellon, Robert I.
Billings, Pliny
Bisby, Hiram
Britten, Zachariah
Bucklin, William
Bump, Henry
Byrne, James
Cady, J. B.
Campbell, Hugh
Campbell, James
Carl, Andrew
Carl, Andrew J.
Carver, Justus M.
Champion, Ezra
Chapin, Scott H.
Chapman, A. A.
Christopher, Daniel
Christy, P.
Cilbert, George
Clagg, George W.
Clark, L. E.
Clements, William M.
Cole, John
Corbin, Alonzo
Cross, Nelson
Crothier, Henry G.
Culver, Allen
Curlen, J
Curry, J.
Daneen, Solon
Daniel, Robert D.
Darling, Hiram G.
Davis, Simon E.

Michigan
(continued)
Defnesty, Hiram
Delamater, Martin
Demmons, S. C.
Dening, Paul
Densmore, William
Doran, James
Dykeman, Michael
Eaton, H. C.
Edson, L. D.
Elkine, Freeman
Emerson, Samuel
Feeter, Stephen
Fisher, Reuben
Foary, J. A.
Follett, Edward
Forkes, George W.
Frossney, Caspar
Gates, John
Gibson, H.
Gohien, Charles G.
Greager, Henry
Grunger, Leonard
Harkness, Darwin
Havens, Egbert L.
Heath, Charles
Hill, C. C.
Hilliard, George H.
Hillman, _____
Hopper, Edward
Hulbert, Chester A.
Hungerford, Robert B.
Jeune, Lot
Johnson, Edwin
Johnson, John
Johnson, Mark
Jones, Thomas D.
Joy, D. M.
Karratt, Clawson
Kelly, W. F.
Kimsden, Evier

Michigan
(continued)
Kircher, J.
Lampman, Peter
Leonard, Orville
Livermore, Rawson
Livingston, Henry
Losee, James
Martell, Richard E.
Marvin, Calvin
Masser, Christian
McClanahan, John
Moore, Amos
Morgan, Levi
Mosher, Aaron
Mott, Sylvanus
Moyer, A.
Nichols, Joseph
Northrup, Lewis
Northrup, William B.
Paine, Ebenezer
Parker, Ira D.
Peak, Jerry
Pendall, Benjamin Z.
Phillips, James
Pierce, James F.
Pitts, Elijah
Porter, Joseph
Relbucks, Milo
Richardson, Geo. H.
Roberts, George
Robinson, Edward
Rogers, Sanford T.
Rows, Thomas
Scaman, Rufus W.
Schultz, Henry
Sharp, William H.
Sheehan, Timothy
Simonson, Stephenson
Smith, Lyman
Spencer, Lewis P.
Spickman, John

Michigan
(continued)
Stewart, James
Stottard, Orlando
Sweet, Kyler
Timber, John D.
Vallean, William
Vanderbeek, William
Vanderman, John
Wallace, H. C.
Warner, Henry
West, Charles
White, William C.
Whiteman, D.
Whitmore, Hiram
Wilder, Hiram
Wilear, Warren
Wilson, J.
Wilson, William E.
Winsman, Abraham
Wood, William
Woodford, J.B.
Wright, James R.
Wyekoff, George
Wyman, Benjamin
Young, Daniel C.

Minnesota
Ames, Gotlieb
Bozank, Joseph
Christianson, O.
Colbath, Richard N.
Ernest, Anthony W.
Glenn, Daniel P.
Godwin, Foss
Henry, Lewis
Hill, W. H.
Hodston, Hannibal
Irish, Alonzo
Lownsberry, John W.
McCullough, J. C.

Minnesota
(continued)
McPhelan, Samuel
Morey, Ira
Plumbaux, William R.
Ryer, Frank
Wallace, William

Mississippi
Hudspetts, J. J.
Logan, E. C.
McGarley, G.
McHenry, A.
Riggs, A.
Riggs, George W.
Robertson, T. C.
Steele, Alfred S.
Stone, G. B.

Missouri
Coffey, Jesse
Crowley, Joseph
Hild, George
Long, George B.
Lord, Francis G.

New Hampshire
Barton, Henry
Bean, Geo. P.
Briggs, William
Brown, John
Cater, E.J.
Chase, Jas. H.
Click, tenin
Cooke, Chas. H.
Davis, Chas. H.
Delevan, Joseph F.
Dinnie, Percy G.
Dudley, G. N.

New Hampshire
(continued)
Frank, John
Godfrey, Charles N.
Goodwin, Abram
Gordon, Scott
Hacket, George H.
Hodgton, Henry C.
Hoppenhoff. _____
Jordon, John
Juan, Antonio
Lange, A. L.
Lillie, L.N.
Longer, Carl
Loring, Andrew
McCarthy, Patrick
McClure, Samuel C.
McCrann, Jas. H.
McKealy, James
McLaughlin, Thomas
Mederal, D. E.
Moodel, Stephen
Moore, Henry C.
Munsey, Geo. F.
Niles, Geo. W.
Norrell, Joseph W.
Osee, Samuel J.
Parker, George
Peavey, Hollis S.
Plum, Edward
Plummer, J. L.
Powell, Russell G.
Raffle, Samuel
Rand, Moses
Riley, Michael
Robin, Agustus
Robinson, Frank B.
Sadonstable, Frank
Scrusier, Henry
Seymour, Joseph
Spaulding, Page
Stacy, S. F.

New Hampshire
(continued)
Stantoungh, James
Stevens, Henry
Stevens, Henry H.
Swaine, Luther G.
Thrall, George H.
Tibbetts, Isaac
Tilton, F.
Welch, Benjamin
White, Moses E.
Wintworth, John
Wood, Charles E.

New Jersey
Bechman, Frank
Blanchard, Martin
Briggs, Henry
Burch, Nathan
Calhoun, John
Cole, John B.
Cook, Peter
Cooper, David J.
Cowell, Edward
Dalton, George
Driver, Patrick
Fober, Francis
Johnson, Thomas
Kimball, J.B.
Kishpaugh, William B.
McKienan, E.
Medare, Joseph
Naley, George
Phillips, Alexander
Popelin, Frederick
Rich, Peter
Rogers, Owen
Sargeant, William
Simkings, S.
Smith, Henry
Smith, John

New Jersey
(continued)
Tenth, Michael
Thompson, William H.
Witheral, David

New York
Abbott, Charles P.
Abrams, James
Abselen, Henry
Accy, C. D.
Ackler, Adam
Ackley, Henry
Ackley, Henry T.
Ackley, John
Adams, Blbert
Adams, Charles
Adams, George
Ade, Henry
Adier, John B.
Aely, Frederick
Agan, Patrick A.
Ager, Alfred
Ager, Mathew
Agnew, William
Albert, Henry C.
Albred, William H.
Albright, Isaac
Aldas, Henry
Alexander, John
Alexander, William
Allen, Henry
Allen, J. H.
Allen, Lawson
Allen, Samuel
Allen, William
Allison, Robert
Allison, Thomas G.
Amos, Henry M.
Anderson, Benjamin
Andews, Charles
Andews, Joseph

New York
(continued)
Andreson, John
Andrews, F.W.
Andrews, John
Apple, Oscar
Archibald, Edward
Argersinger, Albert
Armstromy, J. F.
Armstrong, M.M.
Armstrong, Thomas
Arndt, Hiram
Arnoff, J. F.
Arnold, James H.
Arnold, John
Arnold, William L.
Arsmstrong, Henry
Artin, M.
Ashcott, Robert
Ashley, Francis H.
Ashner, Robert A.
Askins, George
Atkins, Lester
Atwood, Henry C.
Augustus, P.
Austin, Albert H.
Austin, Freeman
Austin, George
Avidson, Avil
Backus, E. H.
Backus, George W.
Bacon, Curtis
Bacon, Ishabel E.
Bacon, Scanole
Bagg, Noah R.
Bailey, George
Bailey, William B.
Baily, Adison D.
Baily, G. W.
Baily, Hugh
Baker, Artem
Baker, Charles S.

New York
(continued)
Baker, Howard A.
Balch, Judson
Baldwin, B. B.
Baldwin, Stephen
Ballard, John
Ballard, Robert
Balleam, T.
Ballenger, Benjamin
Balls, Benjamin
Bancroff, Charles
Banker, George H.
Barbe, James A.
Barden, M.
Bare, Urea
Barlow, W.
Barnes, Charles G.
Barnes, H.
Barnes, Peter
Barnhard, Archer
Barnum, ____
Barob, W.
Barr, John
Barrett, William
Barritt, James
Barrows, B. Franklin
Barton, Alexander M.
Barton, Augustus
Barton, William H.
Batch, Ambrose
Bathgate, James
Batt, George
Batterbury, John
Bayem, Peter
Beach, Amos S.
Beadle, O. H.
Beagy, John
Beatten, Samuel S.
Beck, Edward
Beckwith, Rufus J.
Beed, Daniel

New York
(continued)
Beeson, William
Beismer, Martin
Belcher, Stephen
Bell, George E.
Bell, Washington L.
Bellcove, Alfred
Bench, John
Bender, Jocob
Benjamin, J. B.
Bennett, Agustus
Bennett, Clras
Bennett, George W.
Bennett, Harrison
Bennett, Irvin S.
Bennett, James A.
Bennett, Richard
Benson, J. W.
Berkley, Charles
Berrian, George N.
Better, Joseph
Bigelow, Samuel
Billing, George
Bird, James
Bird, Thompson
Birmingham, J.
Bishop, Robert U.
Black, Valentine
Blake, Thomas
Blakeley, G.W.
Blanchard, Aaron
Blanchard, Wesley
Bland, Taylor
Blinn, Clinton A.
Blodgett, A.C.
Bloomer, Hans
Blunt, Henry
Blyman, Ennis
Blyth, George T.
Boarding, Davis
Bogart, Wallace

New York
(continued)
Bohrmens, W.
Boisvert, Adolph
Bond, Edwin H.
Bonerty, Levi
Bostwick, Joseph
Bosworth, Jndson A.
Bouin, John R.
Bowditch, W.
Bower, Godfrey
Bower, Harvey
Bowley, H. W.
Bowman, John
Bowman, Joseph M.
Bowman, R. D.
Bownell, Augustus
Bowsit, Miller
Boyce, James H.
Boyd, John
Boyem, Peter
Boynton, E. P.
Bradley, H.
Bradley, J.
Brady, Nathaniel
Brady, Patrick C.
Bragg, William J.
Bramer, Thomas S.
Branell, Henry
Brannin, John M.
Brennan, Michael
Brewer, Ernest
Brewer, John C.
Brichter, John
Bridane, Andrew
Bridges, John F.
Briggs, Charles
Briggs, James
Briggs, Lewis
Brigham, T. W.
Brindle, J.
Brise, Isaac

New York
(continued)
Bristol, L. J.
Britten, Henry C.
Broadback, Frederick
Broadheart, Abel
Broadwell, William
Broderich, John
Bromer, Johnson
Brooks, Oben
Brown, Andrew
Brown, Anthony D.
Brown, Charles J.
Brown, Coburn
Brown, Cyrus
Brown, E. A.
Brown, E. B.
Brown, George
Brown, George W.
Brown, Isaiah
Brown, James
Brown, John
Brown, John E.
Brown, Joseph
Brown, Lewis
Brown, Martin
Brown, Paul
Brown, T.
Brown, Thomas
Brown, Thomas J.
Brown, William
Brown, William H.
Browner, John E.
Brumer, Henry
Brundage, John
Brundage, L. D.
Bruse, George F.
Bruster, James
Brynart, Joseph
Bualeson, Rufus
Buchannan, August
Buck, Thomas

New York
(continued)
Buckler, Nicholas
Buckner, Samuel B.
Bulgen, James
Buliss, Eugene
Bull, John
Bullis, Simeon
Bunch, John
Bunn, Albert
Burch, Adam
Burch, Thomas
Burdick, G. A.
Burgie, ___
Burlingame, William F.
Burlingame, Z.
Burnes, John
Burns, John
Burns, Patrick
Burns, Thomas
Burnside, Frank
Burr, Lewis M.
Burrell, Decatur
Burton, Winslow
Butler, Anthony A.
Butler, Charles
Cady, Dennis
Calahan, Patrick
Calburton, Edward A.
Callahan, Jerry
Callen, James
Cambell, Charles
Cameron, Benton
Campbell, Richard
Campton, S. B.
Canada, James
Canfield, Francis M.
Cannon, John
Canter, Michael
Caple, Hamilton
Carey, John
Carl, Charles

New York
(continued)
Carl, James
Carliman, Benjamin
Carnahah, Lorenzo
Carpenter, Albert
Carpenter, J. A.
Carr, George W.
Carr, Thomas A.
Carroll, Alexander
Carroll, Thomas
Carteppe, Andrew
Carter, George W.
Carter, William
Cartie, Robert
Cartie, Roiln M.
Cartwright, Joseph
Carver, George
Carver, Lewis
Case, Reuben M.
Casedo, William T. L.
Casia, Joseph
Casley, James
Cassidy, John
Casterline, William
Castle, William S.
Caston, Theodore
Cauldwell, George
Cavey, William
Chambers, Isaac
Chambers, Legrand
Chambers, R. B.
Champlain, George
Chandley, William
Chapman, Woshington
Chase, John F.
Chesbrough, Spicer
Chilpers, Levy
Chilson, King A.
Chinn, George
Christmas, Jacob
Churchill, Calvin

New York
(continued)
Clansy, John
Clarch, Charles
Clark A. B.
Clark, Alexander
Clark, David
Clark, James
Clark, John T.
Clark, Joseph M.
Clark, Martin L.
Clark, Orris
Clark, Patrick
Clark, Samuel L.
Clark, Wesley
Clark, William A.
Clark, William J.
Clarke, William F.
Clase, Nathan
Clavenaugh, Joseph M.
Cleland, William
Clement, Hudson
Clement, Therome
Clinton, Horace
Clough, J. H.
Coats, James
Cogan, John
Colby, William
Colchoss, Henry
Colcord, Lewis
Cole, Alvah
Cole, Amos E.
Cole, Lewis H.
Cole, Riley
Collins, Cornelius
Collins, Peter
Colson, Frederick
Colvert, John A.
Condaint, Joseph
Condon, James
Conine, Lewis
Conklin, Edward S.

New York
(continued)
Conklin, Francis
Conklin, John
Conn, Asa T.
Connel, Thomas
Connelly, Edward
Connigan, John
Connoly, Valentine
Conrad, W.
Conradt, John
Conroy, William
Coodall, C. A.
Cook, Edward
Cook, Jacob
Cook, John
Cool, J.
Cooper, Daniel
Cooper, George T.
Cooprin, Nathan
Copper, Geo. W.
Cordell, Charles T.
Corey, Elijah
Corn, Charles
Corn, George
Cornalls, Edgar
Cornell, A.
Corroran, Joseph
Cosart, Lewis
Couch, Charles
Cough, Bruce
Coughlan, John
Counteman, Charles
Courter, Collin
Courtney, W.
Covey, Alfred C.
Cowles, Nathan
Coyle, James
Craig, Stacy
Crandall, John D.
Crane, Lewis H.
Crane, Lewis II

New York
(continued)
Cranston, Michael
Crawford, Peter
Crawford, Thomas
Creighton, Sturtevant
Croncerr, Lafyette
Cronin, P.
Cross, Lewis
Cross, Sonathan
Crow, W. G.
Crowin, Ambrose
Crusy, Samuel
Culkins, James
Cullen, James
Culver, George M.
Cumming, William
Cummings, David
Cummings, John
Cunningham, Jacob
Curch, Jonathan
Curtis, Daniel
Curtis, Hiram C.
Curtis, J. R.
Curtis, James
Curtis, Theodore C.
Cussle, Shedras F.
Custis, George
Dachman, Joseph
Daly, M.
Daly, Peter
Damond, Albert H.
Daniel, Thomas
Dannigan, James
Darnold, James L.
Darow, C.
Darum, Edward
David, John
Davidson, Lewis
Davis, Agustus
Davis, Almond
Davis, Charles E.

New York
(continued)
Davis, David
Davis, Edward E.
Davis, Edwin
Davis, Henry
Davis, James K.
Davis, Moses
Davis, Robert
Davis, William
Davis, William G.
Dawley, Alexander C.
Day, George W.
Day, John
Day, Pratt
Daymon, Ebenezer
Dayton, Henry C.
Dean, Daniel
DeBrodt, Charles
DeCamp, Leander
Deck, Edward
Decker, John
Deenbwung, Jeremiah
Deland, Alvin S.
Delany, Andrew
Delong, Peter
Demerest, Baptist
Demond, B. V.
Denald, Charles
Denel, Asa
Dennis, Elihu
Depert, Z.
Dermian, Conrad
Dervey, Otis C.
Dessert, Gustavas
Devoy, Calvin
Dewitt, W.H.
Dexter, Levi
Dickson, Samuel
Dillon, S.
Diueheart, George
Dodge, Francis R.

New York
(continued)
Doerson, Robert
Dominu, Priest
Donahue, Henry
Donahue, Thomas
Dondelly, Z. B.
Donnely, James
Donner, Henry
Donnety, C. A.
Donovan, Francis
Donovan, Michael
Dooner, Henry
Dorn, John J.
Douglass, David
Dowling, William
Down, Stephen
Downing, William E.
Drake, Edwin L.
Draper, George W.
Drew, John
Driscoll, Dennis
Drummond, Alexander
Dudley, J.
Duffer, George E.
Duffle, Stacy K.
Dullord, W. F.
Dunkle, Watson
Dunlop, _____
Dunn, Peter
Dunn, William H.
Dunson, John or Jo
Dunton, David A.
Dupruy, Hugh
Durand, John
Durham, Abraham
Dusenbuy, Henry
Dusseldorf, Peter
Dye, Abel
Dye, Lewis
Dyer, H. D.
Dykenan, Martin

New York
(continued)
Dymond, George
Eames, John E.
Early, Edward
Eastman, D.
Eastman, Dwight
Eddy, J.
Edmund, James II
Eggleston, Abraham
Ehler, Israel
Ehler, Julius
Eicklin, John
Eldridge, John W.
Eldridge, Solomon
Elkery, Henry
Ellard, George
Ellenwood, Frank
Elliott, Ezekiel
Elliott, L. B.
Ellis, Daniel
Ellis, H.
Ellis, Henry
Ellis, Hiram
Ellis, Samuel
Elmer, Henry
Emerson, John
Emery, M. A.
Emory, William
Enenger, R.
Engham, John M.
Engles, Charles M.
Enright, David
Ernest, Samuel
Ernstein, Ernest
Erslee _____
Evan, George
Evans, James
Evans, John II
Evans, W.
Evans, Wesley
Evans, William D.

New York
(continued)
Evans, William M.
Everts, Harvey
Eye, Andy
Fadden, Isaac
Fadron, William H.
Fagan, Michael
Fahren, John D.
Fairbanks, Lafayette
Fairchild, Addison
Fairman, James A.
Farmer, Daniel
Farr, George C.
Farrell, Patrick
Fastell, Charles
Fay, Frederick
Fay, W. M.
Feague, Rufus II
Fellman, Phinneas
Ferrill, Chester
Ferry, Orlon E.
Fiefer, Frank
Fieg, Henry
Field, Charles B.
Fields, Henry
Figee, James
Finch, Daniel
Finch, Eugene
Finch, Francis
Finckler, Lewis
Finlayson, Henry
Finnerty, John
Firtzgerald, Owen
Fisher, _____
Fisher, Lewis
Fitts, Richard B.
Fitzpatrick, Hugh
Flagg, Samuel
Flagge, John
Flaherty, Patrick
Fland, John D.

New York
(continued)
Fleming, II. J.
Fleming, John
Fletcher, Delbut
Flood, John
Flue, Arthur
Fluhart, William B.
Flynn, James
Flynn, Edward
Fogarty, Bartley
Folbrook, William
Folder, Robert
Foley, J.
Foley, Owen
Foote, S. II
Ford, Dwight
Ford, L.
Ford, Thomas
Forest, Samuel
Forhaity, Martin
Forresti, Samuel C.
Forstell, Charles
Forster, George M.
Foss, Charles
Foster, C.
Foster, Edward C.
Fox, Herman
Francis, John A.
Frank, R. C.
Franklin, Charles
Freeland, George
Freer, Moses
French, Ira J.
Freslerbuch, Peter
Fressler, Ralph S.
Frey, James S.
Fricks, William W.
Friese, Thomas
Frulkner, Robert
Fryer, Edward
Fullee, Joseph P.

New York
(continued)
Furnum, Thomas
Gage, Franklin
Gage, Josiah H.
Gainer, John
Gall, Robert
Gallagher, T.
Gallman, Patrick
Gallman, William
Gallup, George
Gamble, Henry C.
Ganton, William
Ganvis, Julius
Gardner, Caleb N.
Gardner, Francis
Gardner, M. P.
Garing, John
Garrison, Henry
Garrison, William H.
Garritt, James
Gartland, Thomas
Garver, J. J.
Gashill, Charles
Gasler, Powell
Gaw, Andrew
Geary, John
Geer, William H.
Gehenger, Alvin
Geiger, Lewis
Geohegan, John
Geohegan, Thomas
George, Charles
Gerhart, John
German, James
Gifford, A.
Gilbert, William
Gillan, Christopher
Gillett, Edgar
Gipple, Henry
Gleason, Michael B.
Gleason, Thomas

New York
(continued)
Goding, G.T.
Goforth, Wm.
Gonell, Solon
Goodman, Peter
Goodrich, Charles II
Goodwin, G. W.
Goodyear, Joseph
Gordephy, Elaezer
Gordon, Daniel
Gordon, James P.
Gordon, John S.
Gordon, William
Gorman, Robert
Gough, L. J.
Gould, ____
Goupp, N.
Grant, David
Grant, James
Grant, John P.
Graver, C. L.
Graves, Franklin
Graves, James P.
Gray, Silas
Green, David
Green, George W.
Green, James
Green, John
Green, Stephen S.
Greer, William H.
Griffin, George W.
Griffin, George H.
Grifllth, Hugh
Griswold, John P.
Grobut, Agustus
Grocer, John C.
Gross, John
Grossner, John
Grove, Absolem
Grundy, Stephen K.
Grunff, Frederick

New York
(continued)
Gurrin, Frederick
Hadwell, Obed
Haglin, Lewis
Hahil, C.
Hahn, William
Haight, T. B.
Haines, John
Halbernut, Lewis
Hale, Walter W.
Haley, Thomas
Hall, Elihu
Hall, Hiram
Hall, John
Hall, John G.
Hall, John W.
Hall, Richard
Hall, William
Haltin, John H.
Ham, George P.
Hamilton, James
Hammill, William
Hammond, Samuel W.
Hamon, Patrick
Hand, William
Handel, Valentino
Handler, John
Hanford, C.
Hanna, E. B.
Hanna, Henry
Hanney, John
Hanson, Charles
Harding, Carpenter
Harding, John C.
Harding, Theodore
Hardwick, H.
Hardy, Benjamin
Hardy, James M.
Hargroff, Edmund
Harlow, Charles
Harmon, B.

New York
{continued}
Harrington, Nelson
Harris, Albert
Harris, John
Harris, N.B.
Harrison, Cruser
Hart, Daniel E.
Hart, John
Hart, Joseph B.
Harth, M. F.
Hartley, William
Hartly, Joseph
Hartman, Edwards
Hartman, Lewis
Harvey, James
Haskins, Charles
Hastie, John
Hatch, George
Hatfield, George
Hattin, John
Haufman, George
Hauston, Ira F.
Haven, Loren
Haverstick, Amos
Haviland, Alfred
Hawkins, Charles
Hawkins, Francis
Hawkins, Walker
Hawkins, William
Hawkins, William C.
Hawley, Edward J.
Hawley, Henry M.
Hawley, James
Hayes, George
Hayes, Michael
Hayner, Hiram
Hays, John
Hazen, Frederick
Heald, William S.
Healy, Thomas
Heday, Francis

New York
{continued}
Hedges, W. W.
Heen, A.
Hegeman, H.
Hellison, Julius
Helminger, C.
Hendermott, Jeremiah
Henderson, John
Henner, Charles II
Hennessy, Mathew
Henry, Levy
Henshaw, George W.
Hertzog, Godfrey
Hescott, Benjamin
Hesse, Harmon
Hesselstine, Follen
Hettmgan, Jacob
Hewiett, Samuel
Hicks, E.
Hill, Benjamin
Hill, Benjamin F.
Hill, Elenor
Hill, James
Hill, William
Hiller, Nicholas
Hilliker, Ellis R.
Hillman, Daniel
Hillock, B.
Hincher, George
Hinckley, Rudolph
Hindelong, Albert
Hins, William g.
Hintze, John
Hoag, Judson
Hoard, Lorenzo
Hodgson, George A.
Hoffman, _____
Hofner, Henry
Holcomb, Seymour
Hollenbock, Henry
Holley, William

New York
(continued)
Holmes, Clarence
Holmes, George
Holmes, Robert
Holsensberger, John
Holt, Henry H.
Honner, Dennis
Hopkins, Charles
Horan, P.
Hordling, C. T.
Horle, Agustus
Horn, C. L.
Hornby, Adam
Hough, John M.
Houghtaling, A. B.
Howard, George W.
Howard, M.
Howard, William
Howe, Orren W.
Howell, Henry B.
Howell, Kedar
Hubachu, Jacob
Hubbard, Francis
Hugam, David J.
Hughes, James
Hull, John D.
Hulsey, Henry W.
Hulsinger, _____
Hund, William
Hunker, John C.
Hunt, Jonathan
Hunt, William B.
Hurbert, Edgar
Hutchinson, Orville
Hyde, Freeman
Hyke, J. H. (or Isaac)
Hyland, Charles
Ingalls, David
Ingersoll, Albert
Ingerson, Frederick
Ingraham, A.

New York
(continued)
Ingram, James A.
Ingram, Thomos
Inman, Nathan
Irving, Farbrothe
Jackson, E.D.
Jackson, Jacob
Jackson, Owen
Jackson, Thomas
Jacquette, A.
Jacquith, George W.
Jagger, Daniel
James, William H.
Jamison, Wm. W.
Janney, Parley
Jaques, Arnold
Jeffers, C.
Jeffers, Philip
Jenner, Edward B.
Johnson, David
Johnson, Edwin
Johnson, J.
Johnson, Jerome
Johnson, John
Johnson, Joseph
Johnson, Nicholas
Johnson, Ruliff
Johnson, Samuel
Johnson, Stephen
Johnson, W.
Johnson, William
Johnson, William
Jones, Aaron
Jones, C.J.
Jones, Charles
Jones, Franklin
Jones, George
Jones, Henry L. S.
Jones, John
Jones, John O.
Jones, L.T.

New York
(continued)
Jones, Martin
Jones, William
Jones, William C.
June, James
Justice, John
Kaiser, Alexander
Kanco, Henry
Kanoll, M. W.
Katon, Thomas
Kean, Thomas
Keely, Silas M.
Keenan, John
Keisters, G.A.
Kellery, George
Kelley, James
Kelsey, Abram
Kemble, Nathaniel
Kemp, Charles J.
Kennedy, F.
Kenney, John
Kenny, David
Kent, Charles
Kent, Charles F.
Kenuy, A.
Kenzie, Nathan
Keough, Peter
Kerschum, Jacob
Ketryn, Joseph II
Kidstenbach, M.
Kiffer, James
King, Alexander
King, Charles S.
King, George H.
King, Henry W.
King, Moses P.
Kingerland, Isaac
Kinpon, Horace A.
Kirchan, Julius
Kitchen, A.B.
Kline, Thomas A.

New York
(continued)
Knapp, Charles E. II
Knickerbocker, Chas. E.
Knight, Jonathan
Knight, Joshua
Korchesky, Alexander
Krell, William
Kubler, John
Kulmer, G.
Kuster, Martin
Lafayette, John
Laflan, Albert
Lahon, W. M.
Lake, George W.
Lambert, Frederick W.
Lambert, J.
Lambra, John
Lamka, Edward
Lamore, Frank A.
Lancaster, Thomas
Lancton, David
Landrells, James P.
Lang, Charles
Langwood, George
Lansdorph, Sergeant
Lapham, Jonathan
Lapham, Simon
Lapoint, Peter
Lasell, John A.
Lathrop, Benjamin
Lawrence, Edward
Lawson, John
Lawson, William
Lawvenger, Oswald
Leary, Daniel
Leasure, John
Leavitt, Sylvester
Ledford, _____
Lee, Charles
Lee, James
Lee, William W.

New York
(continued)
Leib, Lewis
Lenerd, Levi
Leonard, Charles G.
Leonard, Joseph
Leonard, Peter
Leonard, William
Letson, J. W.
Levey, B. F.
Levi, Barney
Levings, Jeremiah
Lewis, Abraham
Lewis, Charles
Lewis, Frank
Lewis, Peter
Lindsay, Edward
Lintern, John B.
List, Harrison
Little, George
Little, Thomas
Lobdell, Isaac
Loewe, Nicholas
Long, Henry
Longe, Joseph E.
Longuar, E.
Looney, William H.
Loop, B. F.
Loper, Lutheran
Lord, M. W.
Lord, M. W.
Lorenz, Martin
Louress, Andrew
Lowell, Joseph
Luffand, Jacob
Lull, E.P.
Lundy, James
Lurouch, William S.
Lust, Hiram II
Lutkin, David H.
Lyman, James C.
Lyman, S. H.

New York
(continued)
Lyons, J.E. M.
Lytlebrand, Charles
Maban, Alexander
Mack, Clark A.
Mackie, John W.
Madden, Thomas
Madison, George M.
Mahan, William
Maher, M.
Mahew, G.W.
Mahon, Michael
Maine, C.
Mairin, Lee
Malford, Albert
Malon, Henry
Malone, Richard
Maloy, Wellington
Mansfield, David
Mansfield, Royal
Mansfield, William L.
Mapes, Selah
March, C.
March, Isaac
Marquaet, Charles
Marsh, Edmund N.
Martin, Christopher
Martin, Frederick
Martin, Hamilton M.
Martin, James
Martin, John
Martin, John J.
Martin, Zeb
Mason, Elvin P.
Mason, L.
Master, Walter P.
Matchkath, Gotlieb
Mathews, E.
Mathews, James
Matoon, E.H.
Matterson, Stillman

New York
(continued)
Maxim, James
Maxwell, James
Maxwell, Samuel
May, Edward
May, James
Maybee, Moses
McAdam, William N.
McAlliston, W.
McBride, Patrick
McBride, W.
McCabe, Alexander
McCandlish, Alex
McCann, James
McCardle, James
McCarty, C.
McCarty, Parick
McCaslin, John G.
McClosky, Francis
McClure, H.
McComber, Lyman
McConnell, John
McCoughel, Charles
McCoy, John H.
McCraig, George
McCue, Edward
McCunn, Dennis
McDaniel, Daniel
McDermott, Edward
McDonald, D.
McDonald, Joseph
McDonnald, John
McDonoly, Michael
McDowell, James Kerr
McElery, Daniel
McElwain, B. W.
McEvony, M. D.
McFall, George
McFarland, Dugand
McFurley, James C.
McGarr, D.

New York
(continued)
McGillis, James
McGony, Barney
McGovern, W. H.
McGrath, James
McGraw, William
McGregor, Richard
McGuire, John
McGuire, Michael
McHenry, James A.
McInleer, Christopher
McIntyre, J.
McIntyre, John
McKay, Reuben
McKenny, John
McKinney, Samuel
McLellan, William
McLorin, U.
McMahon, Edward
McMahon, J.
McMahon, Michael
McMullen, Daniel
McNamara, Thomas
McOwen, B.
McPherson, George
McQuinn, Owen
McSweeny, Mitchell
McTaugh, John
McTye, Michael
McWilliams, J.
Mead, Francis
Mecum, William
Megher, James
Meitzler, Francis
Melburn, George E.
Mellville, ____
Meng, Philip
Mentz, W. W.
Merchael, Sylvanus c.
Meridith, Oswall
Merrill, John

New York
(continued)
Merritt, David
Meyer, Herman
Midlaugh, Stewart D.
Miles, James
Millam, Christian
Miller, Caleb
Miller, Charles
Miller, F.
Miller, G. C.
Miller, John
Miller, Joseph
Miller, William
Miller, William H.
Miner, Joseph
Minnes, Joseph
Minor, Charles W.
Mitchell, Alfred
Mitchell, Edward
Mitchell, Henry
Molcott, Vicar
Monay, James
Monch, Hans Peter
Monsod, James
Monson, M.
Moody, _____
Moon, William
Moore, Benjamin F.
Moore, Charles
Moore, Edward A.
Moore, George W.
Moore, James
Moore, John
Moore, L. R.
Moore, Orlando
Moore, Stephen
Moran, J. T.
Moray, Philip
Moreau, Peter
Morel, John
Morgan, Patrick

New York
(continued)
Morley, James
Morris, James
Morris, Lewis
Morris, William
Morrison, Peter
Morrissy, George
Morse, James
Morton, E. D.
Mosier, Martin F.
Moule, Henry A.
Moulton, William H
Mueller, Oswald
Mulligan, Edward
Murphy, Daniel
Murphy, J. M.
Murphy, James
Murphy, John
Murphy, Michael
Murray, Daniel
Murray, David
Murray, William II
Myerhalt, _____
Myers, Peter
Mynard, Norman
Nash, O.
Natyke, William
Nay, Horace
Neal, Arthur
Neal, E. V.
Neal, Robert
Newcomb, Benjamin
Newcomb, Seth P.
Newell, H. G.
Newell, George W.
Newland, Alfred M.
Newman, George
Newton, Orville
Nicholas, James
Nichols, A. A.
Nichols, Benjamin

New York
(continued)
Niel, James II
Nilan, Thomas
Nix, Angevine
Noble, William L.
Nolan, James
Nolly, Owen
Noonan, Patrick
Norman, John
Northing, John
Noze, C. II
Nutter, Lewis
Nye, Adam
O'Brien, John
O'Brien, John O.
O'Haran, Parick
O'Niel, John
Ogden, John H.
Ogle, J. H.
Oldenheinze, Albert
Olembad, Philo
Oliff, George
Oliver, James
Oliver, James
Olmstead, Charles
Ormsby, James
Orr, Ansel
Ostrom, Thomas J
Otis, John
Ott, John
Ould, Leonard
Outland, Milton
Owens, E.
Owens, Edward W.
Page, David L.
Page, Moses P.
Page, Theodore L.
Paine, James F.
Palmer, Charles
Palmer, James
Palmer, M.

New York
(continued)
Palmer, Thomas P. W.
Parish, Jesse M.
Parker, A.
Parker, C. T.
Parker, George
Parker, James
Parks, Carlas
Partridge, W. H.
Paterson, J.
Patridge, William
Patten, J. N.
Patterson, F.
Paugh, Evan D.
Pauls, John
Payne, George
Pazay, Joseph
Pearee, Arthur
Pease, John
Peck, Alfred
Peck, Alpheus
Pedley, James
Peet, John
Pennoy, William
Pepler, C. H.
Perkins, Martin J. H.
Persons, Alexander
Peterman, Ralph
Peters, John
Peterson, William
Pettingill, James A.
Phelps, Joseph
Phillips, Joseph
Phillips, Shedrick
Phillips, Simeon
Pierce, Henry
Pierce, Henry II
Pierson, Abraham C.
Pike, Irving
Piquard, Emile
Pitsinger, E.G.

New York
(continued)
Pitsley, Henry
Place, Jonathan
Place, Robert
Planter, William II
Platt, Sylvester
Plummer, Charles
Pollard, John
Poole, James E.
Pope, Luke
Pope, William
Potter, Henry C.
Potter, Merreth
Powell, Charles
Powell, William
Powers, William
Pratt, Silas
Pratt, Thomas
Preble, O.
Prentice, Myron
Prentice, Simeon
Prentice, Thos. W.
Prescott, Lyther O.
Preston, Sidney
Price, Anthony
Price, Nathan S.
Prior, William
Pritchard, William
Proctor, H. H.
Punty, Patrick W.
Purdy, John
Putnam, Israel
Quinn, James
Radeliffe, ____
Radley, Erastus
Raesner, Henry
Ragin, Daniel
Ralph, Thomas
Ramsey, J.
Randall, Abner E.
Randleman, J. H.

New York
(continued)
Ranhausen, Isaac
Rasse, U. H.
Raven, Peter C.
Raymond, George
Raynor, Henry
Reamer, William
Reckley, William
Redcliff, William
Reed, H. A.
Reed, Jeremiah II
Reeds, Morris
Reedy, William
Reese, Harland P.
Regan, Cornelius
Regan, Peter M.
Reid, Charles S.
Reisch, Charles
Rempster, Francis
Remy, D.
Restin, Elijah L.
Retchman, Jacob
Retson, Mathew
Reynold, Richard
Reynolds, James
Reynolds, Leonard
Ribert, John
Rice, Anthony L.
Rice, James
Rich, Joseph
Richardson, Edward
Richardson, John
Richardson, L. G.
Richardson, M.
Ridgway, Henry
Ridgway, James
Riggs, Michael S.
Riley, Michael
Ring, James A.
Risedolps, D. G. H.
Risenlark, W.D.

New York
{continued}
Ritter, William H.
Ritterbash, Charles
Roach, N. E.
Robbins, Samuel
Roberts, Edward C.
Roberts, Henry B.
Roberts, John
Robertson, Joseph
Robinson, J.
Robinson, Smith
Robinson, William
Robnett, Lawson C.
Robotham, George
Rodden, M. S.
Rogers, Albert
Rogers, Ephraim J.
Rogers, Henry
Rogers, Nicholas
Rogil, John
Rolader, J. S.
Rolle, John
Rollins, Adolphus
Roper, John
Roreothy, John
Rose, Warren
Rosenstrauch, Saligman
Roser, E.P.
Ross, Thomas
Ross, William
Ross, William J.
Rouche, J.
Rounds, D. H.
Rowell, Enos S.
Rowland, Robert
Rubner, A.
Ruderlauck, Ezra
Rulfrew, B. W.
Rummings, Emory C.
Rush, Isaac S.
Rusling, Ludlow

New York
{continued}
Russell, George
Ryan, Patrick
Salcer, John
Sammis, Alcott
Sammis, John
Sampson, B.
Sandberg, John
Sandfut, Charles
Sands, Michael B.
Sargeant, Aaron
Saul, Peter
Savage, Horace
Savine, Samuel
Saxe, Henry
Scammel, E.
Scarlet, Frederick
Schaff, S. M.
Schaffer, Charles
Schaffer, Christian
Schaule, Henry
Schiefner, William
Schlottemau, Henry
Schmidt, George
Schmidt, John
Schnauben, Philip
Schneider, John
Schock, Clement
Schofield, Emelie
Schoonmaker, Frank
Schopp, Peter
Schreyer, William
Schumaker, Benjamin
Schwartz, Martin
Schweder, Francis J.
Schwindt, L. I.
Scolon, John
Scolton, John W.
Scott, E. B.
Scott, John
Scott, Robert

New York
(continued)
Scott, W. W.
Searles, Joseph
Sears, Benjamin
Sears, George
Seasley, Lewis
Seatterfield, G. A.
Sedbittle, Wade
Seiber, Jacob
Selway, Thomas
Seren, G. H.
Seren, George H.
Serme, James
Sever, Philip
Severs, James
Seward, _____
Seward, William H.
Sewiers, George b.
Seymour, Robert M.
Shaffner, Lewis
Shampine, P.
Sharp, Joseph
Shatyford, George
Shaw, Martin
Shea, John
Shea, John
Shea, Thomas
Shepherd, Jeremiah
Sherman, Morris
Shield, James H.
Shields, Patrick
Shiels, John
Shinman, William
Shipley, George
Shufile, Jacob
Shults, William
Shurber, R.
Shurtz, John
Sidmoyo, Franklin
Silliman, Jeremiah
Sillsby, John

New York
(continued)
Silsbee, Philo O.
Simons, Lauren B.
Simpson, _____
Singleton, William
Sink, Solomon
Sitel, Robert
Slauch, Gotleib
Sleeper, George
Sleeper, John
Sleghpaugh, H.
Slocum, Edward
Small, Joseph
Smeales, _____
Smith, A.
Smith, A. P.
Smith, Allen C.
Smith, Charles
Smith, E.
Smith, E. H.
Smith, Emery W.
Smith, F. J.
Smith, Harris
Smith, Henry
Smith, Herman R.
Smith, Isaac
Smith, J.
Smith, Jacob A.
Smith, James
Smith, John
Smith, John B.
Smith, Lawrence
Smith, Lewis
Smith, N. H.
Smith, Nathan
Smith, Robert
Smith, Samuel
Smith, Simpson
Smith, Stephen
Smith, Thomas
Smith, Thomas G.

New York
(continued)
Smith, Tilton D.
Smith, W. C.
Smith, William
Smith, William N.
Snelzer, John C.
Snowberger, David
Snyder, _____
Soder, Charles W.
Somers, Issacher
Sommer, Eben
Spaulding, O. K.
Speigelholder, John
Sperry, E. S.
Spicer, A. D.
Spring, James
Sprouls, F. J.
Spullberg, _____
Stage, William
Stahl, Jacob
Staler, William B.
Stanley, Jetho
Stanton, Willard L.
Stark, Jacob
Steele, Albert
Steeples, Orlando
Stefan, Frank
Steinberger, William
Stenebrook, John
Stephens, J.
Stephenson, J.
Sternwick, Adolph
Stevens, John
Stevens, W. J.
Stevenson, Frank
Stevnes, Benjamin
Stewart, William F.
Stiles, S.
Stillson, Amos H.
Stone, Charles
Stone, J. W.

New York
(continued)
Stone, Robert
Stormout, William
Story, William
Stover, Andrew W.
Stowell, Byron S.
Stratton, Alfred
Stratton, George F.
Stratton, Walker
Street, Jacob
Striken, William
Striker, William
Strinle, William
Strogen, Thomas
Strothers, George
Stubbs, Henry S.
Sullivan, John
Sullivan, John
Sullivan, Thomas
Sullivan, William
Sullivan, Willis
Sutherland, Michael
Sutherland, William
Swacole, Alonzo
Swart, John A.
Sweeney, William
Sweet, James
Sweitzer, Theodore
Swink, L.
Sykes, George
Symmes, Albert A. C.
Talcott, E. C.
Tarpenerig, S.
Tasker, Dolphus
Tates, _____
Taylor, George W.
Taylor, John
Taylor, Joseph
Taylor, Randolph
Teisley, Jacob
Terry, Albert W.

New York
(continued)
Tetus, Caleb
Tews, Samson
Thibault, Augustus
Thomas, Robert
Thomas, Samuel
Thomas, Stephen H.
Thomas, Warren
Thomas, William
Thompson, A.
Thompson, Benjamin F.
Thompson, C.
Thompson, C. E.
Thompson, James
Thompson, John
Thompson, Silas W.
Thompson, Thomas
Thompson, William
Thornton, J. G.
Thorp, Samuel
Thorpe, George M.
Thurston, Quincy F.
Tierney, Richard
Tiffany, J.
Tiffrey, Cornelius
Tilson, Sylvester
Titus, David S.
Tompkins, W.
Topen, Aretem
Tousley, Ebenezer
Towell, Chauncey
Tower, W. H.
Town, Enoch L.
Towsley, James
Track, Joseph
Trash, Alfred
Trederer, Theodore
Tripp, J. N.
Troberg, Gustavus
Tryer, Charles
Tryon, R.P.

New York
(continued)
Tubbs, Malvin
Turepy, Henry
Turk, William H.
Tuttle, Solomon
Tyler, Emory H
Tyler, James
Van Arsdale, _____
Van Arsdale, Thomas
Van Decker, Hiram
Van Dike, _____
Van Dyke, John
Van Gilder, Rufus
Van Kleeck, Charles H.
Van Tassel, John
Van Tyle, D.
Van Valkenburgh, Jacob
Van Vleck, George S.
Van Vleet, Darius
Van Wager, Levi
Van Wermer, _____
Van Wert, James C.
Van Winkle, David
Van Zandt, Jacob
Vance, Simeon
Vaugh, Robert
Vibbard, Seymour
Vickery, Thomas W.
Vincent, Horace J.
Vinett, Fabian
Virgin, August
Vohb, Charles
Wade, C. F.
Wadsworth, Benjamin
Wagner, John
Wakefield, Harry M.
Waldron, Charles
Waldron, Cortlandt
Walker, Francis G.
Walker, Lee
Walker, Philip

New York
{continued}
Walkins, W. H.
Wallace, Thomas
Walsh, Michael
Walsh, William
Walter, Albert
Ward, James
Ward, John W.
Ward, William
Wardell, George A.
Warden, E. S.
Ware, H. S.
Warmermaker, William
Warner, Charles H.
Warner, Joseph
Warner, P. F.
Warner, Sherman H.
Warren, Patrick
Warrick, W. P.
Waterman, Arthur S.
Waters, Patrick
Watson, Anthony
Watts, Daniel
Waves, Charles
Weber, S. J.
Weeks, Maryatt
Weir, Thomas
Welch, H. F.
Welch, Reuben
Wells, Francis
Wells, George W.
Wells, Henry
Welsh, James
Welsh, John
Weltz, David
Wentwsorth, John
Wescott, James
Weshurd, Henry
West, Harlan P.
Westcott, Assia
Westmuller, Conrad

New York
{continued}
Westover, Charles
Whalen, Charles
Wheat, Charles L.
Wheelan, Albert
Wheelan, George
Wheeler, Francis
Wheeler, Sylvester
Whilton, Isaac
Whipple, A. S.
Whipple, John
Whitaker, Christopher
Whitaker, Edward W.
White, E.
White, Moses
White, Orville
White, Richard
White, William E.
Whitehead, John (Colored)
Whitehead, William
Whitehouse, Russell
Whither, Daniel
Whitney, Angrew
Whittenmore, Alonzo
Whuna, Stephen
Wickham, Isaac
Wiebeck, John
Wilber, Stephen
Wilcox, William
Wilke, Thomas A.
Will, George
Willard, Patrick
Willebaugh, Samuel
Williams, Allen
Williams, Edward
Williams, George
Williams, Henry P.
Williams, Jeremiah
Williams, John
Williams, John
Williams, Peter

New York
(continued)
Williams, R. F.
Williams, Smith
Williams, Tunis
Wills, John
Wilson, _____
Wilson, Charles
Wilson, David A.
Wilson, H. S.
Wilson, William
Wine, Eli
Winehan, James
Winkler, _____
Winn, Samuel
Winset, Charles
Wirker, N.
Wise, Robert
Withe, J.
Withrington, Rich
Wolf, Christian
Wolvert, Charles
Wood, E. C.
Wood, H.
Wood, Ira
Wood, William H.
Woodhouse, Georg
Woodman, Thomas
Woodruff, Richard
Wosman, Nicholson
Wricklish, Otto
Wright, Henry S.
Wright, Solomon
Wright, Thomas E.
Wrinckle, Lawrence
Wurtz, C. H.
Wyael, James
Wyman, George B.
Wynn, William D.
Yager, Antoine
Yeomans, Samuel
York, Thomas F.

New York
(continued)
Yost, Alexander
Young, David
Young, John
Young, Richard
Youngs, Hiram
Zehnder, Jacob
Zickley, John R.
Zugler, John A.

North Carolina
Allen, Robert
Barton, James W.
Bass, Jethro
Beekman, W. M. H.
Bird, Josiah
Blannership, John
Blood, L. W.
Boyett, Stephen
Brown, John
Campbell, Robert
Carthlend, Francis
Chambers, George W.
Champion, W. M.
Clark, Alfred
Clifton, George
Coleman, Aseh
Contrain, Jackson
Cox, C.
Crawford, A. G.
Davenport, M. E.
Davis, Allen
Early, H. T.
Edwards, John H.
Edwards, Thomas D.
Eldridge, David
Elliott, J. T.
Elmore, J.
Estis, John M.
Faust, Jacob
Ferguson, George A.

North Carolina
(continued)
Few, M. D.
Fulk, Joseph
Gordon, Jonathan
Grady, W. S.
Green, Martin
Griffin, David G.
Hall, Joseph T.
Harmon, Daniel
Hassell, John W.
Helm, A. J.
Helton, Alfred
Hennison, _____
Henson, W. B.
Hill, Jesse
Hodges, A.
Howard, J. C.
Howell, W. M.
Irving, A.
Jenkins, _____
Johnson, Fleet
Johnson, Stephen
Jones, Wilson
Keeny, Sampson
Knight, Thomas C.
Kransanbrink, William
Kufham, William H.
Mann, C. D.
Marsings, Robert
Massey, R. B.
McDonald, John C.
McDowell, William
McGill, John
McKetheand, J.
McViear, William
Middleton, H.P.
Miles, Gilbert
Mitchel, John W.
Montgomery, William
Morarit, John
Morris, Robert T.

North Carolina
(continued)
Murdoch, J. C.
Norwood, Joseph, J.
Nowell, J. H.
Owen, William H.
Patterson, N.
Pearsall, Leonidas
Perry, N. E.
Phillips, Richmond
Phipps, John
Pinckney, James
Powell, Andrew
Priestwood, E.
Proctor, S. D.
Quackenbush, John G.
Rape, Samuel M.
Reeves, Sanders
Riddix, James
Roberson, James
Rogers, James B.
Roland, Charles
Royal, William H.
Sawyer, W. B.
Seigle, N. W.
Sharp, Washington
Shaw, Hugh
Shore, William H.
Simpson, R.
Smith, E. N.
Smith, J. H.
Starr, Robert
Staton, M.
Steely, F.
Stowe, J.
Thomas, J. W.
Vaughn, William L.
Wadsworth, Eli W.
Ward William H.
White, Franklin
Wilbanks, W.
Williams, C. D.

North Carolina
(continued)
Williams, S.
Wilson, George S.
Wilson, James E.
Wilson, John W.
Winston, H. N.
Wright, Henry V.
Yow, John W.

Nurses
Busch, Mrs. Joanna
Cummings, Henry
Lemoin, Henry
Russell, James
Stimpson, Mrs. Mary

Ohio
Ackerly, Catlin
Adams, George W.
Amber, John
Balser, Peter
Barnhardt, Samuel
Barr, Lewis J.
Bebout, Andrew G.
Belford, J.
Belford, John
Boal, William F.
Bogley, Irvin
Bolestell, David
Brispham, J. P.
Brown, Joseph
Burke, Lewis F.
Burkhardt, John
Canaga, O. C.
Carll, Peter
Champlin, Lewis
Chase, Dennis
Clark, Lewis G.
Clark, R. W.

Ohio
(continued)
Clements, M. D.
Clergy, Jesse H.
Coit, William H.
Collard, George
Creuthers, Christopher
Dahlin, Jeremiah
Dart, William
Dees, Joseph P.
Dildine, John H.
Dunkel, Jacob
Edwards, John
Elliot, P.
Ellsworth, Sylvester
Evans, William
Fenton, William
Flems, Henry
Fletcher, William
Flookner, John
Ford, Joseph E.
Fought, Simon
Fowler, S. H.
Fritz, J.
Frothbart, Ferdinand
Fullen, O.
Gillespie, D.
Gray, Newton
Green, Henry
Gunckel, George
Gunner, John
Hart, Jacob
Hashier, N. A.
Heller, Elias
Heller, Elias
Hendrick, Peter
Hickey, William B.
Hine, Charles
Hoffman, Lewis
Horner, James
Horsman, James
Huffman, M.

Ohio
(continued)
Ingrall, Robert L.
Jackson, Cyrus J.
Jamison, J.H.
Jamison, John R.
Jaylond, Alphonzo
Joy, Albert S.
Joy, Cornelius
Kadle, B.
Kapp, Augustus
Keyser, William
King, Lysander
Kraichill, Isaac
Kutzer, James
Listy, W. L.
Little, Charles
Longworth, Jackson
Mackey, William
Mager, C. H.
Malson, William E.
Mapes, John
Marshall, Seth
McCarty, Thomas B.
McCollen, J. B.
McDill, Robert
McDonald, J.
McDonald, John
McFee, David
McGee, Patrick
McNeil, E. R.
McReynolds, John
McVey, Daniel
Merrick, John
Milligan, Robert
Ming, Philip
Monelthori, Horace
Morris, William
Mount, Henry
Nash, W. H.
Noarks, George
Olcott, George

Ohio
(continued)
Palmerston, J. S.
Palmeter, Allen
Pitt, Philip
Plumer, Amzi T.
Plummer, George M.
Ponet, James H.
Pray, Denison P.
Randall, David
Reaser, Peter
Reed, David
Reed, Hinas
Rees, John
Richardson, Henry
Rogers, Hugh S.
Ross, George A.
Rowe, John N.
Sammery, John S.
Sanderson, James N.
Schoonmaker, A.
Scott, Alexander
Shaw, Marvin
Shelberry, Perry E.
Shelly, William G. S.
Sheridan, Andrew
Shuler, Andrew J.
Shuler, George
Skinner, Joseph
Souther, _____
Sprague, Delos
Spurgeon, Elias
Stebbins, W. W.
Stewart, Robert
Storer, Ignatz
Stull, Joshua
Sutton, Charles E.
Svringle, D. M. L.
Swallow, William W.
Thompson, Samuel
Truax, William H.
Walter, James

Ohio
(continued)
Watts, Henry
Way, Addison, A.
White, Wilbur
Wilder, L.
Wilkerson, Lewis
Williamson, H. C.
Wilson, George H.
Wilson, John W.
Wood, William J.
Wright, Sylvester
Young, Clark

Pennsylvania
Albro, William
Allspatch, David J.
Altemus, George
Arnaud, Abner
Auchenbach, William
Bailey, John W.
Baldnye, David
Banks, Phillip
Barger, Jacob
Barr, S.
Baupp, _____
Belford, David
Bell, David
Bennet, Henry C.
Bimerand, George
Bisbing, J.
Block, Joseph
Bond, S.
Boner, Adam
Booth, John
Borden, J. W.
Boyce, Thomas D.
Brabson, W. F.
Bringle, William
Broughton, William
Browe, Isaac W.

Pennsylvania
(continued)
Brown, B. F.
Brown, Henry
Brown, James
Brown, William
Bruper, John
Bryant, G. S.
Buck, Osborne
Buckhardt, Charles
Burkhart, Andrew
Bushfield, Thomas
Byers, William
Cain, A. N.
Camp, William H.
Canahan, Benjamin
Carman, Samuel D.
Carney, William
Chamberlin, Willsam
Chase, Simon
Chuoniger, E.
Clark, Charles
Cline, Milton
Cole, Chauncey
Collins, Robert
Comack, John
Comet, Romanus
Conley, Thomas
Coppersmith, Thomas
Coxey, James
Cozard, Edward
Creamer, George
Critchlow, Adam W.
Critone, Alfred
Crofut, Levi
Crosby, Matthias
Culver, Parmenas
Datzins, Philip W.
Davis, B. F.
Davis, John
Dawagan, John
Devow, Isaac

Pennsylvania
(continued)
Dinst, John
Divins, David
Doty, William
Drackenmuller, John
Drake, John B.
Dunkle, Benjamin
Dunlap, S. R.
Dunn, Thomas
Eaven, George A.
Eckhert, H.
Entry, Isaac
Esbach, J. W.
Finley, Anthony
Firth, Thomas J.
Fisher, George
Fisk, Erastus
Flanagan, B.
Fogles, N.
Forlet, H.
Fossnacht, Samuel B.
Foster, Charles
French, James
Gates, George
Gealy, Cyrus
Geslach, Michael
Gilgon, Samuel P.
Gillen, John
Grace, Samuel G.
Graeder, George
Graham, William H.
Green, Samuel
Grenan, John
Guinard, Virgil
Haborn, John
Haffner, Michael
Hall, George A.
Hall, Jacob
Hall, John
Hamans, James
Hamilton, James

Pennsylvania
(continued)
Hanagan, W.
Hanna, Thomas
Harmon, Johnson
Harris, William
Hart, Samuel
Harvey, James B.
Haven, Charles
Hayes, William
Hazel, Henry
Hener, Guelph
Henrick, George O.
Hentzer, J. B.
Herring, Levi
Hickman, James W.
Hickson, Thomas
Hiler, Jonathan
Hill, James
Hirsch, Levi
Hitherton, Edward H.
Hoge, Henry H.
Hollinger, E. W.
Holmes, Henry
Holt, James
Holt, Norman F.
Horn, Caleb
Hoster, Samuel
Hough, John M.
Huggins, John
Hull, William C.
Huntsman, J. C.
Ingle, Almon
Ingle, William
Johnson, John W.
Jones, E.
Jones, William W.
Kellinger, Joseph
Kerns, Enoch B.
Kertlein, Fred
Kesse, Thomas
Kinsley, Benjamin

Pennsylvania
(continued)
Kirkpatrick, Henry
Kirmi, John E
Kline, George
Kramer, David
Kreger, Daniel B.
Kreps, Jacob
Kunze, Solomon
Larue, James W.
Laubach, William S.
Leary, Michael
Lee, Henry
Lemereaux, S. H.
Lester, George
Lewis, John C.
Liebrand, G.
Lingfellow, Charles
Logan, Newton
Ludwig, Albert
Lydeck, Eli P.
Macklemry, B. C.
Magan, W. C.
Malony, Daniel
Mansfield, Stephen
Massey, John
Mathey, Robert
McCasky, James
McClemen, Hugh
McConnell, James
McCrist, John
McCuster, John K.
McDermond, L.
McGraw, Michael
McIsaac, Daniel
McJenkin, J. S.
McKenna, Patrick
McKiester, Joseph
McMullin, Joseph
Meltack, Henry
Menia, John
Miller, Daniel

Pennsylvania
(continued)
Miller, James
Monday, C.
Moock, James A.
Mooney, Daniel C.
Moore, George
Morris, James
Myers, James
Nelman, John A.
Neville, Robert
Newman, Benjamin
Nicholson, James
Panrocle, James
Park, Nicholas
Parkinson, James
Patterson, David
Pearce, Jeremian
Pettit, Lorenzo M.
Pine, William
Pinnert, Isaac B.
Poole, Josiah
Powler, C.
Quigley, James B.
Radcliff, James
Ramford, Joseph
Rarick, O. R.
Ray, James
Reed, Joel
Reed, Monroe F.
Reeves, John A.
Reib, Henry
Reyner, Charles
Rice, Henry
Riskine, Henry
Roach, Nathan
Robb, C.
Roberts, G. T.
Rogers, Augustus
Rouse, G. W.
Rover, Phillip
Rudolph, Emmer

Pennsylvania
(continued)
Ruffenburg, Abraham
Russell, James
Rutter, Isaac B.
Sailor, S. H.
Salamo, Thomas
Samerill, James
Sanders, Daniel
Schoonmaker, H. E.
Severn, John
Shadow, John
Sheever, Joseph
Shields, Thomas
Smith, David C.
Smith, Jacob
Smith, Lewis
Smith, William H.
Snyder, Franklin
Snyder, William H.
Stackhouse, Samuel W.
Starch, William
Stark, A. D.
Stevens, Victor
Stiter, John
Stonesifer, Josiah
Stover, John
Streightliff, Jacob
Strunk, William C.
Sturns, Oscar R.
Sweeny, Edward
Taylor, D. W.
Taylor, Isaac
Thomas, John
Thompson, Andrew
Tilley, William H. H.
Van Arsdale, Thomas
Van Arsdale, William
Vannettel, Charles
Wagner, Jacob
Walker, John
Walter, Frederick

Pennsylvania
(continued)
Waltman, Sylvanus
Watson, William
Weaver, Charles
Weaver, L.
Weekly, James W.
Wertson, John
Wesner, Frank
Whigand, Robert
Wiggins, Charles
Williams, L. D.
Wilson, Henry
Wilty, Jacob
Winkleburgh, George
Wirbaugh, Henry
Wolf, Frederick
Wolfe, John
Wood, Thomas
Wright, John J.
Young, Edward C.
Yous, George

Rhode Island
Allen, George M.
Bound, Philip
Franklin, Edward
Good, H.
Jefferson, George
Johnson, John
Merrech, John
Weaver, Alton

South Carolina
Beard, J.H.
Boughman, Henry L.
Brown, H.E.
Brown, J.J.
Burdick, E. W.
Cain, S.

South Carolina
(continued)
Calvert, John
Campbell, Elisha
Carroll, Joseph
Carthen, Timothy
Chaisley, A. M.
Covington, Elijah
Crowder, William
Darin, Berry
Davis, James R.
DeBar, Lewis W.
Duggens, Robert
Dunlap, J.S.
Durixs, C. L.
Durm, Berry
Evan, Jay
Farmer, John L.
Fedden, Stephen
Fogle, William
Franklin, R. L.
Frieman, John
Gardner, F. M.
Gilliland, A.
Glasson, James N.
Glover, John B.
Gooding, Thomas
Griffin, Silas
Hair, W. J.
Haliburton, A. G.
Harris, E. J.
Henley, Charles C.
Hill, J. A.
Hollenfield, Jacob
Hughes, John
Hute, Charles
Hute, J. M.
Inabimet, Archibald
Johnson, Murdoch D.
Jowers, J. W.
Korn, J. A.
Lunday, James

South Carolina
(continued)
Matthis, Thomas
McCurry, H. S.
Morrison, Angust
Murphy, Enoch E.
Myer, J. H.
O'Connell, Patrick
Otts, Martin
Parker, James
Poor, John M.
Pridgin, J. O.
Rollins, Thomas
Rost, William R.
Sale, W. A.
Shaver, William
Snow, Jesse
Still, Isaac
Still, Tobias
Strone, G. R.
Swalt, Simeon
Templeton, H. B.
Tilley, William
Tindall, Henry T.
Weatherby, J. B.
Wherry, James
White, Elisha
Younginer, Joseph

Tennessee
Allen, H. W.
Barnett, Andrew
Flower, Franklin
Gordon, John
Griesber, James H.
Haddox, H. M.
Moore, Gabriel E.
Roberts, William D.
Smith, Alonzo M.
Stokes, B. R.

Tennessee
(continued)
Willis, James
Wilson, Nathaniel
Wood, E. C.

Texas
Atterbury, Charles
Ellis, J.
Green, Benjamim M.
Grumbles, P.B.
Himpson, Samuel
Porter, John
Wright, H.C.

United States Colored Troops (USCT)
_____, Henry
_____, Isaac
_____, James
_____, James M.
_____, Joseph
_____, Samuel
Allen, William
Anderson, John
Bailey, Benjamin
Bam, Wesley
Banks, Amos
Barton, Ary
Bash, Samuel
Baxter, John
Bay, Thomas
Baza, James S.
Bellamy, Harvey
Black, Charles
Blake, John
Blake, Thomas
Boney, Richard
Boston, Stephen
Boyer, Jacob
Boyer, Jesse

USCT
(continued)
Boyer, W. H.
Brooks, Jacob
Brown, George
Buck, Charles
Bunce, Clarence
Burgett, Lewis F.
Butler, _____
Butler, Samuel
Canby, John
Carmen, William
Carter, Isaac
Cartha, Edward
Chambers, J.
Charleston, George
Chase, August
Chase, Lewis
Christian, Thomas
Cole, Benjamin
Cook, Moses
Copeland, George
Cornish, Thomas
Curtis, Maber
Datterson, Charles
Davis, Edward
Delong, Silas H.
Dewitt, William
Dix, George
Douglas, John W.
Dozier. Major
Dubois, Charles
Dubois, Isaiah
Fayette, James A.
Fidgett, Oswald
Ford, James
Fox, Lorenzo
Frisbee, Charles
Fuller, George
Gabriel, James
Gaines, James
Garrison, Charles

USCT
(continued)
Gartham, John M.
Gilbert, George
Gray, Francis
Greeley, Horace
Green, Benjamin
Green, James
Gromer, Solomon
Harris, Walter
Hart, Andrew D.
Harvey, Albert G.
Hayes, Hannibal
Hill, Henry
Hooper, William H.
Hooting, Jesse
Horlem, Joseph
Howard, Wilson
Hubertson, _____
Hughes, Wesley
Hulett, George
Hutchins, Thomas
Hydlems, Joseph
Jackson, Charles
Jackson, Edward
Jackson, George
Jackson, James
Jackson, John
Jackson, Thomas
Jackson, William
Jager, Peter
Jennings, George W.
Johnson, Alfred
Johnson, Augustus
Johnson, C.
Johnson, Charles L.
Johnson, Diggs
Johnson, George
Johnson, Henry
Johnson, Sylvester
Johnson, Thomas
Johnston, Abraham

USCT
(continued)
Jones, George
Jones, John T.
Jones, Michael
Kelly, John
King, Lewis
Lancaster, L. L.
Larry, Daniel
Lee, Jerome
Lee, William H.
Linnett, John H.
Lloyd, Charles
Lucas, C.
Lyons, R.
Mack, James H.
Mann, Jesse
Marshall, Joseph
McDowell, Andrew
McGee, James
McGlocklin, Joseph
Merritt, Alfred
Miller, Frank
Miller, Herman
Minard, Henry
Mitchell, T.
Moffat, William
Moore, Thomas
Mordise, Nelson
Morton, Benjamin
Mowber, Aaron
Munday, Gordon
Murray, Beverly
Neuber, George
Nevins, Alexander
Newby, William
Ourtman, J.
Owens, James
Owens, W. H.
Park, John
Parker, Nathan
Parker, Robert

USCT
(continued)
Pennington, James
Pero, John
Perry, Thomas
Petty, Edward
Pinto, John
Pleasant, George N.
Porterfield, N.
Portland, Samuel
Powell, James
Prime, Charles
Prince, Alexander
Princeton, Reuben
Richard, Christopher
Richards, Henry
Rickson, Henry
Robertson, John
Root, Marcus
Sampson, Peter
Sanders, James B.
Scott, James
Scott, John
Scott, Richard
Scott, Samuel
Shadrach, Woodland
Sharpe, George
Sharpe, Joshua
Shell, William
Sigley, James
Silwood, Silas A.
Simmons, Frank
Smith, Charles
Smith, Augustus
Smith, Benjamin
Smith, Major
Smith, William
Snowden, Samuel
Soggs, Henry
Somers, Harrison
Sparrowgrass, J. T.
Taylor, George

USCT
(continued)
Taylor, W. J.
TenEyck, Anthony
TenEyck, Charles H.
Thomas, Charles
Thompson, Albert
Thompson, Henry
Townsend, William
Tripp, William
Van Arsdale, John
Van Loo, Francis
Vandermarker, Jacob
Vollerth, Garret
Walker, Alfred
Washington, Charles
Webb, Christopher
Webster, James
Weeks, Nathaniel
Weeks, Thomas M.
Wells, Alex.
Wells, Nelson
Wenkoop, George
White, Edward
White, James
White, Joseph
Williams, Nathaniel
Williams, William
Wilson, Daran
Wright, Francis J.
Wright, Jacob
Young, David
Young, John
Young, William

Vermont
Bailey, B. C.
Barrett, Benjamin
Barry, Charles E.
Bartlett, Thos. J.

Vermont
(continued)
Bigelow, John L.
Buryes, Edwin D.
Cammel, Joseph
Chamberlin, Wm.
Cook, Clarke C.
Dommin, Priest
Downs, Thomas
Drury, W. G.
Farewell, Francis M.
Fass, Jacob
Fuller, Henry W.
Fulton, Geo. E.
George, Reuben G.
Hamblin, Jesse B.
Hill, Frank
Holt, Henry C.
Lang, A. W.
Newton, John
Norris, Horace
Perementor, Frank
Poridges, Alfred
Robinson, M.W.
Roddy, Terrence
Sanders, Andrew
Stoddard, Charles
Taylor, Benjamin
Taylor, Joseph W.
Wheeler, A.

Virginia
Anderson, Joseph R.
Baxter, Alfred
Bellshaw, John
Blake, E. P.
Boulden, N. H.
Branaham, William
Brown, Henry
Cabbage, John
Clark, Joseph W.

Virginia
(continued)
Clark, W. F.
Conetrey, Jeff.
Cook, A. L.
Cousins, James A.
Cramden, J. S.
Driff, Benjamin R.
Duff, James A.
Early, Silas D.
Fletcher, Charles
Giles, Richard
Gilmore, H. J.
Good, A. H.
Hair, John B.
Hammock, J. H.
Hazelgrove, Andrew S.
Hill, Jehu
Hogan, Walker K.
Johnson, S. A.
Jones, Robert
Keefe, Irvin H.
Kegby, William
Lantrop, William
Lemon, William
Light, C. M.
Litton, George
Lowber, S. B.
Lybe, S. A.
Lynch, Geo. E.
Mattox, R. F.
May, William H.
McCann, Austin
McCarthy, Michael
McDowell, David C.
Mewell, Hudson
Murray, Michael
Overfelt, Robert
Owens, John
Phillips, E. W.
Pollard, G. W.
Redman, S. C.

Virginia
(continued)
Reese, Samuel U.
Short, Robert
Skelton, Alexander
Southard, William
Thompson, H. F.
Tyree, William H.
Way, John M.
Wilkinson, George
Woods, John B.

Washington
Schmas, Joseph

Wisconsin
Aldrich, A. R.
Allen, Robert
Baker, Chauncey C.
Beach, Cyrus T.
Birge, Nelson W.
Bosell, John
Boyd, Joshua
Burdick, Joel G.
Campbell, George W.
Clark, Hugh
Combs, James W.
Cooper, Samuel
Dark, George
Darling, Truman
Davis, George M.
Dinja, John
Dixon, William
Edson, Alonzo
Elliot, Thomas
Ellverson, E.
Fairbanks, Cyrus
Fibay, John W.
Foss, Daniel
Goodman, Austin
Graves, Thomas T.

Wisconsin
(continued)
Hagness, Matheas
Hamlett, Horace
Haynard, Franklin
Hollister, James D.
Hurst, Charles
Jackson, James
Kenshaw, Jacob
King, Edgar
Knoble, Kaspan
Landis, John
Lane, Benjamin W.
Langbeag, James
Lilbaugh, Philip
McClug, James
Meigs, John H.
Millard, Johu J.
Murphy, James
Oslin, Amos
Ourey, Henry
Paddock, E. R.
Porter, John R.
Pulk, Henry
Rice, Orson E.
Rivers, Alfred
Roscoe, Boardman
Rouse, Benjamin
Sanders, Harvey
Sanders, Nathan
Sawyer, Reuben G.
Schlitter, Casper
Schons, Henry
Senney Henry C.
Shepherd, George T.
Sprague, B.D.
Taplin, Charles H.
Taylor, Henry
Weymouth, Owen
Wood, Joseph
Zbilowsky, Joseph

FORT COLUMBUS
New York

Fort Columbus was located on Governor's Island in New York City's Harbor. Not only was the fort a vital defensive position, but during the war Confederate POWs were held there. Burials continued in the post cemetery until at least 1876; however, the Quartermaster General's General Order 11, issued in 1873, was supposed to have ended the burials. One of the last soldiers buried here was Capt. Thomas B. Weir of the 7th Cavalry. Weir survived Custer's ill-fated 1876 expedition only to die suddenly at home the following December.

In 1886 between 500 and 1,000 bodies from the post cemetery were moved to the Cypress Hills National Cemetery on Long Island.

Name	Rank	Co	Unit
_____, Courtney			Civilian
Abbott, Robt. O.	Col-Surgeon		
Abernethy, W.		H	37th NC
Aikens, Adolph	Pvt	C	General Service
Allen, Charles	Corp	K	7th US Inf
Allen, Emiline			Civilian
Andrews, Hiram	Pvt	F	4th US Art
Armstrong, Samuel	Lt		US Art
Auman, Bessie			Civilian - Child
Auther, Geo. H.	Pvt	D	General Service-USA
Barbury, J.E.		D	28th NC
Bartley, Smith			
Bennett, Henry	Pvt	B	Music Boys
Besamore, Charles	Pvt	B	Union Boys
Blunt, _____			CSA
Bodgerson, _____			CSA
Boyer, Henry	Pvt	D	General Service-USA
Boyle, James	Major		1st US Art
Bringart, Francis		D	Select Recruit
Broderich, Lawrence	Musician	B	General Service-USA
Brown, _____			CSA
Brown, Eliza F.			Civilian
Brown, Julia A.			Civilian
Burke, Frank	Pvt	A	General Service
Burke, John	Pvt	A	General Service

Name	Rank	Co	Unit
Burke, Peter	Pvt	D	General Service-USA
Bush, John	Pvt	D	General Service-USA
Byrne, Patrick	Pvt	E	General Service
Carr, James	Musician		
Carroll, Henry	Pvt	E	General Service
Casey, James	Pvt	A	General Service-USA
Chemington, William			
Christopher, Henry	Pvt	C	Perm Party
Churchill, Helen S.			Civilian
Colden, Patrick	Pvt	E	General Service
Cole, Mary			Civilian
Colgan, James	Pvt	E	General Service
Collins, Mary R.			Civilian
Conkly, Patrick	Pvt	H	28th Mass Inf
Conners, James			Prisoner
Coster, Martin	Pvt	D	General Service-USA
Creamer, Peter	Pvt	B	Music Boys
Cummings, Alex.	Col		
Cummings, T.	Pvt	A	Perm Party
Curtis, William F.	Pvt	E	General Service
Daily, Hubert	Pvt	D	General Service-USA
Dallye, Ernest	Pvt	A	Perm Party
Daly, Patrick	Pvt	E	General Service
De Kamp, James C.			Civilian
DeKamp, Susan			Civilian
DeLagenl, Julius A.	Capt		
DeLagnet, Sarah E.			Civilian
Dennis, Albert B.	Pvt	E	General Service
Dillman, Charles	Pvt	B	Union Boys
Donnelly, Charles	Pvt	J	General Service-USA
Dunford, Daniel	Musician	B	General Service-USA
Eckert, _____		D	28th _____
Elliot, Joseph C.	Pvt	D	General Service
Emmerson, Joseph	Pvt	D	General Service-USA
Erving, David	Prisoner	B	General Service-USA
Etzold, John H.			General Service
Farrell, Ellen			Civilian
Fish, John	Pvt	E	91st NY Inf
Fleck, David	Corp	A	Perm Party
Flickinger, Andrew	Pvt		General Service-USA
Flynn, Thomas	Pvt	D	General Service

Name	Rank	Co	Unit
Fogarly, M.J.			
Fogarty, George T. (Sr.)	Sgt		Depot Band
Fogarty, George T. (Jr.)	Pvt	B	Music Boys
Fogarty, John M.			
Fogerty, Emma			Civilian
Ford, Andrew J.	Corp	C	Perm. Party
Ford, Cornelius	Pvt	D	General Service-USA
Forney, David	Pvt	D	General Service-USA
Freeman, Constant			Civilian
Fried, John	Sgt	B	Union Boys
Fried, William T.			
Frye, Chas.			
Furgenson, Emanuel	Pvt		9th US Inf
Gallagher, Frank	Pvt	D	General Service-USA
Gass, George	Pvt	D	General Service
Gates, Collinson R.	Major		
Gates, Lydia			Civilian
Gates, Sarah			Civilian
Gates, William	Bvt Brig Gen		General Service
Gibson, William	Pvt	E	Perm. Party - Colored
Glandon, Peter	Pvt	D	General Service-USA
Gninert, E.D.			Civilian - Child
Gobel, F.A.	Bvt Major		General Service
Gousin, P.A.	Sgt	A	Perm Party
Green, James	Capt		2nd US Art
Gregory, _____			CSA
Griffin, P.	Pvt	H	1st US Inf
Gross, Carl	Pvt	D	General Service-USA
Gulick, William	Sgt	F	Perm. Party
Haefeli, Jacob	Sgt	C	Perm Party
Hainz, Fred			Civilian - Child
Hainz, Julia			Civilian - Child
Hainz, Mary			Civilian - Child
Hamilton, Bobby			Civilian - Child
Hamstreet, Harman L.			Music Boys
Hanke, Ann			Civilian
Hanna, George E.			Civilian - Child
Harrington, William		C	Permt. Party
Harrison, Josiah	Musician	B	General Service-USA
Harry, Louis A.	Pvt		General Service-USA
Hart, Patrick	Pvt	D	General Service-USA

Name	Rank	Co	Unit
Hassel, _____			CSA
Haynes, Alfred B.	Pvt	B	Music Boys
Head, William N.			
Head, William	Sgt		
Heaton, Robert	Lt.		2nd US Art
Henion, John	Pvt	B	Music Boys
Henke, Charles	Sgt	B	Music Boys
Herberger, John	Pvt	D	General Service-USA
Hercher, Oliver	Pvt	D	General Service-USA
Hillier, William	Pvt	D	General Service-USA
Holfride, F.	Pvt	F	1st US Art
Holmes, Laura			Civilian
Hooker, Casfer	Sgt	A	Perm Party
Hooker, John			Civilian - Child
Hooker, Samuel			Civilian - Child
Hooley, John	Pvt		General Service
Hooper, Franz	Pvt	A	Perm Party
Horan, John	Recruit		
Hovan, Jessie			
Howe, Charles	Pvt	D	General Service-USA
Hoyt, Alex. D.			Civilian - Child
Huber, Charles	Pvt	D	General Service
Huckbone, W.I.	Pvt	I	91st NY Inf
Hughes, Martha			Civilian
Hughs, John	Sgt		4th US Art
Hyler, John	Pvt		General Service
Hynes, John	Ordnance Sgt.		
Ivens, Elizabeth G.			Civilian
J.T.F.	Lt.		3rd US Art
Jennings, _____			CSA
Jern, Robert F.	Pvt	C	General Service
Johnson, Frederick W.	Pvt	D	General Service-USA
Johnson, J.	Pvt	C	6th US Inf
Jolly, _____			CSA
Jones, Frank	Pvt	D	General Service-USA
Jones, John	Corp	C	General Service-USA
Kaimer, Rudolph	Musician	B	General Service-USA
Karberg, Andrreas P.	Pvt	D	General Service-USA
Keckyman, Frank	Pvt	D	General Service
Kelcher, James		E	General Service-USA
Kendall, Charlotte			Civilian

Name	Rank	Co	Unit
Kendall, William			
Kennedy, John	Pvt	A	General Service
Kilborn, Walter	Pvt	K	91st NY Inf
King, Francis	Pvt	D	General Service-USA
Kinsell, Michael	Pvt	E	General Service - Recruit
Kyte, _____			CSA
Lagelarrer, Albert			
Lagenbauer, Gustau W.			
Leonard, Martin	Pvt	D	General Service-USA
Leonard, Patrick	Corp	C	Perm. Party
Lieberson, Daniel	Pvt	D	General Service-USA
Liesbert, Christ.	Pvt	D	General Service-USA
Littlefield, Catherine			Civilian
Lnyon, Thomas	Pvt	E	General Service
Lockwood, Stephen D.	Pvt	A	Perm. Party
Lowe, Anna M			Civilian - Child
Luck, Peter		E	General Service-USA
Magrine, Adeline			Civilian
Maguire, P.	Pvt	G	28th Mass Inf
Maning, John B.			
Mann, James	Surgeon		
Martin, Christopher	Pvt	B	Music Boys
Marton, Thomas	Pvt	D	General Service-USA
Mathison, Fritz	Pvt	D	General Service-USA
McBride, W.	Pvt	F	Perm. Party
McClellan, _____			CSA
McCoglan, John	Musician	B	General Service-USA
McCormick, C.	Pvt	A	Perm Party
McCormick, Chas.	Col		Surgeon
McFarland, William	Pvt	E	General Service-USA
McGrath, Thomas	Prisoner	J	General Service
McHugh, John	Pvt	A	General Service-USA
McHugh, Thomas	Pvt	D	General Service
McIntyre, William	Sgt		US Inf
McKellop, James			General Service
McKelsey, Monroe	Pvt	C	General Service-USA
McKeon, Charles	Pvt	D	General Service-USA
McLaughlin, _____	Pvt		VRC
McMahon, John	Pvt	B	General Service-USA
Meades, Samuel	Pvt	E	General Service - Recruit
Meridith, William	Pvt	D	General Service-USA

Name	Rank	Co	Unit
Mertins, Jacob	Sgt	A	Perm. Party
Miller, Ward			Civilian - Child
Mills, Madison	Surgeon		USA
Miltowe, Hutchinson	Pvt	A	Perm. Party
Modlin, _____			CSA
Monohiff, Ann			Civilian
Moore, Alexander	Pvt	M	2nd US Art
Moore, John	Pvt	D	General Service-USA
Moore, John A.	Pvt	D	General Service-USA
Morris, Elias	Pvt	D	General Service-USA
Morrison, Ann E. L.			Civilian
Morrison, Douglas			
Morrison, J.	Pvt	G	98th NY Inf
Morrison, Jane			Civilian
Morrissey, Michael	Pvt	C	22nd US Inf
Muller, William	Pvt	D	
Murray, Thomas	Pvt	E	General Service - Recruit
Neland, James	Pvt	D	General Service-USA
Noble, Christ.	Pvt	B	General Service
Noonan, William	Pvt	D	General Service-USA
Nowlan, Daniel			
Oliver, Fred			Civilian - Child
Oliver, Winfred			Civilian - Child
Page, Wm. J.			
Patson, Thos.	Pvt	D	General Service-USA
Patterson, William	Sgt		
Peck, Henry	Pvt		
Pfefferley, Ester T.			Civilian
Pierce, B.T.	Lt Col		1st US Art
Pilt, Alfred	Pvt	E	98th NY Inf
Pinchard, John B.			
Pinehard, Maria			Civilian
Plymfrton, Joseph	Col		1st US Inf
Rathbame, Henry	Pvt	A	Perm. Party
Reynolds, Fred			Civilian - Child
Reynolds, Mela			Civilian - Child
Rickard, Joseph	Recruit	D	General Service-USA
Riley, Patrick	Pvt	D	General Service-USA
Rixford, George	Pvt	D	General Service-USA
Robinson, _____			CSA
Robinson, Isaac J.	Pvt	D	General Service-USA

Name	Rank	Co	Unit
Rodgers, Adelbert	Pvt	D	General Service
Rodgers, James			Civilian - Soldier's son
Russell, Joseph P.	Asst. Surgeon		
Russell, Joseph P. (Jr.)			
Russell, Samuel L.	Capt		2nd US Inf
Saltinyer, Christopher	Pvt	D	General Service-USA
Sanberg, John	Pvt	D	General Service-USA
Schager, Rudolt			Civilian - Child
Schear, Carl			General Service
Schlegel, Henry	Pvt	D	General Service-USA
Schlessing, Justis	Pvt	E	General Service - Recruit
Scott, Robert	Pvt	A	Perm. Party
Serry, William	Pvt	E	General Service - Recruit
Shackleford, L.M.	Lt.		2nd US Art
Shelly, William	Pvt	M	5th US Art
Shields, Francis	Sgt	L	Perm Party
Shipley, Henry	Pvt	D	General Service-USA
Shultz, Simon S.			Civilian - Child
Simmons, W.	Pvt	J	91st NY Inf
Simpson, ____			CSA
Smith, Francis			
Smith, James	Pvt	D	General Service-USA
Smith, John	Pvt	A	General Service
Smith, John R.P.			
Smith, Sidney	Lt.		1st US Art
Snyder, Ferando			General Service
Souder, M.K.			Civilian
Soust, Francis	Pvt	D	General Service-USA
Stanley, Charles	Musician		
Steinman, Julis	Pvt	E	General Service - Recruit
Stigler, Magdalen, wife of Bandmaster			Civilian
Storms, Peter	Sgt	A	Perm Party
Stuart, Bridget			Civilian
Stuart, Mary J.			Civilian
Stuart, Rosanna			Civilian - Child
Stuart, William P.			
Sullivan, Thomas	Pvt	E	General Service-USA
Swain, William	Pvt	D	General Service
Themble, James	Sgt	G	Perm Party
Tilterton, ____			CSA

Name	Rank	Co	Unit
Tisdale, John			
Tisdale, Sarah L.			Civilian
Tolten, John H.	Pvt	D	General Service-USA
Townsend, G.		E	27th NC
Traub, Frederick	Pvt	D	General Service-USA
Tryer, Edward	Pvt	D	General Service-USA
Tyson, _____			CSA
Vassil, Louis	Pvt	J	General Service-USA
Villenger, Joseph	Pvt	E	General Service - Recruit
Walk, Abraham	Pvt	B	General Service-USA
Wallen, Samuel G.			
Walsh, David L.	Sgt		
Walters, Katie			Civilian
Weber, Henry	Pvt	C	General Service
Weil, Fred.	Prisoner		General Service
Weir, Thomas B.	Capt		7th US Cav
died Dec 9, 1876			
West, Willet C.	Fifer	B	Music Boys
Wheeler, Thomas	Pvt	D	General Service-USA
Whitehurst, _____			CSA
Wier, Henry	Pvt	D	General Service-USA
Williams, Benjamin	Pvt	D	General Service
Wise, Alexander	Pvt	D	General Service-USA
Woll, Robert	Pvt	D	General Service-USA
Young, Lewis			

FORT NIAGARA
New York

Fort Niagara, located near Youngstown, was established in 1841. These names came from an undated list in the Quartermaster's files.

Name	Rank	Co	Unit
Brunner, John			1st US Art
Chrysty, John			
Co____y, Barnabas	Lt		2nd US Art
Dimarest, William	Sgt		
Hadley, Geo. F.	Artificer		1st US Art
drowned 4 May 1871			
Hobbe, Geo. T.	Corp		1st US Art
drowned 4 May 1871			
McCamen, Michael			
McHarrison, Robert	Lt		2nd US Inf
Mooney, Patrick	Pvt		1st US Art
drowned 4 May 1871			
Morris, Francis W.			Civilian
child of Capt. Morris			
Norris, J.L.	Lt		US Art
Pender, Michael	Pvt		42nd US Inf
Poe, Thomas	Adj		Penn Vols
Powle, Geo.	Pvt		1st US Art
drowned 4 May 1871			
Price, Francis	Pvt		1st US Art
drowned 4 May 1871			
Pully, _____			
Rolsaubin, M.V.			Art
Shane, Thos.	Pvt		1st US Art
drowned 4 May 1871			
Sherman, Adden P.			
Snow, Amasa	Sgt		2nd US Inf
Stoddart, Rob't			1st US Art
Young, James	Capt		2nd US Inf

FORT WADSWORTH
New York

In 1886 Fort Wadsworth's assistant post quartermaster requested headstones for these soldiers.

Name	Rank	Co	Unit
Brumsltmell, Wm. C.	Pvt	B	1st US Art
Miller, Melehier	Pvt	B	1st US Art
Pringle, John	Pvt	B	1st US Art

JAMESTOWN
New York

Name	Co	Unit
Ollyses, S. Henry	B	72th Reg
Simmons, Obed	B	72th Reg
Wilcox, S.V.		

NEWBURGH
New York

The Ellis Post # 52 of the GAR sent the War Department this listing of Civil War soldiers buried at Newburgh. Most of these soldiers died during the war.

Name	Rank	Co	Unit
Barltey, Jacob	Pvt	D	19th NY
Barrett, _____	Pvt		
Brown, Richard	Pvt		1st Colored
Clark, George	Pvt	E	19th NY
Clark, Lewis	Pvt		71st NY
Corwin, D.C.	Pvt	A	56th NY
Depeu, William	Pvt		48th NY
Dous____, Soloman	Pvt	B	3rd NY
Dowling, Roe I.	Pvt	I	71st NY
Estabrook, Sanford T.	Sgt		124th NY
Goodman, Samuel B.	Pvt		
Hawley, Abraham	Pvt	A	124th NY
Jennings, John	Seaman		
Johnson, John F	Pvt		19th NY
Lightman, Daniel	Pvt		26th Colored
Luadsurrtl, Joseph	Pvt		18th NY
Mabu, Michael	Pvt		56th NY
Many, Leazu G.	Pvt	B	3rd NY
Mautthews, Henry	Pvt		26th Colored
Millsiau__, Miller	Pvt	B	36th NY
Price, theodore L.	Pvt	B	3rd NY
Sanxay, Fred. D.	Pvt		7th NY
Stevson, William	Pvt		124th NY
Underhill, L.	Seaman		USS Grand Gulf
Wright, Fred. E.L.	Pvt	B	14th
Wright, George	Pvt.		5th NY

ONEIDA COUNTY
New York

Most of these soldiers died in the South during the war; however, a few apparently died after the war. Soldiers buried in the New Fork Mill Cemetery are marked with an "*". The soldiers without a burial site listed were buried in the Oriskany Cemetery.

Name	Rank	Co	Unit
Ashley, George *		C	117th NY Inf
Baerlift, Wm.		A	26th NY Inf
Bayne, James *		B	106th NY Inf
Benedict, Charles S.		B	146th NY Inf
Whiteboro Cemetery			
Davis, Jas.		F	117th NY Inf
Fish, Dan E.		E	2nd NY Hvy Art
Fosen, J.A.		E	3rd NY Lt Art
Innman, Samuel *		D	117th NY Inf
Kelly, Geo.		K	18th NY Cav
Kelly, Wm.		F	117th NY Inf
Lowell, James		A	117th NY Inf
Whiteboro Cemetery			
Martin, Thomas *	Sgt. Major		76th NY Inf
Nicholson, T.M.		A	1st NY Lt. Art
Palmer, Lorin A.		M	15th NY Cav
Paul, Thos.			33rd NY
Ringrose, Christopher		F	117th NY Inf
Rowland, Edward *		F	26th NY Inf
also served in the 2nd NY Inf			
Tryone, Wm. H.			Wisconsin
Walcott, John M. *		D	117th NY Inf
Williams, Edward *		D	117th NY Inf
Wilson, Ira		I	3rd NY Inf
Wood, Eugen K.		K	26th NY Inf
Whiteboro Cemetery			

WEST POINT
New York

These names are from an 1886 headstone request.

Name	Rank	Co	Unit
Allen, Jaber	Pvt		USMA Det Cav
Austin, Frank	Pvt	A	Engineers
Conner, James	Pvt		USMA Det Art
Diestel, Bernard	Pvt		MSMA Det. Art
Huff, David A.	Pvt		MSMA Det. Art
Ireezerling, Peter	Musician		USMA Band
Maher, Timothy	Pvt		MSMA Det. Art
Maxwell, Henry	Pvt		USMA Det Cav
McGraue, Bernard	Corp		MSMA Det. Art
Miller, Andrew	Pvt		MSMA Det. Art
Monaghau, Michael	Pvt		MSMA Det. Art
Peck, Louis	Pvt		MSMA Det. Art

COVE CREEK ROAD
North Carolina

These names are from an 1866 report. There were eleven unknown US soldiers and one unknown soldier from the United States Colored Troops buried here also. Apparently at least some of these soldiers were killed by bushwhackers.

Name	Unit
Dawson, ____	
Dodson, Bloomington	1st Ark Cav

FORT MACON
North Carolina

Construction on Fort Macon was begun in 1826. This list is dated 1873. It is unclear if these bodies were moved to a national cemetery after the fort closed in 1877; however, other bodies from the fort were moved to the Newberne National Cemetery shortly after the end of the war.

Name	Rank	Co	Unit
Alexander, Peter	Pvt	I	40th US Inf
Brown, Charles F.			37th US Inf
Browne, William	Pvt	I	40th US Inf
Brunn, Emile Ann	Child		Civilian
Donowey, William	Pvt.	A	8th US Inf
Jones, William	Pvt	I	40th US Inf
Martin, John	Pvt	K	4th US Art
McAllister, Patrick	Pvt.	I	8th US Inf
Sedgwick, George W.	Pvt	B	40th US Inf
Sinington, William			Prisoner
Thurnberr, Louis	Pvt	K	4th US Art
Unknown (Woman)			Civilian

FORT YATES
North Dakota

Fort Yates, established in 1878, was named for Capt. George W. Yates who was killed with Custer. This list of burials in the post cemetery was made in 1892. The post closed in 1903. Later these bodies were moved to the Keokuk (Iowa) National Cemetery.

Name	Rank	Co	Unit
Brown, Henry	Sgt	H	11th Inf
Fisher, James	Pvt	I	12th Inf
Fisher, John	Pvt	I	12th Inf
Goddard, Charles	Surgeon		
Harrington, Wm.	Commissary Sgt		
Saut, Louis	Pvt	H	12th Inf
Stevens, Merritt	Artificer	H	12th Inf

GLEASON
Ohio

Name
Dingman, Wm
Heindle, Jay
Jackson, Jasper
Lee, Geg.
Lovel, Lewis
Mcleoy, Charles
McNulty, Patrick
Perice, George
Ray, Henry
Romey, John
Sarmtman, Wm
Shutts, Wm
Spurgeon, Heaerison
Wolford, Charles
Wolford, Saul

HANNIBAL
Ohio

In 1888, J.F. Thonen, manufacturer of Limburger cheese, wrote the War Department requesting headstones for the following soldiers.

Name	Co	Unit
Brunii, John	H	77th Ohio
Dunby, Bendicht	H	77th Ohio
Kernen, John	A	77th Ohio
Rothacken, John	E	116th Ohio
Wetter, John	E	116th Ohio
Wiso, John	J	20th Ohio

HARMON
Ohio

In 1884, Harmon's GAR post applied for headstones for these soldiers:

Name	Co	Unit
Daby, Wm.	L	1st Ohio Cav
Duder, Charles	D	77th Ohio Battery
Finch, Henry	K	2nd Ohio Heavy Art
Haines, George W.	H	3rd W Va Inf
Huntsman, Josiah		
Whiting, Theodur	N	39th Ohio
Wilson, Wm.	K	148th
Yearing, Joseph	L	1st Ohio Cav

LEBANON
Ohio

These soldiers are listed on an 1888 headstone request.

Name
Bell, James B.
Bradley, Wm. R.
Brill, Samuel
Cochran, Wm. L.
Dondell, John R.
Doudell, Benj. F.

FORT KLAMATH
Oregon

This is a list of burials in Fort Klamath's post cemetery from 1864 to 1884. The graves of women and children were not listed. These bodies were moved to the San Francisco National Cemetery.

Name	Rank	Co	Unit
Albin, James E.	Pvt	A	4th US Art
Archer, Edward T.	Pvt	B	4th US Art
Benson, John	Pvt	F	21st US Inf
Bloom, Louis	Pvt	A	4th US Art
Brown, John J.	Pvt		Org Vols
Cavanaugh, Daniel	Pvt	K	1st US
Donohue, William	Pvt	G	1st US Cav
Eggling, Christ	Pvt	B	1st US Cav
Everett, Henry	Pvt	G	12th US Inf
Flynn, Michael	Pvt	L	12th US Inf
Gallagher, Daniel	Pvt	B	1st US Cav
Garelle, Chas. W.	Pvt	G	1st US Cav
Gilienthol, Lewis	Pvt	K	23rd US Inf
Gorden, Waldmer	Pvt	F	21st US Inf
Greebong, Pedro	Pvt	A	1st Cav Org Vols
Hallack, Stephen I.	Pvt	I	1st Inf Org Vols
Harrie, James	Pvt	B	1st US Cav
Herman, Christ.	Pvt	K	1st US Cav
Laib, Fred. M.	Pvt	L	12th US Inf
Mlooney, Lawrence	Corp	A	4th US Art
Moore, Harry De. W.	1st Lt		21st US Inf
O'Brian, Richard	Pvt	G	1st US Cav
Packard, McKenan	Pvt	L	1st Cav Org Vols
Seeling, Hearmon	Sgt	A	4th US Art
Simmers, George A.	Hospital Steward		US Army
Smith, Sydney A.	Pvt	G	1st US Cav
St. Clair, Julius	Corp	L	12th US Inf
Welsh, John	Pvt	G	12th US Inf

CAMP CADWALADER
Pennsylvania

This is an undated list of burials at Camp Cadwalader.

Name	Rank	Co	Unit
Aermes, David	Pvt	E	81st Pen Vol
Allen, James	Pvt	G	10th NY Art
Arlow, Samuel	Q.M. Sgt	C	10th NY Art
Armstrong, Frank	Corp	M	10th NY Art
Babcock, Lug Erastns	Lt	B	10th NY Art
Bachman, Felix	Pvt	G	215th Pen
removed by friends			
Bachtel, David	Pvt	J	203rd Pen
Baker, Daniel	Pvt	J	10th NY Art
Baker, David	Pvt		NY
Baker, Lewis L.	Pvt	C	203rd Regt
sent home			
Ballauer, Frederick	Pvt		198th Pen
body sent home			
Barney, David T.	Pvt	E	10th NY Art
Bennett, Stephen	Pvt	M	10th NY Art
Bradley, Patrick	Pvt	C	97th Pen
Britzki, Carl	Pvt	M	10th NY Art
Bruce, Charles C.	Pvt	H	10th NY Art
Brunch, Jacob	Pvt		Independent Co
removed by friends			
Buk, Michael	Substitute		
Burch, Niles	Pvt	J	10th NY Art
Bush, William H.	Pvt	M	10th NY Art
body sent to Jeff. Co.			
Busler, Morgan	Pvt	J	10th NY Art
body sent to Jeff. Co.			
Cacker, Gideon	Pvt	E	6th NC
Cancy, Albert	Pvt	D	10th NY Art
Carmoell, J.	Sgt	J	10th NY Art
Clark, Morseman	Pvt	K	10th NY Art
Clark, Peter J.	Pvt	J	51___ Vol
Cline, Watson	Pvt	M	10th NY Art
Covey, Charles	Corp	D	10th NY Art
Crawford, Charles	Pvt	C	203___ Vol

Name	Rank	Co	Unit
Cunningham, Martin	Pvt		5th Pen Cav
body sent home			
Dague, Aaron	Pvt	J	215th Pen
Deacon, _____			10th NY Art
Den, Richard W.	Pvt	H	187th Pen
removed by friends			
Denny, Frederick	Pvt		195th Pen
Donnell, John O.	Pvt	E	11th NY Inf
Dugan, John	Pvt	B	187th Pen
sent home			
Dunnire, Jacob	Pvt	J	98th Pen
Ecker, John J.	Pvt	A	10th NY Art
Ehrgood, John H.	Pvt		214th Pen
Elert, George	Pvt		202nd Pen
Elin, Charles	Substitute		
removed by friends			
Elliott, Henry	Pvt	C	7th Battery NY Art
Elwood, _____	Pvt	K	10th NY Art
Ervings, Johnson	Pvt	H	10th NY Art
Evans, E.	Pvt	C	10th NY Art
Flaharity, Porter	Pvt	H	10th NY Art
Ford, Milan H.	Pvt	J	10th NY Art
Fox, Jacob	Pvt	D	98th Pen
Fraim, Miller			Independent Battery
Gardner, Jermiah	Pvt		47th Pen
body sent home			
Gardner, Peter	Pvt	A	10th NY Art
Garrison, Silas	Pvt	C	10th NY Art
Gatz, John B.	Pvt	J	199th Pen
Gilfrin, Wm. G.	Pvt		214th Pen
removed by friends			
Goodman, Benj. F.	Pvt	A	187th Pen
Griffin, William	Corp	E	6th USCT
Groover, Charles	Pvt	B	187th Pen
removed by friends			
Guming, Lenard	Pvt	K	95th Pen
Hall, John	Pvt	D	213th Pen
taken by friends			
Herr, John	Pvt	A	203rd Pen
Herrick, Geo. W.	Corp	M	10th NY Art
Hewitt, Lorenzo	Pvt	C	10th NY Art

Name	Rank	Co	Unit
Huck, Francis	Pvt	C	7th NY Art
Hughes, Edward	Pvt	D	VRC
moved by friends			
Hull, Jacob			
Ingason, Cyrus	Musician	H	10th NY Art
Irvin, Joseph	Pvt	G	187th Pen
James, Alonzo L.	Pvt	G	10th NY Art
Jerrard, John	Pvt	J	10th NY Art
Jones, Seth	Pvt	B	10th NY Art
Judd, A. C.	Pvt	A	10th NY Art
Keifer, George	Pvt		Independent Company
Keyes, John W.	Pvt	G	10th NY Art
Kramer, Henry	Pvt	A	5th Pen
Krantz, John	Pvt	L	15th TVC
Kruge, Josiah	Pvt		187th Pen
Lambert, David	Pvt		Codwaterder Guards
removed by friends			
Lawton, Eugene	Pvt		10th NY Art
Lewis, Hart	Pvt		10th NY Art
Logue, David	Pvt		103rd Pen
body sent home			
Madden, Aaron W.			
sent home			
Magor, George	Pvt	B	203rd Pen
sent home			
Mahon, Milton	Pvt	D	214th Pen
removed by friends			
Maltby, Warren	Pvt	A	10th NY Art
Mammeur, John	Pvt	H	187th Pen
Manfred, Jenkins	Pvt	B	10th NY Art
Merriman, Campbell	Pvt	J	67th Pen
MoCue, _____	Pvt	M	10th NY Art
Naner, Rudolph	Pvt	J	10th NY Art
Niles, Loyd	Pvt	M	10th NY Art
O'Bryan, Albert	Pvt	D	47th Pen
O'Neill, Edward	Pvt	J	95th Pen
removed by friends			
Ragott, Charles	Pvt	J	10th NY Art
Refoler, John	Pvt		203rd Pen
Rickley, John	Pvt	J	21st VRC
Risley, Zachary		H	1st Art

Name	Rank	Co	Unit
Robbins, George	Pvt		18th NY Art
Roberts, Vincent	Pvt	K	12th NJ
Safse, Charles W.	Pvt		5th Pen Cav
Sanford, Albert	Pvt	M	10th NY Art
Sherman, Edward	Pvt	G	10th NY Art
Shook, John	Pvt	J	64th Pen
Snyder, Henry	Pvt	K	88th Pen
Spatsberry, Edward	Pvt	C	10th NY Art
Speer, David	Pvt	H	10th NY Art
St. John, Jerry	Pvt	C	10th NY Art
Sulger, James	Pvt	G	215th Pen
Tassey, Thomas E.	Pvt	E	10th NY Art
Thomas, Charles	Pvt	K	32nd USCT
Tierco, Clark F.	Pvt	M	10th NY Art
Veteabough, James			
Vomasdale, Milton	Pvt		214th Pen
Ward, Owen T.	Pvt	E	10th NY Art
Werkhuser, John	Pvt	H	34th P. V.
Williams, Samuel C.	Pvt	A	10th NY Art
Winters, Henry	Substitute		

CAMP CURTIN
Pennsylvania

Camp Curtin was the first mobilization point for Union recruits in Pennsylvania. The dead were buried in a soldiers' lot in Harrisburg Cemetery. The lot was in poor "condition" according to an 1881 report that estimated between 150 and 200 burials in the lot. These names are from an undated burial list.

Name	Rank	Co	Unit
Barker, H.L.	Pvt	A	8th Maine
Bigler, Michael	Recruit		
Bricker, Sameal J.	Pvt	H	20th Ten Vol
body delivered to wife			
Brown, John	Pvt		101th Pen
Cheeseman, Wm. M.	Sgt	K	184th Pen
body delivered to his brother			
Dailey, John R.	Pvt	A	15th VRC
Elliott, Lewis	Pvt	I	45th Pen
Encell, Joseph	Pvt	A	6th NJ
Ennis, John	Pvt	H	29th Pen
Fay, Issac	Sgt	A	15th VRC
Fornoy, Sammel	Pvt		103th Pen
body delivered to his wife			
Hanigan, Patrick	Pvt	K	15th VRC
Hoffman, D.	Pvt	D	195 Pen
Hoke, Francis	Pvt	L	14th Pen Cav
Kimbal, W.C.	Corp	K	16th VRC
Kingon, Jab. W.	Pvt	I	26th Mich
Kohrig, Martin	Pvt	K	74th Pen
Lightinger, David	Pvt	H	16th VRC
Lyons, Joh G.	Recruit		
Maxwell, Jacob C.	Pvt	B	52th Pen
McClane, Gilbert	Pvt	A	49 Pen
McMilledge, Robert	Pvt	A	16th VRC
Morgan, Dennis	Pvt	B	184th Pen
Pameter, James	Sgt	H	19th Pen
Parks, Joseph	Recruit		
Perkins, William	Pvt	C	6th _____
Plank, John A.	Pvt	J	195th Pen
Quick, John	Corp	C	126th NY

Name	Rank	Co	Unit
Runhard, John	Pvt	B	5th Pen Cav
Spiglemire, J.A.	Pvt	I	181st Pen
Stout, Josiah	Pvt	I	52nd Pen
Summers, Rufus	Pvt		53rd Ind
Wamming, James	Pvt	Lt	100th Pen
Watson, Charles	Pvt	G	16th VRC
Willman, Joseph	Pvt	K	16th VRC
Yafrlo, S.J.	Pvt		Va Cav
Zerfaf, David			Pen Vols

SHOHOLA
Pennsylvania

On July 15, 1864, a railroad accident near Shohola killed 49 Confederate POWs and 17 of their guards, who were members of the 11th Veterans Reserve Corps. The victims were buried near the accident scene. In 1911 the Commissioner for Marking Confederate Graves had these bodies moved to the Woodlawn National Cemetery at Elmira, New York. Because individual graves could not be identified, a granite monument was erected over the reburial site. Bronze tablets with the names of the dead soldiers were attached to the monument.

After the accident, two badly injured Confederates were moved to Barryville, New York, where they died. Their graves, in the Barryville Cemetery, were marked in 1911.

Name	Rank	Co	Unit
Adams, Joseph	Pvt	A	51st NC - CSA
Baker, Jesse E.	Pvt	F	51st NC - CSA
Baxley, John W.	Pvt	A	31st NC - CSA
Bessent, J.H.	Corp	G	51st NC - CSA
Bird, J.H.	Pvt	I	26th VA - CSA
Bowers, W.	Pvt	B	48th NC - CSA
Briggs, R.	Pvt	E	31st NC - CSA
Bright, J.W.	Pvt	A	26th VA - CSA
Bryant, Travers S.	Pvt	I	51st NC - CSA

Name	Rank	Co	Unit
Callehan, C.	Pvt	C	10th ____ Cav - CSA
Caln, M.	Pvt		Pegram's VA Batty - CSA
Cary, J.W.	Pvt	I	51st NC - CSA
Center, C.O.	Pvt	H	52nd NC - CSA
Cornell, William H.	Pvt	I	11th VRC
Davis, John D.	Pvt	I	51st NC - CSA
Dever, N.H.	Pvt	I	51st NC - CSA
French, Henry	Pvt	E	11th VRC
Fuller, Byam	Pvt	H	24th GA - CSA
Gatton, W.F.	Pvt	B	35th VA Cav - CSA
Green, Henry	Pvt	A	9th VA - CSA
Ham, William B.	Sgt	E	8th NC - CSA
Hardison, J.J.	Pvt	I	51st NC - CSA
Hart, John A	Pvt	H	11th VRC
Hatch, J.S.	Pvt	H	53rd GA - CSA
Haynes, R.P.	Sgt	H	26th Va - CSA
Jackson, Isaac	Pvt	A	11th VRC
Jackson, William M.	Pvt	C	53rd GA - CSA
Jeffrey, Thomas M.	Pvt	A	11th VRC
Johnson, John D	Pvt	B	31st NC - CSA

injured in wreck - died and buried at Barryville, NY

Name	Rank	Co	Unit
Johnson, Michael	Pvt	I	8th NC - CSA

injured in wreck - died and buried at Barryville, NY

Name	Rank	Co	Unit
Joiner, A.	Pvt	C	13th VA - CSA
Jones, William A	Pvt	D	22nd VA - CSA
Lee, S.W.	Pvt	K	8th NC - CSA
Linco, Joseph	Pvt	A	11th VRC
Manning, Wallace	Pvt	F	31st NC - CSA
Martin, John S.	Pvt	F	11th VRC
McCorquadale, Malcolm	Pvt	I	51st NC - CSA
McCurvey,, T.W.	Pvt	K	16th GA - CSA
McQuaque, A.	Pvt	B	31st NC - CSA
Mitchell, Joseph	Pvt	B	42nd VA Cav - CSA
Munroe, Duncan	Pvt	I	51st NC - CSA
Parks, J.C.	Pvt	H	22nd VA - CSA
Patrick, J.N.	Pvt	H	26th VA - CSA
Pelks, J. D.	Pvt	E	47th VA - CSA
Pitchford, R.D.	Pvt	E	1st NC Cav - CSA
Plass, Edmund	Pvt	F	11th VRC
Pope, D.W.	Pvt	I	51st NC - CSA
Price, Richard	Pvt	H	11th VRC

Name	Rank	Co	Unit
Reaser, Philip	Pvt	D	26th Va Bat - CSA
Reuls, J.W.	Pvt	E	31st NC - CSA
Samkins, T.C.	Pvt	C	2nd GA Cav - CSA
Sanford, J.F.	Pvt	A	44th NC - CSA
Sangford, W.B.	Pvt	K	16th Ga - CSA
Sapt, F.W.	Pvt	E	22nd NC - CSA
Smatley, G.C.	Pvt	C	GA Legion - CSA
Smith, David	Pvt	K	11th VRC
Spicer, Daniel	Pvt	C	11th VRC
Stauffer, Napoleon B.	Pvt	D	42nd NC - CSA
Strickland, Thomas J.	Pvt	I	51st NC - CSA
Vanalstine, Hart W.	Pvt	E	11th VRC
Vannorman, Ozro	Pvt	A	11th VRC
Vaughen, Henry	Pvt	E	47th VA - CSA
Voltz, Cotlie	Pvt	E	11th VRC
Watson, Samuel D.	Sgt	F	51st NC - CSA
Wetherby, Lyman	Pvt	F	11th VRC
Wilkinson, Adam	Pvt	F	11th VRC
Williams, James H.	Pvt	K	53rd GA - CSA
Witchery, Philip	Pvt	C	11th VRC

FORT ADAMS
Rhode Island

From 1799 until 1953 Fort Adams guarded the seacoast near Newport, Rhode Island. These names were taken from an 1886 headstone request and a list of burials in the post cemetery for 1889 and 1890.

Name	Rank	Co	Unit
Armstrong, Joseph	Pvt	F	15th Inf
Bassett, Franklin E.	Pvt	H	3rd Art
Beish, Henry W.	Pvt	A	2nd Art
Bonvall, William H.	Pvt	H	3rd Art
Brown, William J.	Pvt	F	2nd Art
Clapp, George W.	Artificer	H	3rd Art
Crib, _____			Civilian
child of Wm Crib, Band. -2nd Art			
Currie, Archibald	Pvt	L	3rd Art
Downs, Dennis	Recruit	A	15th Inf
Dumbell, Michael	Pvt	E	3rd Art
Egan, Edward	Pvt	B	3rd Art
Ferguson, John	Hospital Steward		USA
Fran, John	Pvt	E	3rd Art
Haley, James C.	Pvt	K	1st Art
Harvard, Edward	Pvt	A	5th Art
Heath, John	Pvt	Band	2nd Art
Holland, Auther G.	Pvt	E	4th Art
Jacobs, William	Pvt	F	5th Art
Johnson, Thos. M.	Pvt	B	3rd Art
Jones, Thos. H.	Pvt	F	5th Art
Koppe, Franz	Pvt	F	1st Art
Mayo, Peter	Pvt	A	15th Inf
McMahon, James	Pvt	J	2nd Art
Meaghen, Daniel	Pvt	F	15th Inf
Moll, Louis W.	Pvt	D	3rd Art
Morrison, George	Ord Sgt		US Army
Newman, Harry			Civilian
son of Pvt Harry Newman			
Olmstead, Chas. S.	Pvt	H	3rd Art
Ove, Chas. W.	Pvt	F	5th Art
Perry, George	Recruit		15th Inf

Name	Rank	Co	Unit
Pew, Oliver	Pvt	J	3rd Art
Phang, ____			Civilian
Reiss, ____			Civilian
child of Ord. Sgt A. Reiss			
Roff, Christian F.	Pvt	F	2nd Art
Rose, Edwin	Pvt	B	3rd Art
Schultz, ____			Civilian
child of 1st Sgt George A. Schultz			
Theeker, Ebenezer	Pvt	F	2nd Art

AIKEN
South Carolina

On May 8, 1882, N.R. Denby from Bergen Point, NJ, requested headstones for his "former comrades" who died while on occupation duty at Aiken.

Name	Rank	Co	Unit
____, J.	Pvt	H	5th US Cav
Buigon, J.	Corp	H	5th US Cav
Bulrick, H.	Corp	H	5th US Cav
Curtis, M.	Pvt	H	5th US Cav
Driscoll, A.	Pvt	H	5th US Cav
Jackson, W.	Pvt	H	5th US Cav
Jbery, M.	Sat	H	5th US Cav
Maple, F.	Pvt	H	5th US Cav
Mascey, C.	"his wife"		5th US Cav
Reiley, J.	Pvt	H	5th US Cav
Stoney, A.	Corp	H	5th US Cav

CHESTER
South Carolina

Charles F. Emerson was 19 when he died while on occupation duty in Chester. Emerson is buried alongside fifty-six unknown Confederates in Chester's Evergreen Cemetery.

Name	Unit
Emerson, Charles F.	15th Maine Veteran Volunteers

ORANGEBURG
South Carolina

Sixteen Union soldiers died while on occupation duty in Orangeburg between May 7, 1865, and December 5, 1865. It is unclear if B.H. Malone was a Union or Confederate POW. In 1879, Mr. Charles S. Bull wrote the War Department about the neglected graves of Union soldiers in Orangeburg. A member of the Quartermaster's Corps stationed in Charleston was dispatched to Orangeburg. After consulting with several residents including Mrs. J.K. Rome, who was "well known for her kind attention in nursing the sick Federal and Confederate soldiers alike," he recommended that nineteen bodies of Union soldiers be moved to the Florence National Cemetery.

Name	Rank	Co	Unit
"Captain"			Civilian- Colored
Deutsch, Geo.	Pvt	D	54th NY
Dickerson, Louis	Pvt	K	55th Mass-Colored
Jackson, Texter	Pvt	G	55th Mass - Colored
Lew, Jimri	Pvt	F	55th Mass-Colored
Malone, B.H. died 4July 1865			POW
Mathews, William	Pvt	G	55th Mass-Colored
Matthews, David N.	Pvt	H	54th NY

Name	Rank	Co	Unit
Matthews, Elias	Pvt	B	102th USCT
Matthews, William	Pvt	E	102th USCT
Nelson, Wm. R.	Pvt	D	102nd USCT
O'Brien, James	Pvt	K	54th NY
Reed, Elijah	Pvt	F	102nd USCT
Shomden, John	Pvt	A	55th Mass - Colored
Sieber, August	Corp	I	54th NY
Stroup, Russell	Pvt	G	54th NY
Walker, Frank	Pvt	C	102nd USCT
Walker, Wilson	Pvt	D	102nd USCT

YORK
South Carolina

Eight Union occupation soldiers were buried in York's Rosehill Cemetery. Buried in the same cemetery is Capt George D. Wallace who survived Custer's ill-fated 1876 expedition only to be killed at the Battle of Wounded Knee, South Dakota, in 1889.

Name	Rank	Co	Unit
Brown, Sam'l		L	7th US Cav
Cash, Adolphus		D	7th US Cav
Garr, Pat'k	Sgt	C	18th US Inf
Quinton, Thos.		C	18th US Inf
Shea, Jno.	Corp	C	18th US Inf
Wallace, George D.	Capt		7th US Cav
Walsh, Pat'k		C	18th US Inf
Whittemore, G.H.		L	7th US Cav
Windsor, G.W.		C	18th US Inf

CAMP EAGLE PASS
Texas

In 1890 the quartermaster at Camp Eagle Pass requested headstones for soldiers buried in the post cemetery between 1868 and 1878. In April 1900, a total of 73 bodies were moved from the post cemetery to the San Antonio National Cemetery.

Name	Rank	Co	Unit
Baker, Thomas	Musician	K	24th Inf
Bidley, Robert	Musician	B	24th Inf
Blackwell, Isasc	Pvt	F	24th Inf
Bradford, J.	Pvt	K	24th US Inf
Breton, Jufus	Pvt	K	24th Inf
Brown, John	Pvt	B	10th Cav
Emory, Robert	Pvt	L	9th Cav
Fox, James	Pvt	M	4th Cav
Green, J.	Teamster		Civilian
Hall, Frank	Pvt	E	4th Cav
Harris, Lafeyette	Corp.	A	24th Inf
Harrison, Milford	Pvt	K	24th Inf
Hawkins, Jordan	Pvt	C	9th Cav
Hooper, Conelius	Pvt	E	4th Cav
Jones, William	Pvt	I	25th Inf
Kardison, Noah	Pvt	K	41st Inf
Martin, Daniel	Pvt	D	24th Inf
McComb, Edward	Surgeon		
Murray, Enos	Pvt	F	24th Inf
Pitts, Anthony	Pvt	A	24th Inf
Price, John	Pvt	A	41st Inf
R_____, Thos. J.	Hospital Steward		USA
Schuhrieman, George	Pvt	K	8th Cav
Schultz, Michael	Pvt	K	8th Cav
Sinclair, Frank	Pvt	K	8th Cav
Strickman, Ernest	Corp	F	10th Cav
Wakee, Robert	Pvt	A	25th Inf
Warren, Henry	Pvt	K	24th US Inf
Williams, Israel	Pvt	C	9th Cav
Zoller, John	Blacksmith		Civilian

CAMP PENA COLORADO
Texas

Camp Pena Colorado was established in 1873. The camp, located in the Big Bend region of Texas, closed in 1893. In 1886 the post quartermaster requested five headstones for unmarked graves in the post cemetery. These bodies were moved to the San Antonio National Cemetery before 1909.

Name	Rank	Co	Unit
Hall, Joseph	Pvt	M	10th Cav
King, Burt	Farrier	M	10th Cav
Robert, Wm. D.	Pvt	C	1st Inf
Ross, Louis	Saddler	M	10th Cav
Weast, Lonenzo G.	Pvt	C	1st Inf

FORT BLISS NATIONAL CEMETERY
Texas

The first US fort in El Paso was established in 1848. The fort was renamed Fort Bliss in 1854. These names are from an 1886 headstone request. At that time there were at least 104 unknowns in the cemetery. It appears that sometime before 1884 a few bodies from the post cemetery were moved to the San Antonio National Cemetery, but most of the bodies were apparently left. In 1939 the post cemetery was enlarged and renamed Fort Bliss National Cemetery. Memorial markers for two soldiers awarded the Congressional Medal Of Honor during the Indian Wars are also located in the cemetery.

Name	Rank	Co	Unit
Albert, John		G	3rd US Inf
Allison, Jacob		K	3rd US Inf
Anderson, Samel		B	5th Inf Col Vols
Appleton, Johnothan B.		B	5th Inf Col Vols
Belval, Lewis		G	3rd US Inf
Boges, Enoch		F	1st Cav Col Vols
Bottsfond, Charles E.	Lt	H	10th US Inf
Bratling, Frank	Corp		8th US Cav
memorial marker - Congressional Medal of Honor			
Brown, Duncan	Pvt	K	10th US Inf
Cahill, William	Pvt	G	23rd US Inf
Car, Robert		A	!st Cav Col Vols
Carletin, Thomas		G	5th Inf Col Vols
Cautillair, David	Pvt	C	23rd US Inf
Corrnues, C.		K	3rd US Inf
Graudjeau, Frederick	Pvt	G	23rd US Inf
Heywood, Bradley	Pvt	K	10th US Inf
Hooker, George	Pvt		5th US Cav
memorial marker - Congressional Medal of Honor			
Johnston, John		F	1st Cav Col Vols
Kmilck, Charles W.		B	1st Inf Col Vols
Lang, Agustus		E	1st Cav Col Vols
Luke, Thomas		C	1st Cav Col Vols
Mathrop, Sherman		D	5th Inf Col Vols
McLaughlin, John	Pvt	K	10th US Inf

Name	Rank	Co	Unit
Milles, Jame		F	1st Col Vols
Osterburg, John	Pvt	D	10th US Inf
Paulus, Jacob		G	3rd US Inf
Sharp, Alinza	Sgt	B	5th US Inf
Wallas, Edward		F	1st Cav Col Vols
Walsh, Micheal		K	3rd US Inf
Y____, Soloman		J	!st Cav N Mex Vols

FORT CLARK
Texas

Fort Clark was established in 1852. These names are from headstone requests made in 1886 and 1889. These bodies were moved to the San Antonio National Cemetery before 1909.

Name	Rank	Co	Unit
Ashley, George W.	Pvt	F	19th US Inf
Barker, John	Pvt	G	8th US Cav
Bates, Hugh	Pvt	G	22nd US Inf
Bellows, _____	Sgt	H	8th US Cav
Brown, James	Pvt	D	8th US Cav
Bryant, Franklin A.	Pvt	H	19th US Inf
Buechi, William	Pvt	G	8th US Cav
Bulleu, James	Pvt	B	19th US Inf
Christian, Jacob	Hospital Steward		USA
Chrles, Crawford	Pvt	B	22nd US Inf
Cloth, Christian	1st Sgt	F	8th US Inf
Daley, Thomas	Pvt	K	8th US Cav
Davise, Frank	Pvt	H	20th US Inf
Diehl, John	Pvt	H	19th US Inf
Dwol, August	Pvt	F	2nd US Art
Eugle, Frank	Pvt	E	8th US Cav
Eus____, Jacob	Pvt	A	4th US Cav
Flecheger, Jacob	Pvt	K	8th US Cav
Fogurty, Patrick	Pvt	H	8th US Inf
Forrest, Frank	Trumpeter	H	8th US Cav

Name	Rank	Co	Unit
Geates, Frederick	Pvt	L	8th US Cav
Gleason, John	Pvt	M	4th US Cav
Going, J.B.	Surgeon		USA
Griffin, Maurice	Pvt	B	19th US Inf
Hayes, Nicholus	Pvt	E	8th US Cav
Hubby, Chester S.	Pvt	E	8th US Inf
Hyland, Michael	Pvt	H	22nd US Inf
Jergb, Ewil	Pvt	A	18th US Inf
Kivglen, Fradinick	Pvt	G	22nd US Inf
Klightou, James C.	Pvt	G	8th US Cav
Lindsay, Fessnien	Pvt	L	8th US Cav
Lynch, John A.	Pvt	M	8th US Cav
Mason, Harr	Pvt	E	8th US CAv
McBride, John	Pvt	B	19th US Inf
McDonald, John	Pvt	K	19th US Inf
Meier, William	Pvt	H	8th US Cav
O'Brian, _____	Pvt	F	19th US Inf
Palmer, James	Pvt	G	10th US Inf
Prame, Hartwell	Pvt	G	1st US Inf
Radcliff, Theodore	Sgt	K	19th US Inf
Roucheslange, John	Pvt	E	20th US Inf
Runge, Christiare	Pvt	D	19th US Inf
Ruth, John F.	Pvt	E	19th US Inf
Schubart, William	Pvt	E	3rd Cav
Smith, William	Pvt	F	19th US Inf
Trump, George W.	Pvt	K	19th US Inf
Ward, William A.	Pvt	B	8th US Cav
Weleer, Rudolph	Pvt	B	22nd US Inf
Wright, Harry A.	Pvt	H	8th US Cav
Wright, John W.	Hospital Steward		USA

FORT DAVIS
Texas

Fort Davis was first garrisoned in October 1854. This list of burials in the post cemetery is dated 1886. The post closed in 1891. Bodies from the post cemetery were moved to the San Antonio National Cemetery sometime before 1909.

Name	Rank	Co	Unit
Asberry, William	Pvt	H	9th Cav
Banks, Benjamin	Pvt	H	10th Cav
Bensford, Harry C.	Pvt	K	16th Inf
Boughten, John Frazer	Surgeon		
Boyd, Daniel	Pvt	K	9th Cav
Brady, Isaac	Pvt	C	9th Cav
Brown, George A	Pvt	Band	25th Inf
Buchanan, Andrew T.	Corp	F	9th Cav
Butcher, Henry	Pvt	C	25th Inf
Butler, Edward	Corp	C	9th Cav
Butler, Henry	Pvt	G	41st Inf
Cass, Austin	Pvt	C	9th Cav
Christopher, Albert	Pvt	H	10th Cav
Coleman, Rueben	Sgt	F	9th Cav
Dallas, George M.	Pvt	G	25th Inf
Daniels, Jermiah	Pvt	F	9th Cav
Davis, John	Corp	F	24th Inf
Duffy, John	Pvt	H	10th Cav
Everett, Thomas	Pvt	K	10th Cav
Ferris, Thomas H.	1st Sgt	F	10th Cav
Fmraman, Jerry R.	Pvt	A	10th Cav
Foster, George	Pvt	M	10th Cav
Gaddess, John	Musician	A	10th Cav
Gardner, James	Pvt	K	10th Cav
Glenn, Frank	Pvt	F	24th Inf
Green, Freeman	Sgt	F	9th Cav
Haggan, George	Pvt	B	41st Inf
Harris, George W.	Sgt	J	9th Cav
Helm, Benjamin	Corp	K	10th Cav
Hill, Charles	Chief Musician		25th Inf
Holcher, John J.	Ord. Sgt		
Holmes, James F.	Musician	K	10th Cav

Name	Rank	Co	Unit
Jackson, Abram	Corp	A	25th Inf
Jackson, Anthony	Sgt.	E	25th Inf
Jackson, Snuih	Sgt	J	9th Cav
Johnson, Amos	Pvt	B	41st Inf
Johnson, David	Pvt	C	9th Cav
Johnson, Dorsey	Pvt	H	10th Cav
Johnson, James	Pvt	H	10th Cav
Johnson, Oliver	Pvt	C	9th Cav
Kelliher, Patrick	2nd Lt		25th Inf
Kinney, Sandford	Pvt	G	25th Inf
Knoll, William	Pvt	H	10th Cav
Lisby, John	Pvt	H	10th Cav
Loomis, Richard	Pvt	F	9th Cav
Lusk, James	Pvt	K	25th Inf
Mapp, Soloman	Pvt	J	25th Inf
Marshall, Nathan	1st Sgt	B	41st Inf
Martin, John	Pvt	H	9th Cav
Martin, Shadruck	Pvt	F	9th Cav
Mason, John H.	Corp	N	10th Cav
Merryweather, Anderson		Band	9th Cav
Meyers, William	Pvt	H	10th Cav
Miller, Henry	Pvt	B	25th Inf
Mitchell, John S.	Pvt	C	10th Cav
Morgan, John	Pvt	H	10th Cav
Muches, John	Pvt	H	10th Cav
Ortez, Rafael	Pvt	Band	1st Inf
Patrick, George	Pvt	J	9th Cav
Patterson, James H. body removed	Corp		25th Inf
Porter, Sanford	Pvt	C	9th Cav
Powell, Toby	Pvt	E	25th Inf
Riley, William	Pvt	J	25th Inf
Roach, Frank	Pvt	C	9th Cav
Robinson, Charles	Pvt	A	10th Cav
Skinner, John	Pvt	L	10th Cav
Smalley, Benjamin	Pvt	C	10th Cav
Smallgood, Eli	Musician	G	25th Inf
Smith, Aanoss	Pvt	H	25th Inf
Smith, Edward	Recruit		25th Inf
Soloman, Henry	Pvt	H	9th Cav
Starks, Soloman	Pvt	F	9th Cav

Name	Rank	Co	Unit
Stewart, James	Pvt	B	10th Cav
Talliferro, David	Corp	J	9th Cav
Taylor, Henry	Pvt	C	9th Cav
Taylor, Joseph	Pvt	F	9th Cav
Washington, Daniel	Pvt	H	9th Cav
Watkins, Morgan	Pvt	J	25th Inf
Wesley, Lane	Pvt	B	10th Cav
Williams, Henry	Pvt	B	41st Inf
Williams, John	Pvt	K	9th Cav
Wilson, George	Pvt	K	25th Inf
Workman, Charles	Pvt	C	9th Cav

FORT HANCOCK
Texas

Fort Hancock was an active post from 1881 to 1895. After the post closed, bodies in the post cemetery were moved to San Antonio National Cemetery.

Name	Rank	Co	Unit
Warmly, George	Saddler	I	10th Cav

FORT RINGGOLD
Texas

Fort Ringgold closed in 1906. In 1911 a total of 146 bodies (16 unknown) were moved to the Alexandria (Louisiana) National Cemetery. These are the only names recorded in the Quartermaster's Department's files.

Name	Unit	Notes
Comnsumcp, Palm.		native of Fla
Woodruff, Frank C.	Civilian	son of Maj. E.C. Woodruff - 9th Inf

SAN ANTONIO NATIONAL CEMETERY
Texas

This is a list of unmarked graves of civilians in the San Antonio National Cemetery as of July 17, 1884. Some of these bodies had been moved to the cemetery from Fort Griffin, Fort Richardson, Fort Bliss, Fort Coucho, and Fort McKavell, Texas. There were seven graves of children marked simply "no record."

Name	
Andrews, Mary Ellen	infant daughter of Trumpeter Andrews
Apel, William	son of Pvt Apel - Troop C, 8th Cav
Augns, Annie	daughter of General C.C. Augns
Averell, C.	laundress - 4th Cav
Bailey, Mrs. ____ and child	
Bauer, Caroline	laundress - Band - 11th US Inf
Bomen, ____	infant son of Ed and Emma Bomen
Bowman, Emma	wife of Edward Bowman
Braddock, A.	laundress

Name

Britt, Alice Emma	daughter of M. Britt - 4th Cav
Broson, ____	child of J.M. Broson - 4th Cav
Brown, Maria	child of Trumpeter Brown - 4th US Cav
Buckley, ____	Q.M. Employee
Caoy, ____	child of Capt Guenther Caoy
Carlton, Ernest	son of D.J. Calton
Cherry, J.D.	Q.M. Employee
Choisy, ____	child of Capt Y.S. Choisy
Cresson, ____	child of Lt Col Cresson
Cumminskey, ____	two children of Pvt Thos. Cumminskey Co I - 4th US Inf
Curry, Charlotte	daughter of Pvt James Curry - Battery 9 - 2nd Art
Edenholm, Carl J.	child of C.J. Edenholm Q.M.
Forbes, Edna Hulda	
French, Ina	daughter of Pvt Ellis French - Co
Gaper, Alexander	son of Com. Sgt. Gaper
Gassman, ____	infant daughter of J. Gassman - 10th US Cav
Gill, ____	child of Pvt Spencer Gill - 24th Inf
Gray, Charlotte	officer's servant
Grimes, Alice	child of Sgt Grimes - 6th US Cav
Hall, ____ (and infant)	wife of Asst Surgeon J.D. Hall
Hall, Ellen	laundress - 6th US Cav
Herzing, ____	infant son of John Herzing
Hooges, ____	child of Ed Hooges - 25th Inf
Hosack, Willie W.	son of W.H. Hosack - Major - US
Jennings, ____	infant son of Corp Charles M. Jennings Co B - 16th Inf
Kelly, ____	infant of Corp W.S. Kelly - Co E - 11th US Inf
Kelly, ____	child of Sgt Kelly - Co I, 10th US
Keys, ____	infant daughter of Capt A.S.B. Keys - US Cav
Lteinmetz, ____	child of Asst. Surgeon Lteinmetz
Mulhen, Ada E.	child of Ord Sgt Mulhen
Mulhen, Joseph	son of Ord Sgt Mulhen
Narper, ____	two children of Sgt Narper - 25th Inf
Nolan, Annie M.	wife of Capt Nolan
Notson, Etla Cara	infant daughter of Asst Surgeon Notson
Notson, Otis	infant son of Asst Surgeon Notson,
Pryor, Frank D.	stepson of Capt D.W. Porter - AQM
Raglin, Polly (and child)	wife of Pvt Raglin
Ross, ____	child of Q.M. Sgt Ross - 11th US Inf
Schleicher, Gustas	member US Congress

Name			
Shoemaker, Frank	son of Lt Shoemaker - 4th Cav		
Sneeney, Daisy	infant daughter of Robert Sneeney - 10th Cav		
Stearns, ____	child of Ord. Sgt Stearns		
Thornton, Austin	employee - QM Dept		
Walsh, Mary E.	daughter of Pvt David and Eliz Walsh Co H - 8th US Cav		
Whiteside, M. Carrock	child of Capt Whiteside		
Williams, Amy	wife of W.W. Williams		
Wood, ____	child of Col M.H. Wood		

FORT CAMERON
Utah

This is an undated list of "bodies taken up at the Fort Cameron Cemetery and re-intered (sic) in the Fort Douglas, Utah, Cemetery."

Name	Rank	Co	Unit
Beall, Robert	Postmaster		Civilian
Bell, John	1st Sgt		
Boen, Maggie			Civilian
Child of Pvt Edw. Boen - Co. L 14th Inf			
Craig, Julia Magdelsna			Civilian
Child of Lt Craig - 8th US Inf			
Farnham, Frank			Civilian
Child of F. Farnham - 8th Inf			
Garrick, Kate L.			Civilian
Member of the Family of Asst. Surgeon H.H. Mason			
Howeit, John			8th Inf
Johnson, Thomas	Pvt	E	8th Inf
King, Frank	Sgt	B	14th Inf
Mason, Rose T.			Civilian
Infant duaghter of Sgt.P.Mason - 14th Inf			
McClay, Thomas	Pvt		
Migh, William	Pvt	J	8th Inf

Name	Rank	Co	Unit
Morton, Eddie			Civilian
Child of Pvt Edm. Morton - CoB - 14th Inf			
Pack, Lewis			Civilian
Son of Pvt John Pack - Co G - 8th Inf			
Raymond, Floyd E.			Civilian
Son of Hospital Steward Charles Raymond			
Riley, Susan Ann			Civilian
Wife of Pvt Riley - 8th Inf			
Shears, Henry F.	Pvt	A	6th Inf
Sullivan, _____			8th Inf
White, James	Pvt	G	14th Inf

FORT DOUGLAS
Utah

Fort Douglas was established in 1862. These names are from an 1886 headstone request. The post cemetery remains an active US Army post cemetery.

Name	Rank	Co	Unit
Bannon, Michail	Pvt	B	13th Inf
Bender, Zacharias	Pvt	E	13th Inf
Blackburn, T.J.	Pvt	E	13th Inf
Blake, Wesley	Sgt		Signal Corps
Devine, Saumel	Pvt	C	13th Inf
Dohn, Adam	Pvt	B	3rd Cav
Erhardt, Fred E.	Corp	G	26th Inf
Fisher, D.	Corp	E	13th Inf
Fitzgerald, Wm.	Sgt	E	13th Inf
Gallahan, P.O.	Pvt	L	13th Inf
Garvey, John	Pvt	F	13th Inf
Geile, John	Pvt	I	13th Inf
Guthrie, Joseph	Pvt	F	13th Inf
Hallard, A.R.	Pvt	G	7th Cav
Hathaway, J.S.	Musician	K	13th Inf
Jeffery, W.	Pvt		6th Cav
Johnson, Wm.	Pvt	E	13th Inf
Lhalon, Edward	Pvt	L	13th Inf
Marsh, James	Musician	C	13th Inf
McDonald, John	Pvt	B	13th Inf
Miller, Chistopher	Pvt	F	13th Inf
Mitchell, Thos.	Pvt	L	13th Inf
Mumehy, W. S.	Sgt	F	13th Inf
Mumique, Mathas	Pvt		6th Cav
O'Brien, Lucius	Hospital Steward		
Portland, A.H.	Corp	G	7th Cav
Theedle, Thomas	Pvt	C	26th Inf

ALEXANDRIA NATIONAL CEMETERY
Virginia

This list is of unmarked civilian graves in the Alexandria National Cemetery. The four quartermaster department employees marked with an " * " drowned April 24, 1865, while pursuing John Wilkes Booth.

Name	Rank	Unit
Carroll, Peter *	Employee	Civilian
Clinchy, Mrs. S. M.	Laundress	Civilian
Farley, Christian	Employee	Civilian
Fink, H.B.	Ambulance Driver	Civilian
Fox, Jno.	Q.M. Dept.	Civilian
Gosnell, Samuel N.*	Employee	Civilian
Gulleyhone, R.	Teamster	Civilian
Hawley, Horace A.	Q.M. Dept.	Civilian
Huntington, Geo. W. *	Employee	Civilian
Leaman, Thomas H.	Q.M. Dept	Civilian
removed from Aquia Creek, Va		
Logan, Richard	Teamster	Civilian
Phares, Jos.	Clk. Sub. Dept	Civilian
Sample, Jno.	Wagonmaster	Civilian
Shammey, Patk. N.	Teamster	Civilian
Taylor, Alonzo M *.	Q.M. Dept.	Civilian
Wallace, Wm. Pem	Teamster	Civilian
Weaver, Jno. B.	Teamster	Civilian
Wills, Thomas	Sub. Dept.	Civilian

APPOMATTOX COURT HOUSE
Virginia

The skirmishes at Appomattox Station and Appomattox Court House on April 8th and 9th, 1865, convinced General Lee that his army's line of retreat was cut off. Lee had no option but to "go and see General Grant," as he put it.

In May of 1865 the ladies of Appomattox met to form an association to preserve the graves of Confederates who were killed in the vicinity. On December 1, 1866, eighteen Confederates (ten unknown) and one unknown Union soldier were reinterred in what is now known as the United Daughters of the Confederacy Cemetery. Other Union soldiers killed at Appomattox Court House were moved to the Poplar Grove National Cemetery near Petersburg.

These Civil War soldiers are buried within the boundaries of the Appomattox Court House National Historical Park:

Name	Rank	Co	Unit
Almond, George		H	18th Va - CSA
buried in Herman Church Cemetery			
Ashby, J.W.			12th Va Cav - CSA
Cogan, Henry J.	Lt	D	188th Pen Inf
married a local girl while on occupation duty here			
buried in the Patterson - Hix Cemetery			
Conner, Jennings		B	46th Va Inf - CSA
buried in the O'Brien Cemetery			
Demesme, O.F.	Sgt		Donaldsonville Art - CSA
Douglas, J.W.			
Hicks, A.B.			26th Va - CSA
Hogan, J.A.			26th Ga - CSA
Hutchins, J.H.			5th Ala - CSA
Macon, Miles C.	Capt		Fayette Art - Va - CSA
Meeks, Lafayette	Pvt		2nd Va Cav - CSA
buried in the Meeks Cemetery			
O'Brien, John G.			25th Va Inf - CSA
buried in the O'Brien Cemetery			
Raine, Charles J.	Capt		Lee Battery -VA Art - CSA
buried in the Raine Cemetery			
Winn, P.F.M.			Battery E 9th Ga Reg - CSA

BALL'S BLUFF NATIONAL CEMETERY
Virginia

The Battle of Ball's Bluff occurred when Federals under Col. Edward Baker crossed the Potomac River near Leesburg on October 15, 1861. Baker's force was pushed back with a loss of 49 killed, 158 wounded, and 714 missing. A Congressional committee called the affair " the most atrocious military blunder in history."

Ball's Bluff National Cemetery contains only 25 headstones (all but one unknown), but it appears that at least 54 Federal soldiers are buried there. Outside the cemetery wall is a marker in memory of Col. Baker. However, his remains were taken to California. In 1940 his remains were moved to the San Francisco National Cemetery. The War Department refused Clinton Hatcher's parents request to bury their son inside the cemetery's walls. His marker is about 120 feet from the fence.

Name	Rank	Co	Unit
Allen, James		H	15th Mass Inf
Baker, Edward D.	Col		71st Pen Inf
Hatcher, Clinton		F	8th Va - CSA

COLD HARBOR NATIONAL CEMETERY
Virginia

In 1909 the State of New York erected a monument with a bronze plaque listing the members of the 8th New York Heavy Artillery who were killed or died of wounds received at the Battle of Cold Harbor, June 3, 1864. Most of these soldiers are buried in the Cold Harbor National Cemetery (1952 interments: 673 known, 1279 unknown, 889 in one mass grave).

Name	Rank	Co	Unit
Agett, James , Jr.	Pvt	I	8th NY Heavy Art
Albert, John	Pvt	M	8th NY Heavy Art
Austin, Edgar	Pvt	C	8th NY Heavy Art
Avery, James	Pvt	I	8th NY Heavy Art
Barber, Ryan A.	Pvt	K	8th NY Heavy Art
Barker, William , Jr.	Pvt	M	8th NY Heavy Art
Bateman, Charles A.	Pvt	C	8th NY Heavy Art
Bauman, William, Jr.	Pvt	F	8th NY Heavy Art
Beals, Benjamin, O.	Pvt	M	8th NY Heavy Art
Bennett, J.A.	Pvt	E	8th NY Heavy Art
Benson, Harvey J.	Pvt	M	8th NY Heavy Art
Bishop, Andrew J.	Pvt	B	8th NY Heavy Art
Boomhower, Conrad	Pvt	M	8th NY Heavy Art
Bordwell, Hiram E.	Pvt	D	8th NY Heavy Art
Bowman, John	Pvt	B	8th NY Heavy Art
Bratt, Cornellus	Pvt	C	8th NY Heavy Art
Brewer, James	Pvt	B	8th NY Heavy Art
Briggs, Charles H.	Pvt	C	8th NY Heavy Art
Brown, Fayette S.	Lt	B	8th NY Heavy Art
Brown, William H.	Pvt	E	8th NY Heavy Art
Burgemeister, Frederick	Pvt	H	8th NY Heavy Art
Caldwell, James H.	Pvt	M	8th NY Heavy Art
Calvert, Walter L.	Pvt	I	8th NY Heavy Art
Campbell, Oliver M.	Lt	M	8th NY Heavy Art
Cardwell. Joseph W.	Lt	A	8th NY Heavy Art
Cartwright, Ezra	Pvt	A	8th NY Heavy Art
Case, Allen W.	Pvt	C	8th NY Heavy Art
Clark, Henry T.	Pvt	I	8th NY Heavy Art
Clark, Ollen	Pvt	C	8th NY Heavy Art
Clinch, John	Pvt	M	8th NY Heavy Art

Name	Rank	Co	Unit
Coe, Elwood	Pvt	B	8th NY Heavy Art
Comstock, Adelbert	Pvt	E	8th NY Heavy Art
Cooper, Peter L.	Pvt	E	8th NY Heavy Art
Cope, Eli	Pvt	H	8th NY Heavy Art
Corwell, Job	Pvt	B	8th NY Heavy Art
Curchwell, Cornellus	Pvt	C	8th NY Heavy Art
Curtis, Nathaniel B.	Pvt	K	8th NY Heavy Art
Day, George W.	Pvt	B	8th NY Heavy Art
Dolan, Peter	Pvt	K	8th NY Heavy Art
Duggan, Dennis	Pvt	D	8th NY Heavy Art
Egelston, Seneca J.	Pvt	K	8th NY Heavy Art
Elton, Washington	Pvt	B	8th NY Heavy Art
Fennen, Irwin	Pvt	H	8th NY Heavy Art
Fennen, William	Pvt	H	8th NY Heavy Art
Folk, John , Jr	Pvt	I	8th NY Heavy Art
Gardner, Alex	Capt	I	8th NY Heavy Art
Gladden, George W.	Lt	M	8th NY Heavy Art
Gors, Richard	Pvt	F	8th NY Heavy Art
Gowett, James	Pvt	D	8th NY Heavy Art
Hanretty, Patrick	Pvt	C	8th NY Heavy Art
Hard, Wallace B.	Lt	K	8th NY Heavy Art
Harrington, Horace R.	Pvt	A	8th NY Heavy Art
Hart, Charles M.	Pvt	D	8th NY Heavy Art
Helmer, Thomas	Pvt	E	8th NY Heavy Art
Henning, Mortimer	Pvt	E	8th NY Heavy Art
Herberger, John	Pvt	C	8th NY Heavy Art
Hillis, Charles	Pvt	C	8th NY Heavy Art
How, David H.	Pvt	B	8th NY Heavy Art
Howell, John	Pvt	B	8th NY Heavy Art
Hoyt, Edward	Pvt	I	8th NY Heavy Art
Ireland, William	Pvt	B	8th NY Heavy Art
Jacobs, Joseph	Pvt	B	8th NY Heavy Art
Johnson, Andrew H.	Pvt	K	8th NY Heavy Art
Johnson, George W.	Pvt	B	8th NY Heavy Art
Jones, George R.	Pvt	M	8th NY Heavy Art
Jones, John	Pvt	M	8th NY Heavy Art
Kent, John W.	Pvt	E	8th NY Heavy Art
Krager, Frederick	Pvt	H	8th NY Heavy Art
Lapworth, Andrew	Pvt	B	8th NY Heavy Art
Lindan, Anthony	Pvt	F	8th NY Heavy Art
Mann, James	Pvt	A	8th NY Heavy Art

Name	Rank	Co	Unit
Maynard, Gustavus	Pvt	B	8th NY Heavy Art
McDaniels, John	Pvt	H	8th NY Heavy Art
McDonald, Milo	Pvt	K	8th NY Heavy Art
Mehwaldt, Charles G.	Pvt	B	8th NY Heavy Art
Meyer, Theodore	Pvt	B	8th NY Heavy Art
Miller, William	Pvt	M	8th NY Heavy Art
Moore, William G.	Pvt	C	8th NY Heavy Art
Moran, Milo	Pvt	M	8th NY Heavy Art
Morasey, James	Pvt	K	8th NY Heavy Art
Morrison, Franklin E.	Pvt	B	8th NY Heavy Art
Murphy, Martin	Pvt	D	8th NY Heavy Art
Niles, Lucien J.	Pvt	D	8th NY Heavy Art
Olds, Alfred S.	Pvt	F	8th NY Heavy Art
Palmer, Jerome	Pvt	M	8th NY Heavy Art
Passmore, Thomas G.	Pvt	L	8th NY Heavy Art
Pease, Spencer A.	Pvt	I	8th NY Heavy Art
Peterson, Nathan Z.	Pvt	B	8th NY Heavy Art
Pier, George W.	Pvt	C	8th NY Heavy Art
Poole, George F.	Pvt	C	8th NY Heavy Art
Putney, Horace	Pvt	M	8th NY Heavy Art
Quayle, Robert	Pvt	M	8th NY Heavy Art
Randall, Abal P.	Pvt	A	8th NY Heavy Art
Rausch, Peter	Pvt	M	8th NY Heavy Art
Reding, Nicholas	Pvt	M	8th NY Heavy Art
Reed, Ogden J.	Pvt	C	8th NY Heavy Art
Rinker, George W.	Pvt	K	8th NY Heavy Art
Rittenburg, Charles	Pvt	E	8th NY Heavy Art
Rivers, John	Pvt	C	8th NY Heavy Art
Robbison, Charles	Pvt	F	8th NY Heavy Art
Rogers, Elijah W.	Pvt	F	8th NY Heavy Art
Romer, Charles C.	Pvt	B	8th NY Heavy Art
Root, John	Pvt	B	8th NY Heavy Art
Rose, Benjamin J.	Pvt	B	8th NY Heavy Art
Saddleson, William H.	Pvt	B	8th NY Heavy Art
Scanlan, John	Pvt	C	8th NY Heavy Art
Seagar, Charles	Pvt	F	8th NY Heavy Art
Senn, Jacob	Pvt	B	8th NY Heavy Art
Siebold, Joseph	Pvt	M	8th NY Heavy Art
Skidmore, Webster J.	Pvt	H	8th NY Heavy Art
Smith, William	Pvt	C	8th NY Heavy Art
Steven, Riley	Pvt	I	8th NY Heavy Art

Name	Rank	Co	Unit
Stevens, Harvey R.	Pvt	L	8th NY Heavy Art
Stiles, Martin W.	Pvt	B	8th NY Heavy Art
Stock, Charles	Pvt	A	8th NY Heavy Art
Stone, William J.	Pvt	E	8th NY Heavy Art
Storrow, Joseph	Pvt	B	8th NY Heavy Art
Strouts, Edward	Pvt	I	8th NY Heavy Art
Tallman, Benjamin F.	Pvt	H	8th NY Heavy Art
Taylor, Edwin J.	Pvt	B	8th NY Heavy Art
Terrey, George W.	Pvt	A	8th NY Heavy Art
Tone, John A.	Pvt	I	8th NY Heavy Art
Torrey, William H.	Pvt	C	8th NY Heavy Art
Van Tassel, Frederick	Pvt	F	8th NY Heavy Art
Walker, Robert, Jr.	Pvt	H	8th NY Heavy Art
Wall, James	Pvt	H	8th NY Heavy Art
Watson, William	Pvt	B	8th NY Heavy Art
Weber, Joseph	Pvt	H	8th NY Heavy Art
Welch, William	Pvt	L	8th NY Heavy Art
Weller, Henry A.	Pvt	M	8th NY Heavy Art
Whitman, Edward A.	Pvt	H	8th NY Heavy Art
Whittan, Charles E.	Pvt	M	8th NY Heavy Art
Wilcox, Emory	Pvt	B	8th NY Heavy Art
Willett, Alpheas C.	Pvt	M	8th NY Heavy Art
Wood, Frank	Pvt	H	8th NY Heavy Art
Wood, Thomas L.	Pvt	C	8th NY Heavy Art
Woodhull, George H.	Pvt	M	8th NY Heavy Art
Wylie, William H.	Pvt	K	8th NY Heavy Art
Zimmerman, John M.	Pvt	H	8th NY Heavy Art

HAMPTON VA NATIONAL CEMETERY
Virginia

Hampton VA National Cemetery was established during a yellow fever epidemic in 1894. Only the bodies of yellow fever victims were buried in the nation's smallest national cemetery (22 interments).

Name	Rank	Co	Unit
Adams, Cassius		G	115th Pen Inf
Atwell, Fred'K		A	19th U.S. Inf
Barker, Abra'hm	Corp	F	88th Pen Inf
Beal, Wm. E.	Hospital Steward		USA
Burke, Wm.	Artif'r	E	1st NY Eng'rs
Chambers, Rob't		E	3rd Pen. Res. Inf
Dalton, Jas.		A	100th Pen Inf
Dietz, C.S.	Corp.	A	68th Pen Inf
Fisher, Wm.		I	18th NY Inf
Goodington, G.V.		G	47th NY Inf
Gordon, W.B.	Musician	F	29th Pen Inf
Hafner, Henry			USA
Halverson, Thor.		I	15th Iowa Inf
Marks, Geo	Corp	G	56th NY Inf
McGovern, Chas.		B	95th NY Inf
Moffitt, J.T.		I	1st U.S. V.V.I.
Mullane, J.E.		I	93rd NY N.G.V.
Richardson, G.W.		F	1st Va Inf
Sanford, A.F.	QM Sgt		40th Mo Inf
Souker, Julius		F	20th NY Inf
Thompson, George H.			USA
Whitfield, H.S.	Sgt	H	1st NJ Inf

US NAVAL HOSPITAL
Portsmouth
Virginia

These sailors are buried in a small cemetery at the US Naval Hospital at Portsmouth. Both were killed in the same naval battle, when the CSS Virginia destroyed the USS Cumberland and the USS Congress on March 8, 1862. A simple stone cairn honors the 337 Union sailors killed in the battle.

Name	Unit
Fay, T.	USS Cumberland
Robinson, William	CSS Beaufort - CSA

FORT SPOKANE
Washington

These names are from an 1885 headstone request.

Name	Rank	Co	Unit
Cassidy, Thomas	Hospital Steward		
Fisher, George	Pvt	H	2nd Cav
Hinkler, Wm	Pvt	I	2nd Inf
Jollprecht, Emil	Pvt	I	2nd Inf
Rizheimer, Lawrence	Sgt	K	2nd Inf
Thompson, Albert	Pvt	H	2nd Cav

FORT WALLA WALLA
Washington

In 1889 the post quartermaster at Fort Walla Walla wrote the Quartermaster General reporting errors in headstones shipped to the post. The headstones that needed correcting were for:

Name	Rank	Co	Unit
Anderson, P.	Pvt	C	1st Cav
Bridges, Wm.	Ordinance Sgt		
Cramblet, Wm.	Pvt	A	1st Inf
Davis, John P.	Pvt	I	1st Drag
Deriff, Francis	Pvt	H	1st Cav
Dorfeldt, Rudolf	Sgt	B	2nd Cav
Heathcote, Theo	Ordinance Sgt		
Huntziger, Eugene	Pvt	E	2nd Cav
Kroose, T. V.	Pvt	B	1st Cav
Leonard, Jacob	Pvt	B	9th Inf
McClure, F.	Pvt	A	1st W.T.Vols
Riley, James	Pvt	D	1st Org. Vol Inf

VANCOUVER BARRACKS
Washington

The first US troops were stationed at Fort Vancouver in 1853. These names are from an 1886 headstone request. Today Vancouver Barracks Post Cemetery remains an active US Army post cemetery.

Name	Rank	Co	Unit
Baker, Charles	Musician	D	10th US Inf
Brown, Daniel			11th Maryland Vols
Carroll, Michael		F	21st Inf
Clarke, Charles	Pvt	I	21st US Inf
removed from Clearwater Indian Territory			
Compton, Alson	Pvt	I	21st US In
removed from Clearwater Indian Territory			
Couglan, D.	Pvt	A	9th In
removed from the Dalles, Oregon.			
Davis, Alfred	Capt		16th Ill
removed from Clearwater Indian Territory			
Doyle, James	Corp	I	21st US Inf
removed from Clearwater Indian Territory			
Gand, Winfried D.		C	21st Inf
Goodenow, Lyman		H	21st Inf
Heinemann, John C.	Musician	I	21st US Inf
removed from Clearwater Indian Territory			
Lundy, Elias J.		D	21st Inf
McDougal, F.D.	1st Lt		2nd Calf Inf
removed from the Dalles, Oregon			
McEuroll, Thomas	Pvt	A	9th Inf
removed from the Dalles, Oregon			
Smith, Thomas	Pvt	A	9th Inf
removed from the Dalles, Oregon.			
Watson, Stephen	1st Lt		1st Org Cav
removed from Fort Watson, Oregon			
Wiggins, A.W.	Surgeon		U.S.A.
removed from Fort Stevens, Oregon			

GRAFTON NATIONAL CEMETERY
West Virginia

Grafton National Cemetery was established in 1867 as a burial site for soldiers who died during the Civil War in West Virginia. The site chosen was near the B and O Railroad, so bodies could easily be moved to the cemetery from other areas of the state. Bodies were moved to the cemetery from the Cloyd Mountain, Droup Mountain, and Rich Mountain Battlefields as well as from Beverly, Philippi, Wheeling, and other sites, some as far as 200 miles away.

By the time Col. Oscar Mack, the Inspector of National Cemeteries, inspected the cemetery in 1874 there had been 1,254 burials in the cemetery, 634 known and 620 unknown.

Name	Rank	Co	Unit
_____	Pvt	G	196th Ohio
___hear,	Pvt	F	9th Ind
Allen, Charles	Pvt	A	11th Ohio
Allen, Nathan	Pvt	K	
Ammerman, George H.		E	15th Ind
Ammon, Edward	Pvt	C	28th Ohio
Anderson, James			
Anderson, Samuel	Corp		15th Ind
Anderson, William J.	Pvt		10th W Va
Armstrong, Issac	Pvt	A	36th Ohio
Arney, John			
Arnold, Charles A.			8th Ohio Cav
Arrowood, Job	Corp		10th Wva
Austin, Theodore	Pvt	K	20th Ill
Auten, J.	Pvt		
Backer, C.			Ohio
Baker, J.			
Baker, J.K.			
Baker, Robert	Pvt	C	107th USCT
Baker, Stillman	Pvt	A	5th NY Heavy Art.
Baldwin, ___	Pvt	G	9th Ind
Ball, Charles H.	Pvt	C	1st NY Cav
Barickman, Aaron	Pvt	K	10th W Va
Barker, James	Pvt	B	7th W Va Cav
Barnard, John	Pvt	D	152th Ind

Name	Rank	Co	Unit
Barnes, David	Pvt	I	7 th W Va Cav
Barnes, James	Pvt	D	6th W Va Cav
Bartholomew, Addison	Pvt	H	15th Ind
Baugh, Sylvester	Pvt	F	15th Ind
Baxter, John D.	1st Sgt	F	10th W Va
Beach, _____	Pvt	F	36th Ohio
Becc_____	Pvt	C	25th Ohio
Beck, Joseph	Pvt	G	8th Ind
Beckley, Edward	Pvt	C	36th Ohio
Beckman, Benjamin E.	Pvt	F	18th Wis
Beighel, Burket	Pvt	I	22th Pen
Belknap, J.D.	Lt	F	14th Ohio
Bell, John R.	Pvt		9th Ohio
Bell, William W.	Pvt	A	106th NY
Bennett, E.	Pvt	H	2nd W Va
Bennett, Elijah		A	116th Ohio
Benton, James F.	Pvt	K	6th W Va Cav
Bishop, Soloman	Pvt	I	7th W Va Cav
Blackburn, Joseph , Jr.	Pvt	E	4th W Va
Blair, Thomas	Pvt	F	36th Ohio
Bleyer, Henry H.	Pvt	C	192th Pen
Bloomer, John	Pvt	G	9th Ind
Board, Joesph Jasper	Pvt	A	15th ___
BoBo, Granville C.	Pvt	C	2nd W Va Cav
Bohon, Paul	Pvt	F	6th W Va
Boice, Beth	Pvt	I	14th W Va
Bolyard, Lewis	Pvt	D	6th W Va
Bosley, Robert L.	Pvt	E	1st W Va Light Art
Boston, James G.	Pvt	D	16th Ky
Boswell, Hezekiah J,	Pvt	H	17th Ind
Bowers, George W.	Pvt	A	3rd Md
Boyd, A.			24th Ohio
Boyd, Robert F.	Corp	I	9th Ind
Bradshaw, William	Pvt	C	36th Ohio
Breckenridge, Norman	Pvt	D	23th Ohio
Briscoe, Thomas S,	Pvt	E	3rd Md
Britz, Henry			
Brommiller, R.H.			
Brothers, Jesse	Pvt	B	32nd Ohio
Brown, David D.	Pvt	D	106th Ny
Brown, James F.	Pvt		12th Ohio

Name	Rank	Co	Unit
Brown, James M.	Pvt	A	74th Pen
Brown, Martian	Pvt	B	25th Ohio
Brown, Oliver	Pvt	H	19th Wis
Brown, T. Bailey	Pvt	B	2nd WVa Inf

first Union soldier killed in the Civil War in West Virginia 22May1861

Name	Rank	Co	Unit
Brunell, Elijah	Pvt	H	___ W Va Cav
Bryson, Charles	Pvt	D	10th W Va
Bull, Joesph	Pvt	B	152nd Ind
Bunnell Nathaniel F,	Pvt		9th Ind
Burdett, Silas A.	Pvt	E	2nd W Va Cav
Burger, Harvey	Pvt	L	6th W Va
Burgess, William P.	Musician	D	36th Ill
Burrell, Frank W.	Pvt	A	23rd Ohio
Bussard, Daniel P.	Pvt	A	150th Ind
Camp, Harry V.	1st Lt		
Campbell, Alexander	Pvt	A	4th W Va
Campbell. Thomas C.	Pvt	C	24th Ohio
Caskadon, William	Pvt	B	21st NY
Cassiday, James C.	Pvt	C	6th W Va
Cavailar, Joesph	Pvt	G	191st Ohio
Chalker, Hiram C.	Pvt	E	174th Ohio
Chambers, Eli	Pvt	A	17th W Va
Channel, Coleman	Corp	H	10th W Va
Channel, Wesley		C	4th W Va
Childs, George C.	Pvt	B	4th W Va
Childs, William H.	Pvt	B	4th W Va
Clardarelli, Joesph M.	Sgt		
Clark, Augustus	Pvt	B	36th Ohio
Clark, John W.	Sgt	D	10th W Va
Clark, Thomas M.	Pvt	D	9th Ind
Clay, Wesley P.		I	174th Ohio
Claybaugh, Jacob	Wagoner	G	2nd W Va
Clyborn, Andrew J.	Pvt	H	23rd Ohio
Coburn, Jacob	Cpt	C	3rd W Va
Cochran, James	Pvt	B	8th W Va
Coffman, Elijah	Pvt	F	15th W Va
Cole, Thomas E.	Pvt	B	17th W Va
Colehouse, John D.	Pvt	F	87th Pen
Coleman, James H.	Pvt	B	20th Ohio
Collin, Charles L.	Pvt	F	25th Ohio
Collins, John C.	Corp	B	8th W Va

Name	Rank	Co	Unit
Collison, Authur	Pvt	F	8th Ohio Cav
Colly, Issac	Pvt	E	32nd Ohio
Cook, Hiram	Pvt	D	8th Ohio
Cooper, Delmar E.	Pvt	A	207th W Va
Cooper, Enos B.	Pvt	I	6th W Va
Cotton, William S.	Pvt	F	9th Ind
Cowan, Michael	Corp	G	3rd W Va
Crammer, Joesph	Pvt	H	23rd Ohio
Crites, Maeshall	Pvt	K	1st W Va Cav
Crowfoot, Lewis	Corp	H	47th Ohio
Cumberlige, Peter	Pvt	H	1st W Va Light Art
Cummings, Augustus	Pvt		___ Ohio
Cunningham. D. L.	Pvt		8th Ind
Cushman, James	Pvt	D	9th Ind
Daikin, Lorenzo D,	Pvt	H	47th Ohio
Daugherty, Albert G.	Pvt	F	7th Iowa
Davis, James	Pvt	A	91st Ohio
Davis, Timothy K.	Pvt	G	6th W Va
Dawson, John J.	Pvt	B	3rd Pen Cav
Dawson, Thomas	Sadler	1	1st W Va Cav
Dawson, William T,	Pvt	F	7th W Va Cav
Delworth Theodore			
Dempster, Francis M.	Pvt	B	24th Ohio
Dennison, Jeremiah E.	Pvt	K	6th W Va
Dermott, David	Pvt	C	20th Mich
Dickerson, Hiram	Pvt	B	30th Ohio
Dight, Henry	Pvt	D	10th W Va
Dillon, Reuben	Pvt		
Ditmore, Julius G.	Pvt	E	23rd Ohio
Dixon, Samuel	Pvt	M	8th Ohio Cav
Dobbins, Joel	Pvt	F	10th W Va
Doepker, Henry	Pvt	I	37th Ohio
Dolhammer, Charles	Pvt	C	22th Ohio
Donohue, Michael	Pvt	A	5th W Va
Dorsey, B.B.	Pvt	A	1st ___
Dorsey, George S.	Pvt	G	6th W Va Cav
Dorston, Joesph	Pvt	C	37th Ohio
Dowler, Jacob	Pvt	C	2nd W Va
Duane, Patrick	Corp	I	10th Ohio
Duffield, William	Sgt	K	15th W Va
Duncan, Edward	Pvt	K	14th Ind

Name	Rank	Co	Unit
Dundon, John	Sgt	G	2nd W Va
Dunn, William B.	Pvt	K	1st W Va
Dunnisch, Theodore	Pvt	F	37th Ohio
Dye, Thomas			
Dyer, John N.	Capt	D	7th Ohio
Dyer, Leroy	Pvt	M	1st NY
Earl, James D.	Pvt	G	14th W Va
Earl, William H.	Pvt	G	9th Ind
Earl. George	Pvt	B	9th Ind
Edmonds, Reuben	Pvt	G	1st Mich Light Inf
Edmonds, Servatus		K	144th Ohio
Egnocheck, Andy P.	Pvt	C	11th
Elkins, Nathan	Pvt	G	7th W Va
Elliott, Cortes	Pvt	A	24th Ohio
Elliott, John	Pvt	F	3rd W Va
Eminghiser, Samuel	Pvt	F	87th Ohio
Emmitt, James	Pvt	H	8th Ind
Endsall, Frank	Pvt	A	53rd Ind
Engle, Paterson	Pvt	C	3rd Md
Euwer, S.B.	Corp	I	15th Pen Cav
Ewing, Joesph	Pvt	B	36th Ohio
Fairbee, Samuel			
Farley, Andrew J.	Pvt	F	5th W Va
Faushear, Wilson	Corp	F	23rd Ohio
Faxon, William H.	Pvt	H	47th Ohio
Fell, Joesph W.	Pvt	A	23rd Ohio
Fisher, H,S,	Pvt	I	3rd W Va
headstone reads Hamden Flesher			
Fisher, William H,	Pvt	I	34th Ohio
Flemming, John	Pvt	K	23rd Ill
Flesher, Hamden	Pvt	K	3rd W Va
Foote, Henry M.	Pvt	L	1st NY Cav
Ford, F.G.D.	Capt	F	15th W Va
Foreman, Joesph M.	Pvt	B	14th Ind
Forth, John W.	Pvt	D	7th W Va
Foster, Richard	Pvt	E	34th Ohio
Fought, Noah	Pvt	I	32th Ohio
Fox, Abner	Pvt	B	1st W Va Light Art
French, David	Pvt	L	13th Ten Cav
Frum, Porter	Corp		6th W Va
Fulwider, Abner	Pvt	K	10th W Va

Name	Rank	Co	Unit
Gabes, Ernst	Pvt	F	75th Ohio
Gallagher, Alfred	Pvt	C	15th Pen
Gallant, J.	Scout		
Gallinger, Frank	Corp		QMC
Gardner, Francis	Pvt	I	82nd Ohio
Garrison, Frank L.	Pvt		17th ___
Garroll, William	Pvt	E	5th W Va
Gates, Willian H.	Pvt	E	36th Ohio
Gatliffe, Benjamin	Pvt	G	122nd USCT
Geho, Joesph C.	Pvt	K	3rd W Va
Geho, L.G.	Pvt	I	6th W Va
Geiss, Adam	Drummer	C	37th Ohio
George, Gustavus	Pvt	E	9th Ind
Giberson, John T.	Pvt	D	7th Ind
Gibson, Jacob	Pvt	D	4th Ind Milroy's Scouts
Gibson, John	Scout		
Gibson, Stewart	Pvt	B	32nd Ohio
Gilbert, Lewis C.	Pvt	F	1st W Va
Gillman. Francis M.	Pvt	I	9th Ind
Goode, George W.	1st Lt	D	12th Ohio
Gordon, Gilbrt B.	Pvt	B	106th NY
Gould, Luther W.	Pvt	G	36th Ohio
Gould, Samuel	Pvt	I	14th W Va
Grabill, Jacob A.	Musician		
Graff, Charles	Pvt	D	28th Ohio
Graham, John F.	Pvt	D	17th Ihd
Gray, J.			
Green, Issac	Pvt	H	14th Ind
Greeno, Elias	Pvt	A	150th Ind
Greer, James W.	Pvt	D	5th W Va
Greimsman, Henry	Pvt	K	29th NY
Griffin, C.	Pvt	D	4th W Va
Griffin, James C.	Pvt	F	47th Ohio
Hagar, William	Pvt	G	7th W Va
Hall, Zachariah	Pvt	H	5th W Va
Hall, Bushrod	Pvt	D	17th W Va
Hall, Jordon C.	Pvt	A	6th W Va
Hamilton, Samauel B.	Pvt	C	2nd W Va
Hams, J.W.		E	34th Ohio
Handrahan, Patrick	Pvt	H	10th Ohio
Hann, William H.	Pvt	G	150th Ind

Name	Rank	Co	Unit
Hannan, James	Pvt	D	192th Pen
Harris, Edmund T.	Pvt	B	15th Ind
Harris, John W.	Pvt	K	6th W Va
Hartley, John	Pvt	F	91st Ohio
Hartness, John D.	Pvt	G	21st NY Cav
Harvey, Albert B.	Sgt	B	12th Ohio
Harvey, Levi P.	Corp	C	75th ___
Hasmer, Johann	Corp	A	37th Ohio
Hastings, Thomas	Pvt	I	5th Wis
Haught, William E.	Pvt	M	6th W Va
Hawkins, John	Pvt	K	10th W Va
Hawkins, Johnathan	Corp	F	10th W Va
Hawks, Andrew J.	Pvt	I	7th W Va
Hayman, Jereman	Pvt	F	9th W Va
Hazard, William D.	Pvt	C	23th Ohio
Hazen, Henery E.	Pvt	A	23rd Ohio
Head, Washington	Pvt	H	1st NY Cav
Hearn, Melville H.	Sgt	I	13th Ohio
Heath, Henry	Pvt	B	23rd Ohio
Helwig, Phillip	Pvt	D	82nd Ohio
Henkle, George	Pvt	F	5th W Va
Henry, James	Pvt	K	21st Mich
Henry, James F.	Pvt	A	196th Ohio
Hensey, Henry W.	Pvt	F	5th W Va
Herrhammer, Andrew		F	28th Ohio
Hersman, Perry	Pvt	M	3rd W Va Cav
Higgins, Daniel	Pvt	C	15 th W Va
Hoagg. J.H.		K	44th Ohio
Hoffman, Peter	Pvt	G	8th W Va
Holland, Issac	Pvt	B	14th Ind
Holley, Charles S.,	Pvt	B	36th Ohio
Hooker, William H.	Pvt	H	10th W Va
Hoover, John W.	Corp	I	2nd W Va Cav
Horton, James t.	Pvt	I	193rd Ohio
House, Reason	Pvt	B	25th Ohio
Householder, Reuben	Pvt	I	152nd Ind
Houtz, Joesph	Pvt	E	30th Ohio
Hunt, William S.	Pvt	C	1st Mich
Husk, John E.	Pvt	H	4th W Va Cav
Hutton, James	Pvt	G	1st NY Cav
Hyde, William	Pvt	A	55th Ohio

Name	Rank	Co	Unit
Iliff, James	Pvt	C	23rd Ohio
Ingram, V.	Pvt		
Inine, Francis	Pvt	A	3rd Ohio
Irey, Cryus	Pvt	H	20th Pen Cav
Isabelle, Frederick	Pvt	K	23rd Ohio
Jacobs, Alexander R.	Corp	F	23rd Ohio
Jacoy, R.		A	55th Ohio
Jefferys, Melker M.	Pvt	E	15th W Va
Jenny, Johann	Pvt	A	37th Ohio
Jobbins, ___	Pvt	G	3rd Pen
John, Henry C.	Pvt	D	9th Ind
Johnson, Charles H.	Pvt	D	7th Ohio
Johnson, J.B.			
Johnson, Jacob	Pvt	F	110th Ohio
Johnson, Thomas H.	Corp	D	34th Ohio
Jones, Albert	Pvt	G	20th Ill
Jones, John	Pvt	H	193rd Ohio
Jones, Richard	Pvt	H	34th Ohio
Junod, August	1st Lt	E	14th Ind
Kail, William H.	Pvt	I	30th Ohio
Kalb, Samuel B.	Pvt	G	1st Ohio
Kelley, W.	Pvt		
Kellison, William	Pvt	M	3rd W Va
Kelly, William J.	Pvt	C	25th Ohio
Kemler, Martin	Sgt	H	15th Mo
Kendell, Eli R.	Corp	K	10th W Va
Kenedy, W.		K	10th W Va
Kent, Peter	Cook	B	7th Iowa
Killgannon, John	Pvt		___Ind
King, Willard H.	Pvt	D	34th Ohio
Kinnear, John	Pvt	D	13th Ind
Kinny, Solon	Corp	G	6th W Va
Kisor, Charles R.	Pvt	G	3rd W Va
Kittle, William H.	Pvt	C	7th Ind
Klinger, Nicholas	Corp	H	152nd Ind
Knapp, Rufus	Corp	D	9th W Va
Knisely, Robert Lee, Jr.	Corp		W Va
Knisley, George W.	Pvt	G	85th Pen
Knotts, Franklin	Pvt	K	6th W Va
Knotts, William Truman	Sgt		W Va
Kowan, James	Pvt	K	3rd W Va

Name	Rank	Co	Unit
Krause, Ferdinand	Pvt	E	28th Ohio
Landers, William		G	10th W Va
Landon, Darius	Pvt	E	34th Ohio
Lather, Andrew J.	Pvt		
Laywell, Milton C.	Pvt	G	8th W Va
Lee, Michael	Corp	D	5th W Va
Leeds, Alexander	Lt	H	6th Mass
Leep, Charles	Pvt		28th Ohio
Leickering, Henry	Corp		3rd Ind Cav
Lescohier, Frederick	Pvt	I	9th Ind
Lewellen, John C.	Pvt	B	17th W Va
Lewis, Henry	Pvt	G	4th W Va
Lickleter, Nicholas H.	Pvt	D	25th Ohio
Lock, Issac	Pvt	K	17th W Va
Lock, Nelinzy L.	Corp	D	5th W Va Cav
Lock, Wm.	Pvt	K	17th W Va
Lockie, George		B	106th NY
Loir, Peter	Lt		
Loop, John A.	Pvt	K	106th NY
Lothes, John		K	37th Ohio
Lovejoy, James W.	Pvt		W Va
Luckey, Bemjiman	Pvt	I	3rd W Va Cav
Luckins, Daniel C.	Pvt	B	20th Ohio
Lynch, James	Pvt	A	13th Ohio
Magill, John L.	Sgt	B	3rd W Va Cav
Malley, Edward C.	Corp	K	5th W Va Cav
Malone, Wilber D.	Pvt	D	7th Ohio
Malone, William	Pvt		
Mann, P.			
Manther, A.			
Martin, Edward	Pvt	K	2nd W Va Cav
Martin, George	Pvt	H	12 US ___
Martin, William	Sgt	K	14th Ohio
Matlick, William H.	Pvt	C	___ W Va
Matthews, Henry C.	Pvt		
Maxwell, John B.	Pvt	G	7th W Va Cav
May, William	Pvt	M	1st W Va Cav
Maze, George Jr.	Pvt		13th W Va
McAnanay, Peter	Pvt	B	11th W Va
McAtee, Richard H.	Pvt	K	5th W Va

Name	Rank	Co	Unit
McCandles, J,E,	Pvt		7th Ohio
McCann, Jacob	Pvt	L	2nd W Va Cav
McCann, John	Pvt	I	63rd Ohio
McCarthy, George S.	Pvt	H	22nd Pen Cav
McCay, Daniel	Pvt	F	5th W Va Cav
McCollum, Thomas	Pvt		___ W Va Inf
McCord, Joshua	Pvt	B	106th NY
McCorkle, Charles M.	Pvt	D	7th W Va Cav
McCoy, William T.	Pvt	L	7th W Va Cav
McCune, Barnabus C.	Pvt	B	9th W Va
McDaniel, John	Pvt	K	7th Ind
McDivitt, John	Pvt	C	1st NY
McDonald, Abraham	Pvt	F	6th W Va Cav
McDougle, Enos E.	Pvt	K	3rd W Va
McDowell, J.D.	Pvt		
McEntyre, Martin	Pvt	C	23rd Ill
McFadden, James L.	Pvt	B	10th W Va
McFolin, Asberry	Pvt		Murphy's State Guard
McGill, George .	Corp	B	17th W Va
McGill, William H.	Pvt	H	4th W Va Cav
McGinnis, John C.			37th Ohio (Zouaves)
McGllvary, F.	Pvt	G	1st W Va
McKinny, Alenerin			
McNeal, Dudley	Pvt	I	36th Ohio
McWhorter, Henry	Sgt	E	3rd W Va Cav
McWilliams, John	Pvt	C	4th W Va Cav
Meek, John A.	Pvt	A	24th Ohio
Meiser, James	Pvt	F	3rd Md
Mench, S.			
Merryman, J.D.	Pvt	C	8th Ohio
Metcalf, Gloster	Pvt	K	115th USCT
Metcalf, William	Pvt	E	8th Ohio Cav
Mettler, Jrank J. (sic)	Sgt	HQ	2nd W Va
Meyer, August	Pvt	A	24th Ohio
Mick, Walter	Pvt	A	10th W Va Cav
Miller, Adam	Pvt		3rd Ohio Cav
Miller, George W.	Pvt	I	10th W Va
Miller, H.J.	Pvt	I	13th W Va
Miller, John	Pvt	K	14th Pen Cav
Miller, Melvin	Sgt		
Miller, Samuel	Pvt		32nd Ohio

Name	Rank	Co	Unit
Minor, Levi J.	Pvt	G	30th Ohio
Moan, John	Pvt	G	1st W Va Light Art
Moats, George W.	Pvt	I	3rd W Va
Montgomery, Robert I.	Pvt	M	3rd W Va Cav
Moore, Daniel	Pvt	B	5th US Art.
Moore, James	Employee		Civilian
Moore, Moses	Pvt	E	2nd W Va Mtd. Inf
Moore, Wilson	Pvt		13th W Va
Moral, Phillip	Pvt	I	7th W Va
Moran, Thomas Joesph	Pvt		
Morell, Frederick	Pvt	E	58th NY
Moyers, William A.	Pvt	D	14th W Va
Mullen, James	Pvt	K	7th W Va Cav
Murley, James	Pvt	D	10th Ohio
Murphy, Jonathan	Pvt	A	13th Ind
Murrell, Thos. J.	Pvt	K	12th Ohio
Myers, Harrison	Pvt	H	14th Ind
Myers, Henry	Corp	C	2nd W Va Mtd. Inf
Neal, Andrew D.	Pvt	I	7th W Va
Neal, William	Pvt	D	91st Ohio
Neff, G.W.	Pvt		US Scouts
Nibert, James M.	Pvt	I	36th Ohio
Nicholson, James W.	QM Sgt	L	2nd W Va Cav
Nieman, Frederick	Pvt	E	28th Ohio
Nobler, James	Pvt	L	2nd W Va Cav
Noeduch, Henry	Pvt		3rd Ohio Cav
O'Brain, Willis	Pvt		122th USCT
O'Donell, Daniel	Pvt	K	2nd W Va
Oerthel, Andrew	Pvt	F	6th Ohio
Okey, James S.	Pvt		25th Ohio
Olson, Olaf	Sgt	H	2nd ___
Orr, James L.	Pvt	A	7th W Va
Osborn, David	Pvt	H	4th W Va
Osborn, Samuel	Pvt	E	36th Ohip
Page, Carlos	Pvt	G	106th NY
Page, H.R.	Pvt		24th Ohio
Palsgrove, David N.	Pvt	B	20th Pen Cav
Park, Elijah H.	Pvt	C	23rd Ohio
Parks, Merritt W.	Pvt	G	1st NY Cav
Patterson, J.R.			
Patton, Thomas	Pvt	C	28th Ohio

Name	Rank	Co	Unit
Paxton, W.R.	Pvt		
Payne, John T.	Pvt	F	3rd W Va
Perkins, James W.	Pvt	F	6th W Va
Peters, Lewis	Pvt	F	3rd Md
Phifer, Leroy J.	Pvt	A	4th Ohio
Phillips, Elijah	Pvt	E	6th W Va Cav
Phillips, John	Pvt	B	24th Ohio
Phillpott, William	Pvt	C	106th NY
Pickering, Lewis	Pvt	B	1st W Va Light Art
Pierce, Thomas	Pvt	D	36th Ohio
Pierpoint, E.A.			Civilian
Plants,____			Civilian
Poe, Nathan H,	Pvt	F	3rd W Va
Pollocj, Enoch	Pvt	D	Pen Cav
Pond, Wesley D.	Pvt	G	9th Ind
Pottger, Simon	Pvt	A	28th Ohio
Potts, Benjamin	Pvt	A	10th W Va
Powell, Henry C.	Pvt	H	4th W Va Cav
Powell, John	Corp	B	13th Ind
Pratt, Henry	Pvt	E	9th Ind
Prew, Allick	Pvt	F	9th Ind
Pritt, Brown W.	Pvt	E	4th W Va
Pullins, Wesley	Pvt	H	10th W Va
Raber, Phillip	Pvt	K	9th W Va
Rader, Henry	Pvt	B	74th Pen
Raines, William F.	Pvt	E	13th W Va
Rankin, William H.	Pvt	C	23rd Ohio
Ransom, Hawley F.	Corp	D	34th Ohio
Ray, W.C.	Pvt	B	36th Ohio
Ream, Charles	Pvt		7th Ind
Reed. Cyrus	Pvt	D	82nd Ohio
Reedy, John	Pvt	I	23rd Ill
Reich, Henry F.	Sgt	G	19th___
Remy, William	Pvt	D	2nd W Va Cav
Rexroad, Lewis	Corp	K	10th W Va
Richardson, Edward	Pvt	I	36th Ohio
Richmond, John	Pvt	E	86th Ohio
Richmond, John			US Scouts
Richmond, Samuel	Pvt		US Scouts
Riddle, John		B	24th Ohio
Riddle, Vanburen	Pvt	G	9th W Va

Name	Rank	Co	Unit
Ridenour, Aaron C.	Pvt	F	6th W Va
Ridenour, David S.	Pvt	K	6th W Va
Riffle, William	Pvt	E	13th Ind
Riley, John	Wagoner	A	6th W Va
Rinera, Deming	Pvt	C	6th Ohio
Ringer, Cryus E.	Sgt	B	6th W Va Cav
Roach, William	Pvt	K	23rd Ohio
Roan, Gibson G.	Pvt	B	3rd W Va Cav
Roberts, William	Pvt	G	55th Ohio
Robey, James N.	Pvt	F	9th Ind
Robins, J.J.	Pvt		
Robinson, James	Pvt	D	17th Ind
Robinson, John	Employee		Civilian
Romiser, Peter	Corp	5	5th W Va Cav
Root, John M.	Sgt	C	24th Ohio
Rose, Burton D.	Pvt	I	3rd W Va Cav
Rose, Marion	Pvt	E	10th W Va
Ross, Daniel A.	Pvt	A	6th Ohio
Ross, John	Pvt	A	23rd Ill
Rossross, S.		E	1st Ohio
Rouk, Benjamine	Sgt	I	7th W Va Cav
Rowland, John	Pvt	F	36th Ohio
Russell, Bemjamin F.	Pvt	I	7th W Va
Rutherford, David			
Rymer, John	Pvt	C	10th Ohio
Sanders, David W.	Pvt	H	10th W Va
Sanders, Harvey	Pvt	A	140th Pen
Sass, Fred	Pvt	C	16th Ill
Saum, _____	Pvt	G	37th Ohio
Saylor, Issac	Corp	I	30th Ohio
Schaupe, William	Pvt	C	37th Ohio
Schlatter, George	Pvt	B	37th Ohio
Schneider, Jacob	Sgt	F	37th Ohio
Schram, _____	Sgt	H	8th Ohio
Schweizer, Joseph	Pvt	K	28th Ohio
Seamon, Jerome B.	Sgt Maj		23rd Ohio
Searl, John R.	Pvt	D	23rd Ohio
Seemann, Charles	Pvt	F	37th Ohio
Seese, George	2Lt	H	13th Ind
Sewell, Issac	Pvt	A	12th Ohio
Sexton, Robert M.	Pvt	B	2nd NY Cav

Name	Rank	Co	Unit
Shanks, Franklin		E	74th Ohio
Sharp, Charles T.			
Shaw, General J.	Pvt	A	10th W Va
Shawver, James H.	Sgt	A	10th W Va
Shepherd, Thomas M.	Pvt	K	34th Ohio
Shimbena, John	Pvt	D	14th W Va
Shinn, Assa	Corp	B	6th W Va
Short, John			
Short, Levi	Pvt	G	10th W Va
Shreffler, William	Pvt	E	91st Ohio
Shrewsberry, Russell B.	Corp	F	13th W Va
Shriver, Marion	Pvt	E	10th W Va
Sickman, Alfred	1st Lt	G	2nd W Va
Sickmiller, John	Corp	C	23rd Ohio
Sidwell, William J.	Pvt	F	6th W Va
Simonton, D.M.	Pvt	E	14th Pen Cav
Sinclair, Eli	Corp	A	89th Ohio
Slavens, James H.	Pvt	E	5th W Va
Smarr, Mathew M.	Pvt	L	1st W Va Cav
Smith, A.J.	Pvt	B	23rd Ohio
Smith, David		A	3rd Ten Cav
Smith, Issac		D	17th W Va
Smith, J.J.	Pvt	A	6th W Va
Smith, James			Civilian
Smith, Mathias C.	Pvt	F	10th W Va
Smith, Mortimer	Pvt	C	25th Ohio
Smith, William H.	Pvt	I	3rd W Va
Snediker, W.H.			
Snodgrass, Robert H.	Pvt	A	13th W Va
Snurr, John D.	Pvt	E	9th Ind
Snyder, Henry	Pvt	E	87th Pen
Snyder, Hugh	Pvt	N	6th W Va
Soulsly, Cuthbert	Pvt	I	5th W Va Cav
Sowders, Leonidas			
Spencer, Jackson	Pvt	D	6th W Va
Standiford, James	Pvt	G	13th Ind
Stanley, Eli M.	Pvt	K	10th W Va
Stanton, E.			
Star, Irvin	Pvt	F	24th Ohio
Steinhagen, Henry	Pvt	A	13th W Va
Stemple, Christopher C.	Pvt	F	15th W Va

Name	Rank	Co	Unit
Stenbeck, John H.	Pvt	I	32th Ohio
Stevenson, Marion M.	Sgt	I	8th Ind
Stewart, Thomas W.	Pvt	G	36th Ohio
Stogden, John W.	Pvt	F	7th W Va Cav
Stokes, Oceander	Corp	I	24th Ohio
Stuckey, Joesph	Pvt	F	6th W Va
Sturgill, James	Pvt	I	5th W Va
Suddard, James	Pvt	C	6th W Va Cav
Suddarth, Josiah	Pvt	H	10th W Va
Suhna, W,A,			
Summers, J,A,	Pvt	K	3rd W Va
Summers, John R.	Pvt	L	2nd W Va Cav
Sweeny, James	Pvt	K	2nd W Va Cav
Swisher, John H, C,	Pvt	G	66th Ohio
Swobeda, William C.	Pvt	G	1st NY Cav
Sypolt, John W.	Musician	F	6th W Va
Taggart, James A.	Sgt	A	10th Ind
Taklenburg, Willaim		H	28th Ohio
Taylor, James J.	Corp	H	20th Pen Cav
Taylor, Simeon M.	Pvt	C	48th Ind
Tennemeyer, William	Pvt	G	9th Ohio
Tenney, Hoyt C.	Pvt	B	23rd Ohio
Tenny, Marshall H.	Pvt	F	18th Wis
Thomas, Benjamin	Pvt	K	17th W Va
Thomas, J.J.	Teamster		
Thomas, John L.	Pvt	D	10th Ind
Thompsan, Henry P.	Pvt		137th NY
Thompson, Hugh	Pvt	D	116th Ohio
Tilton, Douglas	Pvt	F	36th Ohio
Todd, Henry	Corp	F	18th W Va
Toland, Issac	Pvt	B	16th Ill
Toms, Sylvester	Pvt	F	3rd Ohio
Towner, John J,	Pvt	K	10 th
Tracy, Ohio O,	Pvt	F	111th Ill
Trader, George A.	Pvt	L	7th W Va
Treadway, James E.	Pvt	A	6th W Va
Trimble, Ebenezer R,	Pvt	E	32nd Ohio
Truax, Edward S.	Pvt	C	23th Ohio
Tumbleton, Thomas	Pvt	F	2nd ___
Turnbull, John	Pvt	A	4th W Va
Tyler, Thomas	Pvt	G	23rd Ill

Name	Rank	Co	Unit
Underwood, Lewis L,H,	Pvt	E	14th W Va
Unlucky, Bemjamin J.	Pvt		
Simmonds Independent Battery Light Artillery			
Utt, James R.	Cpt	D	3rd W Va
Vangorden, Nelson	Musician	E	8th Ohio
Vanscoy, Abel	Pvt	F	17th W Va
Vansickle, David	Pvt	H	3rd W Va
Vansickle, David	Pvt	L	1st W Va
Varner, Asa	Pvt	H	1st W Va
Varner, J.	Pvt		
Vass, J.P.	Sgt	I	
Wabill, Hiram	Pvt	F	152nd ___
Wable, John W.G.	Pvt	C	17th W Va
Wagner, Ernest C.			
Walker, Martin	Pvt	K	147th Ind
Walls, Milton F.	Pvt	C	14th W Va
Walter, Emanual	Sgt	G	5th W Va
Walter, James	Pvt	B	36th Ohio
Waltz, Harrison	Pvt	K	6th Ohio
Warhob, Henry D.	Pvt	F	9th Ind
Waterman, Josiah C.	Pvt	F	9th Ind
Watkins, Samuel	Pvt	B	3rd Pen Cav
Watson, John	Pvt	I	6th W Va
Weise, F, Joseph	Musician	B	9th ___
Welcher, William	Pvt	G	7th W Va Cav
Wheeler, Orin	Pvt	H	25th Ohio
Whitcomb, Leverett H.	Pvt	I	5th Ohio
White, David K.	Musician	B	55th Ohio
White, James H.	Pvt	B	36th Ohio
White, James W.	Pvt	F	30th Ohio
White, William	Corp	E	22nd Pen Cav
White, William H.	Pvt	E	36th Ohio
Whitehair, Emery D.	Corp	F	6th W Va Cav
Whitehair, Henry J.	Pvt	H	12th W Va
Whitehair, S.	Pvt	F	6th W Va Cav
Whitlatch, Solomon	Pvt	G	15th W Va
Wight, John Elias	Pvt	C	23rd Ohio
Wilhelm, Joseph	Pvt	A	37th Ohio
Wilkerson, W,			
Williama, Williams	Pvt	F	13th Ohio
Williams, George W.	Sgt	H	6th Cav

Name	Rank	Co	Unit
Williams, John	Pvt	B	9th Ind
Williams, Thomas	Pvt	K	177th Ohio
Wills, Charles E.	Musician	D	36th Ohio
Wilson, Andrew J.	Corp	F	15th Ind
Winchel, Chauncey	Pvt	K	36th Ohio
Windle, William	Pvt	K	5th W Va
Wiseheart, Philander	Pvt	F	8th Ind
Wittmann, Wilhelm	Pvt	C	28th Ohio
Wolcott, Lewis	Sgt	F	36th Ohio
Wolf, John	Pvt	G	13th Ind
Woods, Carry	Pvt	C	7th W Va Cav
Woody, Benjamin C.	Pvt	E	14th Pen Cav
Workman, Newton	Pvt	I	9th W Va
Worth, Benjamin F.	Pvt	G	7th Ind
Wright, Eli C.		A	55th Ohio
Wright, James M.	Sgt	D	34th Ohio
Wright, Joesph	Pvt	B	2nd W Va
Wright, Stephen H.	Pvt	E	154th Ind
Young, John	Pvt	I	13th _____

FORT D.A. RUSSELL
Wyoming

These names are from an 1887 list of burials in Fort Russell's post cemetery. There were nine unknown burials and 59 burials of civilians.

Name	Rank	Co	Unit
Aadis, James	Pvt	L	3rd US Cav
Alexander, John	Pvt	F	23rd US Inf
Andrewsm Hugh	Corp	G	9th US Inf
Bannon, William	Pvt	C	14th US Inf
Barker, William H.	Bugler	H	2nd US Cav
Bbum, Guslowe A.	Pvt	A	9th US Inf
Bee, W.W.	1st Lt		18th US Cav
Brady, Roger W.	Chaplin		USA
Brown, William	Pvt	L	3rd US Cav
Cahill, James	Capt	K	2nd US Cav
Camp, Burton W.	Pvt	I	5th US Cav
Cassidy, James	Pvt	K	8th US Inf
Cobb, Joseph	1st Sgt	E	5th US Cav
Condree, Peter H.	Sgt	M	3rd US Cav
Condrill, William H.			
Cox, Samuell P.	Sgt	H	3rd US Cav
Coxe, John W.	Sgt	D	4th Inf
Curran, Williams	Pvt	G	30th US Inf
Day, William H.	Pvt	E	5th US Cav
Donahee, Michael T.	Pvt	J	3rd US Cav
Duncnan, John	Pvt	A	18th US Inf
Dwyer, Charles	Pvt	A	3rd Cav
Gilliland, Wilson S.	Pvt		14th US Inf
Goman, Maurice	Pvt	G	30th US Inf
Gower, Henry L.	Pvt	D	9th Inf
Gurtin, John J.	Sgt	A	5th US Cav
Hachell, Daniel	Sgt	G	9th US Inf
Haley, Edward	Pvt	B	9th US Inf
Haley, Michau	Pvt	D	9th US Inf
Hallon, Charles	Pvt	E	2nd US Cav
Ham, Lewis	Pvt	E	2nd US Cav
Herman, Frans	Pvt	L	3rd US Cav
Hill, Amos B.	Pvt	J	5th US Cav
Keeney, John	Bugler	F	2nd US Cav

Name	Rank	Co	Unit
Kierman, James			
King, James	Pvt	D	5th US Cav
Kirby, Thomas	Pvt	G	3rd US Cav
Kirkbridge, Joseph B.	Sgt	H	5th US Cav
Larisch, Richard	Pvt	I	9th US Inf
Lineburner, John A.	1st Sgt	D	5th US Cav
Logan, John	Pvt	H	9th US Inf
Lord, Francis	Pvt	J	5th US Cav
Low, Peter	Sgt	B	14th US Inf
Maloney, Thomas	Pvt	H	30th US Inf
Mason, George F.	1st Lt		5th US Cav
Massey, Wm. A.	Corp	E	9th US Inf
McCarlin, Hugh	Recruit		5th Inf
McGinnis, Harry L.	Pvt	D	18th US Inf
McGis, Owen	Pvt	H	27th US Inf
McGraih, Maiheu	Pvt	E	9th US Inf
McWillen, Leo	Pvt	B	5th US Cav
Mills, Henry		L	3rd US Cav
Miur, Jacob	Pvt	G	9th US Inf
Murray, Thomas	Pvt	J	5th US Cav
Nelson, John	Pvt	I	4th US Inf
O'Rilly, Francis	Pvt	F	23rd US Inf
Phibbe, D.M.	Pvt	A	3rd Cav
Potter, Charles	Q.M.S.	D	30th US Inf
Rendiu, Edwin	Recruit		9th Inf
Sandus, John W.	Pvt	G	30th US Inf
Sekayer, James	Pvt	K	5th US Cav
Shoemaker, Stephen	Pvt	D	30th US Inf
Shuban, William	Pvt	K	2nd US Cav
Smith, Charles	Pvt	H	9th US Inf
Smith, Geddis	2nd Lt		23rd US Inf
Smith, John	Pvt	M	5th US Cav
Smith, Joseph	Pvt	J	3rd Cav
Stacy, William	Pvt		21st Cav
Suminus, Richard	2nd Lt	G	9th US Inf
Thompson, Robert	Sgt	J	9th US Cav
Thompson, William		Band	9th US Inf
Tony, John	Pvt	J	9th US Cav
Trutchzschler, Ulrich	Pvt	K	8th US Inf
Vaugh, Charles	Pvt		14th US Inf

Name	Rank	Co	Unit
Vaugham, Thomas	Recruit		5th Cav
Ward, Henry	Pvt	G	30th US Inf
Williams, John	Pvt	D	3rd US Cav
Williams, John B.	Pvt	D	9th US Inf
Williams, Wright	Pvt	K	5th US Cav
Wilson, George K	Pvt	I	5th US Cav

FORT LARAMIE
Wyoming

Fort Laramie was established 1n 1849. These names are from an 1886 headstone request. These bodies were eventually moved to the Fort McPherson National Cemetery.

Name	Rank	Co	Unit
Annedal, James	Pvt	H	7th US Inf
Banke, Gordon	Pvt	H	4th Wis Inf
Baston, J.J.	Pvt	D	3rd US Cav
Brown, Hugo	Pvt	H	14th US Inf
Cain, Avery B.	Capt		4th US Inf
Cammer, William M.	Pvt	H	14th US Inf
Canham, Alper	Corp	H	4th Wis Inf
Clemens, William H.	Pvt	A	2nd Wis Cav
Clifford, Timonthy	Pvt	F	4th US Inf
Cofcant, Rollin	Pvt	G	4th US Inf
Collins, James	Pvt	H	7th Inf
Colman, John C.	Corp	K	2nd US Cav
Dizzlry, Edward T.	Pvt	D	4th US Inf
Donovan, John	Corp	K	4th US Inf
Draulin, Robert	Pvt	b	4th US Inf
Dunamoor, John	Pvt	J	18th Wis Inf
Dutn, John	Pvt	B	4th US Inf
Edgan, George M.	Corp	G	3rd US Cav
Farbull, William	Corp	A	2nd Wis Cav
Fellhaur, Ed.	Pvt	J	2nd US Cav
Foster, Columbus	Pvt	K	5th US Cav
Garrons, Louis	Pvt	G	3rd US Cav

Name	Rank	Co	Unit
Gaus, Christian	Musician	K	4th Wis Inf
Gosty, Felix A.	Pvt	J	3rd US Cav
Hallamer, John	Pvt	H	
Hamington, Thomas	Pvt	H	14th US Inf
Hommall, Daniel	Sgt	J	4th Wis Inf
Huffman, Robert	Sgt	A	14th US Inf
Jahlbug, Dennis	Pvt	C	2nd US Cav
Johnson, J. J.	Pvt	E	14th US Inf
Larson, Christian M.	Pvt	J	5th US Cav
Lasell, Nace A.	Pvt	A	3rd US Cav
Lavill, Francis A.	Pdvt	H	4th Wis Cav
Layet, Paul	Pvt	K	14th US Inf
Lonnins, Timothy	Pvt	H	3rd US Cav
Looney, Richard	Pvt	K	3rd US Cav
Mailard, Anthony	Musician	Band	4th US Inf
McGruger, John	Pvt	K	2nd US Cav
McKay, Robert	Pvt	E	4th Wis Inf
McKrnzio, John	Pvt	F	7th US Inf
Merill, Loring	Capt	B	14th US Inf
Molitor, John	Pvt	D	4th US Inf
Moll, John A.	1st Sgt	A	3rd US Cav
Morris, Moore	Pvt	G	3rd US Cav
Murphy, Thomas	Pvt	D	4th Wis Inf
O'Brien, J.	Pvt	G	4th US Inf
Parnick, Peter	Pvt	G	4th Wis Cav
Reynolds, Alexander	Musician	H	14th US Inf
Ritchie, Robert	Pvt	J	4th Wis Inf
Robinson, John J.	Pvt	K	5th US Cav
Ryan, Michail	Pvt	H	14th US Inf
Sather, Robert	Pvt	K	3rd US Inf
Sealn, John	Pvt	K	2nd US Cav
Shatey, John	Pvt	F	3rd US Cav
Shimpsin, Charles E.	Pvt	H	5th US Cav
Smith, John	Pvt	E	4th US Inf
Sullivan, Patrick	Pvt	E	9th US Inf
Tasker, Warren C.	Pvt	K	2nd US Cav
Taylor, William	Pvt	G	3rd US Cav
Trugin, Chawes W.	Pvt	K	4th US Inf
Vance, Wm. H.	Pvt	A	3rd US Cav
Wheeler, Charles	Pvt	E	4th Wis Inf
Wiggens, C.A.	Pvt	D	3rd US Cav

Name	Rank	Co	Unit
Williams, L.T.	Pvt	H	7th US Inf
Zello, Casper E.	Pvt	A	9th US Inf

FORT McKINNEY
Wyoming

In 1886 the post quartermaster at Fort McKinney (1876-1894) requested 15 headstones for soldiers buried in the post cemetery.

Name	Rank	Co	Unit
Armstrong, Charles	Pvt		6th US Cav
Bacon, Adlors		E	8th US Inf
Bird, Wm. N.	Pvt	C	5th Cav
Brddinbury, Wm.		H	8th US Inf
Burke, Richard	Pvt	A	9th Inf
Coodick, Thomas	Pvt	E	5th Cav
Frantz, Albert H.	Pvt		6th US Cav
Jackson, Joseph	Corp	K	9th Inf
Jones, Go.	Farrier	I	5th Cav
McLauyhillus, Erasunns	Pvt	K	9th Inf
Miller, Simon		A	8th US Inf
Punrray, Thomas	Pvt	K	9th Inf
Rurger, Joseph	Pvt	D	9th Inf
Shuld, Juo. A.	Pvt	C	5th Cav
Skiorrh, Dan'l	Sgt	E	5th Cav

FORT WASHAKIE
Wyoming

These names are from an 1890 report. There were at least 49 unknown burials in the post cemetery in 1890.

Name	Rank	Co	Unit
Corcoran, Redmond	Pvt	G	5th US Cav
Kelly, James	Sgt	K	5th US Cav
O'Grady, John	Pvt	L	5th US Cav
Regan, Patrick	Pvt	B	2nd US Cav
Rodgers, James	Pvt	G	5th US Cav
Rogers, James			Civilian
Snell, Willie			Civilian
son of Pvt. C.M. Snell Co I 7th Cav			
Stanard, Charles	Pvt	B	18th US Inf
Warren, William	Pvt	C	2nd US Cav
Watson, James	Pvt	C	2nd US Cav

FORT YELLOWSTONE
Wyoming

Congress established Yellowstone National Park on March 1, 1872. The US Army established Fort Yellowstone to protect the park. The post cemetery was established near Mammoth Hot Springs in 1888. By 1909 a total of 56 burials of soldiers and their dependents had been made in the cemetery. On July 4-5, 1917, the remains of 20 soldiers were moved to the Custer Battlefield National cemetery.

Fourteen civilians are buried in a cemetery on a knoll near the Mammoth Hot Springs Hotel.

Name	Rank	Co	Unit
Harner, Walter		C	3rd Cav
King, ____			Civilian
infant child of 1st Lt. Harry L. King			
Monaghan, Frank F.	Pvt	H	1st Cav
O'Connor, William H.			Employee
Schmidt, Frank			Civilian
infant child of Joseph Schmidt, employee Yellowstone Hotel Association			
Symonds, John N.			Employee

GRATTAN MASSACRE
Wyoming

On August 19, 1854, Lt. John L. Grattan and 28 of his men were killed in what has become known as the Grattan Massacre. Gratton was attempting to recover a cow that had strayed into an Indian village from a passing wagon train. When Gratton found the cow had been killed, he ordered his men to fire on the Indians. Chief Brave Bear, who was noted for his efforts to establish peace between the white man and the Indians, was killed. The Indians were incensed and returned the fire killing Gratton and his entire command.

The soldiers' bodies were buried at nearby Fort Laramie. In 1891 the remains of the enlisted men were moved to Fort McPherson National Cemetery and buried in a mass grave. Lt. Gratton's remains were then reinterred in Leavenworth National Cemetery.

Name	Rank	Co	Unit
Boyle, Anthony	Pvt	G	6th Inf
Burkle, Cha's	Pvt	G	6th Inf
Cameron, W'm.	Pvt	G	6th Inf
Collins, Michael	Pvt	G	6th Inf
Coutenay, John	Pvt	G	6th Inf
Donahoe, John	Pvt	G	6th Inf
Faren, W'm. P.	Sgt	G	6th Inf
Fitzpatrick, James	Pvt	G	6th Inf
Flinn, John	Pvt	G	6th Inf
Grattan, John L.	Lt	G	6th Inf
Hammill, David	Pvt	G	6th Inf
Krapp, H.A.	Musician	G	6th Inf
Lewis, H.E.	Musician	G	6th Inf
Mayu, John	Pvt	G	6th Inf
McNulty, Chas.	Corp	G	6th Inf
MCNulty, John	Pvt	G	6th Inf
Meldon, John	Pvt	G	6th Inf
Murley, Patrick	Pvt	G	6th Inf
Murray, Walter	Pvt	G	6th Inf
O'Bourke, Patrick	Pvt	G	6th Inf
Platenis, Cha's	Pvt	G	6th Inf
Rushing, S.H.	Pvt	G	6th Inf
Sanienski, Stan's	Pvt	G	6th Inf
Smith, Thomas	Pvt	G	6th Inf

Name	Rank	Co	Unit
Stevens, Edward	Pvt	G	6th Inf
Sweetman, John	Pvt	G	6th Inf
Whitford, W.M.	Pvt	G	6th Inf
Williams, John	Pvt	G	6th Inf

Name Index

"Captain"	172	Adams, Albert	29
___, Mamie	30	Adams, Alex.	45
___, James C.	77	Adams, B.P.	39
___,J.	171	Adams, Blbert	107
___, Courtney	144	Adams, Cassius	194
___, Katherine M.	77	Adams, Charles	107
___, S. H.	77	Adams, George	28
___, Evelyn	77	Adams, George	107
___, F. H.	77	Adams, George E.	64
___, Henry	139	Adams, George W.	132
___, Isaac	139	Adams, Henderson	74
___, Joseph	139	Adams, Jesse	88
___, Wm. M	25	Adams, Joseph	167
___, James	139	Ade, Henry	107
___, Samuel	139	Adier, John B.	107
___, ___	139	Aely, Frederick	107
___, James M.	139	Aermes, David	162
___, Thompson	20	Agan, Patrick A.	107
___	198	Ager, Alfred	107
___gyrald, John	11	Ager, Mathew	107
___hear,	198	Agett, James , Jr.	190
Aadis, James	215	Agnew, William	107
Abbing, Charles	45	Agoost, William	97
Abbott, Charles P.	107	Aikens, Adolph	144
Abbott, James	104	Airey, Thomas	94
Abbott, Robt. O.	144	Alarick, John H.	102
Abernethy, W.	144	Albers, John	11
Abrams, James	107	Albert, Henry C.	107
Abselen, Henry	107	Albert, John	176
Accy, C. D.	107	Albert, John	190
Ackerly, Catlin	132	Alberts, James S.	71
Ackerman, Fred'k	30	Albin, James E.	161
Ackler, Adam	107	Albred, William H.	107
Ackley, Henry	107	Albright, Isaac	107
Ackley, Henry T.	107	Albro, William	134
Ackley, John	107	Aldas, Henry	107
Ackley, William	100	Aldbigh, Frank	30
Adair, Italia	30	Aldrich, A. R.	143
Adams, A. B.	95	Alegan, Hopkins	77

Alexander, Isasc	6
Alexander, John	107
Alexander, John	215
Alexander, Peter	157
Alexander, William	107
Algar, Bloomfield	88
Alimany, Jacob	104
Allan, Fred C.	64
Allem. John	2
Allen, Amony L.	18
Allen, Charles	144
Allen, Charles	198
Allen, Emiline	144
Allen, Emma	35
Allen, George M.	137
Allen, H. W.	138
Allen, Henry	107
Allen, J. H.	107
Allen, Jaber	156
Allen, James	100
Allen, James	162
Allen, James	189
Allen, Joseph	87
Allen, Joshua	18
Allen, Lawson	107
Allen, Lizzie	77
Allen, Musgrove	88
Allen, Nathan	198
Allen, Robert	130
Allen, Robert	143
Allen, Samuel	107
Allen, W.L.	88
Allen, William	107
Allen, William	139
Alley, George	50
Alley, L.T.	50
Allison, F. S.	97
Allison, Jacob	176
Allison, Robert	107
Allison, Thomas G.	107
Allspatch, David J.	134
Almon, Jacob H.	9
Almond, George	188
Almoudinger, Anthony	10
Altemus, George	134
Alwood, Charles H.	100
Amber, John	132
Ames, David	95
Ames, Gotlieb	105
Ammerman, George H.	198
Ammon, Edward	198
Amos, Henry M.	107
Anderson, Augastus	94
Anderson, Bascom C.	41
Anderson, Benjamin	107
Anderson, Homer	35
Anderson, James	198
Anderson, John	77
Anderson, John	139
Anderson, Joseph R.	142
Anderson, Leroy	102
Anderson, Mrs. S.J.	35
Anderson, P.	196
Anderson, S.	100
Anderson, Samel	176
Anderson, Samuel	198
Anderson, Thomas S.	41
Anderson, William J.	198
Andews, Charles	107
Andews, Joseph	107
Andreson, John	108
Andrew, Leroy	96
Andrews, A.	4
Andrews, C.B.	90
Andrews, F.W.	108
Andrews, Hiram	144
Andrews, J.T.	30
Andrews, Jacob B.	98
Andrews, John	108
Andrews, Luerren	102
Andrews, Mary Ellen	182
Andrews, William	64
Andrewsm Hugh	215
Angle, David	100

Name	Page
Annedal, James	217
Ansboro, Martin	3
Aollington, W.S.	57
Apel, William	182
Apple, Oscar	108
Appleby, Simon	96
Appleton, Johnothan B	176
Aqueira, Julain	4
Archer, Edward T.	161
Archer, Elire	71
Archibald, Edward	108
Argambright, ___	30
Argersinger, Albert	108
Arlington, N	77
Arlow, Samuel	162
Armsby, John	53
Armstromy, J. F.	108
Armstrong, Alexander	15
Armstrong, Charles	219
Armstrong, Frank	162
Armstrong, Goble	2
Armstrong, Issac	198
Armstrong, John E.	75
Armstrong, Joseph	170
Armstrong, M.M.	108
Armstrong, Ralph	48
Armstrong, Samuel	144
Armstrong, Thomas	108
Armstrong, William	41
Armstrong, Wm.	100
Arnaud, Abner	134
Arndt, Hiram	108
Arney, John	198
Arnoff, J. F.	108
Arnold, Charles A.	198
Arnold, James H.	108
Arnold, John	108
Arnold, William	53
Arnold, William L.	108
Arrowood, Job	198
Arsmstrong, Henry	108
Arthur, Thomas	94
Artin, M.	108
Asberry, William	179
Asdell, A. N.	98
Ash, David B.	102
Ash, Robert	41
Ashborough, Andrew	21
Ashby, J.W.	188
Ashcott, Robert	108
Ashley, Francis H.	108
Ashley, George	155
Ashley, George W.	177
Ashner, Robert A.	108
Ashton, Thomas	102
Askins, George	108
Assadley, Anthony	64
Atchison, A.C.	28
Atchison, James Jr.	11
Atchison, Thomas	64
Atkins, Lester	108
Atoli, Jno.	30
Atterbury, Charles	139
Atwell, Fred'K	194
Atwood, Henry C.	108
Auchenbach, William	134
Augle, John	49
Auglunyer, J. H.	49
Augns, Annie	182
Augustus, P.	108
Auman, Bessie	144
Austin, Albert H.	108
Austin, Edgar	190
Austin, Frank	156
Austin, Freeman	108
Austin, George	108
Austin, Theodore	198
Austin, Thomas	100
Auten, J.	198
Auther, Geo. H.	144
Averell, C.	182
Averill, Edward	100
Avery, James	190
Avidson, Avil	108

Ayers, Austin E.	77	Baker, Gilford D.	97
B_____, A.	48	Baker, Howard A.	108
B_____, T.	48	Baker, J.	198
Ba_er, W.B.	11	Baker, J.K.	198
Baader, Lee	71	Baker, Jesse E.	167
Babcock, Elmer	64	Baker, Joseph	104
Babcock, Lug Erastns	162	Baker, Lewis L.	162
Bacen, Fred. A,	45	Baker, Robert	30
Bachman, Felix	162	Baker, Robert	198
Bachtel, David	162	Baker, Stillman	198
Backer, C.	198	Baker, Thomas	174
Backus, E. H.	108	Baker, William H.	64
Backus, George W.	108	Baker, Wm.	11
Bacon, Adlors	219	Baker, Wm. M.	11
Bacon, Curtis	108	Bakers, Wm.	77
Bacon, Ishabel E.	108	Balch, Judson	108
Bacon, Julius	45	Baldnye, David	134
Bacon, Scanole	108	Baldwin,	48
Badface	36	Baldwin, ___	198
Baerlift, Wm.	155	Baldwin, B. B.	108
Bagg, Noah R.	108	Baldwin, Jerome	100
Bahr, Conrad	77	Baldwin, Luserne	96
Bailey, B. C.	141	Baldwin, M.L.	49
Bailey, Benjamin	139	Baldwin, Stephen	108
Bailey, C.	11	Ball, Charles H.	198
Bailey, Edmond	53	Ballagher, John	23
Bailey, George	108	Ballard, John	108
Bailey, Henry A.	64	Ballard, Robert	108
Bailey, John W.	134	Ballauer, Frederick	162
Bailey, Mrs. ___ an	182	Balleam, T.	108
Bailey, Thomas	51	Ballenger, Benjamin	108
Bailey, William B.	108	Balls, Benjamin	108
Baily, Adison D.	108	Balser, Peter	132
Baily, G. W.	108	Bam, Wesley	139
Baily, Hugh	108	Bancroff, Charles	108
Baker, Artem	108	Banderberg, J.	104
Baker, Charles	197	Banes, James	95
Baker, Charles S.	108	Banke, Gordon	217
Baker, Chauncey C.	143	Banker, George H.	108
Baker, Daniel	162	Banks, Amos	139
Baker, David	162	Banks, Benjamin	179
Baker, Edward D.	189	Banks, M_____	11

Banks, Phillip	134		Barnum, Homer B.	16
Bannon, Michail	185		Barob, W.	108
Bannon, William	215		Barr, John	108
Barbe, James A.	108		Barr, Lewis J.	132
Barber, A.J.	87		Barr, Robert	100
Barber, Ryan A.	190		Barr, S.	134
Barboun, William	30		Barr, Samuel	11
Barbour, Amos	87		Barrett, _____	154
Barbury, J.E.	144		Barrett, Benjamin	141
Barcheis, F.	53		Barrett, E.C.	21
Barden, M.	108		Barrett, William	108
Bare, Urea	108		Barritt, James	108
Barett, W.S.	21		Barrows, B. Franklin	108
Barger, Jacob	134		Barry, Charles E.	141
Barhard, Annie May	77		Barry, John	64
Barickman, Aaron	198		Barry, R. M.	77
Barker, Abra'hm	194		Barry, Robert M.	14
Barker, H.L.	166		Barry, Thomas	53
Barker, James	198		Barstow, Elijah H.	104
Barker, John	177		Bartell, John	61
Barker, R.C.	102		Bartels, Charles F.J.	77
Barker, William , Jr.	190		Barth, Frances	87
Barker, William H.	215		Barth, Robert	64
Barlow, F. R.	100		Bartholomew, Addison	199
Barlow, W.	108		Bartlett, Alice	77
Barltey, Jacob	154		Bartlett, Mathew	77
Barnard, Frank	50		Bartlett, Thos. J.	141
Barnard, John	198		Bartley, Smith	144
Barnes, Charles G.	108		Barton, Alexander M.	108
Barnes, David	199		Barton, Alfred	94
Barnes, H.	108		Barton, Ary	139
Barnes, I.M.	30		Barton, Augustus	108
Barnes, James	199		Barton, Henry	106
Barnes, Jas. T.	102		Barton, James W.	130
Barnes, Peter	108		Barton, William H.	108
Barnett, Andrew	138		Bash, Samuel	139
Barney, Benj. G.	11		Bass, Jethro	130
Barney, David T.	162		Basseter, Wm. C.	102
Barney, Redmond	100		Bassett, Franklin E.	170
Barnhard, Archer	108		Bassett, Patrick	16
Barnhardt, Samuel	132		Baston, J.J.	217
Barnum, _____	108		Batch, Ambrose	108

Batchilclan, John	59	Beatten, Samuel S.	108
Bateman, Charles A.	190	Beatty, M.	11
Bates, Albert	77	Bebout, Andrew G.	132
Bates, Alfred	38	Becc_____	199
Bates, Charles S.	104	Bechman, Frank	107
Bates, Hugh	177	Beck, Charles	74
Bathgate, James	108	Beck, Edward	108
Bathlain, J. A.	104	Beck, Joseph	199
Bathurst, Benjamin M.	90	Beckley, Edward	199
Batt, George	108	Beckman, Benjamin E.	199
Batterbury, John	108	Beckwith, Rufus J.	108
Batteree, Thos. J.	43	Bee, W.W.	215
Batty, William H.	71	Beecham, Wm.	30
Bauer, Caroline	182	Beed, Daniel	108
Baugh, Sylvester	199	Beehler, F.	15
Bauman, William, Jr.	190	Beehler, Fred'k	77
Baupp, _____	134	Beekman, W. M. H.	130
Baur, Frederick	74	Beer, Joseph	96
Baxley, John W.	167	Beerman, August	77
Baxter, Alfred	142	Beers, James	102
Baxter, John	139	Beeson, William	109
Baxter, John D.	199	Beighel, Burket	199
Bay, Thomas	139	Beish, Henry kW.	170
Bayard, Oliver	20	Beismer, Martin	109
Bayard, Wm. kThomas	20	Belcher, Stephen	109
Bayem, Peter	108	Belden, Henry	102
Bayne, James	155	Beldin, J.	23
Baza, James S.	139	Belding, Jasper L.	23
Bazeman, M.	97	Belford, David	134
Bbum, Guslowe A.	215	Belford, J.	132
Beach, ___	199	Belford, John	132
Beach, Amos S.	108	Belknap, J.D.	199
Beach, Cyrus T.	143	Bell, David	134
Beadle, O. H.	108	Bell, Frank	3
Beagy, John	108	Bell, George E.	109
Beal, Wm. E.	194	Bell, James B.	160
Beall, Robert	184	Bell, John	57
Beals, Benjamin, O.	190	Bell, John	184
Bean, Geo. P.	106	Bell, John R.	199
Beard, Alexander	104	Bell, Washington L.	109
Beard, J.H.	137	Bell, William W.	199
Beating, A. H.	100	Bellamy, Harvey	139

Name	Page
Bellcove, Alfred	109
Bellon, Robert I.	104
Bellows, _____	177
Bellshaw, John	142
Bellville, Louis F.	2
Belval, Lewis	176
Beman, James	41
Bench, John	109
Bender, Jocob	109
Bender, Zacharias	186
Benedict, Charles S.	155
Benjamin, J. B.	109
Bennet, Geo. N.	102
Bennet, Henry C.	134
Bennett, Agustus	109
Bennett, Andrew S.	71
Bennett, Clras	109
Bennett, E.	199
Bennett, Elijah	199
Bennett, George W.	109
Bennett, H.E.	9
Bennett, Harrison	109
Bennett, Henry	144
Bennett, Irvin S.	109
Bennett, J.A.	190
Bennett, James A.	109
Bennett, Joshua	88
Bennett, Richard	109
Bennett, Stephen	162
Bennett, Theopholis	102
Bensford, Harry C.	179
Benson, Harvey J.	190
Benson, J. W.	109
Benson, John	161
Bently, John	21
Benton, Daniel	23
Benton, George W.	100
Benton, James F.	199
Berkley, Charles	109
Berlinn, Chas.	77
Berrian, George N.	109
Berry Wm. H.	88
Berry, John	11
Berry, Joseph	88
Berry, Lewis	98
Berry, W. J.	78
Bersee, Seth	45
Bertsch, Jacob	90
Beruly, Simeon	50
Besamore, Charles	144
Bessent, J.H.	167
Betkic, John	3
Better, Joseph	109
Betts, B. W.	100
Beutly, Orin	61
Bice, A.F.	4
Bice, George	40
Bickner, George	28
Bid, Andrew	78
Biddle, J.W.	71
Bidley, Robert	174
Bigelow, Barnard	97
Bigelow, John L.	142
Bigelow, Samuel	109
Bigger, Robert M.	90
Bigler, Michael	166
Billing, George	109
Billings, Pliny	104
Bimerand, George	134
Biordan, John	23
Birberick, Geo.	30
Bird, J.H.	167
Bird, James	28
Bird, James	109
Bird, James (Jr.)	88
Bird, Josiah	130
Bird, Srunder	28
Bird, Thompson	109
Bird, Wm. N.	219
Birge, Nelson W.	143
Birmingham, J.	109
Bisbing, J.	134
Bisby, Hiram	104
Bishop, Andrew J.	190

Bishop, Joseph	16	Bloomer, John	199
Bishop, Robert U.	109	Blum, Frank	3
Bishop, Soloman	199	Blunt, _____	144
Bishop, William H.	97	Blunt, E. H.	97
Bison, Jacob S.	53	Blunt, Henry	109
Black, Charles	139	Blyman, Ennis	109
Black, Valentine	109	Blyth, George T.	109
Blackburn, Joseph, J	199	Bnonson, Aug. E.	16
Blackburn, T.J.	186	Boal, William F.	132
Blackman, James	45	Board, Joesph Jasper	199
Blackman, Louis A.	41	Boarding, Davis	109
Blackwell, Isasc	174	Bobo, Edwin	64
Blackwood, Rob't	78	BoBo, Granville C.	199
Blair, Andrew M.	94	Bobtail Bull	75
Blair, Thomas	199	Bodgerson, _____	144
Blair, William	7	Bodine, Napoleon	96
Blair, William	45	Boen, Maggie	184
Blake, E. P.	142	Bogart, John	98
Blake, John	139	Bogart, Wallace	109
Blake, Mathew	4	Boges, Enoch	176
Blake, Samuel A.	94	Bogger, Alex.	100
Blake, Thomas	109	Bogley, Irvin	132
Blake, Thomas	139	Bohon, Paul	199
Blake, Wesley	186	Bohrmens, W.	109
Blakeley, G.W.	109	Boice, Beth	199
Blanchard, Aaron	109	Boisvert, Adolph	109
Blanchard, Martin	107	Bokinger, George	98
Blanchard, Wesley	109	Bolestell, David	132
Bland, Taylor	109	Boloton, George H.	3
Blannership, John	130	Bolyard, Lewis	199
Bledsoe, David R.	98	Bomen, _____	182
Bleyer, Henry H.	199	Bonaparte, Wilson	102
Blinn, Clinton A.	109	Bond, Edwin H.	109
Bliss, E.W.	57	Bond, F.W.	78
Bliss, Seth	97	Bond, S.	134
Block, Joseph	134	Boner, Adam	134
Blodgett, A.C.	109	Bonerty, Levi	109
Bloo_____, Philamer	53	Boney, Richard	139
Blood, L. W.	130	Bonthron, James	45
Bloody Knife	75	Bonvall, William H.	170
Bloom, Louis	161	Boomhower, Conrad	190
Bloomer, Hans	109	Boos, William	18

Booth, Cyrus	39	Boyce, James H.	109
Booth, John	134	Boyce, Thomas D.	134
Booth, Ler____	2	Boyd, A.	199
Booth, Wm.	39	Boyd, Daniel	179
Boothwick, William	98	Boyd, John	109
Borber, A. J.	57	Boyd, Joshua	143
Borden, J. W.	134	Boyd, Robert F.	199
Bordwell, Hiram E.	190	Boyd, Thomas	98
Borrers, James	102	Boyem, Peter	109
Bosell, John	143	Boyer, Henry	144
Bosley, Robert L.	199	Boyer, Jacob	139
Boston, James G.	199	Boyer, Jesse	139
Boston, Stephen	139	Boyer, W. H.	139
Bostwick, Joseph	109	Boyett, Stephen	130
Boswell, Hezekiah J,	199	Boyle, Anthony	222
Bosworth, Jndson A.	109	Boyle, James	11
Bott, John A.	78	Boyle, James	144
Bottsfond, Charles E.	176	Boyle, Owen	64
Botzer, Edward	75	Boynton, E. P.	109
Botzer, Edward	75	Bozank, Joseph	105
Boughman, Henry L.	137	Brabson, W. F.	134
Boughten, John Frazer	179	Brachett, Ambrose	59
Bouin, John R.	109	Bradbury, Wiley	97
Boulden, N. H.	142	Braddock, A.	182
Bound, Philip	137	Bradfield, George E.	90
Bounke, Thomas	10	Bradford, J.	174
Bowditch, W.	109	Bradford, M.J.	26
Bowen, Philip	21	Bradigan, Martin	53
Bower, Godfrey	109	Bradley, ____	95
Bower, Harvey	109	Bradley, H.	109
Bowers, George W.	199	Bradley, J.	109
Bowers, W.	167	Bradley, James H.	63
Bowers, William	3	Bradley, Patrick	162
Bowley, H. W.	109	Bradley, Robert K.	90
Bowman, Emmal	182	Bradley, William	7
Bowman, John	109	Bradley, Wm. R.	160
Bowman, John	190	Bradshaw, J.P.	95
Bowman, Joseph M.	109	Bradshaw, William	199
Bowman, R. D.	109	Brady, Francis	2
Bownell, Augustus	109	Brady, Isaac	179
Bowsit, Miller	109	Brady, Nathaniel	109
Bowyer, W.L.	29	Brady, Patrick C.	109

Brady, Roger W.	215	Brigham, T. W.	109
Brady, William	64	Bright, J.W.	167
Bragg, W.	53	Brightfield, John	64
Bragg, William J.	109	Brill, Samuel	160
Braitsch, Charles	70	Brindle, J.	109
Bramer, Thomas S.	109	Bringart, Francis	144
Branaham, William	142	Bringle, William	134
Brandon, Benjamin	64	Brinton, Della	30
Brandon, Wm.	78	Briody, John	64
Branell, Henry	109	Briscod, James	51
Brannin, John M.	109	Briscoe, Thomas S,	199
Bransom, B.F.	53	Brise, Isaac	109
Bratling, Frank	176	Brispham, J. P.	132
Bratt, Cornellus	190	Bristol, L. J.	110
Bray, T.E.	100	Britt, Alice Emma	182
Brayden, John J.	100	Britt, James	11
Brddinbury, Wm.	219	Britten, Henry C.	110
Breath, James	28	Britten, Zachariah	104
Breckenridge, Norman	199	Britton, Henry	18
Brede, H.	25	Britz, Henry	199
Breneman, Finally	40	Britzki, Carl	162
Brennan, Michael	109	Broadback, Frederick	110
Breton, Jufus	174	Broadheart, Abel	110
Brewer, Ernest	109	Broadhurst, Joesph H.	64
Brewer, James	190	Broadwell, William	110
Brewer, John C.	109	Broderich, John	110
Brich, James	41	Broderich, Lawrence	144
Brichter, John	109	Broetz, Herman	63
Brick, John	96	Brogan, James	64
Bricker, Sameal J.	166	Brogau, James	87
Bridane, Andrew	109	Bromer, Johnson	110
Bridges, John F.	109	Brommiller, R.H.	199
Bridges, Wm.	196	Brook, William	61
Briggs, R. J.	97	Brookings, A. L.	100
Briggs, Charles	109	Brooks, Jacob	139
Briggs, Charles H.	190	Brooks, Jno.	78
Briggs, Henry	107	Brooks, Oben	110
Briggs, James	109	Brooksea, Tederick	5
Briggs, John H.	100	Broson, ___	182
Briggs, Lewis	109	Brossis, William S.	95
Briggs, R.	167	Brothers, Jesse	199
Briggs, William	106	Broughton, William	134

Browe, Isaac W.	134
Brower, John M.	90
Browly, O.K.	26
Brown, _____	144
Brown, Alva W.	78
Brown, Andrew	110
Brown, Anthony D.	110
Brown, B	11
Brown, B. F.	134
Brown, Benjamin F.	64
Brown, Bernard E.	11
Brown, Brodish	100
Brown, Charles	45
Brown, Charles F.	157
Brown, Charles J.	110
Brown, Coburn	110
Brown, Cyrus	110
Brown, Daniel	3
Brown, Daniel	197
Brown, David D.	199
Brown, Duncan	176
Brown, E. A.	110
Brown, E. B.	110
Brown, Eliza F.	144
Brown, F. M.	100
Brown, Fayette S.	190
Brown, Geoge C.	64
Brown, George	87
Brown, George	110
Brown, George	139
Brown, George A	179
Brown, George W.	110
Brown, H.E.	137
Brown, Henry	103
Brown, Henry	134
Brown, Henry	142
Brown, Henry	158
Brown, Hugo	78
Brown, Hugo	217
Brown, Isaiah	110
Brown, J.H.	30
Brown, J.J.	137
Brown, J.T.	48
Brown, James	45
Brown, James	110
Brown, James	134
Brown, James	177
Brown, James F.	199
Brown, James M.	200
Brown, James W.	78
Brown, John	51
Brown, John	94
Brown, John	106
Brown, John	110
Brown, John	130
Brown, John	166
Brown, John	174
Brown, John E.	110
Brown, John J.	161
Brown, John L.	31
Brown, Joseph	110
Brown, Joseph	132
Brown, Julia A.	144
Brown, Lewis	110
Brown, Maria	182
Brown, Martian	200
Brown, Martin	110
Brown, Matthew F.	71
Brown, Oliver	200
Brown, P.C.	53
Brown, Paul	110
Brown, Peter	61
Brown, Richard	154
Brown, Sam'l	173
Brown, T.	110
Brown, T. Bailey	200
Brown, Theodore	97
Brown, Thomas	110
Brown, Thomas J.	110
Brown, W.J.	43
Brown, William	11
Brown, William	64
Brown, William	110
Brown, William	134

Brown, William	215	Buckhamman, John W.	38
Brown, William H.	110	Buckhardt, Charles	134
Brown, William H.	190	Buckhart, G.	97
Brown, William J.	170	Buckler, Nicholas	110
Brown, Wm. S.	100	Buckley, _____	182
Browne, James	97	Bucklin, William	104
Browne, William	157	Bucknell, Thomas J.	64
Browner, John E.	110	Buckner, Samuel B.	110
Browney, John	3	Buechi, William	177
Brownfield, Stephen N	31	Buegler, William	53
Brownwell, Dan'l	78	Bugman, Adolph	61
Bruce, Charles C.	162	Bugsell, Ida	31
Bruce, Patrick	64	Buigon, J.	171
Brumer, Henry	110	Buk, Michael	162
Brumsltmell, Wm. C.	153	Bulgen, James	110
Brunch, Jacob	162	Bulhand, Joseph L.	78
Brund, G.W.	78	Buliss, Eugene	110
Brundage, John	110	Bull, Joesph	200
Brundage, L. D.	110	Bull, John	110
Brunell, Elijah	200	Bulleu, James	177
Brunii, John	159	Bullis, Simeon	110
Brunn, Emile Ann	157	Bullock, Charles	61
Brunner, John	152	Bulrick, H.	171
Bruper, John	134	Bump, Henry	104
Bruse, George F.	110	Bunce, Clarence	139
Bruster, James	110	Bunch, John	110
Bryan, J. P.	95	Bungnity, Julius	7
Bryan, T.D.	78	Bunn, Albert	110
Bryant, Franklin A.	177	Bunnell Nathaniel F,	200
Bryant, G. S.	134	Bunting, John	26
Bryant, Travers S.	167	Burch, Adam	110
Bryce, Petter	57	Burch, Charles	45
Brynart, Joseph	110	Burch, Nathan	107
Bryson, Charles	200	Burch, Niles	162
Bualeson, Rufus	110	Burch, Thomas	110
Bucey, Lillie	31	Burdett, Aaron	103
Buchanan, Andrew T.	179	Burdett, Silas A.	200
Buchannan, August	110	Burdick, G. A.	110
Buck, Charles	139	Burdick, E. W.	137
Buck, Daniel W.	18	Burdick, Joel G.	143
Buck, Osborne	134	Burgemeister, Frederi	190
Buck, Thomas	110	Burger, Harvey	200

Name	Value	Name	Value
Burgess, William	100	Burnside, Frank	110
Burgess, William P.	200	Burr, Lewis M.	110
Burget, Henry	31	Burrell, Decatur	110
Burget, Henry	31	Burrell, Frank W.	200
Burgett, Lewis F.	139	Burrell, Green	98
Burgie, ___	110	Burry, W.	53
Burgner, David W.	90	Burt, Chas. E.	74
Buring, J.L.	26	Burt, Chas. H.	96
Burk, Thomas	45	Burton, Erwin	35
Burk, W. B.	48	Burton, Horace	96
Burke, ___	31	Burton, James	97
Burke, Frank	144	Burton, Winslow	110
Burke, Jno	78	Buryes, Edwin D.	142
Burke, John	64	Busch, Mrs. Joanna	132
Burke, John	144	Buser, Charles	41
Burke, Lewis F.	132	Bush, Henry	53
Burke, Peter	145	Bush, John	145
Burke, Richard	219	Bush, William H.	162
Burke, Wm	78	Bushfield, Thomas	134
Burke, Wm.	194	Bushing, _____	95
Burket, Casper	48	Bushy, Henry	103
Burkhant, Emanuel	48	Busler, Morgan	162
Burkhardt, John	132	Bussard, Daniel P.	200
Burkhart, Andrew	134	Bustard, James	65
Burkle, Cha's	222	Butcher, Henry	179
Burleigh, Charles J.	74	Butler, _____	139
Burlingame, William F	110	Butler, Anthony A.	110
Burlingame, Z.	110	Butler, Charles	110
Burmann, Jno.	78	Butler, Edward	179
Burnes, John	110	Butler, Henry	179
Burnham, Lucien	65	Butler, James	65
Burns, A.P.	100	Butler, Jno.	31
Burns, Daniel	94	Butler, John	61
Burns, James	45	Butler, Samuel	139
Burns, James	94	Butler, William	90
Burns, James T.	98	Butterly, Mathew	63
Burns, John	98	Byerly, John B	16
Burns, John	110	Byers, William	134
Burns, Patrick	110	Byerson, Chas.	78
Burns, Thomas	110	Byrne, Geo.	78
Burns, William	61	Byrne, James	104
Burns, John	10	Byrne, Patrick	145

C.T.J.	78
Cabbage, John	142
Cable, Joseph A.	71
Cacker, Gideon	162
Cadey, Hurbert	57
Cady, Dennis	110
Cady, J. B.	104
Caffin, G.	48
Caffrey, Bernard	78
Cahill, James	215
Cahill, William	176
Cain, A. N.	134
Cain, Avery B.	217
Cain, S.	137
Cain, William S.	91
Calahan, Patrick	110
Calburton, Edward A.	110
Caldwell, Alvin A.	14
Caldwell, Earl H.	31
Caldwell, James H.	190
Caldwell, W. R.	97
Calhoun, James	65
Calhoun, John	107
Callahan, Andrew	98
Callahan, Geo.	91
Callahan, Jerry	110
Callahan, John J.	65
Callehan, C.	168
Callen, James	110
Calleng, ___	31
Caln, M.	168
Calvert, John	138
Calvert, Walter L.	190
Calvin, Moses	29
Cambell, Charles	110
Cameron, Benton	110
Cameron, W'm.	222
Cammel, Joseph	142
Cammer, William M.	217
Camp, Burton W.	215
Camp, Harry V.	200
Camp, William H.	134
Campbell, Alexander	200
Campbell, Edward R.	21
Campbell, Elisha	138
Campbell, George W.	143
Campbell, Hugh	104
Campbell, James	104
Campbell, John W.	97
Campbell, Oliver M.	190
Campbell, R. J.	95
Campbell, Richard	110
Campbell, Robert	130
Campbell, thomas	53
Campbell. Thomas C.	200
Campton, S. B.	110
Canada, James	110
Canaga, O. C.	132
Canahan, Benjamin	134
Canby, John	139
Cancy, Albert	162
Candage, Geo. B.	101
Canfield, Francis M.	110
Canham, Alper	217
Cannon, John	97
Cannon, John	110
Canter, Michael	110
Caoy, ___	183
Caple, Hamilton	110
Car, Robert	176
Caraley, James	87
Cardwell. Joseph W.	190
Carey, John	110
Cargill, George M.	91
Carl, Andrew	104
Carl, Andrew J.	104
Carl, Charles	110
Carl, James	111
Carletin, Thomas	176
Carleton, David J.	8
Carleton, James	97
Carliman, Benjamin	111
Carll, Peter	132
Carlton, Ernest	183

Carlton, Eugene	87
Carlyon, Thos.	39
Carman, Samuel D.	134
Carmen, William	139
Carmichael, Wm.	4
Carmoell, J.	162
Carnahah, Lorenzo	111
Carney, James	65
Carney, William	134
Carnhill, Charles	95
Carpenter, Albert	111
Carpenter, J. A.	111
Carr, Dennis	11
Carr, George W.	111
Carr, James	145
Carr, Michael	7
Carr, Thomas A.	111
Carrick, William	37
Carroll, Albert	95
Carroll, Alexander	111
Carroll, Eugene	52
Carroll, Hazel Beatri	35
Carroll, Henry	145
Carroll, John C	4
Carroll, Joseph	138
Carroll, Michael	197
Carroll, Peter	187
Carroll, Thomas	111
Carry, Rodgers	45
Carson, Ezra	100
Carson, Robert	52
Cartell, M.J.	35
Carteppe, Andrew	111
Carter, B.	78
Carter, George W.	111
Carter, Isaac	139
Carter, William	111
Cartha, Edward	139
Carthen, Timothy	138
Carthlend, Francis	130
Cartie, Robert	111
Cartie, Roiln M.	111
Cartright, John	103
Cartwright, Ezra	190
Cartwright, Joseph	111
Carver, George	111
Carver, Justus M.	104
Carver, Lewis	111
Cary, J.W.	168
Case, Allen W.	190
Case, Reuben M.	111
Casedo, William T. L.	111
Casey, James	145
Cash, Adolphus	173
Cash, P.C.	95
Cash, William	20
Cashan, William	65
Casia, Joseph	111
Caskadon, William	200
Casley, James	111
Cass, Austin	179
Cass, John M.	4
Cassel, George A.	98
Cassiday, James C.	200
Cassidy, James	215
Cassidy, John	111
Cassidy, Richard	11
Cassidy, Thomas	195
Castell, George	61
Casterline, William	111
Castle, William S.	111
Caston, Theodore	111
Cater, E.J.	106
Cather, Armantheus D.	65
Caual, Charles	87
Cauldell, Sam'l	96
Cauldwell, George	111
Cautillair, David	176
Cavailar, Joesph	200
Cavanaugh, Daniel	161
Cavender, James S.	45
Cavey, William	111
Center, C.O.	168
Chace, Seth	50

Chaffin, Henry W.	87		Cheale, William	41
Chalk	31		Cheeseman, Wm. M.	166
Chaisley, A. M.	138		Cheever, Ami	65
Chalker, Hiram C.	200		Chein, John	59
Chamberlain, Francis	100		Chemington, William	145
Chamberlin, A.J.	11		Cherry, J.D.	183
Chamberlin, Willsam	134		Chesbrough, Spicer	111
Chamberlin, Wm.	142		Chew, Andrew	57
Chambers, Eli	200		Childers, J.	48
Chambers, George W.	130		Childs, George C.	200
Chambers, Henry	87		Childs, William H.	200
Chambers, Isaac	111		Chilpers, Levy	111
Chambers, J.	139		Chilson, King A.	111
Chambers, Legrand	111		Chindler, ____	78
Chambers, Lewis	29		Chinn, George	111
Chambers, R. B.	111		Chiveral, Alexander	91
Chambers, Rob't	194		Choal, Charles	50
Chambers. Harvey	95		Choisy, ____	183
Champion, Ezra	104		Chon, Lewis	78
Champion, W. M.	130		Chorpening, Samuel	78
Champlain, George	111		Chrain, John	50
Champlin, Lewis	132		Christ, C.S.	21
Chandler, Harvey P.B.	21		Christ, Dan'l	78
Chandler, Richard	94		Christian, Jacob	177
Chandley, William	111		Christian, R.A.	41
Channel, Coleman	200		Christian, Thomas	139
Channel, Wesley	200		Christianson, O.	105
Chapin, Scott H.	104		Christie, Thomas	37
Chapman, A. A.	104		Christmas, Jacob	111
Chapman, Herbert J.	25		Christopher, Albert	179
Chapman, Woshington	111		Christopher, Daniel	104
Charles, James H.	103		Christopher, Henry	145
Charleston, George	139		Christopher, Rex	36
Charley, Vincent	75		Christy, P.	104
Charm, Thomas	97		Chrles, Crawford	177
Chase, August	139		Chrysty, John	152
Chase, Dennis	132		Chueer, Samuel A.	53
Chase, E.B.	16		Chum, Barney	100
Chase, Jas. H.	106		Chuoniger, E.	134
Chase, John F.	111		Church, Wm.	59
Chase, Lewis	139		Churchill, Calvin	111
Chase, Simon	134		Churchill, Helen S.	145

Name	Page
Ciane, Gilbert R	18
Clardarelli, Joesph M	200
Cilbert, George	104
Clagg, George W.	104
Clansy, John	111
Clapp, George W.	170
Clarch, Charles	111
Clark A. B.	111
Clark, Alexander	111
Clark, Alfred	130
Clark, Amy	31
Clark, Augustus	200
Clark, Ben H.	31
Clark, Charles	134
Clark, David	111
Clark, George	3
Clark, George	98
Clark, George	154
Clark, George L.	41
Clark, Henry T.	190
Clark, Herman	31
Clark, Hugh	143
Clark, James	45
Clark, James	111
Clark, Jerome G.	97
Clark, Jno.	31
Clark, Jno.	78
Clark, John T.	111
Clark, John W.	200
Clark, Joseph M.	111
Clark, Joseph W.	142
Clark, Julia	31
Clark, L. E.	104
Clark, Lewis	154
Clark, Lewis G.	132
Clark, Martin L.	111
Clark, Mary	31
Clark, Morseman	162
Clark, Ollen	190
Clark, Orris	111
Clark, Patrick	111
Clark, Peter J.	162
Clark, Phillip	31
Clark, R. W.	132
Clark, Samuel L.	111
Clark, Sevi	57
Clark, Thomas M.	200
Clark, W. F.	142
Clark, Wesley	111
Clark, William A.	111
Clark, William F.	98
Clark, William F.	102
Clark, William J.	111
Clarke, _____	95
Clarke, Charles	197
Clarke, J.C.	11
Clarke, William	52
Clarke, William F.	111
Clarry, Edward B.	101
Clary, Blanche Irene	78
Clary, Kelly	31
Clase, Nathan	111
Claudell, Nicholas	97
Clavenaugh, Joseph M.	111
Clawson, John	11
Clay, Henry	36
Clay, Wesley P.	200
Claybaugh, Jacob	200
Clear, Elihu F.	75
Clear, Elihu F.	75
Clear, G.W.	78
Cleaveland, John E.	71
Cleland, William	111
Clemens, A.	103
Clemens, W.H.	78
Clemens, William H.	217
Clement, Hudson	111
Clement, Therome	111
Clements, M. D.	132
Clements, William M.	104
Clendersing, Andrew	98
Clergy, Jesse H.	132
Click, tenin	106
Clifford, Timothy	217

Clifford, Timothy	78	Colby, Henry	96
Clifton, George	130	Colby, William	111
Clinch, John	190	Colchoss, Henry	111
Clinchy, Mrs. S. M.	187	Colcord, Lewis	111
Cline, Milton	134	Colden, Patrick	145
Cline, Watson	162	Cole, Alvah	111
Clinton, Horace	111	Cole, Amos E.	111
Clise, Oscar	45	Cole, Benjamin	139
Clitz, John	60	Cole, Chauncey	134
Cloe, John	31	Cole, John	104
Cloth, Christian	177	Cole, John B.	107
Clough, J. H.	111	Cole, Lewis H.	111
Clover, Eugene	37	Cole, Mary	145
Cloyd, Charles L.	52	Cole, Riley	111
Clyborn, Andrew J.	200	Cole, Thomas E.	200
Cmigan, Patrick	45	Colehouse, John D.	200
Cnofuk, Chas.	16	Coleman, Aseh	130
Cnuneu, Michael	45	Coleman, Charles	65
Co____y, Barnabas	152	Coleman, Daniel T.	98
Coats, James	111	Coleman, James	31
Coats, R.S. (Mrs.)	78	Coleman, James H.	200
Cobb, Franklin B.	101	Coleman, Jordon	41
Cobb, Joseph	215	Coleman, Rueben	179
Coburn, Isaiah	101	Colgan, James	145
Coburn, Jacob	200	Collamore, F. H.	101
Cochran, James	200	Collard, George	132
Cochran, Wm. L.	160	Collin, Charles L.	200
Coe, Elwood	191	Collins, Charles F.	9
Cofcant, Rollin	217	Collins, Cornelius	111
Coffey, Dan'l	78	Collins, E. A.	29
Coffey, Jesse	106	Collins, James	78
Coffin, Charles	50	Collins, James	217
Coffman, Elijah	200	Collins, John C.	200
Cogan, Henry J.	188	Collins, Lewis	53
Cogan, John	87	Collins, Mary R.	145
Cogan, John	111	Collins, Mich'l	31
Cogswell, H.F.	12	Collins, Michael	222
Coit, William H.	132	Collins, Peter	111
Coker, J.W.	78	Collins, Robert	134
Colbath, Richard N.	105	Collins,James	95
Colbur, J.C.	78	Collison, Authur	201
Colburn, J.C.	15	Colly, Issac	201

Name	Page	Name	Page
Colman, John c.	217	Connoly, Valentine	112
Colson, Peter	52	Conoway, William H.	91
Colson, Frederick	111	Conrad, W.	112
Colson, John O.	101	Conradt, John	112
Colvert, John A.	111	Conroy, William	112
Colyer, Clarence R.	78	Considine, Martin	75
Comack, John	134	Contrain, Jackson	130
Combs, James W.	143	Conway, J.M.	45
Combs, Robert W.	10	Coodall, C. A.	112
Comedy, Philo	103	Coodick, Thomas	219
Comet, Romanus	134	Cook, A. L.	142
Comforth, John	98	Cook, C.P.	91
Commiky, Phillip	100	Cook, Clarke C.	142
Comnsumcp, Palm.	182	Cook, Edward	112
Compton, Alson	197	Cook, Fred	58
Comstock, Adelbert	191	Cook, Hiram	201
Comstock, WLm. LE.	16	Cook, Isaac	98
Conally, James	87	Cook, Jacob	112
Condaint, Joseph	111	Cook, John	112
Condin, Michael	12	Cook, M.B.	35
Condon, James	111	Cook, Moses	139
Condree, Peter H.	215	Cook, Peter	107
Condrill, William H.	215	Cook, S. T.	97
Conetrey, Jeff.	142	Cook, Urban S.	91
Conine, Lewis	111	Cooke, Chas. H.	106
Conklin, Edward S.	111	Cooke, William W.	65
Conklin, Francis	112	Cookes, James M.	91
Conklin, John	112	Cookman, William	97
Conkly, Patrick	145	Cool, J.	112
Conley, Thomas	134	Coombs, George E.	101
Conn, Asa T.	112	Cooper, Daniel	112
Conn, George W.	97	Cooper, David J.	107
Connel, Thomas	112	Cooper, Delmar E.	201
Connelly, Edward	112	Cooper, Enos B.	201
Conner, Edward	65	Cooper, George T.	112
Conner, James	156	Cooper, Peter L.	191
Conner, Jennings	188	Cooper, Samuel	143
Conners, James	145	Cooprin, Nathan	112
Conners, Thomas	65	Cope, Eli	191
Connigan, John	112	Copeland, George	139
Conniss, Michael O.	98	Copper, Geo. W.	112
Connolly, Patrick	101	Coppersmith, Thomas	134

Corbin, Alonzo	104	Cox, Harley W.	31
Corcoran, Edmond	78	Cox, Samuell P.	215
Corcoran, Redmond	220	Coxe, John W.	215
Cordell, Charles T.	112	Coxey, James	134
Corey, Elijah	112	Coy, John Hamer	50
Cormell, Michael	45	Coy, William	50
Corn, Charles	112	Coyle, James	112
Corn, George	112	Cozard, Edward	134
Cornalls, Edgar	112	Crabtre, John W.	18
Cornell, A.	112	Craig, Julia Magdelsn	184
Cornell, William H.	168	Craig, L.S.	10
Cornish, Thomas	139	Craig, Stacy	112
Corpium, James	97	Cramblet, Wm.	196
Corrnues, C.	176	Cramden, J. S.	142
Corroran, Joseph	112	Crammer, Joesph	201
Cortell, Edw'd	78	Crammer, Josiah N.	88
Corwell, Job	191	Cramston, Authur	12
Corwin, D.C.	154	Crandall, John D.	112
Cosart, Lewis	112	Crane, Lewis H.	112
Costello, Wm.	79	Crane, Lewis II	112
Coster, Martin	145	Cranston, Michael	112
Cotton, William S.	201	Crawford, A. G.	130
Couch, Charles	112	Crawford, Charles	162
Cough, Bruce	112	Crawford, John M.	91
Coughlan, John	112	Crawford, Peter	112
Couglan, D.	197	Crawford, Thomas	112
Coulthart, W. A.	100	Creamer, George	134
Counteman, Charles	112	Creamer, Peter	145
Courter, Collin	112	Creighton, Sturtevant	112
Courtney, W.	112	Cressey, E. P.	7
Cousins, James A.	142	Cresson, ____	183
Coutenay, John	222	Creuthers, Christophe	132
Covey, Alfred C.	112	Crib, _____	170
Covey, Charles	162	Criddle, Christopher	65
Covington, Elijah	138	Crier, Sam'l	79
Covington, Hugh	1	Crimp, James	95
Cowan, Michael	201	Crisfield, William B.	65
Cowden, George H.	97	Crisholm, Samuel	7
Cowell, Edward	107	Critchlow, Adam W.	134
Cowles, Nathan	112	Crites, Maeshall	201
Cowperthwait, Joseph	91	Critone, Alfred	134
Cox, C.	130	Crittenden, John J.	65

Crofut, Henry B.	16		Cummings, John	112
Crofut, Levi	134		Cummings, T.	145
Croht, Henry	103		Cummins, John	38
Croker, John	2		Cumminskey, ___	183
Croker, S.A.	79		Cunip, Henry W.	18
Croker, Wm.	79		Cunningham, ___	79
Croncerr, Lafyette	112		Cunningham, Jacob	112
Cronin, P.	112		Cunningham, Martin	163
Crosby, Matthias	134		Cunningham, Sorvell	101
Crosey, John	79		Cunningham. D. L.	201
Cross, Lewis	112		Curch, Jonathan	112
Cross, Nelson	104		Curchwell, Cornellus	191
Cross, Sonathan	112		Curl, William	88
Cross, Warnell	91		Curlen, J.	104
Crothier, Henry G.	104		Curley, Patrick	7
Crow, W. G.	112		Curran, Williams	215
Crowder, William	138		Currie, Archibald	170
Crowfoot, Lewis	201		Curry, Charlotte	183
Crowin, Ambrose	112		Curry, J.	104
Crowley, Joseph	106		Curtis, Daniel	112
Crown, Joseph	52		Curtis, Edward S.	26
Crusy, Samuel	112		Curtis, Hiram C.	112
Crutchfield, Isabella	12		Curtis, J. R.	112
Crutchfield, James	12		Curtis, James	112
Crutchfield, Joseph	12		Curtis, Joseph	98
Cuddy, Charles	37		Curtis, M.	171
Culkins, James	112		Curtis, Maber	139
Cullen, James	112		Curtis, Nathaniel B.	191
Cullen, Patrick	41		Curtis, Theodore C.	112
Culoer, Theodore	53		Curtis, William F.	145
Culvay, C.W.	45		Cushing, Louis	12
Culver, Allen	104		Cushman, James	201
Culver, George M.	112		Cussle, Shedras F.	112
Culver, Parmenas	134		Custer, George A.	65
Cumberlige, Peter	201		Custer, Thomas W.	65
Cumier, J. H.	59		Custis, George	112
Cumming, Lester A	79		Cutling, Horatio A.	103
Cumming, William	112		D_____, H.	48
Cummings, Alex.	145		Daby, Wm.	160
Cummings, Augustus	201		Dachman, Joseph	112
Cummings, David	112		Dagram, Nicholas	98
Cummings, Henry	132		Dague, Aaron	163

Dahlin, Jeremiah	132	Daugherty, Albert G.	201
Daikin, Lorenzo D,	201	Davenport, A.R.	29
Dailey, John R.	166	Davenport, M. E.	130
Daily, Hubert	145	Davenport, Samuel	45
Daily, John H.	7	Davern, Edward	65
Dale, Thomas	20	David, John	112
Daley, Daniel	103	Davidson, E. H.	98
Daley, Jeremiah	103	Davidson, John	21
Daley, Thomas	177	Davidson, Lewis	112
Dalious, James	75	Davidson, W. F.	95
Dalious, James	75	Davidson, W.D.	12
Dallas, George M.	179	Davidson, William	59
Dally, Michael	103	Davis, Agustus	112
Dallye, Ernest	145	Davis, Alfred	197
Dalton, George	107	Davis, Allen	130
Dalton, Jas.	194	Davis, Almond	112
Daly, M.	112	Davis, B. F.	134
Daly, Patrick	145	Davis, Charles E.	112
Daly, Peter	112	Davis, Chas. H.	106
Damond, Albert H.	112	Davis, David	12
Dandall, Isaiah	101	Davis, David	79
Dandridge, Richard	41	Davis, David	113
Daneen, Solon	104	Davis, Edward	139
Daniel, Robert D.	104	Davis, Edward E.	113
Daniel, Thomas	112	Davis, Edwin	53
Daniels, Jermiah	179	Davis, Edwin	113
Daniels, O.E.	12	Davis, Fred	28
Daniels, Patrick	16	Davis, George L.	103
Dannigan, James	112	Davis, George M.	143
Dany, Bernard	79	Davis, Henry	45
Darin, Berry	138	Davis, Henry	113
Dark, George	143	Davis, James	45
Darling, Hiram G.	104	Davis, James	101
Darling, Truman	143	Davis, James	201
Darnold, James L.	112	Davis, James K.	113
Darow, C.	112	Davis, James R.	138
Darrell, Geo.	53	Davis, Jas.	155
Darris, John	65	Davis, John	134
Dart, William	132	Davis, John	179
Darum, Edward	112	Davis, John D.	168
Datterson, Charles	139	Davis, John P.	196
Datzins, Philip W.	134	Davis, Joshua	25

Davis, Moses	113	Deck, M.	97
Davis, Robert	113	Decker, Isaac	12
Davis, Sampson	95	Decker, John	113
Davis, Simon E.	104	Deddridge, Benj.F.	10
Davis, Timothy K.	201	Deem, William	91
Davis, William	65	Deenbwung, Jeremiah	113
Davis, William	98	Dees, Joseph P.	132
Davis, William	113	Defnesty, Hiram	104
Davis, William G.	113	DeGraft, Matthew J.	21
Davise, Frank	177	DeJrak, E.L.	74
Davison, James	97	DeKamp, Susan	145
Dawagan, John	134	DeLagenl, Julius A.	145
Dawilson, Charles E.	101	DeLagnet, Sarah E.	145
Dawley, Alexander C.	113	Delamater, Martin	104
Dawsen, William J.	61	Deland, Alvin S.	113
Dawsey, David E.	72	Delaney, Augustus	37
Dawson, ____	157	Delaney, John	12
Dawson, John J.	201	Delany, Andrew	113
Dawson, Rich'd	79	Delarid, J.M.	79
Dawson, Thomas	201	Delevan, Joseph F.	106
Dawson, William T,	201	Dell, Peter	2
Day, George W.	113	Delong, Peter	113
Day, George W.	191	Delong, Silas H.	139
Day, Ira W.	98	Delworth Theodore	201
Day, John	113	Demerest, Baptist	113
Day, N. K.	79	Demes, John	2
Day, Pratt	113	Demesme, O.F.	188
Day, William H.	215	Demming, Macy	16
Daymon, Ebenezer	113	Demmons, S. C.	104
Dayton, Henry C.	113	Demond, B. V.	113
De Brady, De Young	95	Dempsey, James	12
De Kamp, James C.	145	Dempster, Francis M.	201
De Llois	87	Den, Richard W.	163
Deacon, _____	163	Denald, Charles	113
Dean, C.	103	Denel, Asa	113
Dean, Daniel	113	Denias, Clement	101
Dean, James	53	Dening, Paul	104
Deanholdt, H.	43	Dennis, Albert B.	145
DeBar, Lewis W.	138	Dennis, E. A.	98
DeBrodt, Charles	113	Dennis, Elihu	113
DeCamp, Leander	113	Dennis, Henry	12
Deck, Edward	113	Dennison, Jeremiah E.	201

Dennison, W.A.	53
Denny, Edward M.	101
Denny, Frederick	163
Denny, Joseph	53
Densmore, William	104
Depert, Z.	113
Depeu, William	154
Derchew, Otto	72
Deriff, Francis	196
Dermian, Conrad	113
Dermott, David	201
DeRussy, R.E.	60
Dervey, Otis C.	113
Dessert, Gustavas	113
Detrick, Eli	98
Deuel, William A.	79
Deutsch, Geo.	172
Dever, N.H.	168
Devine, Saumel	186
Deviney, James	6
Devow, Isaac	134
Devoy, Calvin	113
DeWams, Geraldo	18
Dewey, Daniel	18
Dewitt, C.	100
Dewitt, W.H.	113
Dewitt, William	139
Dewn'e, Thomas	31
DeWolf, James M.	75
Dexter, Levi	113
Dickerson, Charles	20
Dickerson, Hiram	201
Dickerson, Louis	172
Dickey, Charles H.	101
Dickey, Madison	103
Dickinson, Barrow	98
Dickman, A. D.	95
Dickson, Samuel	113
Diehl, John	177
Diescher, Lewis	103
Diestel, Bernard	156
Dietz, C.S.	194
Dietz, John	91
Diffley, Edward T.	79
Dight, Henry	201
Dikman, William	16
Dildine, John H.	132
Dillman, Charles	145
Dillon, Reuben	201
Dillon, S.	113
Dimarest, William	152
Dimock, Joseph J.	18
Dingee, J.	12
Dingman, Wm	159
Dinja, John	143
Dinnie, Percy G.	106
Dinst, John	135
Dispenett, Newton	98
Ditmore, Julius G.	201
Diueheart, George	113
Divins, David	135
Dix, George	139
Dixon, John J.	97
Dixon, Samuel	201
Dixon, William	101
Dixon, William	143
Dizzlry, Edward T.	217
Dobbins, Joel	201
Dodd, John	97
Dodge, Francis R.	113
Dodge, Joseph	91
Dodge, W.	53
Dodson, Bloomington	157
Doe, Patrick	96
Doe, Patrick	96
Doepker, Henry	201
Doerson, Robert	113
Dohman, Anton	65
Dohn, Adam	186
Doi, Edward	79
Dolan, John	21
Dolan, John	31
Dolan, Peter	191
Dolan, Thomas	79

Dolhammer, Charles	201	Dorsey, George S.	201
Dolin, Steverson	57	Dorston, Joesph	201
Dollen, F.M.	31	Doss, Henry C.	65
Dollis, J. J.	97	Doty, William	135
Dominu, Priest	113	Doudell, Benj. F.	160
Dommin, Priest	142	Dougherty, William	3
Donahee, Michael T.	215	Doughty, Robert H.	101
Donaho, Thomas I.	7	Douglas, George E.	72
Donahoe, John	222	Douglas, J.W.	188
Donahue, Henry	113	Douglas, John W.	139
Donahue, John	15	Douglass, David	113
Donahue, Thomas	113	Douglass, James	45
Dondell, John R.	160	Dous____, Soloman	154
Dondelly, Z. B.	113	Dowen, Andrew J.	21
Donely, John	91	Dowler, Jacob	201
Doner, Frank	95	Dowling, Roe I.	154
Donnell, John O	163	Dowling, William	113
Donnelly, Charles	145	Down, Stephen	113
Donnelly, Michael	41	Downer, Job	98
Donnelly, Timothy	65	Downey, John	101
Donnely, James	113	Downey, Thomas	37
Donner, Henry	113	Downing, Fritz R.	91
Donnety, C. A.	113	Downing, Thomas P.	65
Donohue, Michael	201	Downing, William E.	113
Donohue, William	161	Downs, Dennis	170
Donovan, Francis	113	Downs, Thomas	142
Donovan, John	217	Doyle, James	197
Donovan, L. Jno.	79	Doyle, Jno.	79
Donovan, Michael	113	Doyle, John	15
Donovan, Michael	1	Doyle, Willliam	14
Donowey, William	157	Dozier. Major	139
Dooner, Henry	113	Drackenmuller, John	135
Door, Joseph	98	Drake, Edwin L.	113
Dorabush, Charles	53	Drake, John B.	135
Doran, James	104	Drake, John L	18
Dorer, William	61	Drake, McKindra L.	63
Dorfeldt, Rudolf	196	Draper, George W.	113
Dorman, Isaiah	75	Draper, Isaac F.	97
Dorn, John J.	113	Draulin, Robert	217
Dorn, Richard B.	75	Drew, John	113
Dorrance, W. B.	98	Driff, Benjamin R.	142
Dorsey, B.B.	201	Driscall, Edw. (Jr.)	89

Driscoll, A.	171
Driscoll, Dennis	113
Driscoll, Edward	65
Driscott, James	103
Driver, Patrick	107
Drummond, Alexander	113
Drummond, William	7
Drury, W. G.	142
Dryer, John	10
Duane, Patrick	201
Dubois, Charles	139
Dubois, Isaiah	139
Duder, Charles	160
Dudley, G. N.	106
Dudley, J.	113
Duff, James A.	142
Duffer, George E.	113
Dufficks, Leroy	61
Duffield, William	201
Duffle, Stacy K.	113
Duffy, Edward	61
Duffy, John	179
Dugan, John	163
Duggan, Daniel	45
Duggan, Dennis	191
Duggan, John	65
Duggens, Robert	138
Duis, William	79
Dullord, W. F.	113
Dumbell, Michael	170
Dummell, Wm. H.	45
Dunamoor, John	217
Dunby, Bendicht	159
Duncan, Austiso	41
Duncan, Edward	201
Duncnan, John	215
Dundon, John	202
Dunford, Daniel	145
Dunham, Daniel J.	101
Dunkel, Jacob	132
Dunkle, Benjamin	135
Dunkle, Watson	113
Dunlap, J.S.	138
Dunlap, S. R.	135
Dunlop, _____	113
Dunn, A.	48
Dunn, Peter	113
Dunn, Russel	50
Dunn, Thomas	135
Dunn, William B.	202
Dunn, William H.	113
Dunnire, Jacob	163
Dunnisch, Theodore	202
Dunson, John	113
Dunton, David A.	113
Dupruy, Hugh	113
Durand, John	113
Durant, Geo	91
Durean, J. G.	4
Durham, Abraham	113
Durixs, C. L.	138
Durm, Berry	138
Dusenbuy, Henry	113
Dusseldorf, Peter	113
Dutn, John	217
Duxburry, J.	53
Dwol, August	177
Dwyer, Charles	215
Dwyer, Philip	8
Dyarnett, _____	98
Dye, Abel	113
Dye, Lewis	113
Dye, Thomas	202
Dye, William	65
Dyer, Fred'k	79
Dyer, H. D.	113
Dyer, John N.	202
Dyer, Leroy	202
Dykeman, Michael	104
Dykenan, Martin	113
Dymond, George	114
Eames, John E.	114
Earl, James D.	202
Earl, William H.	202

Earl. George	202
Early, Edward	114
Early, H. T.	130
Early, Silas D.	142
Eastman, Chas. A.	101
Eastman, D.	114
Eastman, Dwight	114
Easton, C.B.	26
Easton, John	100
Eastwood, Cysus	16
Eaton, F.	101
Eaton, H. C.	104
Eaton, Horato D	18
Eaven, George A.	135
Ecker, John J.	163
Eckert, _____	145
Eckhert, H.	135
Eckler, Peter	98
Eddy, J.	114
Edenholm, Carl J.	183
Edgan, George M.	217
Edgar, L..G.	79
Edgeworth, Robert L.	63
Edmonds, Reuben	202
Edmonds, Servatus	202
Edmund, James II	114
Edson, Alonzo	143
Edson, L. D.	104
Edwards, E. H.	98
Edwards, Isaac J.	98
Edwards, John	132
Edwards, John H.	130
Edwards, Thomas D.	130
Edwards, William	87
Edwards. Marion	24
Egan, Edward	170
Egelston, Seneca J.	191
Eggleston, Abraham	114
Eggling, Christ	161
Egh-e-jar	3
Egnocheck, Andy P.	202
Ehler, Israel	114

Ehler, Julius	114
Ehrgood, John H.	163
Eicklin, John	114
Eigleston, Jno.	91
Eikius, Peter	41
Eiseman, George	65
Eisenhut, Jacob	63
Elam, Charles	46
Eldridge, C.L.	29
Eldridge, David	130
Eldridge, John W.	114
Eldridge, Lewis	101
Eldridge, Solomon	114
Elert, George	163
Elia, Lizzie	79
Elin, Charles	163
Elkery, Henry	114
Elkine, Freeman	104
Elkins, Nathan	202
Ellard, George	114
Ellenberger, Charles	18
Ellenwood, Frank	114
Ellerty, J.	98
Ellige, William	98
Elliot, Joseph C.	145
Elliot, P.	132
Elliot, Thomas	143
Elliott, Cortes	202
Elliott, Ezekiel	114
Elliott, Henry	163
Elliott, J. T.	130
Elliott, Joel H.	37
Elliott, John	202
Elliott, L. B.	114
Elliott, Lewis	166
Elliott, Mary	31
Ellis, Daniel	114
Ellis, H.	114
Ellis, Henry	114
Ellis, Hiram	114
Ellis, Hiram W.	59
Ellis, J.	139

Ellis, John	21	Erslee_____	114
Ellis, Samuel	114	Erving, David	145
Ellis, Wm	50	Ervings, Johnson	163
Ellison, C.	79	Esaac, Frederick	98
Ellsworth, Henry S.	53	Esbach, J. W.	135
Ellsworth, James B.	18	Eskew, Henry	98
Ellsworth, Sylvester	132	Estabrook, Sanford T.	154
Ellverson, E.	143	Estis, John M.	130
Elmer, Henry	114	Etzold, John H.	145
Elmore, J.	130	Eubank, Wm.	31
Elton, Washington	191	Eugene, Max	53
Eltz, Frederick	79	Eugle, Frank	177
Elwood, _____	163	Eus____, Jacob	177
Emerson, Charles F.	172	Eusworth, John	18
Emerson, John	114	Euwer, S.B.	202
Emerson, Samuel	104	Evan, George	114
Emery, M. A.	114	Evan, Jay	138
Eminghiser, Samuel	202	Evans, E.	163
Emmeroth, Peter	101	Evans, Geo.	91
Emmerson, Joseph	145	Evans, James	114
Emmitt, James	202	Evans, John II	114
Emory, Robert	174	Evans, W.	114
Emory, W.H.	53	Evans, Wesley	114
Emory, William	114	Evans, William	132
Encell, Joseph	166	Evans, William D.	114
Endsall, Frank	202	Evans, William M.	114
Enenger, R.	114	Everett, Henry	161
Engham, John M.	114	Everett, Thomas	179
Engle, Gustave	65	Everett, Wm. W.	87
Engle, Paterson	202	Everly, Martha	79
Engles, Charles M.	114	Everts, Harvey	114
English, William	63	Evitts, Joseph	24
Ennis, John	166	Ewing, Joesph	202
Enright, David	114	Eye, Andy	114
Entry, Isaac	135	F.H.	57
Erhardt, Fred E.	186	F__nch, George	58
Erhardt, Wm. F.	31	Fadden, Isaac	114
Ericksin, Louis M.	46	Fadron, William H.	114
Ernest, Anthony W.	105	Fagan, Michael	61
Ernest, Samuel	114	Fagan, Michael	114
Ernstein, Ernest	114	Fahren, John D.	114
Erskine, John	101	Fair, H. H.	98

Name	Page	Name	Page
Fairbanks, Chas. H.	103	Feeter, Stephen	104
Fairbanks, Cyrus	143	Feeterle, E.	79
Fairbanks, Lafayette	114	Fell, Joesph W.	202
Fairbee, Samuel	202	Fellhaur, Ed.	217
Fairchild, Addison	114	Fellman, Phinneas	114
Fairman, James A.	114	Felons, John C.	95
Fallure, Jas.	31	Felton, Frederick	98
Fanning, Thomas M.	98	Fennen, Irwin	191
Farbull, William	217	Fennen, William	191
Faren, W'm. P.	222	Fenno, James A.	58
Farewell, Francis M.	142	Fenton, William	132
Farley, Andrew J.	202	Fera, C.F.	79
Farley, Christian	187	Ferguson, George A.	130
Farley, Lewis	46	Ferguson, John	170
Farllng, E.J.	31	Ferrill, Chester	114
Farmer, John L.	138	Ferris, Thomas H.	179
Farmer, Daniel	114	Ferry, Orlon E.	114
Farmer, William F.	97	Fetra, Jeremiah	103
Farnham, Frank	184	Few, M. D.	131
Farr, George C.	114	Fibay, John W.	143
Farrand, James	65	Fidgett, Oswald	139
Farrar, G.W.	21	Fiefer, Frank	114
Farrell, Ellen	145	Fieg, Henry	114
Farrell, Patrick	114	Field, Charles B.	114
Farrell, Richard	65	Field, Janet Geraldin	31
Farrell, Wm	8	Fieldman, Wm.	94
Farrington, Henry	103	Fields, Henry	114
Farrington, John	102	Figee, James	114
Fass, Jacob	142	Filbery, Albert	41
Fastell, Charles	114	Filder, Chester G.	100
Faushear, Wilson	202	Fileson, George	98
Faust, Jacob	130	Filmore, Willston	41
Faxon, William H,H,	202	Finch, Daniel	114
Fay, Charles	39	Finch, Eugene	114
Fay, Frederick	114	Finch, Francis	114
Fay, Issac	166	Finch, Henry	160
Fay, T.	195	Finckle, August	65
Fay, W. M.	114	Finckler, Lewis	114
Fayette, James A.	139	Fink, H.B.	187
Feague, Rufus II	114	Fink, J.E.	79
Feay, C.F.	79	Finlayson, Henry	114
Fedden, Stephen	138	Finley, Anthony	135

Finley, Jeremiah	65
Finn,	79
Finnerty, John	114
Finnig, Rich'd	31
Fires, J.P.	60
Firth, Thomas J.	135
Firtzgerald, Owen	114
Fish, Dan E.	155
Fish, John	145
Fish, Leo M.	48
Fish, Mary J.	79
Fishborne, Wm.	12
Fisher, _____	114
Fisher, Charles	50
Fisher, Chas.	60
Fisher, Chas. A.B.	4
Fisher, D.	186
Fisher, George	135
Fisher, George	195
Fisher, H.S.	202
Fisher, J.W.	53
Fisher, Jacob	46
Fisher, James	158
Fisher, John	158
Fisher, Lewis	114
Fisher, Lulu	79
Fisher, Reuben	104
Fisher, Richard	6
Fisher, S. J.	26
Fisher, U. W.	100
Fisher, William H,	202
Fisher, William M.	100
Fisher, Wm.	194
Fisk, Erastus	135
Fisk, James	79
Fitts, Richard B.	114
Fitzgerald, Jas.	12
Fitzgerald, Richard	12
Fitzgerald, Wm.	186
Fitzpatrick, Hugh	114
Fitzpatrick, James	222
Fitzpatrick, Thomas	37
Fitzsimmons, John	94
Flagg, Samuel	114
Flagge, John	114
Flaharity, Porter	163
Flaherty, Daniel	94
Flaherty, Patrick	114
Flanagan, B.	135
Flanagan, Jeremiah	61
Fland, John D.	114
Flecheger, Jacob	177
Fleck,David	145
Flemer, John	98
Fleming, II. J.	115
Fleming, J. E.	95
Fleming, John	46
Fleming, John	115
Fleming, Will	7
Flemming, John	202
Flems, Henry	132
Flesher, Hamden	202
Fletcher, Charles	142
Fletcher, Delbut	115
Fletcher, William	132
Flickinger, Andrew	145
Flinn, John	222
Flood, John	115
Flookner, John	132
Florian, W.M.	35
Flower, Franklin	138
Flowers, William H.	91
Floyd, Robert	98
Floyd, William	46
Flue, Arthur	115
Fluhart, William B.	115
Flynn, James	115
Flynn, Michael	61
Flynn, Michael	161
Flynn, Thomas	145
Flynn, Thos.	79
Flynn,Edward	115
Fmraman, Jerry R.	179
Foary, J. A.	104

Fober, Francis	107		Forresti, Samuel C.	115
Fogarly, M.J.	146		Forstell, Charles	115
Fogarty, Bartley	115		Forster, George M.	115
Fogarty, George T.	146		Forsyth, James	24
Fogarty, George T. (Jr)	146		Forth, John W.	202
Fogarty, John M.	146		Fosen, J.A.	155
Fogerty, Emma	146		Foser, William	103
Fogg, Geo. K.	101		Foss, Charles	115
Fogle, William	138		Foss, Daniel	143
Fogles, N.	135		Fossnacht, Samuel B.	135
Fogurty, Patrick	177		Foster, C.	115
Folbrook, William	115		Foster, Charles	135
Folder, Robert	115		Foster, Charles A.	50
Foley, J.	115		Foster, Columbus	217
Foley, John	65		Foster, Edward C.	115
Foley, Owen	115		Foster, G. W.	101
Folger, Henry	101		Foster, George	179
Folger, James	51		Foster, Joseph	46
Folk, John , Jr	191		Foster, Richard	202
Follett, Edward	104		Foster, Rufus	100
Folsom, Ephraim P.	102		Foster, Thomas	26
Foote, Henry M.	202		Fought, Noah	202
Foote, S. II	115		Fought, Simon	132
Forbes, Edna Hulda	183		Foulk, Stephen	20
Ford, Andrew J.	146		Fouts, William	79
Ford, Cornelius	146		Fowler, George	91
Ford, Dwight	115		Fowler, S. H.	132
Ford, F.G.D.	202		Fox, Abner	202
Ford, James	139		Fox, Cyrus	80
Ford, Joseph E.	132		Fox, E. J.	96
Ford, L.	115		Fox, Herman	115
Ford, Milan H.	163		Fox, Jacob	163
Ford, Thomas	115		Fox, James	174
Foreman, Joesph M.	202		Fox, Jno.	187
Forest, Samuel	115		Fox, Lorenzo	139
Forhaity, Martin	115		Foyle, T. W.	101
Forkes, George W.	104		Fraim, Miller	163
Forlet, H.	135		Fraiton, William	97
Forney, David	146		Fran, John	170
Fornoy, Sammel	166		Francis, George	8
Forrest, Frank	177		Francis, J.H.	53
Forrest, J. A.	79		Francis, John A.	115

Francis, Joseph	103
Frank Dennis	16
Frank, Geo.	53
Frank, John	106
Frank, R. C.	115
Frankenfield, Leonard	24
Franklin, Charles	115
Franklin, Edward	137
Franklin, Jonathan	98
Franklin, R. L.	138
Franklin, Robert	98
Frantz, Albert H.	219
Fraser, Edwin	98
Fraser, Moser B.	24
Frass, Lewis A.	31
Frawley, James	80
Fredinian, Alley	51
Freeland, George	115
Freeman, ___	31
Freeman, Constant	146
Freeman, Horace H.	18
Freeman, James	91
Freer, Moses	115
French, David	202
French, G.Q.	53
French, Henry	168
French, Henry E.	65
French, Ina	183
French, Ira J.	115
French, James	135
Freslerbuch, Peter	115
Fressler, Ralph S.	115
Frey, James S.	115
Fricks, William W.	115
Fried, John	146
Fried, William T.	146
Frieman, John	138
Friese, Thomas	115
Frisbee, Charles	139
Fritz, J.	132
Froendall, Theodore	80
Frossney, Caspar	104
Frothbart, Ferdinand	132
Frulkner, Robert	115
Frum, Porter	202
Frye, Chas.	146
Frye, J.L.	59
Fryer, Edward	115
Fugan, Jacob	41
Fuiens, William H.	51
Fulk, Joseph	131
Fullee, Joseph P.	115
Fullen, O.	132
Fuller, Amos L.	103
Fuller, Byam	168
Fuller, George	98
Fuller, Henry W.	142
Fuller, T.P.	96
Fulller, George	139
Fulton, Geo. E.	142
Fulwider, Abner	202
Funcy, Michael	36
Funcy, Michael	36
Funk, Phlip	3
Furber, Ralph	31
Furgenson, Emanuel	146
Furlong, Ruel	50
Furner, Benjamin	101
Furnham, Thomas F.	95
Furnum, Thomas	115
Fyher, Hirman	51
Gabes, Ernst	203
Gaboiel, Jules	15
Gabriel, James	139
Gabriel, Jules	80
Gaddess, John	179
Gaffery, Thos.	80
Gage, Franklin	115
Gage, Josiah H.	115
Gainer, John	115
Gaines, Harry	41
Gaines, James	139
Gaines, Leven	41
Gale, Henry C.	80

Name	Page
Gale, John A	89
Gale, Oliver	89
Gale, William	89
Gall, Robert	115
Gallagher, Alfred	203
Gallagher, Daniel	161
Gallagher, Frank	146
Gallagher, Michael	63
Gallagher, T.	115
Gallahan, P.O.	186
Gallanher, F.	9
Gallant, J.	203
Gallinger, Frank	203
Gallman, Patrick	115
Gallman, William	115
Gallon, Charles	91
Gallon, Charles	91
Gallup, George	115
Galvan, James J.	66
Gamble, Henry C.	115
Gand, Winfried D.	197
Gangert, Dorotha	12
Ganham, Alf'd	80
Ganton, William	115
Ganvis, Julius	115
Ganzert, G.	12
Gaper, Alexander	183
Garcia, Marerlino	8
Gardiner, William	66
Gardner, Alex	191
Gardner, Caleb N.	115
Gardner, F. M.	138
Gardner, Francis	115
Gardner, Francis	203
Gardner, James	179
Gardner, Jermiah	163
Gardner, M. P.	115
Gardner, Peter	163
Gardner, W.H.	103
Gardner, William	52
Garelle, Chas. W.	161
Garing, John	115
Garr, H.	80
Garr, Pat'k	173
Garrett, Samuel	98
Garrick, Kate L.	184
Garrison, Charles	139
Garrison, Frank L.	203
Garrison, Henry	115
Garrison, Silas	163
Garrison, William H.	115
Garritt, James	115
Garroll, William	203
Garrons, Louis	80
Garrons, Louis	218
Gartham, John M.	140
Gartland, Thomas	115
Gartner, Albert T.	101
Garver, J. J.	115
Garvey, John	186
Garvin, George	21
Gary, Charles	101
Gashill, Charles	115
Gashill, Reuben	89
Gaskill, James R.	89
Gasler, Powell	115
Gass, George	146
Gass, Henry	50
Gassman, ___	183
Gates, Collinson R.	146
Gates, George	135
Gates, John	104
Gates, Lydia	146
Gates, Lydia	146
Gates, Sarah	146
Gates, William	146
Gates, Willian H.	203
Gatliffe, Benjamin	203
Gatt, Jacob	95
Gatton, W.F.	168
Gatz, John B.	163
Gaus, Christian	80
Gaus, Christian	218
Gaw, Andrew	115

Name	Page
Gay, Abner	101
Gay, N.	95
Gaylord, Albert	96
Gealy, Cyrus	135
Gear, John	98
Geary, John	115
Geary, R.	23
Geary, Wm. F.	96
Geates, Frederick	178
Geer, John	50
Geer, William H.	115
Gehenger, Alvin	115
Geho, Joesph C.	203
Geho. L.G.	203
Geiger, Lewis	115
Geile, John	186
Geiss, Adam	203
Geohegan, John	115
Geohegan, Thomas	115
George, Charles	115
George, Gustavus	203
George, John	37
George, Reuben G.	142
Georghegan, Thomas	72
Gerald, Geo. W.	101
Gerhart, John	115
German, James	115
Gerrh, J.A.	48
Geslach, Michael	135
Gesselmen, John	49
Getts, John	87
Gibbs, George T.	95
Giberson, John T.	203
Gibson, Charles	102
Gibson, H.	104
Gibson, Jacob	203
Gibson, John	203
Gibson, Stewart	203
Gibson, William	53
Gibson, William	146
Gice, E. M.	95
Gice, E. M.	95
Gice, E. M.	95
Gier, Laurnice	94
Gifford, A.	115
Gilbert, George	140
Gilbert, James	98
Gilbert, Lewis C.	203
Gilbert, William	115
Gilbert, William H.	66
Gilder, G. A.	95
Giles, Richard	142
Gilfrin, Wm. G.	163
Gilgon, Samuel P.	135
Gilienthol, Lewis	161
Gill, _____	183
Gillan, Christopher	115
Gillberg, Edw'd	80
Gillen, John	135
Gillespie, D.	132
Gillett, Edgar	115
Gillette, David C.	66
Gillette, William H.	21
Gillian, James K.	91
Gilliland, A.	138
Gilliland, Wilson S.	215
Gillman. Francis M.	203
Gilmor, George	39
Gilmore, F. W.	31
Gilmore, H. J.	142
Gipple, Henry	115
Girick, Wm.	74
Girle, William	3
Glackousaky, Frank	72
Gladden, George W.	191
Gladding, Edward	103
Glandon, Peter	146
Glaser, Lizzie	32
Glasgow, Adam (Colored)	53
Glass, Ferd.	80
Glass, Ferdinand	14
Glasson, James N.	138
Glasspot, Otto	8
Glatts, Henry	20

Name	Page	Name	Page
Glears, Henry	54	Goodloc, F.J.	26
Gleason, Dan'l	80	Goodman, Austin	143
Gleason, John	178	Goodman, Benj. F.	163
Gleason, Michael B.	115	Goodman, Peter	116
Gleason, Thomas	115	Goodman, Samuel B.	154
Glenn, Daniel P.	105	Goodrich, Charles II	116
Glenn, Frank	179	Goodwin, Abram	106
Glenn, Samuel R.	98	Goodwin, Edwin	36
Glidden, Benj. F.	101	Goodwin, G. W.	116
Glisman, Frank	41	Goodwin, Jinus	18
Gloltery, John	46	Goodwin, Samuel	101
Glover, Harrison	103	Goodyear, Joseph	116
Glover, John B.	138	Gorden, Waldmer	161
Glover, Peter	80	Gordephy, Elaezer	116
Gninert, E.D.	146	Gordon, charles	46
Gnman, Michael	46	Gordon, Daniel	116
Gobel, F.A.	146	Gordon, Gilbrt B.	203
Goble, Jno.	80	Gordon, Henry	75
Goddard, Charles	158	Gordon, James P.	116
Godfrey, Charles N.	106	Gordon, John	138
Godfrey, G.M.	16	Gordon, John S.	116
Godfrey, Mary L.	80	Gordon, Jonathan	131
Goding, G.T.	116	Gordon, Scott	106
Godskesen, Seneus	39	Gordon, W.B.	194
Godwin, Foss	105	Gordon, William	116
Goffer, Corneilus	2	Gore, Robert	80
Goforth, Wm.	116	Gorman, John	3
Gohien, Charles G.	104	Gorman, Robert	116
Going, J.B.	178	Gors, Richard	191
Golden, Pat M.	75	Gorton, George W.	21
Goldhofer, J.	60	Gosnell, Joshua	102
Goldsmith Alex.	32	Gosnell, Samuel N.	187
Goman, Maurice	215	Gosty, Felix A.	218
Gonell, Solon	116	Gough, L. J.	116
Goocll, Lewis	20	Gould, _____	116
Good, A. H.	142	Gould, Joshua	103
Good, H.	137	Gould, Luther H.	101
Good, Wm. H.	87	Gould, Luther W.	203
Goode, George W.	203	Gould, Samuel	203
Goodenow, Lyman	197	Goupp, N.	116
Gooding, Thomas	138	Gousin, P.A.	146
Goodington, G.V.	194	Gove, Geo.	101

Gowan, Martin G.	98
Gowan, San	54
Gower, Henry L.	215
Gowett, James	191
Grabill, Jacob A.	203
Grace, Samuel G.	135
Grade, August	91
Grady, J. O.	80
Grady, W. S.	131
Graeder, George	135
Graff, Charles	203
Graff, Leo	96
Graham, Charles	66
Graham, Charles	96
Graham, Henry M.	91
Graham, John F.	203
Graham, Rob't	32
Graham, William H.	135
Granger, H.W.	60
Grant, David	116
Grant, James	116
Grant, John P.	116
Grant, Theo	1
Grattan, John L.	222
Graudjeau, Frederick	176
Graver, C. L.	116
Graves, Franklin	116
Graves, James P.	116
Graves, Thomas T.	143
Graves, Wm. H.	80
Gray, Albert J.	101
Gray, Charlotte	183
Gray, Francis	140
Gray, Henry	80
Gray, J.	203
Gray, John	101
Gray, Newton	132
Gray, Silas	116
Gray, Thomas	70
Grayard, Jno.	32
Grayson, James	1
Greager, Henry	104
Greebong, Pedro	161
Greeley, Horace	140
Green, Benjamim M.	139
Green, Benjamin	140
Green, David	116
Green, Freeman	179
Green, George	41
Green, George W.	116
Green, Henry	132
Green, Henry	168
Green, Issac	203
Green, J.	174
Green, James	116
Green, James	140
Green, James	146
Green, John	46
Green, John	116
Green, Martin	131
Green, Martin V.	87
Green, Samuel	135
Green, Stephen S.	116
Green, Wlilliam H.	61
Greeno, Elias	203
Greer, James W.	203
Greer, William H.	116
Gregg, Thomas D.	20
Gregory, _____	146
Gregory, William	43
Greimsman, Henry	203
Grelen, L.G. (Mrs)	80
Grenan, John	135
Grey, Francis	101
Grey, Thomas	12
Grey, Washburn	101
Griesall, John	98
Griesber, James H.	138
Griesner, Julius	15
Griesner, Julius	80
Griffen, Patrick	66
Griffih, C.C.	35
Griffin, C.	203
Griffin, Daniel	3

Griffin, Daniel	80		Guinard, Virgil	135
Griffin, David G.	131		Guire, J.D.	80
Griffin, George W.	116		Gulick, William	146
Griffin, George H.	116		Gulleyhone, R.	187
Griffin, J.	98		Gullum, Nancy Patrici	32
Griffin, James C.	203		Guming, Lenard	163
Griffin, Maurice	178		Gunckel, George	132
Griffin, P.	146		Gunner, John	132
Griffin, Silas	138		Gunther, Jacob	94
Griffin, Thos.	101		Gunther, Jacob	94
Griffin, William	163		Gurney, Windfield	58
Griffith, F. O.	97		Gurrin, Frederick	116
Grifllth, Hugh	116		Gursmann, Wm.	96
Grimes, Alice	183		Gurtin, John J.	215
Grinstaff, Green	100		Guthrie, Joseph	186
Grist, James K	8		H____, B.E.	48
Griswold, Eugene W.	18		H____, Jno.	80
Griswold, John P.	116		H_____, C.T.	48
Grobut, Agustus	116		Habl, Richard	46
Grobut, Augustus	103		Haborn, John	135
Grocer, John C.	116		Hachell, Daniel	215
Gromer, George	98		Hacket, George H.	106
Gromer, Solomon	140		Hackney, George	18
Groms, Benj.	80		Haddo, John	72
Grooms, Edward	91		Haddox, H. M.	138
Groover, Charles	163		Hadley, Geo. F.	152
Gross, Carl	146		Hadwell, Obed	116
Gross, George H.	66		Haefeli, Jacob	146
Gross, John	116		Haffner, Michael	135
Gross, LD.N.	59		Hafner, Henry	194
Grossman, Ira	80		Hafty, Paul	2
Grossner, John	116		Hagan, Thomas	66
Grove, Absolem	116		Hagar, William	203
Grover, Dennis	101		Hageman, Otto	75
Gruaway, J.T.	26		Hagen, Michael	80
Gruber, Charles	51		Haggan, George	179
Gruber, Wm	51		Haglin, Lewis	116
Grumbles, P.B.	139		Hagner, Andrew	98
Grundy, Stephen K.	116		Hagness, Matheas	143
Grunff, Frederick	116		Hahil, C.	116
Grunger, Leonard	104		Hahn, William	116
Guard, Samuel	103		Haidt, M.L.	12

Haight, Geo.	54
Haight, T. B.	116
Hailman, Martin	80
Haines, Chas. S.	46
Haines, George W.	160
Haines, John	116
Hainz, Fred	146
Hainz, Julia	146
Hainz, Mary	146
Hair, John B.	142
Hair, W. J.	138
Halbernut, Lewis	116
Halbwachs, Lillian G.	32
Hale, August	5
Hale, Owen	72
Hale, P. P.	95
Hale, Walter W.	116
Haley, Edward	215
Haley, James C.	170
Haley, Michael	46
Haley, Michau	215
Haley, Owem	94
Haley, Owen	94
Haley, Thomas	116
Haliburton, A. G.	138
Hall, Zachariah	203
Hall, _____	183
Hall, Bushrod	203
Hall, C.H.	54
Hall, Elihu	116
Hall, Ellen	183
Hall, Frank	174
Hall, G.C.	32
Hall, George A.	135
Hall, Hiram	116
Hall, Jacob	135
Hall, John	116
Hall, John	135
Hall, John	163
Hall, John G.	116
Hall, John W.	116
Hall, Jordon C.	203
Hall, Joseph	175
Hall, Joseph T.	131
Hall, Richard	116
Hall, Weruer	61
Hall, William	116
Hall, Wm.	16
Hallack, Stephen I	161
Hallamer, John	218
Hallard, A.R.	186
Hallauer, Jno	80
Hallenbeck, William	98
Halliley, Dennis	80
Hallohun, John	12
Hallon, Charles	215
Halloran, Michael	26
Halstead, Albert Prin	16
Halt, Thomas	36
Haltin, John H.	116
Halverson, Thor.	194
Ham, George P.	116
Ham, Lewis	215
Ham, William B.	168
Hamans, James	135
Hamblin, Jesse B.	142
Hamilton, Bobby	146
Hamilton, Edw. C.	91
Hamilton, George	28
Hamilton, Henry	66
Hamilton, James	98
Hamilton, James	116
Hamilton, James	135
Hamilton, Louis M.	37
Hamilton, Samauel B.	203
Hamilton, William	32
Hamington, Thomas	218
Hamlett, Horace	143
Hamley, Louis F.	32
Hamm, Frank	32
Hammill, David	222
Hammill, William	116
Hammock, J. H.	142
Hammon, George W.	66

Hammond, A. M.	80	Hardy, Benjamin	116
Hammond, Oliver	98	Hardy, James M.	116
Hammond, Samuel W.	116	Hardy, James M.	116
Hammond, Thomas B.	10	Harford, John W.	101
Hamon, Patrick	116	Hargroff, Edmund	116
Hampton, J.	48	Harkell, Abraham	103
Hams, J.W.	203	Harkness, Darwin	104
Hamstreet, Harman L.	146	Harlow, Charles	116
Hamwood, Andrew J.	59	Harmon, B.	116
Hanagan, W.	135	Harmon, Daniel	131
Hanaway, Rob't	80	Harmon, James	98
Hand, William	116	Harmon, Johnson	135
Handel, Valentino	116	Harner, Walter	221
Handler, John	116	Harney, James V.	98
Handrahan, Patrick	203	Harrie, James	161
Hanford, C.	116	Harrigom, Q.A.	32
Hanford, Joseph	101	Harrington, A.J.	54
Hanigan, Patrick	166	Harrington, G.	102
Hanke, Ann	146	Harrington, Henry M.	66
Hanley, L.F.	32	Harrington, Horace R.	191
Hanley, Pal'k	32	Harrington, Nelson	117
Hanlon, Peter	14	Harrington, Weston	66
Hanlon, Peter	80	Harrington, William	146
Hann, William H.	203	Harrington, Wm.	158
Hanna, E. B.	116	Harris, Albert	117
Hanna, George E.	146	Harris, Benjamin	98
Hanna, Henry	116	Harris, E. J.	138
Hanna, Thomas	135	Harris, Edmund T.	204
Hannagan, Mich'l	32	Harris, George W.	179
Hannan, James	204	Harris, John	117
Hanney, John	116	Harris, John W.	204
Hanretty, Patrick	191	Harris, Lafeyette	174
Hanrey, _____	48	Harris, N.B.	117
Hanscome, T. P.	101	Harris, Walter	140
Hanson, Charles	116	Harris, William	135
Hany, Robert	51	Harris, Wm.	32
Hard, Wallace B.	191	Harrison, Cruser	117
Harding, Carpenter	116	Harrison, Josiah	146
Harding, John C.	116	Harrison, Milford	174
Harding, Theodore	116	Harrison, William	52
Hardison, J.J.	168	Harrison, William H,	66
Hardwick, H.	116	Harrley, Patrick	32

Harry, Louis A.	146	Hatch, J.S.	168
Hart, Andrew D.	140	Hatcher, Clinton	189
Hart, Charles M.	191	Hatchett, J.	46
Hart, Daniel E.	117	Haterman, William F.	61
Hart, Francis T.	96	Hatfield, George	117
Hart, Jacob	132	Hathaway, J.S.	186
Hart, John	117	Hattin, John	117
Hart, John A	168	Haudy, Charles	61
Hart, Joseph B.	117	Haufman, George	117
Hart, Patrick	146	Haugge, Louis	66
Hart, Samuel	135	Haughey, James A.	80
Hart, William H.	91	Haught, William E.	204
Hartersall, James	66	Hauser, Emil Henry	32
Hartfield, John	97	Hauser, Herman	32
Harth, M. F.	117	Hauston, Ira F.	117
Hartland, David	52	Havell, William	98
Hartley, John	204	Haven, Charles	135
Hartley, William	117	Haven, Loren	117
Hartly, Joseph	117	Havens, Egbert L.	104
Hartman, David	98	Haverstick, Amos	117
Hartman, Edwards	117	Haviland, Alfred	117
Hartman, Lewis	117	Hawkins, Charles	117
Hartness, John D.	204	Hawkins, Francis	117
Harvard, Edward	170	Hawkins, John	204
Harvey, Albert B.	204	Hawkins, Johnathan	204
Harvey, Albert G.	140	Hawkins, Jordan	174
Harvey, James	117	Hawkins, Marcy	32
Harvey, James B.	135	Hawkins, Walker	117
Harvey, Levi P.	204	Hawkins, William	117
Hashier, N. A.	132	Hawkins, William C.	117
Hasken, Richard	3	Hawks, Andrew J.	204
Haskins, Charles	117	Hawley, Abraham	154
Haskins, James D.	103	Hawley, Daniel	103
Haslmck, Augustus	6	Hawley, Edward J.	117
Hasmer, Johann	204	Hawley, Henry M.	117
Hassel, _____	147	Hawley, Horace A.	187
Hassell, John W.	131	Hawley, James	117
Hassley, John	91	Hayden, Charles	80
Hastie, John	117	Hayden, Henry	18
Hastings, Thomas	204	Hayes, A.A.	12
Hatch, Charles	5	Hayes, George	117
Hatch, George	117	Hayes, Hannibal	140

Name	Page
Hayes, Michael	117
Hayes, Nicholus	178
Hayes, William	135
Hayman, Jereman	204
Haynard, Franklin	143
Hayner, Hiram	117
Haynes, Alfred B.	147
Haynes, R.P.	168
Hays, John	117
Haywood, John P.	18
Hazard, William D.	204
Hazel, Henry	135
Hazelgrove, Andrew S.	142
Hazen, Frederick	117
Hazen, Henery E.	204
Hazer, M.	35
Head, William N.	147
Head, Washington	204
Head, William	147
Heald, William S.	117
Healy, M.	80
Healy, Thomas	117
Hearn, Melville H.	204
Heath, Charles	104
Heath, George W	80
Heath, Henry	204
Heath, John	170
Heath, W.H.	80
Heath, William H.	66
Heathcote, Theo	196
Heaton, Robert	147
Heday, Francis	117
Hedges, W. W.	117
Heen, A.	117
Heenan, Hugh	103
Heff, Jacob	57
Hegeman, H.	117
Heindle, Jay	159
Heinemann, John C.	197
Heintz, B.E.	12
Heiser, Thos. R.	46
Heller, Elias	132
Heller, Elias	132
Hellison, Julius	117
Helm, A. J.	131
Helm, Benjamin	179
Helm, John	66
Helmer, Thomas	191
Helminger, C.	117
Helton, Alfred	131
Helwig, Phillip	204
Hemer, Samuel	98
Hendermott, Jeremiah	117
Henderson, James	80
Henderson, John	46
Henderson, John	66
Henderson, John	91
Henderson, John	117
Henderson, Sykes	66
Henderson, W.H.	12
Hendrick, Moses B.	98
Hendrick, Peter	132
Hendricks, Jas J.	98
Hendricks, M.	97
Hener, Guelph	135
Henhoefer, alexander	91
Henion, John	147
Henke, Charles	147
Henkle, George	204
Henley, Charles C.	138
Henneck, Jas. W.	103
Henner, Charles II	117
Hennessy, Mathew	117
Henning, Mortimer	191
Hennison, _____	131
Henrick, George O.	135
Henry, Levy	117
Henry, James	204
Henry, James F.	204
Henry, Lewis	105
Hensey, Henry W.	204
Henshaw, George W.	117
Henson, W. B.	131
Hentzer, J. B.	135

Herberger, John	147
Herberger, John	191
Hercher, Oliver	147
Herforth, Wm.	32
Herline, Alonzo	74
Herman, Christ.	161
Herman, Frans	215
Herr, John	163
Herrhammer, Andrew	204
Herrick, Geo. W.	163
Herrin, John	91
Herring, Charles	25
Herring, Levi	135
Hersman, Perry	204
Hertzog, Godfrey	117
Herzing, ___	183
Hesaton, Semer C.	40
Hescott, Benjamin	117
Hesse, Harmon	117
Hesselstine, Follen	117
Hetsimer, Adam	66
Hettmgan, Jacob	117
Hewiett, Samuel	117
Hewitt, Lorenzo	163
Hewlings, Nyent	89
Hewliu, Wm.	25
Heywood, Bradley	176
Hian, Elijah (Colored)	26
Hibband, John	8
Hickey, William B.	132
Hickman, James W.	135
Hicks, A.B.	188
Hicks, E.	117
Hicks, Jacob A.	95
Hickson, Thomas	135
Hieber, William	66
Higgins, Daniel	204
Higgins, William	36
Higgins, William	91
Highland, James	81
Highterver, J.F.	81
Hikle, Jared B.	9
Hild, George	106
Hildreth, Norris	61
Hiler, Jonathan	135
Hiley, John	66
Hill, Amos	91
Hill, Amos B.	215
Hill, Anthony	3
Hill, Benjamin	117
Hill, Benjamin F.	117
Hill, C. C.	104
Hill, Charles	179
Hill, Elenor	117
Hill, Frank	142
Hill, Henry	140
Hill, J. A.	138
Hill, James	54
Hill, James	117
Hill, James	135
Hill, Jehu	142
Hill, Jesse	131
Hill, W. H.	105
Hill, William	46
Hill, William	117
Hiller, Nicholas	117
Hilliard, George H.	104
Hillier, William	147
Hilliker, Ellis R.	117
Hillis, Charles	191
Hillman, ___	104
Hillman, Daniel	117
Hillock, B.	117
Hills, Albert M.	18
Hillson, David F.	16
Himpson, Samuel	139
Hincher, George	117
Hinckley, Rudolph	117
Hindelong, Albert	117
Hindman, David	30
Hindman, John	29
Hine, Charles	132
Hines, A.G.	81
Hines, William	15

Hines, Wm.	81		Holifield, Gotthold	10
Hinkler, Wm	195		Holland, Auther G.	170
Hinley, John E	87		Holland, Issac	204
Hins, William g.	117		Hollenbock, Henry	117
Hinsworth, Henry	20		Hollenfield, Jacob	138
Hinsworth, Thomas	20		Hollerfield, Joseph	98
Hintze, John	117		Holley, Charles S.,	204
Hinze, Wm.	81		Holley, Ester Mae	32
Hirsch, Levi	135		Holley, William	117
Hitchhen, Daniel	101		Hollinger, E. W.	135
Hitherton, Edward H.	135		Hollingsworth, W__	97
Hizelberger, Joseph	54		Hollis, Frank	3
Hleole, _____	48		Hollis, H.P.	48
Hoag, Judson	117		Hollister, James D.	143
Hoagg. J.H.	204		Holmer, Julius	75
Hoard, Lorenzo	117		Holmes, Charles	3
Hobbe, Geo. T.	152		Holmes, Clarence	118
Hockersmith, George	100		Holmes, Desato	24
Hodges, A.	131		Holmes, Dewis	61
Hodgson, Benjamin (II)	75		Holmes, George	118
Hodgson, George A.	117		Holmes, H. P.	101
Hodgton, Henry C.	106		Holmes, Henry	135
Hodston, Hannibal	105		Holmes, James F.	179
Hoerle, Bernard	21		Holmes, Jonoas	54
Hoffman, _____	95		Holmes, Katherine	32
Hoffman, _____	117		Holmes, Laura	147
Hoffman, Charles	54		Holmes, Robert	118
Hoffman, D.	166		Holmes, Thomas	10
Hoffman, Lewis	132		Holmsley, Randolph L.	9
Hoffman, Peter	204		Holse, Charles	54
Hofner, Henry	117		Holsensberger, John	118
Hogan, J.A.	188		Holt, Armstead	32
Hogan, Michael	63		Holt, Henry C.	142
Hogan, Walker K.	142		Holt, Henry H.	118
Hoge, Henry H.	135		Holt, James	135
Hogebloom, David L.	21		Holt, Norman F.	135
Hoke, Francis	166		Holtzman, William	21
Holbrook, W.A.	103		Holway, Theodore	8
Holcher, John J.	179		Holycross, _____	32
Holcomb, Edward P.	66		Hommall, Daniel	218
Holcomb, Seymour	117		Honner, Dennis	118
Holfride, F.	147		Honse, William	18

Hooges, ___	183		Houtz, Joesph	204
Hooker, Casfer	147		Hovan, Jessie	147
Hooker, George	176		How, David H.	191
Hooker, John	147		Howard, ___ zo	32
Hooker, Samuel	147		Howard, Chas.	32
Hooker, William H.	204		Howard, George W.	118
Hooley, John	147		Howard, Henry	103
Hooper, Conelius	174		Howard, J. C.	131
Hooper, Franz	147		Howard, Joseph Edward	32
Hooper, William H.	140		Howard, M.	118
Hooting, Jesse	140		Howard, Tom	39
Hoover, John W.	204		Howard, William	118
Hope, John	12		Howard, Wilson	140
Hopkins, Charles	118		Howe, Charles	147
Hoppenhoff. ___	106		Howe, Henry H.	101
Hopper, Edward	104		Howe, Orren W.	118
Horan, John	147		Howeit, John	184
Horan, P.	118		Howell, George	66
Hordling, C. T.	118		Howell, Henry B.	118
Horle, Agustus	118		Howell, James	2
Horlem, Joseph	140		Howell, James	8
Horn, C. L.	118		Howell, John	191
Horn, Caleb	135		Howell, Kedar	118
Horn, Marion E.	66		Howell, W. M.	131
Hornby, Adam	118		Howerth, James	16
Horner, James	132		Hoyard, Michael	12
Horsman, James	132		Hoyh, E.	16
Horton, J.F.	25		Hoyt, Alex. D.	147
Horton, James	9		Hoyt, Edward	191
Horton, James t.	204		Hubachu, Jacob	118
Hosack, Willie W.	183		Hubbard, Francis	118
Hosey, John	3		Hubbard, George M. C.	101
Hosffle, Theodore	14		Hubbard, T.W.	9
Hoster, Samuel	135		Hubbard, Thomas	101
Hough, John M.	118		Hubby, Chester S.	178
Hough, John M.	135		Huber, Charles	147
Houghtaling, A. B.	118		Hubertson, ___	140
Houghtaling, Chas. H.	15		Huck, Francis	164
House, Israel W.	98		Huckbone, W.I.	147
House, Reason	204		Hudspetts, J. J.	106
Householder, Reuben	204		Huff, David A.	156
Houston, Samuel	54		Huffman, M.	132

Huffman, Robert	218	Huntington, Geo. W.	187
Hufletin, Elijah S	21	Huntsman, J. C.	135
Hugam, David J.	118	Huntsman, Josiah	160
Hugely, Argine	81	Huntziger, Eugene	196
Huggins, J.C.L.	54	Hurbert, Edgar	118
Huggins, John	135	Hurdick, George	72
Huggins, W. M.	98	Hurley, James	81
Hughes, _____	91	Hurley, John	26
Hughes, Anthony	95	Hurley, Timonthy	94
Hughes, Edward	164	Hurst, Charles	143
Hughes, Francis T.	66	Hurt, Josh.	57
Hughes, J.	60	Husk, John E.	204
Hughes, James	81	Husker, Leander	98
Hughes, James	118	Hutchings, George	101
Hughes, James Allen	32	Hutchins, Abel W.	91
Hughes, John	138	Hutchins, J.H.	188
Hughes, Martha	147	Hutchins, Thomas	140
Hughes, Martin	101	Hutchinson, ___	81
Hughes, Robert H.	66	Hutchinson, Orville	118
Hughes, Wesley	140	Hutchinson, V.A.A.	81
Hughs, John	147	Hutchison, Blanche	81
Hulbert, Chester A.	104	Hute, Charles	138
Hulett, George	140	Hute, J. M.	138
Hull, Grahame	16	Hutten, Wm. H.	32
Hull, Jacob	164	Hutton, James	204
Hull, John D.	118	Hyatt, Wm.	16
Hull, Marion	54	Hyde, Freeman	118
Hull, William C.	135	Hyde, William	204
Hulse, Peter	87	Hydlems, Joseph	140
Hulsey, Henry W.	118	Hyke, J. H. or Isaac	118
Hulsinger, _____	118	Hyland, Charles	118
Humes, David M.	91	Hyland, Michael	178
Humphrey, A. M.	98	Hyler, John	147
Humphrey, J. J.	95	Hyman, _____	57
Humphries, NJ	46	Hynes, John	147
Hund, William	118	Ibwin, Basgom G.	81
Hungerford, Robert B.	104	Iliff, James	205
Hunker, John C.	118	Ilsoone, T.B.	43
Hunt, James	81	Imboden, Eli	98
Hunt, Jonathan	118	Inabimet, Archibald	138
Hunt, William B.	118	Indian Child	32
Hunt, William S.	204	Indian, Billy	96

Name	Page
Ingalls, David	118
Ingason, Cyrus	164
Ingersoll, Albert	118
Ingerson, Frederick	118
Ingle, Almon	135
Ingle, William	135
Ingraham, A.	118
Ingrall, Robert L.	133
Ingram, James A.	118
Ingram, Thomos	118
Ingram, V.	205
Ingrass, Hardin	41
Inho, George W.	51
Inine, Francis	205
Inman, Nathan	118
Innman, Samuel	155
Ireezerling, Peter	156
Ireland, William	191
Irey, Cryus	205
Irish, Alonzo	105
Irvin, Joseph	164
Irving, A.	131
Irving, Farbrothe	118
Irving, John	72
Isabelle, Frederick	205
Ivens, Elizabeth G.	147
Iynde, Henry	52
J.T.F.	147
Jackson, Abraham	96
Jackson, Abram	180
Jackson, Anthony	180
Jackson, Charles	140
Jackson, Cyrus J.	133
Jackson, E.D.	118
Jackson, Edward	140
Jackson, Geo. W.	98
Jackson, George	140
Jackson, H.G.	48
Jackson, Isaac	168
Jackson, Jacob	118
Jackson, James	140
Jackson, James	143
Jackson, Jasper	159
Jackson, Joel P.	97
Jackson, John	140
Jackson, Joseph	219
Jackson, Nathaniel N.	25
Jackson, Owen	118
Jackson, Snuih	180
Jackson, Texter	172
Jackson, Thomas	118
Jackson, Thomas	140
Jackson, Thomton	41
Jackson, W.	171
Jackson, William	140
Jackson, William M.	168
Jaco, Wm.	57
Jacobs, Alexander R.	205
Jacobs, Joseph	191
Jacobs, William	170
Jacoy, R.	205
Jacquette, A.	118
Jacquith, George W.	118
Jager, Peter	140
Jagger, Daniel	118
Jagger, Franklin	18
Jahlbug, Dennis	218
James, Alonzo L.	164
James, Henry	52
James, Thomas	43
James, William B.	66
James, William H.	118
Jamison, J.H.	133
Jamison, John L.	18
Jamison, John R.	133
Jamison, Wm. W.	118
Janney, Parley	118
Jaques, Arnold	118
Jarboe, L.C.	29
Jarrard, Thomas	52
Jaylond, Alphonzo	133
Jbery, M.	171
Jeffers, C.	118
Jeffers, Philip	118

Jefferson, George C.	137	Johnson, Dorsey	180
Jeffery, W.	186	Johnson, Edwin	104
Jefferys, Melker M.	205	Johnson, Edwin	118
Jeffrey, Thomas M.	168	Johnson, Fleet	131
Jenings, Alb't	32	Johnson, Frederick W.	147
Jenkins, _____	131	Johnson, George	140
Jenkins, Hiram	101	Johnson, George W.	191
Jenkins, L	81	Johnson, H.	9
Jenkzer, Walter Kendi	74	Johnson, Henry	140
Jennan, George	96	Johnson, Israel M.	33
Jenner, Edward B.	118	Johnson, J.	118
Jennings, _____	183	Johnson, J.	147
Jennings, George W.	140	Johnson, J. J.	218
Jennings, Harry	32	Johnson, J.B.	205
Jennings, John	154	Johnson, Jacob	205
Jennings, _____	147	Johnson, James	180
Jenny, Johann	205	Johnson, Jerome	118
Jergb, Ewil	178	Johnson, John	104
Jern, Robert F.	147	Johnson, John	118
Jerrard, John	164	Johnson, John	137
Jeune, Lot	104	Johnson, John D	168
Jobbins, _____	205	Johnson, John F	154
John , _____	7	Johnson, John K.	20
John, Henry C.	205	Johnson, John W.	135
John, Thomas	46	Johnson, Joseph	72
Johnson,	32	Johnson, Joseph	118
Johnson, ___	32	Johnson, Joseph H.	38
Johnson, Alfred	140	Johnson, Mark	104
Johnson, Almond	81	Johnson, Michael	168
Johnson, Amos	180	Johnson, Murdoch D.	138
Johnson, Andrew H.	191	Johnson, Nicholas	118
Johnson, Augustus	140	Johnson, Oliver	180
Johnson, C.	140	Johnson, Peter	81
Johnson, Charles	46	Johnson, Richard	7
Johnson, Charles	87	Johnson, Ruliff	118
Johnson, Charles H.	205	Johnson, S. A.	142
Johnson, Charles L.	140	Johnson, Samuel	118
Johnson, David	98	Johnson, Stephen	118
Johnson, David	118	Johnson, Stephen	131
Johnson, David	180	Johnson, Sylvester	140
Johnson, Davin	98	Johnson, Thomas	98
Johnson, Diggs	140	Johnson, Thomas	107

Johnson, Thomas	140	Jones, Joseph	43
Johnson, Thomas	184	Jones, Julien D.	75
Johnson, Thomas H.	205	Jones, L.T.	118
Johnson, Thomas N.	98	Jones, Martin	119
Johnson, Thos. M.	170	Jones, Mary	12
Johnson, W.	118	Jones, Michael	140
Johnson, W.M.	91	Jones, Richard	205
Johnson, William	118	Jones, Robert	142
Johnson, Wm.	186	Jones, Seth	164
Johnston, Abraham	140	Jones, Thomas A.	33
Johnston, Edward	41	Jones, Thomas D.	104
Johnston, J.F.	81	Jones, Thos. H.	170
Johnston, John	176	Jones, Timothy W. Jon	89
Joiner, A.	168	Jones, Wilber	54
Jollprecht, Emil	195	Jones, William	119
Jolly, _____	147	Jones, William	157
Jolman, Moses B.	101	Jones, William	174
Jones, Aaron	118	Jones, William A	168
Jones, Adams	98	Jones, William C.	119
Jones, Albert	205	Jones, William W.	135
Jones, B.R.	43	Jones, Willis	98
Jones, C.J.	118	Jones, Wilson	131
Jones, C.L.	81	Jones, Wm.	57
Jones, Charles	118	Jones, Wm.	81
Jones, Charles W.	57	Jordan, Hanson	40
Jones, E.	135	Jordan, Harmon	26
Jones, Frank	147	Jordan, John J.	97
Jones, Franklin	118	Jordan, Mary Louisa	24
Jones, Fred. O.	103	Jordon, John	106
Jones, G.D.	33	Jordon, Jos	81
Jones, George	118	Jorgensen, Julius	3
Jones, George	140	Joshlyn, Joseph J.	40
Jones, George R.	191	Jost, William	81
Jones, Go.	219	Jowers, F. M.	96
Jones, Henry	81	Jowers, J. W.	138
Jones, Henry L. S.	118	Joy, Albert S.	133
Jones, John	118	Joy, Cornelius	133
Jones, John	147	Joy, D. M.	104
Jones, John	191	Juan, Antonio	106
Jones, John	205	Judd, A. C.	164
Jones, John O.	118	Judkins, Moses H.	101
Jones, John T.	140	Judson, E.W.	16

Judson, Wm	16		Keifer, George	164
Julin, Lilly Sophia	81		Keisters, G.A.	119
June, James	119		Keith, James F.	4
Junker, Joesph	46		Kelcher, James	147
Junod, August	205		Kellery, George	119
Justice, John	119		Kelley, James	36
Kadle, B.	133		Kelley, James	119
Kahn, John	61		Kelley, John	4
Kail, William H.	205		Kelley, John	98
Kaimer, Rudolph	147		Kelley, John D.	8
Kaiser, Alexander	119		Kelley, W.	205
Kalb, Samuel B.	205		Kelliher, Patrick	180
Kaley, Joh G.	87		Kellinger, Joseph	135
Kanco, Henry	119		Kellison, William	205
Kanoll, M. W.	119		Kellog, Bernard	87
Kapp, Augustus	133		Kelly, ____	183
Karberg, Andrreas P.	147		Kelly, Bernard	91
Kardison, Noah	174		Kelly, Charles F.	38
Karratt, Clawson	104		Kelly, Geo.	155
Karsy, Patrick	54		Kelly, James	220
Kartins, Teter	9		Kelly, John	8
Katon, Thomas	119		Kelly, John	41
Kavanagh, Thomas G.	66		Kelly, John	66
Keah, Wilber D.	41		Kelly, John	140
Kean, Thomas	119		Kelly, John D.	61
Kearns, A.	81		Kelly, John J.	97
Kearns, Jos.	33		Kelly, Lewis	72
Keasy, M. H.	100		Kelly, Patrick	66
Keating, James	81		Kelly, Rob't	81
Keaton, W.	54		Kelly, Robert	41
Keckyman, Frank	147		Kelly, Thamos	61
Keeb, Louis	81		Kelly, Thomas P.	6
Keefe, Irvin H.	142		Kelly, Wille	12
Keefer, Barney	81		Kelly, William J.	205
Keeffee, Maurice	2		Kelly, Wm.	155
Keeler, C.B.	12		Kelly,W. F.	104
Keely, Silas M.	119		Kelsey, Abram	119
Keenan, John	119		Kelsey, Edward	46
Keeney, John	215		Kelsey, James	81
Keeny, Sampson	131		Kelton, Joh V.	12
Kegby, William	142		Kemble, Nathaniel	119
Keichaels, K.	49		Kemler, Martin	205

Kemp, Charles J.	119		Keyser, William	133
Kemp, Sam'l	33		Kglin, R.A.	49
Kemple, Jacob	98		Khaupp, Frank	72
Kendall, Charlotte	147		Khiner, ____	81
Kendall, William	148		Kidstenbach, M.	119
Kendell, Eli R.	205		Kiefe, Maurice	8
Kenedy, W.	205		Kierman, James	216
Kenedy, Walter	37		Kiffer, James	119
Kennedy, F.	119		Kihok, Richard	41
Kennedy, George	98		Kilborn, Walter	148
Kennedy, John	22		Kile, Joseph W.	61
Kennedy, John	148		Killen, Malachi	12
Kennedy, Patrick	97		Killgannon, John	205
Kennedy, Robert	43		Kimbal, W.C.	166
Kenney, John	119		Kimball, J.B.	107
Kenney, Thos. S.	43		Kimball, Moses F.	101
Kenny, David	119		Kimsden, Evier	104
Kenny, Michael	66		King, ____	221
Kenshaw, Jacob	143		King, Alex	33
Kent, Charles	119		King, Alexander	119
Kent, Charles F.	119		King, Anthony H.	98
Kent, John W.	191		King, Burt	175
Kent, Peter	205		King, Charles S.	119
Kenuy, A.	119		King, Chas.	81
Kenwood, A.C.	35		King, Edgar	143
Kenzie, Nathan	119		King, Francis	148
Keogh, Myles W.	66		King, George H.	119
Keough, Peter	119		King, Henry W.	119
Kernen, John	159		King, James	216
Kerns, Enoch B.	135		King, John	66
Kerr, William	46		King, Joseph H.	36
Kerris, Th. E.	54		King, Frank	184
Kerschum, Jacob	119		King, Lewis	140
Kertlein, Fred	135		King, Lysander	133
Kesner, ____	81		King, M.	97
Kesse, Thomas	135		King, Moses P.	119
Ketryn, Joseph II	119		King, Peter	6
Key, L.E.	35		King, Samuel L.	5
Keyes, John W.	164		King, Thomas J.	95
Keys, ____	183		King, Willard H.	205
Keyser, Gustovo	2		Kingerland, Isaac	119
Keyser, William	96		Kingon, Jab. W.	166

Kinnear, John	205		Knight, Thomas C.	131
Kinney, Sandford	180		Knisely, Robert Lee,	205
Kinny, Solon	205		Knisley, George W.	205
Kinpon, Horace A.	119		Knoble, Kaspan	143
Kinsch, Charles	36		Knoll, William	180
Kinsell, Michael	148		Knost, John	52
Kinsley, Benjamin	135		Knotts, Franklin	205
Kinsley, Dennis	92		Knotts, William Truma	205
Kirby, D.	25		Knowles, George	4
Kirby, Thomas	216		Knox, Wm.	101
Kirchan, Julius	119		Kober, William	42
Kircher, J.	105		Koch, D.	102
Kirkbridge, Joseph B.	216		Kohler, Joseph	72
Kirkpatrick, Henry	136		Kohrig, Martin	166
Kirkpatrick, Wm.	98		Koltzbucher, Henry	75
Kirmi, John E	136		Koppe, Franz	170
Kirrney, Isaac	46		Korchesky, Alexander	119
Kishpaugh, William B.	107		Korn, J. A.	138
Kisor, Charles R.	205		Kowan, James	205
Kitchen, A.B.	119		Kraesuer, Charles	42
Kitchen, W.M.	81		Krager, Frederick	191
Kittle, William H.	205		Kraichill, Isaac	133
Kivglen, Fradinick	178		Kramer, David	136
Klein, Gustave	66		Kramer, Henry	164
Klies, John	63		Kramer, William	66
Klightou, James C.	178		Kransanbrink, William	131
Klimbeck, James	12		Krantz, John	164
Kline, George	136		Krapp, H.A.	222
Kline, Thomas A.	119		Krause, Ferdinand	206
Klinger, Nicholas	205		Kreger, Daniel B.	136
Klink, Fred	46		Krell, William	119
Klippl, Adam	2		Kreps, Jacob	136
Kmilck, Charles W.	176		Kriser, Christian	46
Knadesville, Forest	46		Krohn, J.M.	81
Knapp, Charles E. II	119		Kroose, T. V.	196
Knapp, Michael	16		Krueger, Paul	25
Knapp, Rufus	205		Kruge, Josiah	164
Knauth, Herman	66		Kruses, D	49
Knecht, Andy	66		Kubler, John	119
Knickerbocker, Chas.	119		Kufham, William H.	131
Knight, Jonathan	119		Kuhn, Daniel	54
Knight, Joshua	119		Kuley, Joh D.	2

Kulmer, G.	119		Landis, John	143
Kunze, Solomon	136		Landon, Darius	206
Kuster, Martin	119		Landrells, James P.	119
Kutzer, James	133		Landrum, John H.	12
Kyndiay, Isael	2		Lane, Benjamin W.	143
Kyte, _____	148		Lane, C.C.	26
L .T. A.	49		Lang, A. W.	142
L____, W.	12		Lang, Agustus	176
L_____mmson, A.C.	60		Lang, Charles	119
Labor, Dones	42		Langbeag, James	143
LaBounsy, Ira	54		Lange, A. L.	106
Lachenal, Andrew	54		Langwood, George	119
Lacombe, Ernest	3		Lanigan, Mary	26
Lafayette, John	119		Lankeu, John	42
Laflan, Albert	119		Lansdorph, Sergeant	119
Laforge, James	92		Lantrop, William	142
Lagelarrer, Albert	148		Lapham, Jonathan	119
Lagenbauer, Gustau W.	148		Lapham, Simon	119
Lahan, Edward	50		Lapoint, Peter	119
Lahnosenle, U.	9		Lapworth, Andrew	191
Lahon, W. M.	119		Lareny, Anderson	36
Laib, Fred. M.	161		Larisch, Richard	216
Laied, John D.	81		Larrimer, John R.	12
Lajorge, John	54		Larry, Daniel	140
Lake, George W.	119		Larsern, Earnst	25
Lamb, Matthew W.	98		Larson, Christian M.	218
Lambert, David	164		Larue, James W.	136
Lambert, Frederick W.	119		Lasell, John A.	119
Lambert, J.	119		Lasell, Nace A.	218
Lambra, John	119		Lasen, Henry	81
Lamka, Edward	119		Lather, Andrew J.	206
Lamont, Thomas	101		Lathrop, Benjamin	119
Lamore, Frank A.	119		Laubach, William S.	136
Lampburg, W.	54		Laueaeyghe, ___	33
Lampman, Peter	105		Laughlin, Th.	54
Lamure, Alphonso	54		Laughlin, William	22
Lanahan, John	33		Lauhoef, August	1
Lancaster, Ezra G.	103		Launders, Edward	58
Lancaster, L. L.	140		Laur., Ephraim	27
Lancaster, Thomas	119		Laurie, John D.	18
Lancton, David	119		Lavarn, Wm. H.	51
Landers, William	206		Lavill, Francis A.	218

Law, Woodward P.	20		Leham, Henry	66
Lawler, Michael	46		Lehman, Frederick	66
Lawlin, James	72		Lehman, N.B.	61
Lawrence, A.	60		Leib, Lewis	120
Lawrence, Edward	119		Leickering, Henry	206
Lawrence, J.	103		Leighty, Roy C.	81
Lawrence, J. L.	97		Lell, George	75
Lawsden, John	95		Lellen, C.B.	81
Lawson, John	119		LeMarquis, Charles A.	8
Lawson, William	119		Lemereaux, S. H.	136
Lawton, Eugene	164		Lemoin, Henry	132
Lawvenger, Oswald	119		Lemon, William	142
Layet, Paul	218		Lenerd, Levi	120
Laywell, Milton C.	206		Lenhart, Paul	100
Lealey, E.M.	42		Lens, Peter	98
Leaman, Thomas H.	187		Leonard, Charles G.	120
Learik, Zacharias	50		Leonard, G.E.	103
Leary, D.	12		Leonard, Jacob	196
Leary, Daniel	119		Leonard, James	103
Leary, Michael	136		Leonard, Joseph	120
Leasure, John	119		Leonard, Martin	148
Leavitt, Sylvester	119		Leonard, Orville	105
Lebel, Joel	6		Leonard, Patrick	148
Ledford, _____	119		Leonard, Peter	120
Lee, Charles	119		Leonard, William	120
Lee, Edward	33		Leonare, Hiram	12
Lee, Geg.	159		Leoy, James	54
Lee, Henry	136		Lerock, William H.	67
Lee, James	33		LeRoy, Eugene	46
Lee, James	119		Lescohier, Frederick	206
Lee, Jerome	140		Lesslon, William	3
Lee, John	8		Lester, George	136
Lee, Michael	206		Letson, J. W.	120
Lee, S.W.	168		Letun, Alexander	10
Lee, William H.	140		Leukel, Wm.	15
Lee, William W.	119		Leunel, Wm.	82
Leeds, Alexander	206		Levee, James	100
Leep, Charles	206		Levey, B. F.	120
Lefrey, F.W.	51		Levi, Barney	120
Leftwich, Wm. L.	29		Levings, Jeremiah	120
Leggih, Robert	42		Levington, J.	49
Legnon, Frank	46		Lew, Jimri	172

Lewellen, John C.	206
Lewis, Abraham	120
Lewis, Charles	120
Lewis, Frank	120
Lewis, George	82
Lewis, Giles B.	98
Lewis, H.E.	222
Lewis, Hart	164
Lewis, Henry	206
Lewis, John	67
Lewis, John C.	136
Lewis, Peter	120
Lhalon, Edward	186
Libbett, Oliver P.	98
Lickleter, Nicholas	206
Liddiard, Herod	67
Liddiard, Herod T.	75
Lieberson, Daniel	148
Liebrand, G.	136
Lieman, Werner L.	67
Liesbert, Christ.	148
Light, C. M.	142
Lightinger, David	166
Lightman, Daniel	154
Lilbaugh, Philip	143
Lillie, L.N.	106
Lillison, Daniel	101
Lilly, Patrick	16
Limpson, William	42
Linch, Joseph	2
Linco, Joseph	168
Lindan, Anthony	191
Linder, John	8
Lindsay, Edward	120
Lindsay, Fessnien	178
Lindsay, Gaff. O.	101
Lineback, Fredinand	37
Lineburner, John A.	216
Lingan, John	26
Lingfellow, Charles	136
Link, M.A.	54
Linnett, John H.	140
Linons, John H.	18
Lintern, John B.	120
Lippincott, John	89
Lisby, John	180
Lissleson, Leoan	54
List, Harrison	120
Listy, W. L.	133
Litel. Bessie M.	35
Little Brave	75
Little, Charles	133
Little, George	120
Little, Henry M.	98
Little, James H.	96
Little, Thomas	120
Little, Walter W.	26
Little, William	49
Littlefield, Catherin	148
Litton, George	142
Litz, Jacob	82
Livermore, Rawson	105
Livingston, Henry	105
Lizieelder, Alvin G.	82
Llewellen, Jacob	98
Lloyd, Charles	140
Lloyd, Edward W.	67
Lloyd, Julia H.	82
Lnyon, Thomas	148
Lobdell, Isaac	120
Lobering, Louis	67
Lock, Issac	206
Lock, Nelinzy L.	206
Lock, Wm.	206
Lockie, George	206
Lockwood, Stephen D.	148
Loewe, Nicholas	120
Loffin, Rufus	51
Logan, E. C.	106
Logan, John	42
Logan, John	216
Logan, Newton	136
Logan, R. J.	98
Logan, Richard	187

Logan, William	63		Lowber, S. B.	142
Logue, David	164		Lowe, Anna M	148
Loir, Peter	206		Lowell, James	155
Long, George B.	106		Lowell, Joseph	120
Long, Henry	120		Lowell, Wm. H.	101
Long, John	92		Lownsberry, John W.	105
Long, Wm. C.	57		Lowton, Charles	54
Long, Wm. R.	43		Lruax, Joesph R.	89
Longe, Joseph E.	120		Lsockson, L.R.	54
Longer, Carl	106		Ltein, John	61
Longer, Samuel	102		Lteinmetz, ___	183
Longuar, E.	120		Luadsurrtl, Joseph	154
Longworth, Jackson	133		Luarin, George H.	51
Lonnins, Timothy	218		Lubeck, H.E.	13
Loolam, Henry	54		Lucas, C.	140
Loomis William T.	18		Lucas, Clinton J.	18
Loomis, Richard	180		Lucas, Isaac J.	82
Looney, Richard	218		Luck, Peter	148
Looney, William H.	120		Luckey, Bemjiman	206
Loop, B. F.	120		Luckins, Daniel C.	206
Loop, John A.	206		Lucksinger, ___	82
Loper, Lutheran	120		Ludwig, Albert	136
Lopert, Thomas C.	100		Luerro, Vivian	5
Lord, Francis	216		Luffand, Jacob	120
Lord, Francis G.	106		Luke, Thomas	176
Lord, J.M.	103		Lull, E.P.	120
Lord, M. W.	120		Lunday, James	138
Lorentz, George	75		Lundy, Elias J.	197
Lorenz, Martin	120		Lundy, James	120
Loreys, Peter	72		Lung, John	43
Loring, Andrew	106		Lurouch, William S.	120
Losee, James	105		Lusk, James	180
Lossee, William A.	67		Luskins, James	101
Lothes, John	206		Lust, Hiram II	120
Louress, Andrew	120		Lustig, Carol	82
Lovejoy, James W.	206		Lutkin, David H.	120
Lovel, Lewis	159		Lutton, George	61
Lovelady, Samuel D.	98		Lutz, Frederic	82
Loveland, Edward L.	103		Lutz, George	42
Lovett, Patrick	22		Lveick, T. A.	28
Low, A.S.	82		Lybe, S. A.	142
Low, Peter	216		Lyce, Daniel F.	3

Lydeck, Eli P.	136
Lyman, Daniel	38
Lyman, James C.	120
Lyman, S. H.	120
Lynch, ___	82
Lynch, Benjamin D.	38
Lynch, Benoni P.	38
Lynch, Geo. E.	142
Lynch, James	206
Lynch, John A.	178
Lynch, Michael	3
Lynch, Patrick	33
Lynch, Patrick	61
Lynch, Thos.	96
Lyons, B.M.	82
Lyons, J.E. M.	120
Lyons, Joh G.	166
Lyons, R.	140
Lytlebrand, Charles	120
Maban, Alexander	120
Mabu, Michael	154
Mack, Clark A.	120
Mack, James	98
Mack, James H.	140
Mack, Tsbias	97
Mackay, James H.	24
Mackey, William	133
Mackie, John W.	120
Macklemry, B. C.	136
Macom, George	5
Macomber, ___	5
Macomber, Lorenzo S.	82
Macon, Miles C.	188
Macy, Charles	51
Madden, Aaron W.	164
Madden, Thomas	120
Maddox, Samuel	82
Madison, George M.	120
Madsen, Anders	82
Madsen, Christian	67
Magan, W. C.	136
Mager, C. H.	133
Magill, John L.	206
Magnam, A.L.	25
Magor, George	164
Magrine, Adeline	148
Maguin, John D.	14
Maguire, P.	148
Mahan, John	74
Mahan, William	120
Mahedy, E.F.	82
Maher, M.	120
Maher, Timothy	156
Mahew, G.W.	120
Mahon, Michael	120
Mahon, Milton	164
Mahoney, Bartholomew	67
Mahoney, Dennis J.	82
Mahoney, John	59
Mailard, Anthony	218
Maine, C.	120
Mains, Herd. S.	101
Mairin, Lee	120
Maker, ___	82
Malcahy, William	103
Malford, Albert	120
Mallatt, Chas.	82
Malley, Edward C.	206
Mallory, John	13
Malon, Henry	120
Malone, B.H.	172
Malone, Jno	35
Malone, Richard	120
Malone, Wilber D.	206
Malone, William	206
Maloney, Jeremiah	22
Maloney, Peter A.	5
Maloney, Thomas	216
Malony, Daniel	136
Maloy, John	43
Maloy, Wellington	120
Malson, William E.	133
Maltby, Warren	164
Mammeur, John	164

Mandvellie, ___	18		Marsh, James	186
Manfred, Jenkins	164		Marshall, Joseph	140
Maning, John B.	148		Marshall, Nathan	180
Manker, C.A.	82		Marshall, Seth	133
Mann, Jesse	140		Marsings, Robert	131
Mann, C. D.	131		Marte, Jas.	82
Mann, Frank C.	75		Martell, Richard E.	105
Mann, James	148		Martin, Augustus	39
Mann, James	191		Martin, B. E.	96
Mann, P.	206		Martin, Christopher	120
Manning, Andrew	22		Martin, Christopher	148
Manning, James	67		Martin, Daniel	174
Manning, Martin	103		Martin, Edward	206
Manning, Thomas	43		Martin, Frederick	120
Manning, Wallace	168		Martin, Frederick	120
Mansfield, Charles	13		Martin, George	206
Mansfield, David	120		Martin, Hamilton M.	120
Mansfield, David B.	16		Martin, James	1
Mansfield, Royal	120		Martin, James	75
Mansfield, Stephen	136		Martin, James	120
Mansfield, T.	13		Martin, John	120
Mansfield, William L.	120		Martin, John	157
Manther, A.	206		Martin, John	180
Mantz, Gottieb	63		Martin, John J.	120
Mantz, Wm.	16		Martin, John S.	168
Many, Leazu G.	154		Martin, Logan	29
Mapes, John	133		Martin, Michael	72
Mapes, Selah	120		Martin, Peter	92
Maple, F.	171		Martin, Shadruck	180
Mapp, Soloman	180		Martin, Thomas	155
Maquire, Peter	46		Martin, William	206
March, C.	120		Martin, William H.	63
March, Isaac	120		Martin, Zeb	120
Mardorf, Wilhelm	82		Martindale, Charles A	72
Mares, William C.	82		Marton, Thomas	148
Marginson, John	29		Marvin, Calvin	105
Marks, Geo	194		Mascey, C.	171
Marquaet, Charles	120		Masherson, John	54
Marquet, George	22		Mason, ___	82
Marsh, Edmund N.	120		Mason, ___	36
Marsh, George H.	18		Mason, Annie	33
Marsh, James	42		Mason, Elvin P.	120

Mason, Geo. H.	103	Maxwell, Thomas E.	67
Mason, George F.	216	May, D.W.	24
Mason, Harr	178	May, Edward	121
Mason, Henry S.	67	May, James	121
Mason, John H.	180	May, William	206
Mason, L.	120	May, William H.	142
Mason, Rose T.	184	Maybee, Moses	121
Masser, Christian	105	Maybrook, Geo.	82
Massey, Dawson	3	Maybrook, George	15
Massey, John	136	Mayer, Gustavo	36
Massey, R. B.	131	Maynard, Gustavus	192
Massey, Wm. A.	216	Maynard, James L.	92
Master, Walter P.	120	Mayo, Peter	170
Matchkath, Gotlieb	120	Mayu, John	222
Mathews, E.	120	Maze, George Jr.	206
Mathews, James	92	McAdam, William N.	121
Mathews, James	96	McAdoo, Major	33
Mathews, James	120	McAllister, J.A.	82
Mathews, William	172	McAllister, Patrick	157
Mathey, Robert	136	McAllister, Wreman	61
Mathison, Fritz	148	McAlliston, W.	121
Mathlenesen, Ludwig	82	McAnanay, Peter	206
Mathrop, Sherman	176	McAtee, Richard H.	206
Matlick, William H.	206	McBride, John	178
Matoon, E.H.	120	McBride, Michael	13
Matott, A	22	McBride, Patrick	121
Matterson, Stillman	120	McBride, W.	121
Matthews, David N.	172	McBride, W.	121
Matthews, Elias	173	McBride, W.	148
Matthews, Henry C.	206	McBryer, Solomon	49
Matthews, William	173	McCabe, Alexander	121
Matthis, Thomas	138	McCabe, Pat'k	82
Mattox, R. F.	142	McCabe, W.	60
Maury, James	54	McCafferey, Daniel	63
Mautthews, Henry	154	McCafferty, James H.	100
Maxim, James	121	McCall, A.	102
Maxon, Richard	97	McCamen, Michael	152
Maxwell, Henry	156	McCandles, J,E,	207
Maxwell, Jacob C.	166	McCandlish, Alex	121
Maxwell, James	121	McCann, Austin	142
Maxwell, John B.	206	McCann, Jacob	207
Maxwell, Samuel	121	McCann, James	121

McCann, John	207
McCanner, William	82
McCardle, James	121
McCarlin, Hugh	216
McCart, James M.	98
McCarthy, Charlrs	67
McCarthy, Daniel	13
McCarthy, George S.	207
McCarthy, Michael	142
McCarthy, Patrick	106
McCartney, Jno.	92
McCarty, C.	121
McCarty, Parick	121
McCarty, Thomas B.	133
McCasey, Benjamin	37
McCasky, James	136
McCaslin, John G.	121
McCauley, Frank	16
McCauley, Jho.	17
McCauly, Mary	33
McCauu, Bernard	72
McCay, Daniel	207
McClanahan, John	105
McClane, Gilbert	166
McClave, John	98
McClay, Thomas	184
McClellan, _____	148
McClemen, Hugh	136
McClernan, John	37
McClosky, Francis	121
McClug, James	143
McClure, F.	196
McClure, H.	121
McClure, Samuel C.	106
McCoglan, John	148
McCole, Daniel	101
McCollen, J. B.	133
McCollister, John W.	92
McCollum, Thomas	207
McComb, Edward	174
McComber, Lyman	121
McConnell, James	136
McConnell, John	121
McConnell, R. T.	97
McCooly, ___	61
McCord, Joshua	207
McCorkle, Charles M.	207
McCormick, C.	148
McCormick, Chas.	148
McCorquadale, Malcolm	168
McCoughel, Charles	121
McCoy, John H.	121
McCoy, William T.	207
McCraby, John	24
McCraig, George	121
McCrann, Jas. H.	106
McCreany, Frank	6
McCrist, John	136
McCue, Edward	121
McCue, Patrick	24
McCullough, J. C.	105
McCune, Barnabus C.	207
McCune, Henry P.	35
McCunn, Dennis	121
McCurry, Edward	13
McCurry, H. S.	138
McCurthy, Daniel	13
McCurvey,, T.W.	168
McCuster, John K.	136
McDaniel, Daniel	121
McDaniel, John	207
McDaniels, F.L.	54
McDaniels, John	192
McDermond, L.	136
McDermott, A. H.	95
McDermott, Edward	121
McDermott, Geo.	72
McDermott, John	101
McDill, Robert	133
McDivitt, John	207
McDonald, Abraham	207
McDonald, Alexander	10
McDonald, Bosswell	33
McDonald, charles	13

McDonald, D.	101
McDonald, D.	121
McDonald, George	82
McDonald, J.	133
McDonald, John	133
McDonald, John	178
McDonald, John	186
McDonald, John A.	36
McDonald, John C.	131
McDonald, Joseph	121
McDonald, Milo	192
McDonald, Samuel	101
McDonell, James	36
McDongal, Stephen	101
McDonnald, John	121
McDonoly, Michael	121
McDougal, F.D.	197
McDougle, Enos E.	207
McDowell, Andrew	140
McDowell, David C.	142
McDowell, J.D.	207
McDowell, James Kerr	121
McDowell, L.	13
McDowell, William	131
McEachern, Alexxander	3
McElery, Daniel	121
McElroy, Thomas	67
McElwain, B. W.	121
McEntyre, Martin	207
McEuroll, Thomas	197
McEvony, M. D.	121
McFadden, James L.	207
McFall, George	121
McFarland, Dugand	121
McFarland, John D.	101
McFarland, Pete	87
McFarland, William	148
McFee, David	133
McFolin, Asberry	207
McFurley, James C.	121
McGarley, G.	106
McGarr, D.	121
McGee, James	140
McGee, Joseph	29
McGee, Patrick	133
McGhee ____	82
McGill, George .	207
McGill, Henry	54
McGill, John	131
McGill, William H.	207
McGillis, James	121
McGin, James	54
McGinnis, Harry L.	216
McGinnis, John C.	207
McGinnis, John J.	75
McGis, Owen	216
McGllvary, F.	207
McGlocklin, Joseph	140
McGony, Barney	121
McGovern, Chas.	194
McGovern, W. H.	121
McGowan, Wm.	82
McGrade, Jerry	103
McGraih, Maiheu	216
McGrath, Thomas	148
McGrath, James	121
McGrath, John	8
McGraue, Bernard	156
McGraw, Michael	136
McGraw, William	121
McGregor, Richard	121
McGruger, John	218
McGucker, ____	67
McGue, Peter	67
McGuire, James	63
McGuire, John	3
McGuire, John	121
McGuire, John H.	17
McGuire, Michael	121
McGuire, Patrick	103
McGuire, W.	54
McHarley, Daniel	95
McHarrison, Robert	152
McHenry, A.	106

McHenry, Charles	98		McLauyhillus, Erasunn	219
McHenry, James A.	121		McLellan, William	121
McHugh, John	61		Mcleoy, Charles	159
McHugh, John	148		McLorin, U.	121
McHugh, Thomas	148		McMahon, Andrew	42
McIlhargey, Archibald	67		McMahon, Edward	121
McInleer, Christopher	121		McMahon, J.	121
McIntire, H.	22		McMahon, James	170
McIntosh, Donald	75		McMahon, John	74
McIntyre, Charles L.	10		McMahon, John	148
McIntyre, J.	121		McMahon, Michael	121
McIntyre, James	5		McMahon, Patrick	61
McIntyre, John	121		McMilledge, Robert	166
McIntyre, Samuel	73		McMillin, John W.	82
McIntyre, Thomas	52		McMorrow, James	6
McIntyre, William	148		McMullen, Daniel	121
McIsaac, Daniel	136		McMullin, Joseph	136
McJenkin, J. S.	136		McNally, Ed	46
McKay, Reuben	121		McNamara, Thomas	121
McKay, Robert	218		McNanny, Owen	10
McKay, Robt	82		McNeal, Dudley	207
McKealy, James	106		McNee, T.	57
McKellop, James	148		McNeil, E. R.	133
McKelsey, Monroe	148		McNeil, Fred	33
McKelvey, Edm'd B.	36		McNeill, Alexander	20
McKenna, Geo.	82		McNulty, Chas.	222
McKenna, Patrick	136		MCNulty, John	222
McKenny, John	121		McNulty, Patrick	159
McKenzie, Hardy T.	97		McNutt, John H.	98
McKenzie, John R.	82		McOwen, B.	121
McKeon, _____	148		McPhee, Angus	92
McKeon, Charles	148		McPhelan, Samuel	106
McKeron, Patrick	2		McPherson, Alex.	13
McKetheand, J.	131		McPherson, George	121
McKienan, E.	107		McPherson, Wright	98
McKiester, Joseph	136		McQuaque, A.	168
McKinney, Samuel	121		McQuinn, Owen	121
McKinny, Alenerin	207		McReynolds, John	133
McKrnzio, John	218		McRielty, Samuel	96
McLaughlin	148		McSwain, Henry	36
McLaughlin, John	176		McSweeny, Mitchell	121
McLaughlin, Thomas	106		McTaugh, John	121

McTye, Michael	121		Mercer, Harry	37
McVey, Daniel	133		Merchael, Sylvanus C.	121
McViear, William	131		Meridith, Oswall	121
McWhorter, Henry	207		Meridith, William	148
McWillen, Leo	216		Merill, Loring	218
McWilliams, J.	121		Mernagh, Michael	82
McWilliams, John	207		Merrech, John	137
Mead, Francis	121		Merrick, John	133
Mead, John B	28		Merrick, Rob't	83
Meades, Samuel	148		Merrifield, Samuel	100
Meador, Thomas B.	75		Merrill, John	121
Meaghen, Daniel	170		Merrill, Loring	83
Meahau, Charles	62		Merrill, Miner	101
Mecum, William	121		Merrill, Thomas J.	13
Medare, Joseph	107		Merriman, Campbell	164
Mederal, D. E.	106		Merritt, Alfred	140
Medlin, Francis	96		Merritt, David	122
Meehan, Joseph	92		Merritt, David	122
Meek, John A.	207		Merryman, J.D.	207
Meeks, Lafayette	188		Merryweather, Anderson	180
Megher, James	121		Mertins, Jacob	149
Meglie, James	82		Metcalf, Gloster	207
Mehwaldt, Charles G.	192		Metcalf, William	207
Meier, Frederick	67		Mettler, J.H.	98
Meier, William	178		Mettler, Jrank J. (sic)	207
Meigs, John H.	143		Mewell, Hudson	142
Meilke, Max	73		Meyer, Albert H.	67
Meine, Amos	98		Meyer, August	67
Meiser, James	207		Meyer, August	207
Meitzel, Conrad	94		Meyer, Herman	122
Meitzler, Francis	121		Meyer, Theodore	192
Melburn, George E.	121		Meyer, William D.	76
Meldon, John	222		Meyers, Edward F.	83
Mellville, ____	121		Meyers, William	180
Meltack, Henry	136		Mich____, Zina	101
Menan, Daniel	24		Michan, And'w	33
Mench, S.	207		Mick, Walter	207
Mender, Lamhel B.	51		Mickel, W. A.	96
Meneely, Wm. A	15		Micku, Peter	54
Meng, Philip	121		Middleton, H.P.	131
Menia, John	136		Midlaugh, Stewart D.	122
Mentz, W. W.	121		Migh, William	184

Miles, Edwin	2		Miller, Simon	219
Miles, Gilbert	131		Miller, Ward	149
Miles, James	122		Miller, William	42
Miles, James W.	98		Miller, William	122
Millam, Christian	122		Miller, William	192
Millard, Johu J.	143		Miller, William H.	122
Millen, Mot.	23		Miller, Wm. M.	87
Miller, Adam	207		Milles, Jame	177
Miller, Andrew	156		Milligan, Robert	133
Miller, Caleb	122		Milligan, William	37
Miller, Carl	96		Millon, James	3
Miller, Charles	122		Mills, Edward	92
Miller, Chistopher	186		Mills, Floyd	96
Miller, Conrad	52		Mills, Henry	216
Miller, Dan'l	92		Mills, J.R.	60
Miller, Daniel	136		Mills, Madison	149
Miller, Daniel H.	83		Mills, William	24
Miller, Edw.	89		Millsiau__, Miller	154
Miller, F.	122		Milton, Francis E.	67
Miller, Frank	94		Milton, Robert	100
Miller, Frank	140		Miltowe, Hutchinson	149
Miller, Fred K.	13		Minard, Henry	140
Miller, G. C.	122		Miner, Joseph	122
Miller, George W.	207		Miner, Joseph	122
Miller, H.J.	207		Ming, Philip	133
Miller, Henry	20		Minnes, Joseph	122
Miller, Henry	42		Minnuns, Wm. H.	59
Miller, Henry	180		Minor, Charles W.	122
Miller, Herman	140		Minor, Levi J.	208
Miller, Jacob	13		Mis___tucitt	33
Miller, Jacob S.	46		Mitcheal, Beng.	51
Miller, James	136		Mitchel, John W.	131
Miller, John	67		Mitchell, _____	101
Miller, John	122		Mitchell, Alfred	122
Miller, John	207		Mitchell, E.	83
Miller, Joseph	122		Mitchell, Edward	122
Miller, Levi	98		Mitchell, Henry	122
Miller, Melehier	153		Mitchell, Henry	122
Miller, Melvin	207		Mitchell, Isaac N.	98
Miller, P.W.	54		Mitchell, John	67
Miller, R.A.	83		Mitchell, John S.	180
Miller, Samuel	207		Mitchell, Joseph	168

Mitchell, T.	140
Mitchell, Thos.	186
Mitchell, William L.	97
Mitchler, Henry	13
Miughes, John	94
Miur, Jacob	216
Mlooney, Lawrence	161
Moan, John	208
Moats, George W.	208
Mocline, E.F.	35
MoCue, _____	164
Modeny, John	101
Modinger, Wm.	33
Modlin, _____	149
Moeging, Wm. C.	17
Moffat, William	140
Moffitt, J.T.	194
Moftitt, Aaron	96
Moiole, Richard W.	43
Molcott, Vicar	122
Molitor, John	218
Moll, John A.	218
Moll, Louis W.	170
Monaghan, Frank F.	221
Monaghau, Michael	156
Monahan, Michael	24
Monahan, Millie	13
Monay, James	122
Monch, Hans Peter	122
Monday, C.	136
Monehousr, E.	54
Monelthori, Horace	133
Monle, Richard W.	43
Monohiff, Ann	149
Monroe, Joseph	67
Monsod, James	122
Monson, M.	122
Montague, J.	13
Montague, James	13
Montanye, Washington	54
Montgomery, Frank	6
Montgomery, J.O.	83
Montgomery, Robert I.	208
Montgomery, William	131
Moock, James A.	136
Moodel, Stephen	106
Moody, _____	122
Moody, H. C.	101
Moody, William	76
Mooly, Thomas	5
Moon, Benj.D.	10
Moon, William	122
Mooney, Daniel C.	136
Mooney, Patrick	152
Moonie, George A.	67
Moore, Alex	51
Moore, Alexander	149
Moore, Amos	105
Moore, Andrew J.	76
Moore, Andrew N.	92
Moore, Benjamin F.	122
Moore, Carlos T.	98
Moore, Charles	122
Moore, Daniel	208
Moore, Edward A.	122
Moore, Ephraim	101
Moore, Gabriel E.	138
Moore, George	136
Moore, George F.	98
Moore, George W.	122
Moore, Harry De. W.	161
Moore, Henry	33
Moore, Henry C.	106
Moore, James	122
Moore, James	208
Moore, James E	17
Moore, John	122
Moore, John	149
Moore, John A.	149
Moore, L. R.	122
Moore, Moses	208
Moore, Orlando	122
Moore, Rebulon	43
Moore, Stephen	122

Moore, Thomas	140	Morris, Theodore	17
Moore, W.	54	Morris, William	122
Moore, William G.	192	Morris, William	133
Moore, Wilson	208	Morrison, Angust	138
Moorehead, Phillip	83	Morrison, Ann E. L.	149
Moorman, Stephen	98	Morrison, Daniel H.	101
Moral, Phillip	208	Morrison, Douglas	149
Moran, J. T.	122	Morrison, Franklin E.	192
Moran, Milo	192	Morrison, George	170
Moran, Thomas Joesph	208	Morrison, J.	149
Morarit, John	131	Morrison, Jane	149
Morasey, James	192	Morrison, Norman	62
Moray, Philip	122	Morrison, Peter	122
Mordise, Nelson	140	Morriss, George C.	67
Moreau, Peter	122	Morrissey, Michael	149
Morel, John	122	Morrissy, George	122
Morell, Frederick	208	Morse, Albert	52
Morey, Ira	106	Morse, James	122
Morey, Ira F.	39	Morton, Benjamin	140
Morey, W.H.	83	Morton, E. D.	122
Morgan, Alfred	98	Morton, Eddie	185
Morgan, D.	23	Morton, Frank A.	46
Morgan, Dennis	166	Morton, G.	83
Morgan, Geo. E.	59	Morton, Gilbert	52
Morgan, John	180	Morton, Thomas	87
Morgan, Levi	105	Morwig, ____	83
Morgan, Maralou	33	Morwig, Fred'k	83
Morgan, Patrick	122	Morwig, L.	83
Morgan, Peley	51	Moses, Joshua	92
Morley, James	122	Moses, Wheeton	17
Morris, Amos	17	Mosher, Aaron	105
Morris, David	83	Mosier, Alason	22
Morris, Elias	149	Mosier, Martin F.	122
Morris, Francis W.	152	Mossey, Jepther	92
Morris, James	122	Mosu, Henry	33
Morris, James	136	Mott, Geo. E.	89
Morris, John	36	Mott, J.	98
Morris, John	46	Mott, Sylvanus	105
Morris, Lewis	122	Moule, Henry A.	122
Morris, Moore	83	Moulton, William H	122
Morris, Moore	218	Mount, Henry	133
Morris, Robert T.	131	Mowber, Aaron	140

Mowery, Alvarado	22		Murphy, Martin	192
Moyer, A.	105		Murphy, Michael	46
Moyers, William A.	208		Murphy, Michael	122
Mremu, Joseph	46		Murphy, Thomas	218
Muches, John	180		Murphy, W.F.	33
Mucker, Viola	33		Murphy, Wm.	83
Mudgett, Frank	2		Murray, ___	83
Mudgett, Frank	8		Murray, Beverly	140
Mueller, Oswald	122		Murray, Daniel	122
Mulcahy, T.F.	33		Murray, David	122
Muldoon, Barney	25		Murray, Enos	174
Mulhen, Ada E.	183		Murray, John	83
Mulhen, Joseph	183		Murray, John	100
Mulholland, J.	13		Murray, Michael	142
Mulkey, Barton	29		Murray, Thomas	149
Mulkey, Bejamin	29		Murray, Thomas	216
Mull, J. H.	97		Murray, Walter	222
Mullane, J.E.	194		Murray, William II	122
Mullen, Hugh	55		Murrell, Thos. J.	208
Mullen, James	208		Musgeire, Jonathan J.	98
Muller, William	83		Muteay, John	83
Muller, William	149		Myer, J. H.	138
Mulligan, Edward	122		Myerhalt, ___	122
Mumehy, W. S.	186		Myers, Carson	37
Mumique, Mathas	186		Myers, George W.	98
Munday, Gordon	140		Myers, Harrison	208
Munroe, Duncan	168		Myers, Henry	208
Munsey, Geo. F.	106		Myers, Herman	83
Munson, Warren	50		Myers, James	136
Murdoch, J. C.	131		Myers, John	37
Murdoch, James	97		Myers, Peter	122
Murley, Patrick	222		Mynard, Norman	122
Murley, James	208		Naley, George	107
Murman, G.	8		Naner, Rudolph	164
Murphey, Wesley	101		Narper, ___	183
Murphy, Daniel	122		Nash, Edward E.	58
Murphy, Enoch E.	138		Nash, John A.	36
Murphy, J. M.	122		Nash, O.	122
Murphy, James	122		Nash, W. H.	133
Murphy, James	143		Natyke, William	122
Murphy, John	122		Nay, Horace	122
Murphy, Jonathan	208		Neal, Andrew D.	208

Neal, Arthur	122		Newton, Orville	122
Neal, E. V.	122		Nibert, James M.	208
Neal, Henry	74		Nicholas, Chas. L.	101
Neal, Robert	122		Nicholas, James	122
Neal, William	208		Nichols, A. A.	122
Neely, George	92		Nichols, Benjamin	122
Neff, G.W.	208		Nichols, Joseph	105
Negis, william	92		Nichols, L.A.	103
Nehl, Joseph A	36		Nichols, Wm. W.	18
Nehnardt, August E.	83		Nicholson, James	136
Neidner, Frederick	92		Nicholson, James W.	208
Neil, Jeff J.	42		Nicholson, T.M.	155
Neil, John F.	103		Nick, John	98
Neill, John O.	10		Niebuhr, Gustaw	33
Neland, James	149		Niel, James II	123
Nelman, John A.	136		Nieman, Frederick	208
Nelson, George	87		Nilan, Thomas	123
Nelson, John	216		Niles, Albert H.	18
Nelson, Jono.D.	25		Niles, Geo. W.	106
Nelson, Otto	57		Niles, Loyd ,	164
Nelson, Th.	55		Niles, Lucien J.	192
Nelson, Wm. R.	173		Nix, Angevine	123
Nesmith, C.E.	46		Nixon, James	6
Ness, William	102		Noarks, George	133
Neuber, George	140		Noble, Christ.	149
Neville, Robert	136		Noble, Hiram	18
Nevins, Alexander	140		Noble, William L.	123
Newby, William	140		Nobler, James	208
Newcomb, Benjamin	122		Noeduch, Henry	208
Newcomb, Seth P.	122		Nohles, Johu P.	70
Newell, H. G.	122		Nolan, Annie M.	183
Newell, George W.	122		Nolan, James	123
Newham, Rudolph	33		Nolan, Matthew	83
Newland, Alfred M.	122		Nolan, Nicholas	94
Newman, Benjamin	136		Nolan, Palmer	46
Newman, George	122		Nolan, Thomas	4
Newman, Harry	170		Noland, H.J.	103
Newman, James	83		Nolen, James	6
Newport, F.H.	103		Nolitor, Jno.	83
Newton, A.S.	83		Nolly, Owen	123
Newton, H.O.F.	58		Noonan, Patrick	123
Newton, John	142		Noonan, William	149

Norcop, Joseph D.	102		O'Bryan, John	67
Norman, John	123		O'Connel, Tim	33
Norrell, Joseph W.	106		O'Connell, Daniel	83
Norris, Charles	97		O'Connell, David J.	67
Norris, Horace	142		O'Connell, John	55
Norris, J.L.	152		O'Connell, Patrick	98
Northing, John	123		O'Connell, Patrick	138
Northrup, Lewis	105		O'Conner, Dominick	63
Northrup, William B.	105		O'Conner, Patrick	67
Norton, Edmond	102		O'Connor, William H.	221
Norton, G. H.	83		O'Day, Michael	3
Norwood, Joseph, J.	131		O'Donell, Daniel	208
Noshang, Jacob	67		O'Donnell, Joesph	43
Notson, Etla Cara	183		O'Donnell, Nicholas	43
Notson, Otis	183		O'Grady, John	220
Nowell, J. H.	131		O'Hara John	83
Nowlan, Daniel	149		O'Hara, Michael	96
Noze, C. II	123		O'Hara, Miles F.	76
Nuchews, Fred. W.	51		O'Haran, Parick	123
Nulte, Conrad	52		O'Laughlin, Michael	24
Nursey, Frederick	67		O'Neal, Anges	83
Nutter, Lewis	123		O'Neil, James	103
Nutter, Lewis	123		O'Neil, James J.	74
Nye, Adam	123		O'Neill, Edward	164
O'Bourke, Patrick	222		O'Neill, Henry	70
O'Brain, Willis	208		O'Niel, John	123
O'Brian, ____	178		O'Riley, Patrick	14
O'Brian, A.E.	60		O'Rilly, Francis	216
O'Brian, Charles	60		O'Rourke, Patrick,J.	83
O'Brian, F. John	63		O'shea, Thomas	8
O'Brian, Richard	161		Ockners, Frederick	98
O'Brien, J.	83		Oerthel, Andrew	208
O'Brien, J.	218		Ogden, John H.	123
O'Brien, James	6		Ogden, John S.	67
O'Brien, James	173		Ogle, J. H.	123
O'Brien, John	123		Okey, James S.	208
O'Brien, John G.	188		Olcott, George	133
O'Brien, John O.	123		Oldenheinze, Albert	123
O'Brien, Lucius	186		Oldham, Walter S.	58
O'Brien, Martin	24		Olds, Alfred S.	192
O'Brien, William	103		Olembad, Philo	123
O'Bryan, Albert	164		Olevica, P. D.	100

Oliff, George	123		Overfelt, Robert	142
Oliver, Fred	149		Overtt, Abijah	92
Oliver, James	123		Oveutt, Lowell	58
Oliver, James	123		Owen, Leverelt B.	19
Oliver, Q.W.	23		Owen, William H.	131
Oliver, Robert	98		Owens, A. P.	96
Oliver, William A.	19		Owens, E.	123
Oliver, Winfred	149		Owens, Edward W.	123
Ollis, John	87		Owens, George	55
Ollyses, S. Henry	153		Owens, J.M.	13
Olmstead, Charles	123		Owens, James	140
Olmstead, Chas. S.	170		Owens, John	142
Olson, Andrew	4		Owens, W. H.	140
Olson, Edward	42		P_____, Charles F.	19
Olson, Olaf	208		P___eth, Hugh	42
Omling, Sebastian	67		Pack, Lewis	185
Orayard, Bertha	33		Packard, McKenan	161
Ormsby, James	123		Paddock, E. R.	143
Orr, Ansel	123		Page, Carlos	208
Orr, James L.	208		Page, David L.	123
Orr, R.	83		Page, Edward	63
Ortez, Rafael	180		Page, H.R.	208
Orudington, A.E.	35		Page, Moses P.	123
Osborn, David	208		Page, Theodore L.	123
Osborn, Samuel	208		Page, Wm. J.	149
Osee, Samuel J.	106		Pager, H.H.	35
Osim, Christopher	17		Paine, Ebenezer	105
Oslin, Amos	143		Paine, James F.	123
Osterburg, John	176		Palmer, Charles	59
Osterhout, Jesse	83		Palmer, Charles	123
Ostrem, A.K.	27		Palmer, James	123
Ostrom, Thomas J	123		Palmer, James	178
Otis, John	123		Palmer, Jerome	192
Ott, Frank	83		Palmer, Lorin A.	155
Ott, John	123		Palmer, M.	123
Otterby, Thos.	33		Palmer, Thomas P. W.	123
Otts, Martin	138		Palmerston, J. S.	133
Ould, Leonard	123		Palmeter, Allen	133
Ourey, Henry	143		Palsgrove, David N.	208
Ourtman, J.	140		Pameter, James	166
Outland, Milton	123		Panrocle, James	136
Ove, Chas. W.	170		Papar, Theodore	46

Name	Page
Pareno, ___	33
Parish, Jesse M.	123
Park, Elijah H.	208
Park, John	140
Park, Nicholas	136
Parker, ___	83
Parker, A.	123
Parker, C. T.	123
Parker, Enoch	89
Parker, George	106
Parker, George	123
Parker, Gustarus	7
Parker, Henry	2
Parker, Henry	42
Parker, Ira D.	105
Parker, James	43
Parker, James	123
Parker, James	138
Parker, John	67
Parker, Joseph	74
Parker, Joshua	89
Parker, Nathan	98
Parker, Nathan	140
Parker, Robert	140
Parkinson, James	136
Parks, Alexander	52
Parks, Carlas	123
Parks, George	52
Parks, Hoyt R.	102
Parks, J.C.	168
Parks, Joseph	166
Parks, Merritt W.	208
Parnick, Peter	218
Parsons, James	83
Partridge, W. H.	123
Pascher, Henry	92
Pashe, Antone	96
Passmore, Thomas G.	192
Patch, Wm.	17
Paterson, J.	123
Patrick, George	180
Patrick, J.N.	168
Patridge, William	123
Patson, Thos.	149
Patten, J. N.	123
Patterson, ___	83
Patterson, Benjamin	96
Patterson, David	136
Patterson, F.	123
Patterson, J.R.	208
Patterson, James H.	180
Patterson, N.	131
Patterson, William	149
Patton, John W.	67
Patton, Thomas	208
Paugh, Evan D.	123
Paul, James P.	19
Paul, Thos.	155
Pauls, John	123
Paulus, Jacob	177
Paxton, W.R.	209
Payne, George	123
Payne, John T.	209
Payne, William H.	63
Pazay, Joseph	123
Peak, Jerry	105
Pearce, Jeremian	136
Pearee, Arthur	123
Pearsall, Leonidas	131
Pease, John	123
Pease, Spencer A.	192
Peavey, Hollis S.	106
Peck, Alfred	123
Peck, Alpheus	123
Peck, Cornelius	55
Peck, Henry	149
Peck, Louis	156
Peckham, Henry	96
Pedley, James	123
Peet, John	123
Pegram, J. E.	96
Pegram, Julia	36
Pelit, Clinton	62
Pelks, J. D.	168

Pelly, Thos.	17	Petty, Edward	141
Pemy, Thomas	2	Pew, Oliver	171
Pendall, Benjamin Z.	105	Pfefferley, Ester T.	149
Pender, Michael	152	Phagan, Sanford	96
Pendergraph, Joshua	55	Phang, _____	171
Pennington, James	141	Phares, Jos.	187
Pennoy, William	123	Phel, Jacob	87
Pepler, C. H.	123	Phelps, David	95
Percival, Simon B.	55	Phelps, Joseph	123
Perementor, Frank	142	Phibbe, D.M.	216
Perice, George	159	Phifer, Leroy J.	209
Perkins, Charles	67	Philbrick, Wm.	13
Perkins, Erskine	94	Phillips, Alexander	107
Perkins, J.R.	13	Phillips, E. W.	142
Perkins, James W.	209	Phillips, Edgar	67
Perkins, Martin J. H.	123	Phillips, Elijah	209
Perkins, Thomas B.	102	Phillips, George	10
Perkins, William	166	Phillips, George N.	92
Permbenton, Robert	59	Phillips, James	105
Pero, John	141	Phillips, John	209
Perry, George	62	Phillips, Joseph	123
Perry, George	170	Phillips, Luther P.	9
Perry, H.B.	97	Phillips, Lyman D.	103
Perry, Jonothan	58	Phillips, Richmond	131
Perry, Louis	60	Phillips, Shedrick	123
Perry, N. E.	131	Phillips, Simeon	123
Perry, Thomas	141	Phillpott, William	209
Perry, William	51	Phipps, John	131
Perry, William	97	Pickering, Lewis	209
Persons, Alexander	123	Pier, Charles	59
Peshall, Richard M.	73	Pier, George W.	192
Peter, Elijah	96	Pierce, B.T.	149
Peterman, Ralph	123	Pierce, Henry	123
Peters, John	123	Pierce, James F.	105
Peters, Lewis	209	Pierce, Thomas	209
Peterson, John	13	Pierpoint, E.A.	209
Peterson, John	55	Pierson, Abraham C.	123
Peterson, Nathan Z.	192	Pierson, F.	102
Peterson, William	123	Pike, Irving	123
Pette, Davis	57	Pike, Meanton	38
Pettingill, James A.	123	Pildermeislie	28
Pettit, Lorenzo M.	136	Pilt, Alfred	149

Pinchard, John B.	149	Plymfrton, Joseph	149
Pinckney, James	131	Pockett, John	22
Pine, William	136	Poe, Nathan H,	209
Pinehard, Maria	149	Poe, Thomas	152
Pinkham, Edward S.	52	Pollard, Barsless	55
Pinkston, James	84	Pollard, G. W.	142
Pinkston, John W.	84	Pollard, John	124
Pinley, Joh	17	Pollocj, Enoch	209
Pinnert, Isaac B.	136	Pollock, Edwin	84
Pinto, John	141	Pomeroy, Noah G.	63
Piquard, Emile	123	Pond, Wesley D.	209
Pitchford, R.D.	168	Ponet, James H.	133
Piterman, Andrew	84	Poojer, Harrison	8
Pitsinger, E.G.	123	Pool, Winfield S.	98
Pitsley, Henry	124	Poole, George F.	192
Pitt, Philip	133	Poole, James E.	124
Pitter, Felix James	67	Poole, Josiah	136
Pitts, Anthony	174	Poor, John M.	138
Pitts, Elijah	105	Pope, D.W.	168
Pitts, Wm. P.	33	Pope, Luke	124
Pix, Edward	67	Pope, William	124
Place, Jonathan	124	Popelin, Frederick	107
Place, Robert	124	Poridges, Alfred	142
Plank, John A.	166	Porter, Ed	57
Planter, William II	124	Porter, James E.	67
Plants,____	209	Porter, John	139
Plark, William H.	24	Porter, John R.	143
Plass, Edmund	168	Porter, Joseph	105
Platenis, Cha's	222	Porter, Sanford	180
Platt, Peter	4	Porterfield, N.	141
Platt, Sylvester	124	Portland, A.H.	186
Playford, Edward	55	Portland, Samuel	141
Pleary, John	24	Post, George	67
Pleasant, George N.	141	Post, William	92
Pletmons, W. C.	96	Potter,____	84
Plotney, Samuel	98	Potter, Charles	216
Plum, Edward	106	Potter, Henry C.	124
Plumbaux, William R.	106	Potter, James	98
Plumer, Amzi T.	133	Potter, Merreth	124
Plummer, Charles	124	Pottger, Simon	209
Plummer, George M.	133	Potts, Benjamin	209
Plummer, J. L.	106	Potts, John	62

Pouler, Tos.	102		Price, Francis	152
Powell, Andrew	131		Price, Henry V.	98
Powell, Charles	124		Price, John	174
Powell, Henry C.	209		Price, Nathan S.	124
Powell, James	141		Price, Richard	168
Powell, James W.	10		Price, Theodore L.	154
Powell, John	209		Prickett, Jacob	43
Powell, Russell G.	106		Prickett, John	29
Powell, Thomas	97		Prickett, John	29
Powell, Toby	180		Pridgin, J. O.	138
Powell, Warren	29		Priestwood, E.	131
Powell, William	124		Prime, Charles	141
Powell,___	10		Prince, Alexander	141
Power, A.	84		Princeton, Reuben	141
Powers, Charles R.	102		Pringle, John	153
Powers, F. L.	102		Pringle, John C.	15
Powers, Larry	6		Prior, William	124
Powers, William	124		Pritchard, William	124
Powle, Geo.	152		Pritt, Brown W.	209
Powler, C.	136		Proctor, H. H.	124
Pownley,___	84		Proctor, S. D.	131
Prame, Hartwell	178		Proffitt, David	25
Prass, Sh.	55		Prowd, Mathew	30
Prater, Wiley	9		Pryor, Frank D.	183
Pratt, Henry	209		Pryor, Richard L.	13
Pratt, Henry C.	62		Pugh, Eli	96
Pratt, Silas	124		Pulk, Henry	143
Pratt, Thomas	124		Pulkley, Charles E.	19
Pray, Denison P.	133		Pulkugton, Patrick	4
Preble, O.	124		Pullins, Wesley	209
Precoss, S.	55		Pully, _____	152
Premens, Patrick	24		Punrray, Thomas	219
Prentice, Myron	124		Punty, Patrick W.	124
Prentice, Simeon	124		Purdy, John	124
Prentice, Thos. W.	124		Purnell, Andrew	98
Prescott, Lyther O.	124		Pusdy, Amos	17
Pressher, Havy	84		Putnam, Henry	59
Preston, Albert W.	13		Putnam, Israel	124
Preston, Sidney	124		Putney, Horace	192
Prew, Allick	209		Pwens, H.G.	13
Price, Anthony	124		Pyle, A. J.	96
Price, Daniel	94		Quackenbush, John G.	131

Quayle, Robert	192
Quera, Euele	4
Quick, John	166
Quigley, James B.	136
Quinn, Albert	4
Quinn, Elias (Colored)	55
Quinn, James	68
Quinn, James	124
Quinn, P.J.	57
Quinn, Th. (Colored)	55
Quinn, Thomas	55
Quintal, Samuel A.	19
Quinton, Thos.	173
R_____, thos. J.	174
Raber, Phillip	209
Rachard, G. R.	102
Radcliff, James	136
Radcliff, Theodore	178
Radeliffe, _____	124
Rader, Henry	209
Radley, Erastus	124
Raesner, Henry	124
Raffle, Samuel	106
Ragen, George	60
Rager, James	92
Ragin, Daniel	124
Raglin, Polly	183
Ragott, Charles	164
Raider, Richard M.	98
Raine, Charles J.	188
Raines, William F.	209
Rainey, James	97
Rais, Jacob F.	92
Ralph, Thomas	124
Ralston, John	92
Ramford, Joseph	136
Ramsay, J. H.	97
Ramsdell, J. F.	102
Ramsdell, James B.	96
Ramsey, J.	124
Ramsey, John	103
Rand, Moses	106
Randall, Abal P.	192
Randall, Abner E.	124
Randall, David	133
Randall, John	100
Randall, Wm. J.	73
Randleman, J. H.	124
Ranhausen, Isaac	124
Rankin, William H.	209
Ransom, Hawley F.	209
Rape, Samuel M.	131
Rapp, John	76
Rarick, M.	55
Rarick, O. R.	136
Rasse, U. H.	124
Rathbame, Henry	149
Ratteree, Thomas J.	43
Rausch, Peter	192
Rauter, John	68
Raven, Peter C.	124
Ray, Henry	159
Ray, James	136
Ray, James M.	84
Ray, W.C.	209
Raymond, Floyd E.	185
Raymond, George	124
Raymond, Joseph W.	17
Rayner, Calvin	102
Raynor, Henry	124
Rayson, Samuel	5
Reahme, Frank	47
Ream, Charles	209
Reamer, William	124
Reames, Elmer E.	84
Reames, Nettie B.	84
Reames, Peter	84
Reardon, Con	87
Reardon, John	13
Reaser, Peter	133
Reaser, Philip	169
Reckley, William	124
Redamore, Columbus	33
Redcliff, William	124

Reder, Charles	96		Reiss, _____	171
Reding, Nicholas	192		Relbucks, Milo	105
Redman, S. C.	142		Remington, Asa	84
Reed, ____	84		Rempster, Francis	124
Reed, Clifton	84		Remy, D.	124
Reed, David	133		Remy, William	209
Reed, Elijah	173		Rendiu, Edwin	216
Reed, Frank	36		Restin, Elijah L.	124
Reed, H. A.	124		Retchman, Jacob	124
Reed, Hinas	133		Retson, Mathew	124
Reed, Jeremiah II	124		Reuls, J.W.	169
Reed, Joel	136		Reur, Gethard	47
Reed, Monroe F.	136		Reussin, Je___	36
Reed, Ogden J.	192		Rexford, D.A.	39
Reed, William	68		Rexroad, Lewis	209
Reed. Cyrus	209		Reyner, Charles	136
Reeds, Morris	124		Reynold, Richard	124
Reedy, John	209		Reynolds, Alexander	218
Reedy, William	124		Reynolds, Charles A.	76
Rees, John	133		Reynolds, Fred	149
Rees, William H.	68		Reynolds, Henry	84
Reese, Harland P.	124		Reynolds, James	124
Reese, Samuel U.	143		Reynolds, Joseph J.	47
Reeves, Henry B.	98		Reynolds, Leonard	124
Reeves, John A.	136		Reynolds, Mela	149
Reeves, Sanders	131		Reynolds, Patrick	103
Refoler, John	164		Ribert, John	124
Regan, Cornelius	124		Rice, Anthony L.	124
Regan, Patrick	220		Rice, Henry	136
Regan, Peter M.	124		Rice, James	124
Reib, Henry	136		Rice, Orson E.	143
Reibel, August	4		Rice, Sylvester W.	19
Reibold, Christan	68		Rice, Wm. J.	62
Reich, Henry F.	209		Rich, Joseph	124
Reid, Charles S.	124		Rich, Peter	107
Reiker, J. H.	98		Richard, Christopher	141
Reiley, J.	171		Richards, B.B.	103
Reiley, James	84		Richards, Henry	141
Reily, John	55		Richards, John	62
Reily, William Van W.	68		Richards, John M.	22
Reintz, Augustus	92		Richardson, Edward	124
Reisch, Charles	124		Richardson, Edward	209

Richardson, Frank D.	6	Rinera, Deming	210
Richardson, G.W.	194	Ring, James A.	124
Richardson, Geo. H.	105	Ringally, Edward	36
Richardson, Henry	133	Ringer, Cryus E.	210
Richardson, John	124	Ringrose, Christopher	155
Richardson, L. G.	124	Rinker, George W.	192
Richardson, M.	124	Risedolps, D. G. H.	124
Richardson, Robert M.	97	Risenlark, W.D.	124
Richardson, Thomas B.	22	Risk, Chester C.	98
Richardson, Wm.	47	Riskine, Henry	136
Richart, F.B.	29	Risley, Zachary	164
Richenbacker, Martin	13	Ritchie, Robert	218
Richmond, John	209	Ritchie, William	92
Richmond, John	209	Rittenburg, Charles	192
Richmond, Samuel	209	Ritter, William H.	125
Rickard, Joseph	149	Ritterbash, Charles	125
Rickets, Geo.	55	Rivers, Alfred	143
Rickley, John	164	Rivers, John	192
Rickson, Henry	141	Rixford, George	149
Riddix, James	131	Rizheimer, Lawrence	195
Riddle, John	209	Roach, Frank	180
Riddle, Vanburen	209	Roach, Henry	84
Ridenour, Aaron C.	210	Roach, Henry	98
Ridenour, David S.	210	Roach, Herman	84
Ridgeway, Edward	33	Roach, N. E.	125
Ridgway, Henry	124	Roach, Nathan	136
Ridgway, James	124	Roach, William	210
Riffle, William	210	Roagh, M.J.	84
Riggs, A.	106	Roan, Gibson G.	210
Riggs, George W.	106	Robb, C.	136
Riggs, Michael S.	124	Robbins, George	165
Righadson, S.N..	84	Robbins, R. R.	98
Riley, James	196	Robbins, Samuel	125
Riley, John	47	Robbison, Charles	192
Riley, John	210	Roberson, James	131
Riley, Michael	106	Robert, Wm. D.	175
Riley, Michael	124	Roberts, Edward C.	125
Riley, Patrick	149	Roberts, A. U.	102
Riley, Peter	55	Roberts, G. T.	136
Riley, Seaskus	29	Roberts, George	105
Riley, Susan Ann	185	Roberts, George M.	97
Riley, William	180	Roberts, Granville	29

Roberts, Harden	98	Rodgers, James	220
Roberts, Henry	68	Rodgers, Jams	150
Roberts, Henry B.	125	Roff, Christian F.	171
Roberts, John	125	Rogers, Albert	43
Roberts, John A. W.	97	Rogers, Albert	125
Roberts, Joseph	24	Rogers, Amscah	47
Roberts, R.F.	84	Rogers, Augustus	136
Roberts, Robert	74	Rogers, David N.	51
Roberts, Vincent	165	Rogers, Elijah W.	192
Roberts, William	84	Rogers, Ephraim J.	125
Roberts, William	210	Rogers, Henry	125
Roberts, William D.	138	Rogers, Hugh S.	133
Robertson, Aaron L.	17	Rogers, James	220
Robertson, John	141	Rogers, James B.	131
Robertson, Joseph	125	Rogers, Nathan	42
Robertson, T. C.	106	Rogers, Nicholas	125
Robey, James N.	210	Rogers, Owen	107
Robin, Agustus	106	Rogers, Sanford T.	105
Robins, J.J.	210	Rogers, Walter B.	68
Robinson, _____	149	Rogil, John	125
Robinson, Charles	180	Rolader, J. S.	125
Robinson, Daniel	29	Roland, Charles	131
Robinson, Edward	105	Rolfe, R.L.	43
Robinson, Frank B.	106	Rolle, John	125
Robinson, Isaac J.	149	Rollins, Adolphus	125
Robinson, J.	125	Rollins, Thomas	138
Robinson, James	94	Rolsaubin, M.V.	152
Robinson, James	210	Roma, Cottlier	84
Robinson, John	210	Roman, Robert	27
Robinson, John J.	218	Romer, Charles C.	192
Robinson, L.L.	84	Romey, John	159
Robinson, M.W.	142	Romey, Michael	42
Robinson, Smith	125	Romiser, Peter	210
Robinson, T.G.	17	Rood, Edward	68
Robinson, William	125	Rook, Gilmore B.	102
Robinson, William	195	Root, John	192
Robinson, William C.	33	Root, John M.	210
Robnett, Lawson C.	125	Root, Marcus	141
Robotham, George	125	Roper, John	125
Rodden, M. S.	125	Roreothy, John	125
Roddy, Terrence	142	Roscoe, Boardman	143
Rodgers, Adelbert	150	Rose, Adolf	25

Name	Page	Name	Page
Rose, Benjamin J.	192	Royster, William A.	7
Rose, Burton D.	210	Rubner, A.	125
Rose, Edwin	171	Rudden, Patrick	68
Rose, James	97	Ruderlauck, Ezra	125
Rose, Jesse M.	9	Rudolph, Emmer	136
Rose, Marion	210	Rudolph, Teadore	48
Rose, Warren	125	Ruffenburg, Abraham	137
Rosenstrauch, Saligma	125	Ruffing, Sharon Kay	33
Roser, E.P.	125	Ruhle, William	22
Rosmbalm, E.A.	27	Rulfrew, B. W.	125
Ross, ____	183	Rum, Phillip	55
Ross, Daniel A.	210	Rummings, Emory C.	125
Ross, Frank	33	Runge, Christiare	178
Ross, George A.	133	Runhard, John	167
Ross, John	210	Rurger, Joseph	219
Ross, Louis	175	Rush, Isaac S.	125
Ross, Robert	47	Rushing, S.H.	222
Ross, Thomas	125	Rusling, Ludlow	125
Ross, William	125	Russell, Auther	34
Ross, William J.	125	Russell, Bemjamin F.	210
Rossbury, John W.	68	Russell, George	125
Rossross, S.	210	Russell, Henry	51
Rost, William R.	138	Russell, James	132
Roth, Francis	73	Russell, James	137
Rothacken, John	159	Russell, James H.	68
Rotheman, Augustus	73	Russell, Joseph	19
Rouche, J.	125	Russell, Joseph P.	150
Roucheslange, John	178	Russell, Samuel L.	150
Rouk, Benjamine	210	Russell, William	62
Rounds, D. H.	125	Russell, William	102
Rouse, Benjamin	143	Ruth, John F.	178
Rouse, G. W.	136	Rutherford, David	210
Rover, Phillip	136	Rutherford, Th	55
Rowe, E.	102	Ruttan, John	89
Rowe, John N.	133	Rutter, Isaac B.	137
Rowell, Enos S.	125	Ryan, A.	15
Rowland, Edward	155	Ryan, Alpheus	84
Rowland, John	210	Ryan, Daniel	68
Rowland, Robert	125	Ryan, James	17
Rows, Thomas	105	Ryan, Jno	84
Royal, William H.	131	Ryan, Michail	218
Royol, Andrew C.	96	Ryan, Patrick	97

Ryan, Patrick	125		Sandus, John W.	216
Ryan, Thomas	84		Sanford, A.F.	194
Ryan, Thos.	84		Sanford, Albert	165
Ryer, Frank	106		Sanford, J.F.	169
Rymer, John	210		Sanfs___, Prim	102
S_____, T.	49		Sangford, W.B.	169
Sa_____idt, Michael	47		Sanienski, Stan's	222
Saardort, Rey F.	84		Sanxay, Fred. D.	154
Sackett, W.H.	19		Sapp, Francis M.	95
Saddleson, William H.	192		Sapt, F.W.	169
Sadonstable, Frank	106		Sargeant, Aaron	125
Safse, Charles W.	165		Sargeant, William	107
Sailor, S. H.	137		Saris, Robert	36
Salamo, Thomas	137		Sarmtman, Wm	159
Salcer, John	125		Sass, Fred	210
Sale, Robert E.	63		Sather, Robert	218
Sale, W. A.	138		Saul, Peter	125
Saltinyer, Christophe	150		Saum, _____	210
Samdt, John	8		Saunders, Charles	47
Samerill, James	137		Saunders, Richard	68
Samkins, T.C.	169		Saut, Louis	158
Sammery, John S.	133		Savage, Baxton	97
Sammis, Alcott	125		Savage, George	102
Sammis, John	125		Savage, Horace	125
Sample, Jno.	187		Savine, Samuel	125
Sampson, B.	125		Sawyer, Reuben G.	143
Sampson, Peter	141		Sawyer, W. B.	131
Sanberg, John	150		Saxe, Henry	125
Sandberg, John	125		Sayers, Thomas	55
Sanderick, Frederick	103		Saylor, Issac	210
Sanders, Andrew	142		Scahouse, Charles	22
Sanders, Daniel	137		Scaman, Rufus W.	105
Sanders, David W.	210		Scammel, E.	125
Sanders, Harvey	143		Scan, Johnathan	92
Sanders, Harvey	210		Scanlan, John	192
Sanders, James B.	141		Scarlet, Frederick	125
Sanders, Nathan	143		Schaeffer, J.F.	84
Sanderson, James N.	133		Schaff, S. M.	125
Sandfut, Charles	125		Schaffer, Charles	125
Sandree, Joseph	103		Schaffer, Christian	125
Sands, John	8		Schager, Rudolt	150
Sands, Michael B.	125		Schaleh, Frdnic	27

Schaule, Henry	125
Schaupe, William	210
Schawb, L.	55
Schear, Carl	150
Schele, Henry	68
Schiefner, William	125
Schiffer, ___	34
Schlatter, George	210
Schlegel, Henry	150
Schleicher, Gustas	183
Schlessing, Justis	150
Schlitter, Casper	143
Schlitz, Chas	25
Schlottemau, Henry	125
Schmas, Joseph	143
Schmidt, Albert	5
Schmidt, Charles	68
Schmidt, Frank	221
Schmidt, George	125
Schmidt, John	125
Schmutz, Magdeline	84
Schnauben, Philip	125
Schneider, Jacob	210
Schneider, John	125
Schneidn, Adolphus J.	2
Schnitz, K.	43
Schock, Clement	125
Schofield, Emelie	125
Schons, Henry	143
Schoonmaker, A.	133
Schoonmaker, Frank	125
Schoonmaker, H. E.	137
Schopp, Peter	125
Schraeder, Samuel E.	96
Schram, ___	210
Schreyer, John	52
Schreyer, William	125
Schubart, William	178
Schuhrieman, George	174
Schultz, ___	171
Schultz, Henry	105
Schultz, Michael	174
Schulz, Rob't	84
Schumaker, Benjamin	125
Schwan, F.	15
Schwan, F.	84
Schwartz, Martin	125
Schweder, Francis J.	125
Schweet, Harry	27
Schweizer, Joseph	210
Schwindt, L. I.	125
Scollin, Henry M.	76
Scolon, John	125
Scolton, John W.	125
Scoss, George	55
Scott, Alexander	133
Scott, B____	36
Scott, Charles	68
Scott, E. B.	125
Scott, Henry	96
Scott, Henry	98
Scott, J.	25
Scott, James	141
Scott, John	125
Scott, John	141
Scott, Louis	84
Scott, Richard	141
Scott, Robert	19
Scott, Robert	125
Scott, Robert	150
Scott, Samuel	141
Scott, Starling	42
Scott, W. W.	126
Scrusier, Henry	106
Scusn, Peter	42
Seafferman, Henry	76
Seagar, Charles	192
Sealn, John	218
Seaman, Chas. D.	89
Seamon, Jerome B.	210
Searl, John R.	210
Searles, Joseph	126
Sears, Adolphus	50
Sears, Benjamin	126

Name	Page
Sears, Geo.	17
Sears, George	126
Seasley, Lewis	126
Seater, John	5
Seatterfield, G. A.	126
Sedbittle, Wade	126
Sedgwick, George W.	157
Seeley, Eli	19
Seeling, Emima	13
Seeling, Hearmon	161
Seemann, Charles	210
Seese, George	210
Seheutte, H.	24
Seiber, Jacob	126
Seigle, N. W.	131
Seiler, John	68
Seinfor, James	96
Seisman, Peter	98
Sekayer, James	216
Selway, Thomas	126
Seneff, Albert	84
Senn, Jacob	192
Senney Henry C.	143
Sephan, Amos	102
Seren, G. H.	126
Seren, George H.	126
Serine, Orrin	17
Serlis, Harry	55
Serme, James	126
Serry, William	150
Sever, Philip	126
Severn, John	137
Severs, James	126
Severson, Leslie C.	100
Seward, _____	126
Seward, William H.	126
Sewart, John	55
Sewell, Issac	210
Sewiers, George b.	126
Sexton, Robert M.	210
Seymour, Joseph	106
Seymour, Robert M.	126
Sfmowl, George	87
Shack, Charles W.	102
Shackleford, L.M.	150
Shade, Samuel	68
Shadow, John	137
Shadrach, Woodland	141
Shaffer, J.E.	34
Shaffner, Lewis	126
Shage, Aaron	55
Shammey, Patk. N.	187
Shampine, P.	126
Shane, Thos.	152
Shanks, Franklin	211
Sharner, Alfred	24
Sharp, Joseph	126
Sharp, Alinza	177
Sharp, Charles T.	211
Sharp, Washington	131
Sharp, William H.	105
Sharpe, Cal	37
Sharpe, George	141
Sharpe, Joshua	141
Shatey, John	218
Shatyford, George	126
Shaver, William	138
Shaw, General J.	211
Shaw, H. C.	36
Shaw, Hugh	131
Shaw, James R.	84
Shaw, John F.	57
Shaw, Martin	126
Shaw, Marvin	133
Shawver, James H.	211
Shay, Michael	50
Shea, Jeremiah	68
Shea, Jno.	173
Shea, John	126
Shea, Thomas	126
Shears, Henry F.	185
Sheaver, David	98
Sheehan, Joseph	96
Sheehan, Timothy	105

Sheever, Joseph	137	Shook, John	165
Sheiner, Ervin	24	Shore, William H.	131
Shelberry, Perry E.	133	Shorrow, William H.	68
Shell, William	141	Short, John	211
Shelly, William	150	Short, Levi	211
Shelly, William G. S.	133	Short, Nahan	68
Shelworth, Samuel	95	Short, Robert	143
Shepard, Benjamin	94	Shreffler, William	211
Shepherd, George T.	143	Shreuger, Charles	73
Shepherd, Jeremiah	126	Shrewsberry, Russell	211
Shepherd, Thomas M.	211	Shriver, Marion	211
Shepler, John W.	211	Shuban, William	216
Sheridan, Andrew	133	Shuber, _____	96
Sheridan, John	100	Shuetters, Austaonio	94
Sheridan, K.	84	Shufile, Jacob	126
Sherman, Adden P.	152	Shuld, Juo. A.	219
Sherman, E.	98	Shuler, Andrew J.	133
Sherman, Edward	165	Shuler, George	133
Sherman, Morris	126	Shults, William	126
Shield, James H.	126	Shultz, Geo. W.	92
Shields, Francis	150	Shultz, Johann	4
Shields, Patrick	126	Shultz, Simon S.	150
Shields, Thomas	137	Shumate, Joseph	34
Shiels, John	126	Shurber, R.	126
Shill, Frank	6	Shurtleff, James F.	19
Shimbena, John	211	Shurtz, John	126
Shimpsin, Charles E.	218	Shutts, Wm	159
Shine, Geo.	43	Sicking, Bernard	85
Shinman, William	126	Sickman, Alfred	211
Shinn, Assa	211	Sickmiller, John	211
Shipley, George	126	Sidmoyo, Franklin	126
Shipley, George F.	27	Sidwell, William J.	211
Shipley, Henry	150	Sieber, August	173
Shipley, Miller O.	96	Siebold, Joseph	192
Shipley, Saul	34	Siefous, Francis W.	68
Shoemaker, C.P.	92	Siemon, Charles	68
Shoemaker, Frank	184	Siemonson, Bent	68
Shoemaker, Stephen	216	Sigley, James	141
Shoenberg,, F.G.	34	Sillmer, Charles H.	27
Shoenberg,, Paul G.	34	Sillsby, John	126
Sholle, Henry	98	Silsbee, Philo O.	126
Shomden, John	173	Silva, Louis	85

Silver, John	98
Silwood, Silas A.	141
Simkings, S.	107
Simmers, George A	161
Simmons, Frank	141
Simmons, Horace	96
Simmons, Obed	153
Simmons, R.	97
Simmons, S__.H.	25
Simmons, W.	150
Simons, Lauren B.	126
Simonson, Stephenson	105
Simonton, D.M.	211
Simpson, _____	150
Simpson, _____	126
Simpson, R.	131
Simpson, Thomas H.	92
Sinclair, Eli	211
Sinclair, Frank	174
Sines, Gotthardt	47
Sing, S.	100
Singleton, William	126
Sinington, William	157
Sink, Solomon	126
Sirethy, James	42
Sirling, C.	55
Sirrine, David	39
Sitel, Robert	126
Siveley, George	100
Six, James	98
Skelton, Alexander	143
Skidmore, Webster J.	192
Skinner, Benj. F.	17
Skinner, John	180
Skinner, Joseph	133
Skiorrh, Dan'l	219
Slater, J. A.	98
Slatterly, John	100
Slauch, Gotleib	126
Slaughter, Selim	96
Slavens, James H.	211
Sleeper, George	126
Sleeper, John	126
Sleghpaugh, H.	126
Slingerland, R.H.	60
Sliver, Stephen	62
Slocum, Edward	126
Slothezse, Henry	102
Small, Chas. S.	17
Small, Daniel	102
Small, J.F.	13
Small, John M.	58
Small, Joseph	126
Smalley, Benjamin	180
Smallgood, Eli	180
Smallwood, William	68
Smarr, Mathew M.	211
Smatley, G.C.	169
Smead, A. L.	85
Smeales, ____	126
Smidt, Frank	87
Smith, Henry C.	19
Smith, Charles	141
Smith, _____	85
Smith, A.	126
Smith, A. P.	126
Smith, A.J.	211
Smith, Aanoss	180
Smith, Albert A.	68
Smith, Algernon	68
Smith, Allen C.	126
Smith, Alonzo M.	138
Smith, Anderson C.	98
Smith, Augustus	141
Smith, B.	98
Smith, Benjamin	102
Smith, Benjamin	141
Smith, Burr N.	100
Smith, Charles	126
Smith, Charles	216
Smith, Charlie	25
Smith, David	169
Smith, David	211
Smith, David C.	137

Smith, E.	126		Smith, John	126
Smith, E. H.	126		Smith, John	150
Smith, E. N.	131		Smith, John	216
Smith, Edward	180		Smith, John	218
Smith, Edward H.	102		Smith, John B.	63
Smith, Emery W.	126		Smith, John B.	126
Smith, Ephraim B.	57		Smith, John R.P.	150
Smith, Euring	47		Smith, Joseph	42
Smith, F. J.	126		Smith, Joseph	85
Smith, Francis	150		Smith, Joseph	216
Smith, Francis E.	103		Smith, L.B.	35
Smith, Fred. C.	103		Smith, Lawrence	126
Smith, G.S.	85		Smith, Lewis	126
Smith, Geddis	216		Smith, Lewis	137
Smith, George	76		Smith, Lyman	105
Smith, George H.	100		Smith, Major	141
Smith, George W.	92		Smith, Marion F.	92
Smith, Harris	126		Smith, Mathias C.	211
Smith, Henry	97		Smith, Mortimer	211
Smith, Henry	107		Smith, N. H.	126
Smith, Henry	126		Smith, Nathan	126
Smith, Herman R.	126		Smith, Phillip	85
Smith, Isaac	126		Smith, Robert	126
Smith, Isaac C.	85		Smith, Samuel	126
Smith, Issac	211		Smith, Sidney	150
Smith, J.	126		Smith, Simpson	126
Smith, J. A.	97		Smith, Stephen	126
Smith, J. H.	131		Smith, Stewart	29
Smith, J.J.	211		Smith, Sydney A.	161
Smith, Jacob	137		Smith, Thomas	126
Smith, Jacob A.	126		Smith, Thomas	197
Smith, James	43		Smith, Thomas	222
Smith, James	68		Smith, Thomas G.	126
Smith, James	126		Smith, Tilton D.	127
Smith, James	150		Smith, W. C.	127
Smith, James	211		Smith, W. G.	85
Smith, James H.	102		Smith, W. R.	95
Smith, Jno.	85		Smith, W.B	57
Smith, John	4		Smith, W.F.	27
Smith, John	42		Smith, W.H.	55
Smith, John	74		Smith, William	98
Smith, John	107		Smith, William	127

Name	Page
Smith, William	141
Smith, William	178
Smith, William	192
Smith, William H.	98
Smith, William H.	137
Smith, William H.	211
Smith, William N.	127
Smith, Wm.	85
Snedeker, Theodore	28
Snediker, W.H.	211
Sneeney, Daisy	184
Sneld, W.M.	85
Snell, Samuel L.	58
Snell, Willie	220
Snelzer, John C.	127
Snodgrass, Robert H.	211
Snow, Amasa	152
Snow, Andrew	68
Snow, Jesse	138
Snow, Philo	103
Snow, W.S.	34
Snowball	7
Snowberger, David	127
Snowden, Samuel	141
Snurr, John D.	211
Snyder, ___	85
Snyder, ___	127
Snyder, Ferando	150
Snyder, Franklin	137
Snyder, Henry	165
Snyder, Henry	211
Snyder, Hugh	211
Snyder, Robert	85
Snyder, William H.	137
Soder, Charles W.	127
Soggs, Henry	141
Soloman, Henry	180
Somers, Harrison	141
Somers, Issacher	127
Sommer, Eben	127
Sonnelly, Jas	85
Soper, Ruben	89
Souder, M.K.	150
Souker, Julius	194
Soulsly, Cuthbert	211
Soupe', Fritz	88
Soust, Francis	150
Southard, William	143
Souther, ___	133
Southwick, ___	85
Sowders, Leonidas	211
Sowe, Max	57
Spain, P. D.	100
Sparks, Joseph W.	92
Sparrow, Jacob	98
Sparrowgrass, J. T.	141
Spatsberry, Edward	165
Spaulding, O. K.	127
Spaulding, Page	106
Spear, Samuel	98
Speckmon, James	92
Speedy, John	92
Speer, David	165
Speigelholder, John	127
Spencer, Cyrus	96
Spencer, F.	15
Spencer, Frederick	85
Spencer, Jackson	211
Spencer, Lewis P.	105
Spenkius, Walter	5
Sperry, E. S.	127
Spicer, A. D.	127
Spicer, Daniel	169
Spicer, John K.	92
Spickman, John	105
Spiglemire, J.A.	167
Spinney, Alex	103
Splain, James B.	103
Spoenla, Moritz	92
Spotted Horse	85
Sprague, B.D.	143
Sprague, Charles A.	92
Sprague, Delos	133
Sprague, Lucus A	58

Spring, Henry G.	103	Starch, William	137
Spring, James	127	Starck. Frank	68
Springer, Charles S.	55	Stark, A. D.	137
Sprouls, F. J.	127	Stark, D. H.	28
Spullberg, _____	127	Stark, Jacob	127
Spurgeon, Elias	133	Starkey, Charles	10
Spurgeon, Heaerison	159	Starkey, Robert	19
Squire, James	28	Starks, Soloman	180
Sreffen, George O.	92	Starr, Benjamin	96
Srewaet, Mrs A.C.	35	Starr, Fred W.	17
Sruler, Wm.	55	Starr, Robert	131
St John, Ludwick	68	Starr, Saml. H.	17
St. Clair, Julius	161	Staton, M.	131
St. Clark, I.W.	8	Statuf, Stephen G.	103
St. John, Jerry	165	Stauffer, Napoleon B.	169
St. Vrain, Felix	92	Stauley, Wm.	25
Stack, H.	49	Stearns, _____	184
Stackhouse, Samuel W.	137	Stebbins, W. W.	133
Stacl[p;e. Eugene	102	Steele, Albert	127
Stacy, F.	102	Steele, Alfred S.	106
Stacy, S. F.	106	Steeley, W.F.	35
Stacy, William	216	Steely, F.	131
Stafford, Benjamin	68	Steeples, Orlando	127
Stage, William	127	Stefan, Frank	127
Stahl, Jacob	127	Steinberger, William	127
Staler, William B.	127	Steinhagen, Henry	211
Staley,	85	Steinman, Julis	150
Stamford, James P.	98	Steison, Charles	58
Stanard, Charles	220	Stella, Alexander	68
Standiford, James	211	Stemple, Christopher	211
Stang, Edward	13	Stenbeck, John H.	212
Stangler, Thomas	43	Stenebrook, John	127
Stanley, Charles	150	Stepfoe, John C.	20
Stanley, Eli M.	211	Stephens, C. S. T.	96
Stanley, Jetho	127	Stephens, F. N.	102
Stanton, E.	211	Stephens, J.	127
Stanton, Willard L.	127	Stephenson, J.	127
Stantough, James	107	Sterlin, Daring	93
Staples, Geo. D.	102	Sternwick, Adolph	127
Staples, Samuel	68	Stetson, Charles	58
Star, Irvin	211	Steven, Riley	192
Starbird, Alfred C.	22	Stevens, Edward	223

Stevens, H.F.	34
Stevens, Harvey R.	193
Stevens, Henry	107
Stevens, Henry H.	107
Stevens, J.M.	59
Stevens, John	127
Stevens, Merritt	158
Stevens, Russell L.	22
Stevens, Steven S.	17
Stevens, Victor	137
Stevens, W. J.	127
Stevenson, Frank	127
Stevenson, Marion M.	212
Stevnes, Benjamin	127
Stevson, William	154
Steward, James	55
Stewart, Esther	13
Stewart, James	105
Stewart, James	181
Stewart, James M.	25
Stewart, Perry	85
Stewart, Robert	74
Stewart, Robert	133
Stewart, Thomas W.	212
Stewart, William F.	127
Stigler, Magdalen,	150
Stiles, Martin W.	193
Stiles, S.	127
Still, Isaac	138
Still, Tobias	138
Stillson, Amos H.	127
Stimpson, Mrs. Mary	132
Stine, Chas.	85
Stinebaker, Thomas P.	63
Stinger, W.D.	49
Stiter, John	137
Stobacus, Frederick	38
Stock, Charles	193
Stoddard, Charles	142
Stoddart, Rob't	152
Stoerza, Henry	103
Stogden, John W.	212
Stogkwell, Wm.	34
Stokes, B. R.	138
Stokes, Oceander	212
Stone, Adonison J.	98
Stone, Charles	127
Stone, G. B.	106
Stone, George	102
Stone, J. W.	127
Stone, Robert	127
Stone, Robert T.	36
Stone, Walter	96
Stone, William J.	193
Stoneham, Mark	22
Stoner, Saul	60
Stonesifer, Josiah	137
Stoney, A.	171
Stonnfer, Cornelius	8
Storer, Ignatz	133
Stormout, William	127
Storms, Peter	150
Storrow, Joseph	193
Stortz, Frederick	63
Story, William	127
Stottard, Orlando	105
Stout, C.A.	35
Stout, Josiah	167
Stout, M.M.	35
Stover, Andrew W.	127
Stover, John	137
Stowe, J.	131
Stowell, Byron S.	127
Stracks, Harman	103
Strang, Wm.	34
Stranpler, George O.	93
Stratton, Alfred	127
Stratton, George F.	127
Stratton, J.H.	34
Stratton, Robert	17
Stratton, Walker	127
Street, Jacob	127
Streightliff, Jacob	137
Streing, Frederick	76

Name	Page
Strewple, C	49
Strickland, Thomas J.	169
Strickman, Ernest	174
Striker, William	127
Strinle, William	127
Strogen, Thomas	127
Stroman, Absden	99
Strone, G. R.	138
Strong, Alex.	85
Strothers, George	127
Stroup, Russell	173
Strouts, Edward	193
Struad, Frank	34
Strunk, William C.	137
Stuart, Alpheus	68
Stuart, Bridget	150
Stuart, Mary J.	150
Stuart, Rosanna	150
Stuart, William P.	150
Stubbs, Henry S.	127
Stuckey, Joesph	212
Stuckman, W.J.	55
Stull, Joshua	133
Stungwitz, Ignatz	68
Sturgill, James	212
Sturgis, James G.	68
Sturns, Oscar R.	137
Suddard, James	212
Suddarth, Josiah	212
Suhna, W,A,	212
Sulger, James	165
Sullivan, _____	185
Sullivan, Dennis	55
Sullivan, J.W.	85
Sullivan, James	85
Sullivan, James	95
Sullivan, Jno.	85
Sullivan, John	76
Sullivan, John	127
Sullivan, P.	13
Sullivan, Patrick	218
Sullivan, Patrick J.	85
Sullivan, Phillip	13
Sullivan, Thomas	127
Sullivan, Thomas	150
Sullivan, Timothy	87
Sullivan, William	127
Sullivan, Willis	127
Sulllivan, James	103
Sulloy, John	1
Suminus, Richard	216
Summers, David	76
Summers, J,A,	212
Summers, John R.	212
Summers, Rufus	167
Sumnor, George H.	42
Suocking, Henry	55
Sutherland, Michael	127
Sutherland, William	127
Sutton, Charles E.	133
Sutton, James	100
Svringle, D. M. L.	133
Swacole, Alonzo	127
Swain, _____	13
Swain, Jas. F.	13
Swain, Laura	13
Swain, Lucinda J.	13
Swain, William	150
Swaine, Luther G.	107
Swallow, William W.	133
Swalt, Simeon	138
Swane, J.	43
Swart, John A.	127
Sweeney, Frank H.	4
Sweeney, William	127
Sweeny, Edward	137
Sweeny, James	85
Sweeny, James	212
Sweeny, P.J.	85
Sweet, James	127
Sweet, Kyler	105
Sweet, T.	102
Sweetman, John	223
Sweitzer, Theodore	127

Swift, Benard	14
Swift, Bernard	85
Swift, Paul	34
Swink, L.	127
Swisher, John H. C.	212
Swobeda, William C.	212
Sykes, George	127
Sykes, Horace F. (Jr)	34
Sylvester, Silas	98
Symmes, Albert A. C.	127
Symms, Darwin L.	68
Symonds, John N.	221
Sypolt, John W.	212
T_____, E.H.	43
Taggart, James	87
Taggart, James A.	212
Tailor, And'w	85
Taklenburg, Willaim	212
Talbot, Thomas	47
Talcott, E. C.	127
Talley, Edwin C.	20
Talliferro, David	181
Tallman, Benjamin F.	193
Tanner, James J.	76
Tapia, Juan C.	5
Taplin, Charles H.	143
Tarbox, Bryon	69
Tarbox, Wm. S.	102
Tarpenerig, S.	127
Tasker, Dolphus	127
Tasker, Warren C.	218
Tassey, Thomas E.	165
Tates, _____	127
Tates, Cyrus	102
Taylor, Alonzo M.	187
Taylor, Benjamin	142
Taylor, D. W.	137
Taylor, Daniel H.	85
Taylor, Edwin J.	193
Taylor, Evan T	13
Taylor, George	141
Taylor, George W.	127
Taylor, Henry	143
Taylor, Henry	181
Taylor, Henry H.	17
Taylor, Isaac	137
Taylor, James J.	212
Taylor, James R.	9
Taylor, John	127
Taylor, Joseph	8
Taylor, Joseph	127
Taylor, Joseph	181
Taylor, Joseph W.	142
Taylor, Randolph	127
Taylor, Richard	29
Taylor, Simeon M.	212
Taylor, T. W.	102
Taylor, W. J.	141
Taylor, William	13
Taylor, William	218
Taylor, Wm.	85
Teal, John H.	57
Teeman, William	69
Teisley, Jacob	127
Tempany, Fred	34
Templeton, H. B.	138
Tenant, Charles H.	19
Tendergust, H.	9
TenEyck, Anthony	141
TenEyck, Charles H.	141
Tennemeyer, William	212
Tenney, Hoyt C.	212
Tenny, Marshall H.	212
Tenth, Michael	107
Teron, Benjamin	102
Terrey, George W.	193
Terry, Albert W.	127
Terry, Charles E.	19
Tessier, Edward D.	69
Tetus, Caleb	128
Tews, Samson	128
Thacher, George W.	93
Thadus, John	69
Tharp, James D.	93

Thayer, James B.	42		Thompson, Robert	216
Theedle, Thomas	186		Thompson, Samuel	133
Theeker, Ebenezer	171		Thompson, Silas W.	128
Themble, James	150		Thompson, T.	55
Thibault, Augustus	128		Thompson, Thomas	128
Thomas, Benjamin	212		Thompson, W.W.	43
Thomas, Charles	47		Thompson, Wellington	47
Thomas, Charles	141		Thompson, William	128
Thomas, Charles	165		Thompson, William	216
Thomas, E.B.	19		Thompson, William H.	107
Thomas, Geo. S.	96		Thomson, Henry	98
Thomas, Henry	47		Thorburn, Alexander	55
Thomas, J. W.	131		Thorington, J.H.	13
Thomas, J.C.	85		Thorne, M. H.	96
Thomas, J.J.	212		Thornton, Austin	184
Thomas, John	137		Thornton, J. G.	128
Thomas, John L.	212		Thorp, Samuel	128
Thomas, John W.	19		Thorpe, George M.	128
Thomas, Robert	47		Thrall, George H.	107
Thomas, Robert	128		Threadway, _____	35
Thomas, Samuel	128		Thurnberr, Louis	157
Thomas, Stephen H.	128		Thurston, Quincy F.	128
Thomas, Warren	128		Tibbetts, Isaac	107
Thompsan, Henry P.	212		Tieney, Dan	85
Thompson, A.	128		Tierco, Clark F.	165
Thompson, Albert	141		Tierney, Richard	128
Thompson, Albert	195		Tiffany, David	29
Thompson, Andrew	137		Tiffany, J.	128
Thompson, Benjamin F.	128		Tiffrey, Cornelius	128
Thompson, C.	128		Tilley, William	138
Thompson, C. E.	128		Tilley, William H. H.	137
Thompson, Frank	42		Tillinghast, Wm. H.	103
Thompson, George H.	194		Tilson, Sylvester	128
Thompson, H. F.	143		Tilterton, _____	150
Thompson, H.W.	35		Tilton, Douglas	212
Thompson, Henry	141		Tilton, F.	107
Thompson, Hugh	212		Timber, John D.	105
Thompson, J.	23		Timmerman, T.	7
Thompson, James	128		Tindall, Henry T.	138
Thompson, John	128		Tindall, Peter	96
Thompson, Jos	85		Tinole, Peter L.	96
Thompson, Josiah	58		Tipper, Joseph	28

Name	Page	Name	Page
Tisdale, John	151	Trestee, Emile	47
Tisdale, Sarah L.	151	Trimble, Ebenezer R,	212
Titus, David S.	128	Tripp, J. N.	128
Tivens, J.C.	85	Tripp, John Ellis	52
Todd, Henry	212	Tripp, William	141
Toland, Issac	212	Troberg, Gustavus	128
Tolten, John H.	151	Trowbridy, Augustus	17
Tolton, Charles	47	Troy, James E.	69
Tompkins, N. M.	102	Truax, Edward S.	212
Tompkins, W.	128	Truax, William H.	133
Toms, Sylvester	212	Trugin, Chawes W.	218
Tone, John A.	193	Trump, George W.	178
Tony, John	216	Trusdell, Seth	100
Topen, Aretem	128	Trutchzschler, Ulrich	216
Torrell, James H.	42	Tryer, Charles	128
Torrey, E.P.	34	Tryer, Edward	151
Torrey, William A.	69	Tryon, R.P.	128
Torrey, William H.	193	Tryon, William L.	96
Totten, J.H.	85	Tryone, Wm. H.	155
Tournbull, Thomas L.	19	Tubbs, Malvin	128
Tousley, Ebenezer	128	Tucker, Bessie	34
Towell, Chauncey	128	Tucker, John	34
Tower, W. H.	128	Tucker, Rob't	9
Town, Enoch L.	128	Tucker, W.T.	55
Towner, John J,	212	Tugan, James	42
Townsend, Edgar	50	Tumbleton, Thomas	212
Townsend, G.	151	Turepy, Henry	128
Townsend, William	141	Turk, William H.	128
Towsley, James	128	Turly, James	76
Toy, Granville W.	102	Turnbull, James L.	19
Track, Joseph	128	Turnbull, John	212
Tracy, George	51	Turner, John	47
Tracy, Ohio O,	212	Turpin, Edward	42
Trader, George A.	212	Turpin, James	55
Trail, Nathan	47	Tutt, John G.	96
Tranler, J. J.	96	Tuttle, Luther	102
Trash, Alfred	128	Tuttle, Solomon	128
Trass, ___	34	Tuttle, William H.	19
Traub, Frederick	151	Tweed, Thomas S.	69
Tray, William	22	Twist, Leon	85
Treadway, James E.	212	Tyler, Emory H	128
Trederer, Theodore	128	Tyler, James	128

Tyler, Thomas	212	Vanalstine, Hart W.	169
Tyree, William H.	143	Vanatta, L.R.	34
Tyrrell, William	85	Vance, James	93
Tyson, _____	151	Vance, Simeon	128
Uhl, Christian C.	98	Vance, Wm. H.	218
Underhill, L.	154	Vanderbeek, William	105
Underwood, Lewis L,H,	213	Vanderman, John	105
Underwood, Robert C.	93	Vandermarker, Jacob	141
Unknown (Woman)	157	Vangorden, Nelson	213
Unlucky, Bemjamin J.	213	Vannettel, Charles	137
Updegraff, Joseph	13	Vannorman, Ozro	169
Urmston, _____	17	Vanousky, Irwin	38
Utt, James R.	213	Vanscoy, Abel	213
V___son, S	34	Vansickle, David	213
Valier, Vincent	43	Vansickle, David	213
Vallean, William	105	VanValkinburg, Peter	55
Van Allen, Garret	69	Varden, Frank E.	69
Van Arsdale, _____	128	Varner, Asa	213
Van Arsdale, John	141	Varner, J.	213
Van Arsdale, Thomas	128	Vass, J.P.	213
Van Arsdale, Thomas	137	Vassil, Louis	151
Van Arsdale, William	137	Vaugh, Charles	216
Van Decker, Hiram	128	Vaugh, Robert	128
Van Dike,	128	Vaugham, Thomas	217
Van Dyke, John	128	Vaughan, A. G.	97
Van Gilder, Rufus	128	Vaughen, Henry	169
Van Hofen, kCart	13	Vaughn, William L.	131
Van Kleeck, Charles H	128	Very, Edwin	19
Van Loo, Francis	141	Veteabough, James	165
Van Moll, John H.	85	Vetter, Michael	69
Van Sant, Cornelius	69	Vi, J. William	95
Van Tassel, Frederick	193	Vibbard, Seymour	128
Van Tassel, John	128	Vickers, Charles	56
Van Tyle, D.	128	Vickery, Thomas W.	128
Van Valkenburgh, Jaco	128	Vickory, John	69
Van Vleck, George S.	128	Vilanalo, A.	25
Van Vleet, Darius	128	Villenger, Joseph	151
Van Wager, Levi	128	Vinal, Lrupet	56
Van Wermer, _____	128	Vincent, Horace J.	128
Van Wert, James C.	128	Vinett, Fabian	128
Van Winkle, David	128	Vircn, Clemens	42
Van Zandt, Jacob	128	Virgin, August	128

Voght, Rich D.	86
Vohb, Charles	128
Voight, Henry C.	76
Vollerth, Garret	141
Voltz, Cotlieb	169
Vomasdale, Milton	165
Von Bramer, Charles	69
Vooman, Adolph	42
Voss, Henry	69
W. S.	49
W_____, J.W.	43
Wabill, Hiram	213
Wable, John W.G.	213
Wade, C. F.	128
Wade, John	100
Wadsworth, Benjamin	128
Wadsworth, Eli W.	131
Wadsworth, Josiah P.	19
Waggott, Henry	34
Wagner, Chris.	24
Wagner, Ernest C.	213
Wagner, Jacob	137
Wagner, John	23
Wagner, John	128
Wagren, Frederick	27
Wail, Henry	50
Wainwright, James M.	25
Wakee, Robert	174
Wakefield, Harry M.	128
Walcott, John M.	155
Waldm, George B.	42
Waldnuff, Jas.	47
Waldron, Charles	128
Waldron, Cortlandt	128
Walk, Abraham	151
Walker, Alfred	141
Walker, Francis G.	128
Walker, Frank	173
Walker, George	69
Walker, H.W.	47
Walker, Jas. F.	5
Walker, John	5
Walker, John	137
Walker, Lee	128
Walker, Martin	213
Walker, Philip	129
Walker, Robert, Jr.	193
Walker, Samuel	52
Walker, Thomas E.	93
Walker, W.A.	39
Walker, Wilson	173
Walkins, W. H.	129
Wall, James	193
Wallace, George D.	173
Wallace, H. C.	105
Wallace, Thomas	129
Wallace, William	106
Wallace, Wm. Pem	187
Wallas, Edward	177
Wallen, Samuel G.	151
Walls, Milton F.	213
Walsh, David L.	151
Walsh, Frederick	69
Walsh, James	62
Walsh, Mary E.	184
Walsh, Michael	129
Walsh, Micheal	177
Walsh, Pat'k	173
Walsh, Sonny	34
Walsh, William	129
Walss, Edw'd	86
Walter, Albert	129
Walter, Emanual	213
Walter, Frederick	22
Walter, Frederick	137
Walter, James	133
Walter, James	213
Walter, Jos.	86
Walter, Thomas	56
Walters, James	93
Walters, Joseph	42
Walters, Katie	151
Walters, William F.	34
Waltman, Sylvanus	137

Walton, Charles M.	102
Walton, Frank	4
Waltz, Harrison	213
Wamming, James	167
Waples, George B.	93
Ward William H.	131
Ward, Ebenezer	102
Ward, Frank J.	34
Ward, Henry	217
Ward, J.W.	86
Ward, James	86
Ward, James	129
Ward, James H.	19
Ward, John W.	129
Ward, Owen T.	165
Ward, William	129
Ward, William A.	178
Wardell, George A.	129
Warden, E. S.	129
Wardnell, William	36
Ware, H. S.	129
Wareham, James	86
Warhob, Henry D.	213
Warmermaker, William	129
Warmly, George	181
Warner, Charles H.	129
Warner, Edward	56
Warner, Henry	105
Warner, Joseph	129
Warner, Oscar L.	69
Warner, P. F.	129
Warner, Sherman H.	129
Warnock, Jessie May	86
Warren, Amos B.	69
Warren, D.	57
Warren, Elijah	27
Warren, George A.	69
Warren, Henry	174
Warren, Patrick	129
Warren, Samuel	42
Warren, William	220
Warrick, W. P.	129

Was_____, Greenbery	56
Washington, Charles	141
Washington, Daniel	181
Washington, John	47
Waskon, Joseph	6
Waterman, Arthur S.	129
Waterman, Josiah C.	213
Waterman, S.F.	56
Waters, Frederick O.	74
Waters, Patrick	129
Waters, Q.H.	27
Watkins, Alex	34
Watkins, Issac	9
Watkins, Morgan	181
Watkins, Samuel	213
Watkins, W.	14
Watson, Anthony	129
Watson, Charles	167
Watson, James	220
Watson, Jefferson	95
Watson, John	213
Watson, Julia A.	86
Watson, Samual	89
Watson, Samuel D.	169
Watson, Stephen	197
Watson, William	137
Watson, William	193
Watson, William W.	63
Watts, Daniel	129
Watts, Henry	134
Watts, William H.	43
Waves, Charles	129
Way, Addison, A.	134
Way, John M.	143
Way, Thomas N.	69
Wayne, Isaac W.	98
We____, T.S.	17
Weast, Lonenzo G.	175
Weatherby, J. B.	138
Weaver, Alton	137
Weaver, Charles	137
Weaver, Henry	102

Weaver, Jno. B.	187		Wells, George W.	129
Weaver, John A.	47		Wells, Henry	129
Weaver, L.	137		Wells, Henry A.	19
Webb, Christopher	141		Wells, Nelson	141
Webb, James	86		Wells, Richard W.	5
Webb, John W.	97		Welsch, E.M.	86
Webb, Wm. F.	96		Welsh, James	129
Webb, Woodbridge	102		Welsh, John	129
Webber, H. S.	102		Welsh, John	161
Weber, Henry	151		Weltz, David	129
Weber, Joseph	193		Wenkoop, George	141
Weber, S. J.	129		Wentwsorth, John	129
Webster, J.C.	86		Werkhuser, John	165
Webster, James	141		Werner, Julius	14
Webster, Porter	34		Wertson, John	137
Weekly, James W.	137		Wescott, James	129
Weeks, Henry	34		Weshurd, Henry	129
Weeks, Levi	97		Wesley, August	42
Weeks, Maryatt	129		Wesley, Lane	181
Weeks, Nathaniel	141		Wesner, Frank	137
Weeks, Thomas M.	141		Wesson, R.	86
Weil, Fred.	151		West, Andrew	87
Weir, Thomas	129		West, Charles	105
Weir, Thomas B.	151		West, Harlan P.	129
Weise, F, Joseph	213		West, Peter G.	8
Welch, Benjamin	107		West, Willet C.	151
Welch, H. F.	129		Westcott, Assia	129
Welch, John S.	10		Westfall, George	100
Welch, Peter	42		Westmuller, Conrad	129
Welch, Reuben	129		Weston, Leverett P.	19
Welch, William	193		Westover, Charles	129
Welcher, William	213		Wetherby, Lyman	169
Weld, Charles T.	19		Wetter, John	159
Weld, Lewis L.	19		Wetzel, Philip	34
Weleer, Rudolph	178		Weymouth, Fred.	102
Weller, Henry A.	193		Weymouth, Owen	143
Wellington, C. Lloyd	20		Weysser, Chas. W.	103
Wellman, John C.	96		Whaland, Thomas	57
Wells, Alex.	141		Whalen, Charles	129
Wells, Benjamin	76		Whaley, William B.	69
Wells, Francis	129		Wheat, Charles L.	129
Wells, Frank	47		Wheelan, Albert	129

Wheelan, George	129		White, Orville	129
Wheeler, A.	142		White, Richard	129
Wheeler, Able M.	17		White, Sellick R.	17
Wheeler, Charles	218		White, Wilbur	134
Wheeler, Chas	86		White, William	213
Wheeler, Francis	129		White, William C.	105
Wheeler, J.B.	57		White, William E.	129
Wheeler, John (Jr.)	34		White, William H.	213
Wheeler, LCurtis	57		Whitehair, Emery D.	213
Wheeler, Maria	34		Whitehair, Henry J.	213
Wheeler, Orin	213		Whitehair, _____	213
Wheeler, Sylvester	129		Whitehead, John	129
Wheeler, Thomas	151		Whitehead, William	129
Wheeler, Wm. N.	40		Whitehouse, Russell	129
Wherry, James	138		Whitehurst, _____	151
Whigand, Robert	137		Whiteman, D.	105
Whilton, Isaac	129		Whiteside, M. Carrock	184
Whipple, A. S.	129		Whitfield, H.S.	194
Whipple, John	129		Whitford, W.M.	223
Whitaker, Christopher	129		Whither, Daniel	129
Whitaker, Edward W.	129		Whiting, Theodur	160
Whitaker, Joshua	98		Whitlatch, Solomon	213
Whitcomb, Leverett H.	213		Whitlow, William	73
White Elk	34		Whitman, Edward A.	193
White, _____	86		Whitmore, Hiram	105
White, David K.	213		Whitney, Angrew	129
White, E.	129		Whitney, Thos. B.	102
White, Edward	141		Whittan, Charles E.	193
White, Elisha	138		Whittemore, G.H.	173
White, Franklin	131		Whitten, C. F.	102
White, J. H.	86		Whittenmore, Alonzo	129
White, James	141		Whitter, Charles	59
White, James	185		Whuna, Stephen	129
White, James H.	14		Wiard, John	56
White, James H.	213		Wickham, Isaac	129
White, James W.	213		Wiebeck, John	129
White, Jnd.	86		Wier, Henry	151
White, John	8		Wiggens, C.A.	218
White, John H.	29		Wiggins, A.W.	197
White, Joseph	141		Wiggins, Charles	137
White, Moses	129		Wight, John Elias	213
White, Moses E.	107		Wilbanks, W.	131

Wilber, Stephen	129		Williams, J.	100
Wilcox, Emory	193		Williams, James F.	38
Wilcox, S.V.	153		Williams, James H.	169
Wilcox, William	129		Williams, JC	86
Wild, John	69		Williams, Jeremiah	129
Wilde, Otto	73		Williams, Jno	34
Wilder, Hiram	105		Williams, John	34
Wilder, L.	134		Williams, John	47
Wilear, Warren	105		Williams, John	129
Wilhelm, Joseph	213		Williams, John	181
Wilis, Robert	86		Williams, John	214
Wilke, Thomas A.	129		Williams, John	217
Wilkerson, Lewis	134		Williams, John	223
Wilkerson, W,	213		Williams, John B.	217
Wilkinson, Adam	169		Williams, L. D.	137
Wilkinson, George	143		Williams, L.T.	219
Wilkinson, John R.	69		Williams, Morgan	7
Wilkman, Lenard	19		Williams, Nathaniel	141
Will, George	129		Williams, Peter	129
Willard, Patrick	129		Williams, R. F.	130
Willcott, E.	103		Williams, S.	96
Willebaugh, Samuel	129		Williams, S.	131
Willett, Alpheas C.	193		Williams, Samuel C.	165
Willett, Elmer G.	34		Williams, Samuel G.	93
William, Sherman	86		Williams, Smith	130
Williama, Williams	213		Williams, Thomas	214
Williams, Allen	129		Williams, Tunis	130
Williams, Amy	184		Williams, W.A.	86
Williams, Benjamin	47		Williams, William	20
Williams, Benjamin	151		Williams, William	102
Williams, C. D.	131		Williams, William	141
Williams, Dennis	102		Williams, Willington	97
Williams, Edward	47		Williams, Wm. A.	15
Williams, Edward	129		Williams, Wright	217
Williams, Edward	155		Williams, _____	96
Williams, George	42		Williamson, H. C.	134
Williams, George	129		Williamson, J. E.	49
Williams, George W.	213		Willis, Charles H.	93
Williams, Henry	181		Willis, James	138
Williams, Henry P.	129		Willman, Joseph	167
Williams, Israel	174		Wills, Charles E.	214
Williams, J.	17		Wills, John	130

Wills, Thomas	187	Windle, William	214
Wiloghy, Marguret	14	Windsor, G.W.	173
Wilson, _____	130	Wine, Eli	130
Wilson, Alfred	8	Winehan, James	130
Wilson, Andrew J.	214	Winkleburgh, George	137
Wilson, Charles	27	Winkler, _____	130
Wilson, Charles	130	Winn, P.F.M.	188
Wilson, Clarence	34	Winn, Samuel	130
Wilson, Cornelius	86	Winney, DeWitte	76
Wilson, Daran	141	Winset, Charles	130
Wilson, David A.	130	Winsman, Abraham	105
Wilson, George	181	Winston, H. N.	131
Wilson, George H.	134	Winston, J. B.	58
Wilson, George K	217	Winters, Henry	165
Wilson, George S.	131	Winters, John	24
Wilson, H. S.	130	Winters, Owen	43
Wilson, Henry	137	Wintworth, John	107
Wilson, Ira	155	Wirbaugh, Henry	137
Wilson, Isaac	20	Wirker, N.	130
Wilson, J.	23	Wise, Alexander	151
Wilson, J.	105	Wise, Robert	130
Wilson, James	100	Wiseheart, Philander	214
Wilson, James E.	131	Wiso, John	159
Wilson, Jno.	86	Witchery, Philip	169
Wilson, John W.	131	Witehall, Edwin B.	14
Wilson, John W.	134	Witharm, Charles O.	59
Wilson, Martha F.	34	Withe, J.	130
Wilson, Nathaniel	139	Withens, George	43
Wilson, R.	86	Witheral, David	107
Wilson, S.S.	86	Withrington, Rich	130
Wilson, Samuel	47	Wittmann, Wilhelm	214
Wilson, Sarsh Alice	34	Wixon, David E.	93
Wilson, William	130	Wlhitney, Wm. H.	57
Wilson, William E.	105	Woclfter, Arnold	14
Wilson, Wm.	86	Wolcott, Lewis	214
Wilson, Wm.	160	Wolf, Christian	130
Wilson, Wm. A.	35	Wolf, Frederick	137
Wilty, Jacob	137	Wolf, John	214
Wimlow, S.M.	51	Wolfe, J.	56
Wims, Peter (Colored)	56	Wolfe, John	137
Winchel, Chauncey	214	Wolford, Charles	159
Winchlon, Paul	4	Wolford, Saul	159

Name	Page	Name	Page
Woll, Robert	151	Woter, Warren	102
Wolvert, Charles	130	Wricklish, Otto	130
Woocox, J. Ira R.	100	Wright, D	86
Wood, ___	184	Wright, Eli C.	214
Wood, Charles E.	107	Wright, Francis J.	141
Wood, E. C.	130	Wright, Fred. E.L.	154
Wood, E. C. C.	139	Wright, George	154
Wood, Enoch	15	Wright, H.C.	139
Wood, Enoch	86	Wright, Harry A.	178
Wood, Eugen K.	155	Wright, Henry S.	130
Wood, Frank	193	Wright, Henry V.	131
Wood, H.	130	Wright, J.	103
Wood, Ira	130	Wright, Jacob	141
Wood, Isral	57	Wright, James M.	214
Wood, J.D.C.	103	Wright, James R.	105
Wood, John	98	Wright, Joesph	214
Wood, Joseph	143	Wright, John A.	42
Wood, Thomas	137	Wright, John J.	137
Wood, Thomas L.	193	Wright, John W.	178
Wood, William	105	Wright, Joseph A.	8
Wood, William H.	130	Wright, Loyd	198
Wood, William J.	134	Wright, Solomon	130
Woodall, Wm.	14	Wright, Stephen H.	214
Woodbury, Charles M.	103	Wright, Sylvester	134
Woodford, J.B.	105	Wright, Thomas	8
Woodhouse, Georg	130	Wright, Thomas E.	130
Woodhull, George H.	193	Wright, Willis B.	69
Woodins, Walter	96	Wrinckle, Lawrence	130
Woodman, Patties A.	35	Wunterlick, Freda___1	35
Woodman, Thomas	130	Wurtz, C. H.	130
Woodruff, Frank C.	182	Wyael, James	130
Woodruff, Richard	130	Wyatt, Charles	6
Woods, Carry	214	Wyekoff, George	105
Woods, John B.	143	Wylie, William H.	193
Woody, Benjamin C.	214	Wyllie, James	100
Woody, E.	49	Wyllyaws, Fred.	47
Wooster, Aaron	102	Wyman, Benjamin	105
Workman, Charles	181	Wyman, George B.	130
Workman, Newton	214	Wyman, Henry	69
Worrie, H.C.	23	Wynn, William D.	130
Worth, Benjamin F.	214	Y___, Soloman	177
Wosman, Nicholson	130	Yafrlo, S.J.	167

Yager, Antoine	130
Yarnall, Symngir	20
Yates, George .	69
Yazel, William	40
Yearing, Joseph	160
Yelle, Casper E.	86
Yeomans, Samuel	130
York, John K.	102
York, P.C.	97
York, Thomas F.	130
Yost, Alexander	130
Yost, Wm. V.	15
Young Old Crow	35
Young, Beverly D.	100
Young, Clark	35
Young, Clark	134
Young, Daniel C.	105
Young, David	130
Young, David	141
Young, Edward C.	137
Young, George W.	38
Young, J.	49
Young, James	152
Young, John	47
Young, John	96
Young, John	130
Young, John	141
Young, John	214
Young, Lewis	151
Young, Milo	96
Young, Richard	130
Young, Robert A.	93
Young, William	141
Younginer, Joseph	138
Youngs, Hiram	130
Yount, Jefferson	86
Yous, George	137
Yow, John W.	131
Yuderiffe, J.	96
Zach, Ermsh	5
Zahn, H.	57
Zbilowsky, Joseph	143
Zehnder, Jacob	130
Zellmeger, Jacob	35
Zello, Casper E.	219
Zerfaf, David	167
Zickley, John R.	130
Zimmerman, F.	8
Zimmerman, John M.	193
Zlarding, J.W.	56
Zoller, John	174
Zugler, John A.	130
Zuinke, James	47
Zumwalk, Simon	98

BIBLIOGRAPHY

National Archives Record Groups

RG92-576. "General Correspondence and Reports Relating to National and Post Cemeteries." 1865-1890.

RG92-587. "Correspondence Relating to the Administration of National Cemeteries." 1907-1919.

RG92-589 "War Department Orders and Circulars Relating to Cemeteries." 1866-1873.

RG92-682. "Abstracts of Officer's Reports Relating to Burial Places of Soldiers, Available Records, and Recommendations." 1866.

RG92-683. "Descriptive List of National Cemeteries." 1867-1870..

RG92-687 " Miscellaneous Cemetery Records." 1867-1898.

Government Publications

Quartermaster General's Department

Folsom, Col. C.W. *Report of the Inspector General of the National Cemeteries.* 1868.

Mack, Col. Oscar A. *Report of the Inspector General of the National Cemeteries for the Years 1870 and 1871.*

Mack, Col. Oscar A. *Report of the Inspector General of the National Cemeteries.* 1874.

Roll of Honor: Names of Soldiers Who Died in Defense of the American Union, Interred in the National Cemeteries. 27 vols. (1865-1871), repr. in 10 vols. Baltimore, 1994.

Statement of the Disposition of Some of the Bodies of Deceased Union Soldiers and Prisoners of War Whose Remains Have Been Moved to National Cemeteries. 4 Vols. (1868), repr. with Vols. XXVI - XXVII of the *Roll of Honor* (above). Baltimore, 1994.

Other Sources

Hughes, Mark. *Bivouac of the Dead: Burial Sites of the United States Soldiers 1861-1865.* Bowie, Md., 1995.

Roberts, Robert. *Encyclopedia of Historic Forts.* New York, 1987.

Wellman, Paul I. *Death on the Prairie.* New York, 1947.

ABOUT THE AUTHOR

Mark Hughes is an electronic technologist who enjoys historical research. He is a graduate of Gaston College (AAS, 1971) and Southeastern Oklahoma State University (BS, 1985, Master of Technology, 1986). He grew up on his parents' turkey farms in the Carolinas. Before becoming a professional educator he was an electronic technician.

A former instructor at Southwestern Oklahoma State University, he returned to the Carolinas in 1989 to establish an Electronics Engineering Technology program at Orangeburg-Calhoun Technical College where he is currently Department Head of the program.

He is author of *Bivouac of the Dead* as well as the place index for and foreword to the *Roll of Honor* that was reprinted by Genealogical Publishing Company in 1994.

He married Patricia Ann McDaniel in 1970. They have one daughter: Anna Grace Hughes (born 1987).

www.ingramcontent.com/pod-product-compliance
Lightning Source LLC
Chambersburg PA
CBHW071229230426
43668CB00011B/1362